Prepared for the Worst

Also by Christopher Hitchens

Karl Marx and the Paris Commune

James Callaghan: The Road to Number Ten
(with Peter Kellner)

Cyprus

The Elgin Marbles

Blaming the Victims
(edited with Edward Said)

Prepared for the Worst

Selected Essays and Minority Reports

Christopher Hitchens

Hill and Wang / New York
A division of Farrar, Straus and Giroux

Library of Congress Cataloging-in-Publication Data
Hitchens, Christopher.
Prepared for the worst.
I. Title.
AC8H58   1988   081   88-10993

The author is grateful to the following publications for
permission to reprint from previously published material:
The Boston Globe, Grand Street, Granta, Harper's, In
These Times, Inquiry, Literary Review, London Review of
Books, Mother Jones, The Nation, New Statesman, The
New York Times, The Observer, Raritan, The Spectator,
The Times Literary Supplement, and The Washington Post

"On Not Knowing the Half of It:
My Jewish Self," copyright © 1988
by Christopher Hitchens and Grand Street
Publications, Inc., reprinted by permission. "Shahak in
Israel" reprinted by permission from Raritan: A Quarterly
Review, *Vol. VI, No. 4 (Spring 1987). Copyright © 1987*
by Raritan, *165 College Ave., New Brunswick, N.J. 08903*

FOR BEN SONNENBERG

Contents

Prepared for the Worst

Introduction

Nadine Gordimer once wrote, or said, that she tried to write posthumously. She did not mean that she wanted to speak from beyond the grave (a common enough authorial fantasy), but that she aimed to communicate *as if she were already dead*. Never mind that that ambition is axiomatically impossible of achievement, and never mind that it sounds at once rather modest and rather egotistic, to say nothing of rather gaunt. When I read it I still thought: Gosh. To write as if editors, publishers, colleagues, peers, friends, relatives, factions, reviewers, and consumers need not be consulted; to write as if supply and demand, time and place, were nugatory. What a just attainment that would be, and what a pristine observance of the much-corrupted pact between writer and reader.

The essays, articles, reviews, and columns that comprise *Prepared for the Worst* do not meet, or approach, the exacting Gordimer standard in any respect. In fact, so far from addressing people posthumously, I feel rather that I'm standing over my collection like an anxious parent. Friends and even acquaintances tend naturally to praise my little son, at least to my face, and I've become used to inserting the descant of allowances for myself: you've got to realize that he's a bit spoiled; he's keener to talk than he is on what he's saying; he's a bit lacking in concentration; and so on. Still, the teacher *did* say just the other day that he was very inquiring and showed distinct promise. Sympathetic, encouraging nods all around.

You don't get that kind of indulgence for your prose. Hopeless, then, to seek to justify the ensuing. Yes, the piece on Reagan's mendacity was written to the tune of an emollient week in the national press; yes, the review of *Brideshead* was composed in response to a TV travesty then in vogue; yes, the report from Beirut understates the horror (didn't everybody?). But then, might it not be said that the Polish article has a dash of prescience? the Paul Scott essay perhaps a hint of perspective? Forget it. Never explain; never apologize. You can either write posthumously or you can't.

Fortunately, Ms. Gordimer does set another example that a mortal may try to follow. She combines an irreducible radicalism with a certain streak of humor, skepticism, and detachment. She is also a determined internationalist. My choice among her novels would be *A Guest of Honor*, wherein the central character sees his beloved revolution besmirched and yet does not feel tempted—*entitled* might be a better word—to ditch his principles. The whole is narrated with an exceptional clarity of eye, ear, and brain, and there is no sparing of "progressive" illusions. The result is oddly confirming; you end by feeling that the attachment to principle was right the first time and cannot be, as it were, retrospectively abolished by the calamitous cynicism that only idealists have the power to unleash.

Most of the articles and essays in this book were written in a period of calamitous cynicism that was actually inaugurated by calamitous cynics. It was—I'm using the past tense in a hopeful, nonposthumous manner—a time of political and cultural conservatism. There was a ghastly relief and relish in the way in which inhibition—against allegedly confining and liberal prejudices—was cast off. In the United States, this saturnalia took the form of an abysmal chauvinism, financed by MasterCard and celebrating a debased kind of hedonism. In Britain, where there were a few obeisances to the idea of sacrifice and the postponement of gratification, it took the more traditional form of restoring vital "incentives" to those who had for so long lived precariously off the fat of the land. In both instances, the resulting vulgarity and spleen were sufficiently gross to attract worried comment from the keepers of consensus.

Now, I have always wanted to agree with Lady Bracknell that there is no earthly use for the upper and lower classes unless they set each other a good example. But I shouldn't pretend that the consensus itself was any of my concern. It was absurd and slightly despicable, in the first decade of Thatcher and Reagan, to hear former and actual radicals intone piously against "the politics of confrontation." I suppose that, if this collection has a point, it is the desire of one individual to see the idea of confrontation kept alive.

Periclean Greeks employed the term *idiotis*, without any connotation of stupidity or subnormality, to mean simply "a person indifferent to public affairs." Obviously, there is something wanting in the apolitical personality. But we have also come to suspect the idiocy of politicization—of the professional pol and power broker. The two idiocies make a perfect match, with the apathy of the first permitting the depredations of the second. I have tried to write about politics in an allusive manner that draws upon other interests and to approach literature and criticism without ignoring the political dimension. Even if I have failed in this synthesis, I have found the attempt worth making.

Call no man lucky until he is dead, but there have been moments of rare satisfaction in the often random and fragmented life of the radical freelance scribbler. I have lived to see Ronald Reagan called "a useful idiot for Kremlin propaganda" by his former idolators; to see the General Secretary of the Communist Party of the Soviet Union regarded with fear and suspicion by the Communist Party of Czechoslovakia (which blacked out an interview with Miloš Forman broadcast live on Moscow TV); to see Mao Zedong relegated like a despot of antiquity. I have also had the extraordinary pleasure of revisiting countries—Greece, Spain, Zimbabwe, and others—that were dictatorships or colonies when first I saw them. Other mini-Reichs have melted like dew, often bringing exiled and imprisoned friends blinking modestly and honorably into the glare. *E pur si muove*—it still moves, all right.

Religions and states and classes and tribes and nations do not have to work or argue for their adherents and subjects. They more or less inherit them. Against this unearned patrimony there have always been speakers and writers who embody Einstein's injunction to "remember your humanity and forget the rest." It would be immodest to claim membership in this fraternity/ sorority, but I hope not to have done anything to outrage it. Despite the idiotic sneer that such principles are "fashionable," it is always the ideas of secularism, libertarianism, internationalism, and solidarity that stand in need of reaffirmation.

GOOD
AND BAD

❏

THOMAS PAINE
The Actuarial Radical

❑

God save great Thomas Paine," wrote the seditious rhymester Joseph Mather at the time:

> His "Rights of Man" explain
> To every soul
> He makes the blind to see
> What dupes and slaves they be
> And points out liberty
> From pole to pole.

As befits an anthem to the greatest Englishman and the finest American, this may be rendered to the tune of "God Save the King" or "My Country 'Tis of Thee." The effect is intentionally blasphemous and unintentionally amiss. Napoleon Bonaparte, when he called upon Paine in the fall of 1797, proposed that "a statue of gold should be erected to you in every city in the universe." He fell just as wide of the mark in his praise as Mather had in his parody. Thomas Paine was never a likely subject for a cult of personality. He still has no real memorial in either the country of his birth or the land of his adoption. I used to think this was unfair, but it now seems to me at least apposite.

How right Paine was to call his most famous pamphlet *Common Sense*. Everything he wrote was plain, obvious, and within the mental compass of the average. In that lay his genius. And, harnessed to his courage (which *was* exceptional) and his pen (which was at any rate out of the common), this faculty of the ordinary made him outstanding. As with Locke and the "Glorious Revolution" of 1688, Paine advocated a revolution which had, in many important senses, already taken place. All the ripening and incubation had occurred; the enemy was in plain view. But there are always some things that sophisticated people just won't see. Paine—for once the old analogy has force—did know an unclad monarch when he saw one. He taught Washington and Franklin to dare think of separation.

The symbolic end of that separation was the handover of America by General Cornwallis at Yorktown. As he passed the keys of a continent to the stout burghers, a band played "The World Turned Upside Down." This old air originated in the Cromwellian revolution. It reminds us that there are times when it is conservative to be a revolutionary, when the world must be turned on its head in order to be stood on its feet. The late eighteenth century was such a time.

"The time hath found us," Paine urged the colonists. It was a time to contrast kingship to sound government, religion to godliness, and tradition to—common sense. Merely by stating the obvious and sticking to it, Paine had a vast influence on the affairs of America, France, and England. Many critics and reviewers have understated the thoroughness of Paine's commitment, representing him instead as a kind of Che Guevara of the bourgeois revolution. Madame Roland found him "more fit, as it were, to scatter the kindling sparks than to lay the foundation or prepare the formation of a government. Paine is better at lighting the way for revolution than drafting a constitution . . . or the day-to-day work of a legislator." And in her 1951 essay "Where Paine Went Wrong," Cecilia Kenyon wrote rather coolly:

> Had the French Revolution been the beginning of a general European overthrow of monarchy, Paine would almost certainly have advanced from country to country as each one rose against its own particular tyrant. He would have written a world series of *Crisis* papers and died an international hero, happy and universally honored. His was a compellingly simple faith, an eloquent call to action and to sacrifice. In times of crisis men will listen to a great exhorter, and in that capacity Paine served America well.

This is to forget that Paine went to France as an official American envoy, not as an exporter of revolution. It also overlooks Paine the committee man and researcher, Paine the designer of innovative iron bridges and the secretary of conventions. The bulk of part 2 of *The Rights of Man* is taken up with a carefully costed plan for a welfare state, the precepts and detail of which would not have disgraced the Webbs, for example:

> Having thus ascertained the probable proportion of the number of aged persons, I proceed to the mode of rendering their condition comfortable, which is,
>
>   To pay to every such person of the age of fifty years, and until he shall arrive at the age of sixty, the sum of six pounds *per ann*. out of the surplus taxes; and

ten pounds *per ann.* during life after the age of sixty. The expense of which
will be,

Seventy thousand persons at £6 *per ann.*	420,000
Seventy thousand ditto at £10 *per ann.*	700,000
	£1,120,000

This decidedly pedestrian scheme was dedicated to the equestrian Marquis
de Lafayette—a man who more closely resembled the beau ideal of Madame
Roland's freelance incendiary.

Paine was even able to rebuke his greatest antagonist for his lack of attention to formality:

> Had Mr. Burke possessed talents similar to the author of "On the Wealth of
> Nations," he would have comprehended all the parts which enter into and, by
> assemblage, form a constitution. He would have reasoned from minutiae to
> magnitude. It is not from his prejudices only, but from the disorderly cast of
> his genius, that he is unfitted for the subject he writes upon.

This argument from Adam Smith is not the style of a footloose firebrand.

Che Guevara, who was bored to tears at the National Bank of Cuba, once
spoke of his need to feel Rocinante's ribs creaking between his thighs. If
Paine ever felt the same, then he stolidly concealed the fact. A large part
of his revolutionary contribution consisted of using the skills he gained as
an exciseman. "The bourgeoisie will come to rue my carbuncles," said Marx
on quitting the British Museum. The feudal and monarchic predecessors of
the bourgeoisie actually did come to regret teaching Paine to count and to
read and to reckon, even to the paltry standard required of a coastal officer.

You may see the doggedness (and, sometimes, the accountancy) of Paine
in numerous passages—almost as if he were determined to justify Burke's
affected contempt for "the sophist and the calculator." The prime instances
are the wrangle over slavery and the Declaration of Independence, and the
negotiation over the Louisiana Purchase. Both involved a correspondence
with Thomas Jefferson, which has, unlike much of Paine's writing, survived
the bonfire made of his papers and memoirs.

Jefferson withdrew a crucial paragraph from the Declaration, consequent
upon strenuous objection from Georgia and South Carolina. In its bill of
indictment of the king, it had read:

> He has waged cruel war against human nature itself, violating its most sacred
> rights of life and liberty in the persons of a distant people who never offended
> him, captivating and carrying them into slavery in another hemisphere, or to
> incur miserable death in their transportation thither. This piratical warfare, the
> opprobrium of INFIDEL powers, is the warfare of the CHRISTIAN king of
> Great Britain. Determined to keep open a market where MEN should be bought

and sold, he has prostituted his negative for suppressing every legislative attempt to prohibit or restrain this execrable commerce. And that this assemblage of horrors might want no fact of distinguished dye, he is now exciting those very people to rise in arms among us, and to purchase that liberty of which he has deprived them by murdering the people on whom he has obtruded them, thus paying off former crimes committed against the LIBERTIES of one people with crimes which he urges them to commit against the LIVES of another.

In his earlier pamphlet against slavery, Paine had written:

These inoffensive people are brought into slavery, by stealing them, tempting kings to sell subjects, which they can have no right to do, and hiring one tribe to war against another, in order to catch prisoners . . . an hight of outrage that seems left by *Heathen* nations to be practised by pretended *Christians*. . . . That barbarous and hellish power which has stirred up the Indians and Negroes to destroy us; the cruelty hath a double guilt—it is dealing brutally by us and treacherously by them.

Either Paine actually wrote the vanquished paragraph or, as William Cobbett said of the Declaration itself, he was morally its author. His biographer Moncure Conway, who fairly tends to find the benefit of any doubt, comments on the excision and summons an almost Homeric scorn to say:

Thus did Paine try to lay at the corner the stone which the builders rejected, and which afterwards ground their descendants to powder.

Conway and Paine both half-believed that revolutionaries make good reformists, a belief obscured by the grandeur of Conway's phrasing.

Anyway, Paine was not always to be Cassandra. As elected clerk to the Pennsylvania Assembly, he labored hard on the preamble to the act which abolished slavery in that state. He is generally, but not certainly, credited with its authorship. At any rate, his clerkly efforts gave him the satisfaction of seeing the act become law on March 1, 1780, as the first proclamation of emancipation on the continent.*

More than two decades later, on Christmas Day, 1802, Paine wrote to Jefferson with a well-crafted suggestion of another kind.

Spain has ceded Louisiana to France, and France has excluded the Americans from N. Orleans and the navigation of the Mississippi: the people of the Western Territory have complained of it to their Government, and the government is

---

* In his *Reflections of a Neoconservative*, Irving Kristol presses anachronism into the service of chauvinism: "Tom Paine, an English radical who never really understood America, is especially worth ignoring."

of consequence involved and interested in the affair. The question then is—
what is the best step to be taken?

The one is to begin by memorial and remonstrance against an infraction of
a right. The other is by accommodation, still keeping the right in view, but not
making it a groundwork.

Suppose then the Government begin by making a proposal to France to
repurchase the cession, made to her by Spain, of Louisiana, provided it be with
the consent of the people of Louisiana or a majority thereof. . . .

The French treasury is not only empty, but the Government has consumed
by anticipation a great part of the next year's revenue. A monied proposal will,
I believe, be attended to; if it should, the claims upon France can be stipulated
as part of the payments, and that sum can be paid here to the claimants.

I congratulate you on the *birthday of the New Sun*, now called Christmas-
day; and I make you a present of a thought on Louisiana.

This is not exactly visionary (the only revolutionary bit is in the valediction),
but it is very good actuarial radicalism. Paine did not foresee the imperial
delusions harbored by Bonaparte—it has to be admitted that Burke was
more prescient on that point—but five years after the Corsican had offered
him a statue of gold, he was still able to take a more solid bargain off him.

Paine was schooled in the rational, down-to-earth style of the English
artisan's debating club. His earliest pamphlet was a technical treatise on the
folly of the Crown in underpaying the excisemen. His fellow workers in his
second trade, that of corset making, were no less steeped in the fundamen-
tals. He never forgot to consider the material substratum that is necessary
for happiness or even for existence.

The Puritan revolutionaries influenced Paine also. In preaching to the
men and women of no property, he was always contrasting man as made by
God to mankind as reduced by priestcraft and monarchy. The echoes of the
Diggers and Levelers, and of Milton's "good old cause," are everywhere to
be found in his prose. And, though he repudiated the suggestion with some
heat, it's very plain that he must have read the second *Treatise on Civil
Government* by John Locke. Paine was a borrower and synthesizer, not an
originator.

Paine's arguments about natural right and human liberty followed the
tiresome fashion of the time in claiming descent from Genesis. Here again,
he put himself in debt to Locke and to the long English Puritan tradition
of asking, "When Adam delved and Eve span, who was then the gentleman?"
He was somewhat wittier and pithier than Locke, but he did continue to
take the arguments of the "Church and King" faction at face value in making
his case:

For as in Adam all sinned, and as in the first electors all men obeyed; as in
the one all mankind were subjected to Satan, and in the other to sovereignty;

as our innocence was lost in the first, and our authority in the last; and as both disable us from reassuming some former state and privilege, it unanswerably follows that original sin and hereditary succession are parallels. Dishonorable rank! Inglorious connection!

Staying in Locke's footsteps, Paine also ridiculed the Normans, whose conquest of Britain was the fount of kingly authority. In fact, this essentially populist ridicule provided the occasion for a wonderful story about Benjamin Franklin, who, while envoy at Paris, received an offer from a man

> stating, first, that as the Americans had dismissed or sent away their King, that they would want another. Secondly, that himself was a Norman. Thirdly, that he was of a more ancient family than the Dukes of Normandy, and of a more honourable descent, his line never having been bastardised. Fourthly, that there was already a precedent in England, of kings coming out of Normandy: and on these grounds he rested his offer, enjoining that the Doctor would forward it to America.

Franklin didn't forward the letter.

Paine was most emphatically a moralist. His stress was always upon *condition*, not upon class. Still, his best writing and his finer episodes are improvisations upon the moment. His most brilliant are of course the exhortations to Washington's army and the splendid rebuff to Admiral Lord Richard Howe ("In point of generalship you have been outwitted, and in point of fortitude, outdone"). His least impressive are the entreaties to the French to spare their king from the knife. It is to Paine's credit that he urged clemency—having once written so dryly of Burke's concern for the plumage rather than the bird—and that he took a frightful personal risk to do so. One is tempted to find in him the figure of a humane moderate, who wanted to temper the French Revolution just as he had itched to spur the American one. John Diggins actually tries this line in *Up from Communism*, where he characterizes Paine as "another fellow-traveller whose revolutionary idealism had drowned in the Jacobin terrors of the Eighteenth Century." But it won't do. For one thing, if Paine was a fellow traveler with anyone, it was with the Girondins. For another, it was all up with the French king, just as it had been all up with the English one. The French had had more to endure than the American colonists and could not put the Atlantic between themselves and those who wished for revenge or reconquest. Paine, for all his scruple and decency, was out of his depth in trying to brake the pace of events. Mather put it well in another of his poems, "The File-Hewer's Lamentation":

> *An hanging day is wanted;*
> *Was it by justice granted,*

> *Poor men distressed and daunted*
> *Would then have cause to sing:*
> *To see in active motion*
> *Rich knaves in full proportion*
> *For their unjust extortion*
> *And vile offences, swing.*

Even so, Paine did not sicken of revolution as a result of his rough handling by the Committee of Public Safety. To the end of his days, which were shortened by the experience, he proudly pointed out that "the principles of America opened the Bastille." He never diluted any of his convictions, regretting, rather, the slackening of respect for the ideals of the Revolution and insisting, for example, that the Louisiana Purchase should be conditional upon emancipation.

Paine passed his last years fending off the jibes of the Federalists and the taunts of the religious. As Carl Van Doren says, he could have survived *The Rights of Man* if he had not written *The Age of Reason*. But the pious were (and are) too crass to see how devotional a book *The Age of Reason* really is. The cry of "filthy little atheist," directed at Paine at the time and resurrected by Theodore Roosevelt on a later occasion, reflects only ignorance. Paine was no more an atheist than Luther (another conservative revolutionary) or Milton (likewise). He was as biblical and sound as any "plain, russet-coated captain" in Cromwell's New Model Army. But even at the close, with clerics gathering around his sickbed in hopes of a recantation, Paine roused himself to make such distinction as he could between faith and superstition. Addressing the reverend gentlemen who had squabbled over the corpse of Alexander Hamilton, he wrote to a clergyman named Mason:

> Between you and your rival in communion ceremonies, Dr Moore of the Episcopal church, you have, in order to make yourselves appear of some importance, reduced General Hamilton's character to that of a feeble-minded man, who in going out of the world wanted a passport from a priest. Which of you was first applied to for this purpose is a matter of no consequence. The man, sir, who puts his trust and confidence in God, that leads a just and moral life, and endeavors to do good, does not trouble himself about priests when his hour of departure comes, nor permit priests to trouble themselves about him.

He remained staunch to his last hour, drawing down a hail of petty abuse and innuendo. The godly did not even refrain from insinuating that Paine was in thrall to the brandy bottle, as if it had been this that sustained him through war, revolution, poverty, incarceration, and the calumny and ingratitude of the American Establishment.

His courage was by no means Dutch and was worthy of a better cause than theism. It required bravery as well as common sense to give the ambitious objective "United States of America" to the enterprise of the thirteen colonies (Paine was the first to employ the name). It required something more than prescience to say plainly, in *The Rights of Man*, that Spanish America would one day be free. And sometimes Paine's *aperçus* give an awful thrill:

> That there are men in all countries who get their living by war, and by keeping up the quarrels of Nations, is as shocking as it is true; but when those who are concerned in the government of a country, make it their study to sow discord, and cultivate prejudices between Nations, it becomes the more unpardonable.

Paine belongs to that stream of oratory, pamphleteering, and prose that runs through Milton, Bunyan, Burns, and Blake, and which nourished what the common folk liked to call the liberty tree. This stream, as charted by E. P. Thompson and others, often flows underground for long periods. In England, it disappeared for a considerable time. When Paine wrote that to have had a share in two revolutions was to have lived to some purpose, he meant France and America, and not the narrow, impoverished island that he had last fled (on a warning from William Blake) with Pitt's secret police on his tail.

But when the Chartists raised their banner decades later and put an end at some remove to the regime of Pitt and Wellington, it was Paine's banned and despised pamphlets that they flourished. Burns's "For a' That, and a' That" has been convincingly shown, in its key verses, to be based upon a passage in *The Rights of Man*.

Marx does not seem to have heard of him, though there is in *The Rights of Man* a sentence that pleasingly anticipates the opening of *The Eighteenth Brumaire*:

> Man cannot, properly speaking, make circumstances for his purpose, but he always has it in his power to improve them when they occur; and this was the case in France.

And, not long ago, I came across the following:

> Let it not be understood that I have the slightest feeling against Henry of Prussia; it is the prince I have no use for. Personally, he may be a good fellow, and I am inclined to believe that he is, and if he were in any trouble and I had it in my power to help he would find in me a friend. The amputation of his title would relieve him of his royal affliction and elevate him to the dignity of a man.

That was Eugene Debs, giving a hard time to the fawners of New York high society in 1907. To say that Debs could not have written in this manner without the influence of Paine is not to diminish Debs, who acknowledged his debt. Traces of the same lineage can be found in the work of Ralph Ingersoll and (a guess) in the finer scorn of Mark Twain and H. L. Mencken. Can it be coincidence that the founding magazine of the NAACP was called *The Crisis?* When Earl Browder spoke of communism as "Twentieth-century Americanism," and when Dos Passos used Paine to counterpose American democracy to communism, they were both straining, to rather less effect, to pay the same compliment.

Yeats used to speak of a "book of the people," in which popular yearning was inscribed and wherein popular memories of triumph over tyranny and mumbo jumbo were recorded. Tom Paine wrote a luminous page of that book. But, just as he was only a revolutionary by the debased standards of his time, he can only be commemorated as one by contrast to the reactionary temper of our own.

(*Grand Street*, Autumn 1987)

THE CHARMER

❑

 Perhaps you might suggest a time when I could reach Mr. Farrakhan by telephone . . . ?"

"Try on Monday."

"Certainly, thank you. Oh—isn't that Columbus Day?"

"Not for us it isn't."

Thus the abortion of one of my several approaches to the office of the *Final Call* in Chicago. I had just been to hear Louis Farrakhan speak at Madison Square Garden on October 7, 1985. Prior to that evening, I had seen only two attention-getting public speeches delivered in the flesh, as it were. One was Edward Kennedy's unctuous address to the Democrats in Philadelphia in June 1982, the other was Mario Cuomo's crowd-pleasing convention "keynote" in San Francisco two years later. Both of these featured invocations of Ellis Island, brave immigrants, and the American dream. Both of them exhibited pride of ancestry and pride in the struggle for a place in the New World.

Immigrant chic, as James Baldwin pointed out two decades ago, is a form of uplift and consolation denied to black Americans. How, I wonder, do blacks feel when they see Lee Iacocca grandstanding about the Statue of Liberty? Many of them, I presume, are too polite to say. But the atmosphere at the Garden could hardly have been in bolder contrast. The opening prayer made repeated reference to the congregation's being "here in the wilderness of North America." In his warm-up speech, Stokely Carmichael, who has named himself Kwame Touré after the two most grandiose and disappointing pan-Africanist despots, eulogized Africa as the mother of religion and culture, and cited Freud as the authority for Moses' having been black. As he entered his peroration against Zionism, attention was distracted from his white dash-iki by the spirited efforts of the interpreter for the deaf to keep in step.

This officer had much less trouble conveying into gestures the clear, honeyed tones of the main attraction. Louis Farrakhan does not do black talk. He does not do jive. He speaks in a clear, remorseless English, varying only the pitch and the speed. A calypso artist called the Charmer until he saw the light in 1955, he wrote a play about the black travail and called it *Orgena*, which is "a Negro" spelled backward. The hit song from this play, which filled Carnegie Hall in its time, was "White Man's Heaven Is a Black Man's Hell (Heed the Call Y'All)." The key verse is from Genesis (15:13–14), promising redemption and revenge. Like Jesus, with whom he frequently compares himself, Farrakhan has not read the New Testament. He sings well on the recording I possess but enjoys cutting short any laughter with a menacing remark: the charmer has a cruel streak.

By now, everybody knows what Farrakhan said that night, and what Farrakhan thinks, about the Jewish people. In particular, and although most New York newspapers prudently played it downpage or not at all, his warning that "you can't say 'Never Again' to God, because when He puts you in the ovens you're there forever" has become defining and emblematic. And in a way that it never was in the days of Malcolm X or even Elijah Muhammad.

In May 1962, just after the Los Angeles Police Department had cut a lethal swath through the members of the local Muslim temple, Malcolm X opened a public meeting with what he called "good news." One hundred and twenty-one "crackers" of the all-white Atlanta Art Association had died in a plane wreck at Orly. There was a tremendous row about this remark, along conventional lines of hate being no answer to hate, but it was clear even then that Malcolm felt that *all* whites—without discrimination, so to say—were courting judgment. It was to become clearer, though, that he was in transition from racial nationalism to radicalism and was a man who could sicken of his own bile. Farrakhan, a much smoother and shallower person, who wrote in *Muhammad Speaks* in December 1964 that "such a man as Malcolm is worthy of death," is, if anything, in transition the other way. Otherwise, to paraphrase an ancient question, Why the Jews?

In her anxious, thoughtful, and unreviewed book *The Fate of the Jews* (New York: Times Books, 1983), Roberta Strauss Feuerlicht describes a series of meetings on black–Jewish tension which were held at Manhattan's 92nd Street Y in the early part of 1981. At the first of these, the black spokesman was the educator Dr. Kenneth Clark, whose study of racial discrimination was cited by the Supreme Court in *Brown v. Board of Education*. He wondered aloud at one point why it should be this relationship, rather than, say, black–Catholic relations, that was so emotionally combustible:

> Clark's rhetorical question was unexpectedly answered a few minutes later. A woman told him he underestimated how important survival is to Jews and said, "One of the reasons there isn't quite as much dialogue with the Catholics is the Catholics aren't worried that the blacks are going to shove them into the oven."
>
> Though the woman continued to talk, Clark winced, as though he had been

physically struck. "My goodness," he said very softly. Then he spoke louder, asking incredulously, "Did you say something about blacks shoving people into ovens?"

At a subsequent meeting:

> A young black woman, who happens to be married to a Jew though she didn't say so, said that Jews are always talking about the 1960s, but what have they done for blacks lately? A few minutes later, someone thrust a note into her hand. It said:
>   Dear Lady,
>   Is the lives of the children of my friends killed in the civil rights march enough for you? That's what some Jews have done for you.

There was no signature, and it was a long way from the spirit of Schwerner, Chaney, and Goodman.

Feuerlicht's book, which is full of anguish and decency, suffers from its implicit belief that anti-Semitism is a prejudice like any other. This belief, though it may be convenient for pluralism and for civilization, is not well founded. Anti-Semites are inhibited from making exceptions or distinctions. All of their worst enemies are Jews. Their weaker brethren—the anti-Catholics and anti-Masons—emulate anti-Semites only in seeing their devils wherever they look. Anti-Semitism is a *theory* as well as a prejudice. It can be, and is, held by people who have never seen a Jew. It draws upon vast buried resources—calling upon Scripture, blood, soil, gold, secrecy, and predestination. It may have special attractions for those who are themselves victimized by their own kind. And typically the anti-Semite has an interest, however sublimated, in a Final Solution. Nothing else will do. The usual outward sign of this is an inability to stay off the subject.

Thus, while it may be true that some of Farrakhan's audience is drawn by resentment of the political *and moral* strength of the American Jews (Jesse Jackson was never more instructive or more honest than when he said that he was tired of hearing about the Holocaust), Farrakhan himself is uninterested in that banal kind of fedupness. For him, the Jews are a question of the Law and the Book. His meeting demonstrated as much by two significant gestures to *white* anti-Semitism which went unreported. The first of these was made by the introducing speaker, who said that "Minister Farrakhan" was a true champion. He had "even knocked Henry Ford out of the ring." Why, Henry Ford was made to apologize for his writings on the international Jew. But Minister Farrakhan, he didn't apologize to anybody, and there was no one around who could make him. This, evidently, was something more than an appeal to black self-respect.

The second such insight came from Farrakhan himself, when he spoke of the power of the Jewish lobby in Washington and of the numbers of congressmen who were honorary members of the Knesset. These people, he said, are "selling America down the tubes." Here is the precise language employed by the Liberty Lobby, the Klan, and the right-wing patriots who surfaced at the time of the oil embargo. Why is Farrakhan, who doesn't vote or care for Columbus Day, and who thinks America is Babylon, so solicitous of this interpretation of its interests? Dr. Clark's question is answered. Yes, somebody did say something about blacks shoving people into ovens. The fact that it was said under the rubric of religious prophecy may console those who respect that kind of thing.

In his book *The Ordeal of Civility*, John Murray Cuddihy wrote of black–Jewish rivalry:

> The cold war at the top, that between the literary-cultural representatives of the contending groups, is a war for status: the status at issue is the culturally prestigeful one of "victim."

At a slightly less elevated level, black demagogy turns on the Jews not in spite of the fact that they are more liberal and more sensitive to the persecuted, but *because* of it. Could rationalism, not to speak of socialism, suffer a worse defeat?

There's no doubt who prevails in Cuddihy's "prestigeful" stakes, at least as far as white sympathy goes. And Farrakhan's repeated claim for the numbers martyred by slavery is a self-conscious competition with the six million rather than (as is interestingly the case with some species of anti-Semite) a denial of them.

The tendency of victims not to identify with one another and even to take on the oppressor's least charming characteristics is strongly marked and has been much recorded. "Asked if he would accept whites as members of his Organization of Afro-American Unity, Malcolm said he would accept John Brown if he were around today—which certainly is setting the standard high."* Invited to consider Jews as allies, while modeling its own myth on that of Zion in captivity, the Nation of Islam is instead set upon the same quest for racial destiny which has led Israelis to emulate European colonialism. What this says about the future of illusion, and about the cost of religion to humanity, is as much as one can bear to contemplate.

(*Grand Street*, Winter 1986)

---

* Eldridge Cleaver, describing Black Muslim prison life in one of the few worthwhile passages of *Soul on Ice*.

HOLY LAND HERETIC

❑

In January 1986, an International Colloquium of the Jewish Press was held in Jerusalem. Its most tempestuous session concerned the various "responsibilities" of the critic. And in this session, which was entitled "The Press and the Preservation of the Jewish People," the most forward participant was Norman Podhoretz. In his remarks, the editor of *Commentary* went somewhat further than he had in "J'Accuse" (*Commentary*, September 1982) and "The State of World Jewry Address" (1983). He stated plainly that "the role of Jews who write in both the Jewish and the general press is to defend Israel, and not join in the attacks on Israel." Turning to the Israeli press proper, he admonished its writers and editors "to face the fact that the internal political debate in Israel, when it reaches a certain pitch of intensity, has an extremely damaging effect in the U.S. and other diaspora countries. It is hard for Israeli journalists to understand how crushing a blow they deal the political fortunes of Israel in the U.S. by calling Israel a fascist country— as many of them do; what damage they do to Israel by blowing the Kahane phenomenon out of proportion." Perhaps in an effort at paradox, Podhoretz declared that "all this helps Israel's enemies—and they are legion in the U.S.—to say more and more openly that Israel is not a democratic country." Or, as he put it later and more gnomically in the same session: "The statement 'freedom to criticize' is only the beginning of the discussion, not the end of it."

In one way, this was the adaptation to Israel of the standard neoconservative three-card monte as it is played in America: America is a democracy which allows demonstrations against its policies; the Soviet Union does not allow such demonstrations; the American demonstrations are therefore a form of aid and comfort to the Soviet Union. Sometimes the first or second card of this trick is ineptly played, resulting in the unintentionally absurd injunction "This is a democracy, so shut up!" or the even flatter injunction that the critical voice should relocate in Moscow. Podhoretz, even as he defends the undemocratic Israeli Right to American audiences, will invoke the very "democracy" that, when he is in Israel itself, he attempts to enfeeble. And the often-heard slogan about "the only democracy in the Middle

East" has its effect on liberal journals like *Dissent* and the new *Tikkun*, which would themselves never pass a Podhoretz loyalty test.

Neither Western nor Israeli "democracy," of course, is a sham. But the conservative defense of it often rests upon a half-truth. Whether in the weak and propagandistic form of a Jeane Kirkpatrick syllogism (authoritarianism is to be preferred to totalitarianism and, in practice, often to democracy also) or in the more muscular form of Reagan's "Free World" rhetoric, the conservative position in Israel and in the United States exhibits the same irony. It consists of the relentless iteration of a "democracy" for which, in the real world, the speaker has contempt. This explains the vicarious envy with which people like Podhoretz write about the "unfettered" freedom of communist dictatorships to act without restraint. In this ideological imagination, freedom is a sort of moral credit, which may be banked but should not be drawn upon. Objectors to this logic may be denounced as communists. If they challenge the deep alliance between the American and Israeli establishments, they may well be called fascists, too. And the striking thing about this fundamentally conservative relationship between facts and values is how much support and justification it gets from liberals. Of no other power relationship between Washington and a foreign government can this be said.

This short preface introduces an Israeli who, over the past decade and more, has won an increasing reputation. Unlike the nonexistent critics whom Podhoretz denounces but never cites, he does not believe that Israel is a fascist country. But he does believe that it is menaced by fascism, and if taken over by it would constitute a fascistic menace to others. Professor Israel Shahak, Holocaust survivor and pioneer Zionist, devotes himself to the study and dissemination of observable currents in Israeli society as evidenced in the Hebrew press. He believes firmly in the virtues of Israeli pluralism and democracy, and has done more to uphold and defend them than most of those who make of them a mere boast. Although he is best known for his stand on the rights of the remaining Palestinian Arabs, he is also heavily engaged in the battle between fundamentalist and secular Jews which now rages so bitterly and which he was among the first to foresee. What follows is an attempt to make his findings and his principles better known and better understood.

In the course of a week's discussion with Shahak, I endeavored to keep each daily session self-contained. As far as possible, this profile and analysis follows the pattern of our discussions and disagreements. We began with biography.

Israel Shahak was born on April 28, 1933, into a religious and Zionist family in Warsaw. Although his father, a leather merchant, was from a long line of rabbis and had qualified to be one himself, he had developed at a slight angle to strict orthodoxy. The young Shahak was educated in Polish and Hebrew. The family home was damaged in the siege of Warsaw in 1939, which was soon followed by the Nazi creation of the ghetto, but he recalls no serious hardship until 1942. News of the Final Solution had come in the form of rumor from other towns and was more intensely discussed by the children and youngsters than their protective parents ever suspected. Each community felt that it might be the one to be spared; in Warsaw, the given reasons for optimism were the presence of embassies from the neutral states and the fact that the Jewish population performed much useful labor for the occupiers. Shahak's father was the Pangloss of the family, and an early memory is of disputes between parents about the advisability of flight. This argument was cut short by the abrupt removal of the Shahaks to Poniatowa concentration camp, but it resumed there. It culminated in Shahak's mother leaving the camp as the barbed wire went up. Assisted by good Polish friends and taking her son, she left her husband behind. Sheltered for a while by a Polish family, and making use of the trade in false passports from Latin America, mother and son were not "selected" for extermination when apprehended, but they did spend some grueling time in Bergen-Belsen. One week before the liberation, they were transported by rail to Magdeburg and rescued on April 13, 1945, by the American army.

It took only a brief while to establish that the father had perished in a mass extermination by shooting and that Israel's older brother, who had left Poland well before the war, had been killed while serving in the Royal Air Force in the Far East. This gave the family the right to settle in England, and young Israel, who now by Jewish custom headed the family, was asked to decide on their future home. He opted unhesitatingly for Palestine, and he and his mother disembarked at Haifa on September 8, 1945. The succeeding six years were, he says, ones of "utmost happiness." He was a good pupil, although occasionally slapped for asking impertinent questions. His mother remarried successfully (having even asked his permission as head of the family), and stepfather and son took to one another at once. Shahak was too young to serve in the 1948 war, but old enough to feel the excitement of delivering messages and running errands. The memory of ghastliness in Central Europe was not erased—he says it comes back vividly when he is ill—but it was overcome.

Shahak knew very well that there were atheist Jews, because his mother abandoned her belief in God as a result of the Holocaust. He also knew that many Jews were anti-Zionist, because he had had a grandmother in prewar Poland who was wont to spit at the mention of Herzl's name. But he remained both Orthodox and a staunch Ben-Gurionist until the 1950s. His repudiation of both religion and Zionism took place over a long period and, though related, are not identical. For convenience, the two anticonversions can be discussed separately.

It was while he was studying Holy Writ for his final examinations that he found a disturbing symmetry between the biblical atrocities and extirpations enjoined by a jealous God and the genocidal propaganda of the Nazis. He feels that the work of Maimonides and Averroës, with its attempted reconciliation between religion and philosophy, may have been at work on his subconscious. But even these two savants had observed the Commandments, which Shahak now found himself unable to obey. In his lengthy essay "The Jewish Religion and Its Attitude to Non-Jews," he sets out his generalized objections to the sectarianism, absolutism, and racialism of Orthodox doctrine and argues that an attempt by Jews is under way to undo the emancipation of Jews by the Enlightenment. I shall return to this, but I want to emphasize meanwhile that Shahak would insist on this position even if there were no "Palestinian problem."

In any case, his misgivings on that score were to come later, with Israel's attack on Egypt in October 1956. He was shocked, he says, by the lying and deception which went into the collusion with Britain and France against Nasser during the Suez crisis. He was even more shocked by Ben-Gurion's boast that the war would establish "the kingdom of David and Solomon." But the Eisenhower-enforced retreat from Suez was so swift, and the subsequent decade so peaceful and prosperous, that it was not until the conquest of the West Bank and Gaza in 1967 that he faced the idea of his adopted country as at once expansionist and messianic. In the intervening years, he had visited the United States as a lecturer in chemistry at Stanford and had had the opportunity to contrast its open atmosphere with the conformist environment at home. He was struck by the rapid advances of the civil rights movement in the Deep South, and the experience taught him, he says, to admire the United States Constitution. He advocates a similar constitution for Israel in his bulletins. (Many who are called "anti-American" by the neoconservatives are in fact admirers of American liberty and would prefer it to the sort of government with which America so often colludes.)

What, now, are his convictions? He is neither a materialist atheist nor a Marxist, preferring to call himself a disciple of Spinoza. "It may not be said of any philosophy or metaphysic that it is true, but it may be said not to be contradictory." The work of Spinoza, he also finds, is "conducive to intellectual happiness and to fortitude in the face of calamity." As a self-defined elitist, Shahak reposes little faith in "the masses," preferring to rely upon "good information that is addressed to educated minorities." And like Spinoza, he is alone. Not a joiner or a party man, he has voted for the Rakah communist candidates in the last three elections, solely because of their stand on Palestinian self-determination. His apartment on Bartenura Street is almost a caricature of the scholarly dissident's warren of tottering files and unsorted shelves, a cartoon of the one-man show. His mimeographed digest of salient admissions in the Hebrew press, which he translates and sends out to friends and contacts all over the world, has, typically, no title. By "salient admissions" I mean the inadvertent manner in which the devout choose to reveal themselves. One might as well say the advertent manner in which they do this, given stories like the following: " 'It is forbidden to sell apartments to non-Jews in Eretz Israel—not even one apartment,' says the Sephardi chief rabbi, Mordechai Eliahu, in response to a question from members of the Shas Party in Jerusalem, who are campaigning against selling and renting apartments to Arabs in the Jerusalem suburb of Neve Ya'akov" (*Ha'aretz*, January 17, 1986). Or:

> Those who initiate meetings between Jews and Arabs are traitors to the nation. This is a destruction. . . . The Arab nation should not be granted education. If they are allowed to raise their heads, and will not be in the condition of hewers of wood and drawers of water, we will have a problem. The education which is given them is destructive.

So writes Rabbi Yekuti Azri'eli, spiritual leader of Zikhron Ya'akov, in the religious weekly *Erev Shabat* on September 20, 1985. Mohammed Miari, member of the Knesset, complained to the Minister of Internal Affairs about this article, pointing out that the malady of racism "causes harm to those who bear it no less than to those against whom it is directed." The Minister of Internal Affairs is Yitzhak Peretz, whom we shall be meeting again. *Kol Ha'ir* of January 10, 1986, reports, under Shahar Ilan's by-line, a proposal from Nisim Ze'ev, deputy mayor of Jerusalem, to clear the Arabs out of the Old City. Rabbi Ze'ev says that "the population density in the Old City is a security hazard." He is just as eloquent when he speaks of the Neve Ya'akov suburb: "Parents are afraid to let their daughters walk outside in the evening, fearing that they may meet an Arab. Arabs live with Jewish women. There is a brothel there with Jewish women and Arab pimps. Such things should be prevented in advance."

Ten or fifteen years ago, when Shahak was being denounced as an alarmist and a crank, such things were being said "on the fringes." But ten or fifteen years ago, most Israelis would not have believed that Gush Emunim and Kach militants would have established armed settlements, set up a military underground, elected a deputy to the Knesset, and forged parallel units in the army and the police. As J. L. Talmon, the conservative historian best known for his severe reflections on "totalitarian democracy" during the French Revolution, wrote in what was almost his last letter:

> Many among the Orthodox had difficulty accepting the Holocaust within the scheme of Providence and Jewish history, for they could not see the death of more than a million innocent Jewish children as punishment for the sins of the whole Jewish people. . . . After the Six Day war, however, the Orthodox were much relieved, for now they could argue that the Holocaust had been the "birth

pangs of the Messiah," that the Six Day war victory was the Beginning of Redemption and the conquest of the territories, the finger of God at work.

Talmon was very much a loyalist of the state, emphasizing in this very letter (which was open and addressed to Menachem Begin in the spring of 1980) that he was "not concerned here with the rights of the Arabs regarding whose past and culture I have little knowledge or interest." But he was a late and probably unwitting convert to the Shahakian view when he wrote:

Any talk of the holiness of the land or of geographic sites throws us back to the age of fetishism.

And:

Is this merely the manifestation of a classically Jewish characteristic, which the Jews may have bequeathed to other monotheistic religions—namely, the need to subordinate oneself to an idea, to a vision of perfection, to an ascetic and ritualistic way of life—instead of treating life as it really is, as did the Greeks, for example, who perceived reality as a challenge and sought to extract from life and nature all the possibilities inherent in them, in order to expand the mind and give pleasure to both body and soul?

We closed our first day of discussion with some differences of emphasis which I believe amount to disagreements of principle. I took, and take, the standard view that derives from Marx's *aperçu* that a nation oppressing another nation cannot itself be free. By extension, I argued rather stolidly, Israel's subordination of nearly three million sullen Palestinians would inevitably debauch Israeli democracy. I called as my witness Danny Rubinstein of *Davar*, who had written famously about a Jewish longshoremen's strike in the port of Ashdod where the police had run amok. The bloodied strikers' leader was interviewed on Israeli television and said indignantly, "What do they take us for? Arabs from the territories?" Here, surely, was a classic illustration of the sort of tension—between poor whites and the "natives"— that Camus had both suffered and described in Algeria.

Shahak, however, detects signs of health and progress in the recent polarization of Israeli Jewish society. These detections are not, as his enemies might suspect, derived from any *politique du pire*. On the contrary, they arise from his oddly uncynical version of realism. France, he points out, was a cruel colonial power during the Dreyfus Affair. The United States was behaving in a beastly manner in Vietnam during the Watergate exposure. He mentions various other examples, including Warren Hastings in England, who ran India for the East India Company, and Fox, who made the case for Hasting's impeachment on grounds of extortion, to rebuke my undialectical opening gambit. And he selects, almost perversely, the year 1977 as the one when matters began to improve. Since 1977—the year of Begin's election— "there has been no further confiscation of Arab private property within pre-1967 Israel. And the state of political and religious liberty for Jews has improved enormously." Shahak allows that things could get rapidly worse in the context of a general or localized war with Israel's neighbors. But he has a great long-term faith in the operations of democracy. "The sign of victory would be an American-type constitution, which separated church from state and made all inhabitants equal before the law. This would also amount to de-Zionization. Can you imagine an American government confiscating Jewish land for the exclusive use of Christians?" I repress the facetious urge to say yes to this last rhetorical question, and admit his point. A few days later, I see George Bush arrive in Jerusalem fully outfitted with a video crew from his personal PAC and an endorsement from Jerry Falwell. In his address to the Knesset, he chooses to stress the symmetry between Israeli and American values and institutions.

Shahak and I agree to meet next day to debate thornier matters.

Employment of the word *Nazi* has an obvious and highly toxic effect on any discussion or argument that involves Israel or the Jews. The merest polemical comparison between certain Israeli and German generals, for example, is enough to ignite torrential abuse and denial. In some cases, the comparison is used demogogically and with the intent to wound. In others, it is invited by the routine, show-stopping denunciation of all criticism of Israel as Nazi or anti-Semitic in inspiration, a routine which does seem designed to arouse the vulgar itch to turn the tables. One may consign this kind of disputation to the propagandists. It remains a fact that within Israel and among Israelis the swastika is a common daub. Instead of being reserved as the ultimate insult, it is freely used to settle arguments about films on the Sabbath, ritual slaughter, and such. It can even be seen on the walls of quarreling religious establishments in the hyper-Orthodox quarter of Mea Shearim in Jerusalem. Amos Oz describes, for instance, in his travelogue *In the Land of Israel*, a scene in Mekor Baruch:

> Here, too, one finds the same slogan that screams in red paint "Touch not my anointed ones" [a quotation from Psalms, meaning, apparently, Do not despoil the innocent children of Israel] and next to it a black swastika. And "Power to Begin, the gallows for Peres"—erased—and then, in anger, "Death to Zionist Hitlerites." And "Chief Constable Komfort is a Nazi," "to hell with Teddy Hitler Kollek." And finally, in relative mildness, "Burg the Apostate—may his name be wiped off the face of the earth," and "There is no kingdom but the kingdom of the Messiah."

Oz also notices, as have other writers, the apparent need even of secular Zionist militants for the promiscuous use of Nazi imagery. At one point, arguing with a certain "Z" who expresses his relish at the idea of Israeli conquest, massacre, and enslavement, he asks "perhaps more to myself than to my host":

Is it possible that Hitler not only killed the Jews but also infected them with his poison? Did that venom in fact seep into some hearts, and does it continue to seep out from there?

One recalls George Steiner's speculations on this question of a subconscious bond between Hitler and the Jewish state in the peroration of his central character in *The Portage of A.H. to San Cristobal*. And I remember a shakedown in the West Bank, where Israeli soldiers scratched numbers on the arms of those arrested. Useless as a disciplinary or holding device, it nevertheless had a certain emblematic power, as if, by invoking a demon, one might exorcise it. Who knows what spring of compulsion may be pumping away here.

These observations are prefatory to our argument. Israel Shahak's bulletins and digests make a regular point of saying that such-and-such a rabbi or politician or policy is "Nazi-like." While not, perhaps, *the* theme of his argument, it is certainly a continuous and vigorous element within it. I questioned him repeatedly not so much about the tactical wisdom as about the propriety of such a metaphor.

He is unrepentant. The biblical texts, as he points out repeatedly, speak not of subduing or subjugating or vanquishing the Canaanites or the Midianites or the Amalekites but of *annihilating* them. The fact that Israel is now a democracy (for Jews) does not at all mean that Nazi ideas cannot come to power by way of the franchise. After all, that's how they came to power in Germany. And the Nazis of 1933 did not speak of extermination, preferring to talk of deportation, Aryanization, and so on. The Israeli press is full of the speeches of rabbis and politicians who "only" want the Arabs to pack up and leave Israel.

This line is persuasive as far as it goes. Yet Shahak couples it with a further irritating paradox. The Nazis, he says, were apparently different from previous and contemporary movements in that they sought the total destruction of a race, down to its last child and seed. Yet, in this they were a blend of modern imperialism—which issued genocidal orders in Tasmania, the Congo, and Namibia—and vulgar Darwinism. He compares this quite deliberately with the teaching of many Orthodox rabbis, including the notorious Kahane (who has never been disowned by the rabbinate), about the Palestinians. It is not unusual to see the citation from Numbers 31:14–15 and 17–18:

> And Moses was wroth with the officers of the host, with the captains over thousands, and captains over hundreds, which came from the battle. And Moses said unto them, "Have ye saved all the women alive? . . . Now therefore kill every male among the little ones, and kill every woman that hath known man by lying with him. But all the women children that have not known a man by lying with him, keep alive for yourselves."

Shahak harries the rabbis who include this and other homely injunctions in their "Torah Today" pamphlets and papers. Yet he insists that there is nothing distinctive or unique about Nazi anti-Semitism. (He has argued this most recently in a public exchange with the partisans of Claude Lanzmann's *Shoah*, some of whom argue for Polish as well as German "bloodguilt.")

I think I understand the reason for his taking such a line—which is the desire to counter Israeli self-righteousness. But I offered him various reasons for taking the other view. Anti-Semitism is age-old and protean, so that even societies without Jews are infected by it. The anti-Semite sometimes thinks that Jews are inferior; on other occasions he will maintain that Jews have a sinister superiority. Nobody thought, while exterminating the Tasmanians or the Hereros, that they were thwarting a plot by Tasmanians or Hereros to take over the world. No other race or religion has ever been simultaneously arraigned for being the evil genius of plutocracy *and* of Bolshevism. One cannot, therefore, easily dismiss the Zionist idea that there is something ineradicable about anti-Semitism.

To this, Shahak has two kinds of answers. His first is mild and self-deprecatory. He has experienced anti-Semitic persecution, but he has never actually met or known or conversed knowingly with an anti-Semite. ("We didn't talk much with the camp guards.") I may, therefore, be right as far as that goes. For him, the argument against the uniqueness of the Holocaust goes hand in hand with his argument that Jews, too, are capable of replicating the horrors of racialism. This opens the second of his answers:

> I was six and a half years of age when I saw my first dead man, during the bombardment of Warsaw. I can remember the stench of the chimneys in Bergen-Belsen, and seeing tractors pulling platforms that were heaped up with naked, emaciated bodies. I also have memories of being saved by Germans. I was once rounded up and taken to the main square by a patrol of Jewish policemen. A Wehrmacht soldier told me to run, saying, "But make it quick!" As children during the Nazi period, we were told by our parents, "If you come to a crossroads and see Ukrainians, Germans, Poles, and Jewish militia—try the Jews last!"
>
> In 1956 a whole Arab village was massacred at Kafr Kasem. What nobody remembers is that one Israeli platoon commander obeyed orders and slaugh-

tered everyone, while another platoon commander refused. From then on, I
made a conscious decision not to blame Germans for Hitler or Gentiles for
racialism.

The preceding night, in occupied Ramallah, I had had dinner with a
Palestinian leftist and an American radical, both of whom had read Shahak's
critique of the Jewish religion. Both, and in particular the Palestinian,
thought it rather extreme. When I mentioned this to him, he replied with
a mixture of irony and reaffirmation:

The famous *Eight Chapters* by Maimonides contain prescriptions on how to
deal with error. The greater the error, the greater must be the correction. You
must strike a bent piece of iron in proportion to the extent of its distortion. So
my rational duty at present is to be extreme.
  Judaism is more like Islam than it is like Christianity. The law is the law
whether or not it is systematically invoked. If a country had anti-Jewish laws
which were not systematically invoked, or which could be circumvented by the
clever or the rich, would you not still be justified in terming it an anti-Semitic
regime? Given that there is great official racialism in Israel, coupled with great
denial of it and great ignorance of it, one can only act in proportion to the real
situation. Who would not say that *formal*—i.e., religious—discrimination
should be abolished first?

Shahak is fond of the word "abolition," as he is of Voltaire's injunction
écrasez l'infâme. He offers me, with a smile, a footnote from Gibbon. One
William Whiston, an extreme Arian millennialist, was arguing with Halley
in defense of his apparent fanaticism. Whiston won the day by saying, "Had
it not been for such men as Luther and myself, you would now be kneeling
before an image of Saint Winifred." I take this point, even though it reminds
me uncomfortably of Conor Cruise O'Brien's favorite quotation from Burke—
that our side being "mobbish" is the best guarantee of their side being
"civilized."
  This might have closed our second day, were it not for a controversy in
The Jerusalem Post which caught my eye. Rabbi Shmuel Derlich, chief Israeli
army chaplain in Judea and Samaria, had sent his troops a thousand-word
pastoral letter urging them to apply to "the enemies of Israel" the biblical
commandment to exterminate the Amalekites. When challenged by the
army's chief education officer to give a definition of Amalekite, this religious
custodian of the occupation had replied "Germans." There are no Germans
on the West Bank, or in the Bible. This apparently redoubled exhortation
to slay all Germans as well as all Palestinians was referred to the Judge
Advocate General. In the meantime, forty other military chaplains came to
Derlich's support in public. The JAG found that he had committed no offense, adding rather feebly that rabbis serving the army should refrain where

possible from making politically tinged sermons. But the Derlich pastoral letter was couched in terms of Holy Writ, not politics. So are the speeches of Meir Kahane. Kahane's extremism is well-enough understood in the United States, but then he is neatly categorized as an "extremist." It is official and semiofficial statements like those of Derlich, which seldom if ever find their way into the American press, that Shahak spends his time in emphasizing and bringing to light. Perhaps a little "mobbishness" is in order after all?

On the third day I asked Shahak if he would accompany me to Masada. He turned up at the appointed hour, wearing headphones so as to listen to classical music and scrutinizing a book of Hebrew poetry. He thus missed the patter of easy Eddie Cantor gags and mild anti-Bedouin jokes with which the guide diverted the party as our bus traversed the Judean wilderness. (I noticed that the guide had a number tattooed on his arm.) Arriving at the foot of the fortress, which he visited as a young pioneer before Yigael Yadin began his world-famous excavation, Shahak produced a battered copy of Flavius Josephus's *The Jewish War*. Did I know, he inquired, that Josephus was the only authority for the Masada legend, with its heady suggestion that besieged Jews might once again choose total annihilation over shameful surrender? Did I know that he had not been translated into Hebrew (from his original Greek and retranslated Christian Latin) until the nineteenth century? There had been a corrupted tenth-century rendition, *Yosifon to the Romans*, but this omitted the Masada story, perhaps because of the prohibitions on suicide. So, in effect, the Masada account in Josephus only became accessible to Jews in the nineteenth century, and even then only to the assimilated ones. It thus forms a part of the self-conscious recasting of history, which, like similar efforts in Ireland, Greece, and elsewhere, distinguished the nationalist revival.

I had to admit that I hadn't appreciated that, and our guide had to admit that the standard account he gave to tourists was deficient in two respects. Under Shahak's probing, he allowed that the Zealot defenders had not "left" Jerusalem but had been expelled by their fellow Jews. He also conceded, as most vernacular accounts do not, that the Zealots had slaughtered their own families (who had not been present at the decisive meeting) before killing each other and themselves. The T-shirt slogan, which is also employed at the swearing-in of Israeli army cadets at the fortress, says Masada Shall Not Fall Again. It might be interesting if those who were paraded there for the ceremony had a guide like mine.

Breaking away from the tour, Shahak took me to the lower of Herod's three palaces. This was in part to show me the pronounced Hellenistic influence that is evident in the architecture and design. Even the name Masada is a Greek rendering of the Hebrew word for fortress. Shahak takes a strong interest in the influence of the Hellenic world on Jewish culture and manners in antiquity, and reveres some of its humanistic results. Later, in the course of a long discussion with Rabbi Meir Kahane, I noticed that the Kahane curse term for assimilated and secular Jews is "the Hellenized." This may not be the worst insult ever leveled, but it shows the persistent influence of the Second Temple and also the contempt in which dilution or internationalism is held by the devout. Talmon seems to have seen this coming.

At about this time I reflect on the preposterous libel of "self-hatred" which is directed at people like Shahak. Although it is noticeably more often employed by the summer soldiers and sunshine patriots of the Diaspora, it is still a brickbat of moral blackmail within Israel itself. I can only say, speaking as a white Anglo-Celtic atheist, that I have met few people more affirmatively Jewish than Israel Shahak. He is steeped—pleasurably steeped—in Jewish literature, poetry, and lore. Part of his revulsion against the fanatics and the racialists comes from their desecration and vulgarization of Jewish tradition. He is always ready with an apposite text from Agnon, from Maimonides, or from Moses ibn Ezra. He may be an internationalist, but, like the best internationalists, he knows exactly where he comes from.

These reflections were brought into a somewhat sharper focus on the fourth day, when we discussed what Shahak calls "the bad years."

Shahak began independent political activity, after much hesitation, in April 1968. As he often puts it, it is one thing to face official or alien persecution and quite another to withstand the social and emotional pressure of one's society and peers. He recalls, for example, a friend who had been with him through Bergen-Belsen saying loudly that the Palestinians were like Nazis and bragging that he had been among the volunteers to drop napalm bombs on Jordan. In his first venture into public protest against the occupation, Shahak agreed with eight students and three faculty members to sit in silence on the steps of a building in the Hebrew University. This was done to protest a no-charge, no-trial administrative detention order on Mohammed Yusuf Sadeq, an Israeli citizen. By the end of the protest, Shahak was completely covered in spittle. He had endured worse in his time, but, as he says, this was Jewish spittle, and it was expectorated not in the public streets but on a university campus. (Sadeq is now professor of Hebrew Literature at the University of Washington.)

In 1970, Shahak was offered and accepted the chair of the Israeli League for Human and Civil Rights. This body had been founded in 1936 (as the Palestine League for Human and Civil Rights) by Mordechai Avi-Shaul, a poet and translator of Thomas Mann whom Shahak describes as an honorable fellow traveler. Its purpose in 1936 was to support and defend the first and almost the only joint Jewish-Arab hunger strike by political prisoners against the British. In order to minimize the influence of pro-Moscow communists in the league, Shahak successfully moved for two standing rules. One was that the league would take no position on any area of the world not under Israeli jurisdiction. The other was that it would limit itself to upholding the 1949 U.N. Declaration of Human Rights. A member, therefore, need take no view on Palestinian self-determination, Afghanistan, South Africa, Iraq, or any other matter. As well as limiting its usefulness to infiltrators, these stipulations also reduced the number of excuses available to those who did not wish to join the league.

This self-limitation of the league's work did not prevent persecution, large and small, from falling on its chairman. Shahak's apartment was burgled several times, with nothing except books and papers taken—most especially books on Arab civilization. Telephone calls warned him of the possibility of a road accident, and he was shadowed by a van (always the same laundry van: secret policemen are stupid the world over) wherever he went. His telephone was ostentatiously tapped, with the occasional voice going so far as to break in angrily when he said something outrageous. His stepfather was approached and asked to apply pressure. But most hurtful of all, Shahak was accused by a planted questioner in a Washington audience of having betrayed his father to the Nazis.

He retains two strong impressions of this period of harassment, which he says came to an end in the late 1970s. The first was of the dishonesty and spite of many liberals, and the second was of the decency and the fortitude of many conservatives. In 1974, for example, he was attacked by Amnon Rubinstein (now a minister and the leader of the Shinui or "Change" Party) in a long article in *Ha'aretz*. Rubinstein argued that there was a strong prima facie case for charging Shahak with treason ("he has a mental perversion worse than Lord Haw Haw and Tokyo Rose during the Second World War") and challenged his right to citizenship, to a passport, and to his teaching post at the Hebrew University. This was for meeting with PLO supporters overseas. Uri Avneri, who is still considered by many to be the *preux chevalier* of Israeli liberalism, wrote that Shahak's "horror propaganda" was "liable to serve as ammunition in the hands of those who aspire to destroy the state"—precisely the accusation that is now leveled against Avneri himself by Likud and Labor propagandists. The *Jerusalem Post* columnist Lea Ben Dor went slightly further, ending her article with no less than four rhetorical questions:

> What shall we do about the poor professor? The hospital? Or a bit of the terrorism he approves? A booby-trap over the laboratory door?

Fortunately, there were no Smerdyakovs around to take up the Ben Dor incitement. More surprisingly, perhaps, there were a number of Establishment figures who mustered in Shahak's defense. His accession to full professorship in the chemistry department was held up three times by the university's nonacademic Board of Regents, until they were addressed by Ernst David Bergmann. Bergmann was a devoted government loyalist and had been the youngest professor of organic chemistry in pre-1933 Germany. He bluntly reminded the board that Shahak was a first-rate chemist and that politics had no bearing on that consideration.

Shahak is, as he puts it, "proud of the Israeli democracy." He admits to being more critical of the government at home than when he is abroad. And he is punctilious about such things as his reserve duty. He served in the infantry and in Chemical Intelligence in his youth, and still does guard duty in Jerusalem. He recalled with amusement the occasion when Menachem Begin was opening the proceedings of the shady rightist Jonathan Institute (that hothouse of value-free terrorism studies and retired security chiefs) at the Hilton Hotel. A conservative officer, whom Shahak had once called a Nazi racist in a public exchange on the Arab question, was overheard as he allotted guards for this event. He inquired of his brother officers whether Shahak might not be insulted by being given the detail. Shahak, on learning of this, said that it made no difference to him, and that he would stand looking like Schweik wherever he was told.

This ambivalence, if it is an ambivalence, was the material for the fifth day, when we considered what it means for an Israeli Jew to be an anti-Zionist.

Shahak's view is deceptively clear. He considers the mass immigration and settlement of Jews in Palestine to have been a mistake ab initio, starting colonialism in the Middle East at just the point where older colonial powers were abandoning it. He no longer believes the Zionist precepts that exile is a disease and that the Jews need a territorial society. But he does believe that, now that the community is established in Palestine, it ought not to be uprooted. After all, as he says, most Arab states are "artificial entities" too. And the "accidental and artificial" character of Alsace-Lorraine did not give Bismarck the right to annex it.

How does one actually live this contradiction? Well, first by striving to point it out; and second, by insisting that every postulate of Zionism, such as a Law of Return for Jews only, be countered by another one, such as the demand for an American-type constitution that would give all subjects equality before the law. Commitment of this kind determines certain adjustments to everyday life. Shahak will meet with declared Zionists only in formal circumstances, choosing his friends exclusively from among cothinkers. And he will no longer visit the West Bank or attend meetings of Palestinians unless they are overseas. This is partly because of the increased danger of police provocation, but even more because it is not possible to talk to a

Palestinian in conditions of equality. Shahak has numerous criticisms of the militarism and nationalism of the PLO, but he considers it indecent and undignified to express them as an Israeli citizen to an occupied people. One may question his *pudeur*, perhaps, while wishing that certain others could exhibit some of the same forbearance.

For this discussion—of how to be an anti-Zionist Jewish Israeli citizen—Shahak invited two of his colleagues from the Hebrew University to join us. Witold Jedlicki is a sociologist who left Poland in the 1970s, and Emmanuel Faradjun is a political economist whose family originated in the Lebanese Jewish community. Both men agree with Shahak that the political atmosphere in Israel is vastly healthier than it was before the Yom Kippur War, which so undermined the oafish complacency of the ruling Establishment, and Jedlicki cites 1982 as the watershed year because the ravaging of Lebanon led to political cooperation between people like himself and the larger world of antiwar Zionists. He believes that the isolation of the principled anti-Zionists is now over. But he has great forebodings about another war, which the military Establishment might choose to launch in the knowledge that the Reagan Administration is, from its point of view, the most indulgent possible. A war, after all, has the not entirely paradoxical effect of demoralizing peace movements. During the attack on Lebanon, Jedlicki recalls with scorn, Peace Now (which does not allow Arabs to join its ranks) made an announcement that it would suspend activities until hostilities were over. It turned out that public opinion, including a large number of reservists, was readier for protest than the patriotic peaceniks believed.

So I ask, What is the duty of an Israeli anti-Zionist in time of war? The question exposes narrow but deep differences among the three men. Jedlicki says he would be fatalistic about an Israeli military defeat, while Faradjun almost seems to say that Israel would deserve it. Shahak dissents, saying that it is important to distinguish between Palestinian nationalism and pan-Arabism. A pan-Arab triumph over Israel would not automatically be a triumph for the Palestinians and might even be a disaster for them. Of course, this is theoretical, since Israel can easily defeat any combination of Arab forces in any foreseeable future conflict. So Shahak is not, in the 1914 sense of a Liebknecht or a Luxemburg, a defeatist. He does say, though, that in the event of an Israeli attack on Jordan or Syria, he would be well satisfied with a reverse for Israeli arms and would consider the defeat merited as well as a possible source of lessons.

Important differences in emphasis appear, too, when the three discuss conscription. Shahak is "devoted to the principle" on standard democratic and egalitarian lines. Faradjun flatly refuses to serve in an army of conquest and occupation. Jedlicki points out that the draft corrupts conscripts into policemen and bullies. It also enforces Arab–Jewish segregation, because Israeli Arabs (contrary to widespread belief) are not *exempted* from the army but are, with the exception of certain Druze and Bedouin, actually *excluded* from it.

We find ourselves, as a result, having a version of the "moral equivalence" debate. Jedlicki, who is an old colleague and friend of Leszek Kolakowski, says that he wrote to him not long ago, after he had lent his name to the Jonathan Institute, comparing Generals Jaruzelski and Sharon. "In the whole of martial law in Poland," he says, "only a handful of deaths occurred. But Sharon murdered and massacred thousands of people. Does this not deserve to be in the moral reckoning?" Shahak adds that, of all the Arab cities within reach of Israel, only Aqaba and Amman have not been bombed, Aqaba because it is too near Saudi Arabia and Amman because King Hussein, too, enjoys a certain protection by the United States. It is the want of restraint, all three agree, that warrants the comparison between Israel and its ally South Africa.

On one point, Shahak and his colleagues are undivided. The official Israeli Left does not deserve the reputation for relative moderation that it enjoys among European social democrats and American liberals. It is the trade unions and the kibbutzim which have always been most systematic in excluding Arabs from membership and in enforcing discrimination. Zionist socialists have always been the most sinuous and deceptive in pretending that a Zionist state need not conflict with the interests of the Arab population. The Right, at least, never went in for that sort of double standard. In this sense, the duty of anti-Zionist radicals is to undertake a sort of permanent confrontation with illusion—especially the illusions about Israel that have been promulgated abroad. It would, says Shahak, obviously come as a surprise to most American liberal sympathizers of Zionism if they heard his demand that there should be equal voting, trade-union, and welfare rights for all Israeli citizens. This is because such people semiconsciously think of Israel as effectively part of the United States and of its professed value system.

Israel Shahak's voice, then, has a timbre that is very rarely heard in American discourse on the Jewish state. It has, I think, two kinds of relevance to that discourse. The first, and the most obvious, concerns the limitless self-deception and indulgence with which official America, and a decisive swath of its intellectual class, views Israeli plans and Israeli practices. To take only the most salient example: the four billions of United States dollars which are the seed of the special relationship are also the enabling fund for the annexation and colonization of the West Bank—a process from which official America then "officially" dissociates itself. Analogues of the same hypocrisy can be found all over the mass media and academia.

The second consequence of Shahak's project is that it locates the problem of religious fundamentalism in "our own" camp and does not relegate discussion of the subject to a morbid critique of the fanaticism and irrationality of "the other." Martin Buber pointed out long ago that, in the religious Jewish account, the world can be redeemed only by the redemption of Israel, and Israel, in the sense of the Jewish people, can be redeemed only by reuniting with the Holy Land. It was this that caused Herzl's movement to reject all consideration of other national homes—in Uganda, say. The same would have applied if postwar Europe had decided to make a proportionate reparation by offering, for instance, Austria. No, it had to be Palestine. Which meant that there had to be a confrontation with the Palestinian Arabs. The essentially secular and humane justifications for this—the debt owed to the Jewish people, the need to guarantee their security, and so forth—are essentially secondary to the biblical ones. Millennial forces are eclipsing the ideology of the founders of the Jewish state. These forces have never denied that this was the case.

One thus has the extraordinary situation of an apparently Western, developed nation, accoutred certainly with all the Western technology of war and accountancy, that spends real time discussing the differences among Genesis 15–18, Numbers 34:2, and Ezekiel 47:15–20 as a guide to policy. Shahak has expended a lot of time and ink in arguing that such disputes are not mere postscripts to the generalized idealizations of Israel commonly offered by Saul Bellow, Elie Wiesel, and others. A school bus from Petah Tikvah is hit by a train, with many children's deaths resulting. It is not Rabbi Kahane but Rabbi Yitzhak Peretz, Minister of Internal Affairs (to whom Mohammed Miari addressed his plea against anti-Arab racism), who describes this as God's judgment on Petah Tikvah for allowing film shows on Friday nights. He says this on television. The Jerusalem paper *Kol Ha'ir* runs an article by the former chief rabbi, Ovadia Joseph, in which it is said that a Jewish driver who sees another Jewish driver in trouble should stop and try to help, but that this obligation is void in the case of a non-Jew in similar straits. A law forbidding racial discrimination is eviscerated in the Knesset by parties who exempt all incitement against infidels that is derived from Scripture.

Shahak, who has long been the sternest opponent of religious brutishness, has also warned against certain counters to it. When the zealots of Mea Shearim began burning bus shelters with "profane" advertisements earlier this year, the response of secular Jewish militants was to invade the religious quarter and desecrate the synagogues with daubings of nude women and pigs. There was also some loose talk about the religious being "crows" (because of their black apparel) and "cowards" (because they do not serve in the army). Shahak opposed these tactics and this style because, he says, they borrow from the baser clichés of European anti-Semitism. Not even the incitement of a Rabbi Peretz should justify such a retort. I take this as an indication of the care and measure with which Shahak approaches matters.

As we concluded our talk over the final weekend, I began to recognize the unifying energy of Shahak's various essays, petitions, and polemics. Unlike the romantic, Gershom Scholem–type narrators, Shahak believes that the European Enlightenment did not merely free the Jews from superstitious discrimination and persecution by Gentiles but also liberated them from rabbinical control over their own stifled communities. His reverence as a Jew is for the attainments of Jews in that period of emancipation and for the achievements of Jews like Spinoza, who in earlier periods had withstood the pressures of orthodoxy. From this perspective, Zionism appears as a repudiation of these gains and an "ingathering" of the Jews under the stewardship of their former oppressors. It has also necessitated a colonial confrontation with the Muslim world and an alliance with the most backward elements (the Lebanese Phalange, the Guatemalan fascists, the American fundamentalists) in the Christian one. By attempting, in what has been a lonely and hazardous enterprise, to defend simultaneously the rights of the Palestinians and the liberties of the Jews, Shahak has been doing humanism an unacknowledged service.

(Raritan, Spring 1987)

CREON'S THINK TANK:
The Mind of Conor Cruise O'Brien

❑

The young man who had bumped against me asked why I didn't clap. I said I didn't clap because I didn't agree with a lot the speaker had said (by this time I had a fair idea that I was going to get a beating and on the whole preferred being beaten without having clapped to clapping and then getting beaten as well). . . . They wanted "to get O'Brien." They hit me several times and I fell down, then they started kicking me. An Apprentice Boy said: "Is it murder ye want?" After a short while they stopped kicking and went away.

(*States of Ireland*, 1972)

It was a warm afternoon, and I was taking a walk in the neighborhood of the Carlton Hotel, where I was staying. There were not many people around—shops and offices close at one o'clock on Saturday—and most of those who were around were black. Suddenly, quietly and quite gently, one of these grasped my arms from behind. Another appeared in front of me, very close. From a distance he might have seemed to be asking for a light. In fact, he had a knife with a four-inch blade pointed at my throat. . . .

So what? the reader may reasonably ask. A person can be mugged in any modern city. I know this. In fact, the last time I had been mugged—almost exactly twenty years before—was in Manhattan, at Morningside Park. Although that event occurred during a break in a Socialist Scholars' Conference at Columbia, it had no political significance.

("What Can Become of South Africa?" *The Atlantic*, March 1986)

In some people, the anecdotes above would appear too elaborately laconic. But there's nothing vicarious—nothing *armchair*—about the politics of Conor Cruise O'Brien. He is, and always has been, an *engagé*. Up at the sharp end in Katanga, mixing it with Nkrumah's boys in Ghana, getting too close to the action at an Orange rally in Northern Ireland (see above), and out and about in Johannesburg (see above also). Even when he held the Albert Schweitzer Chair in the Humanities at New York University—a title which gave great pleasure to his friends and enemies alike—he was not content with mere "teach-ins" against the Vietnam War. He had to go on the pavements too, leading to a memorably farouche duet with the forces of law and order and to the reflection, offered in *The New York Review of Books*, that "when a New York cop kicks you, you stayed kicked." The nicknames he acquired in the hard school of Dublin politics ("the Cruiser," "the Bruiser," "Conor Cruise O'Booze," "Camera Crews O'Brien") reflect his perennial attachment to the concrete and the earthy. When flown with argument or otherwise seized with emotion, O'Brien has often been heard by friends to cry, "I am Griboyedov!" In the case of most of our contemporary "columnists" and pundits, a claim to kinship with a Decembrist author, lynched in the Russian embassy in Teheran in 1829, would be laughable, pitiable, or both. In the case of the Cruiser, it comes out as a pardonable if quixotic exaggeration. Only his most parsimonious critic would deny that he submits his prejudices to the tests of experience and adventure.

Let me borrow from the audacity of my subject and admit at once that this review of his work is written by a socialist and a former as well as current admirer. How often have I heard, among the sodality of his friends and colleagues and former followers, "Conor's really sold out this time. How can you bother with that windbaggery?" How many times have they said later, and not always with contrition, "Did you read O'Booze on the Sandinistas? Rather good, considering"? I hew to my own chosen course, which is to say that O'Brien is far better—and much worse—than his enemies will credit.

Any consideration of his effort must begin with Ireland, that "damnable question" the petrifying intransigence of which was so well caught by Winston Churchill in a speech in 1922:

> Great empires have been overturned. The whole map of Europe has been changed. The modes of thought of men, the whole outlook on affairs, the grouping of parties, all have encountered violent and tremendous changes in the deluge of the world. But as the deluge subsides and the waters fall short we see the dreary steeples of Fermanagh and Tyrone emerging once again. The integrity of their quarrel is one of the few institutions that has been unaltered in the cataclysm which has swept the world.

It is as an Irishman that O'Brien has been incarnated in his roles of politician, diplomat, academic, and journalist. As a politican he has sat only as a member of Dáil Eireann, the lower house of the legislature of Ireland. As a diplomat, he was launched as Ireland's envoy to the United Nations. As a scholar, he was formed by the tension between the Catholic and Protestant educational institutions of his homeland. As a journalist, he has taken the subject of colonialism and anticolonialism for his own, and, as was once

famously said in *The Eighteenth Brumaire*, has translated each new language
back into the language of his birth.

Ireland, then. A fragment of memoir may be in order. O'Brien's agnostic
father died in 1927, when the boy was ten, and left his practicing Catholic
mother with a difficulty not easily resolved:

> For a Catholic parent at this time to send a child to a Protestant school was
> adjudged a mortal sin. Battle for my soul (and my mother's) went on over my
> head . . . my mother was in the middle. So I had gone to a Protestant preparatory
> school, then to the Dominican Convent at Muckross, Dublin, for first Com-
> munion. After that to Sandford Park, and more mortal sin.
>
> After my father's death, the pressure on my mother to withdraw me from
> this school must have been strong. Another widow, in a similar position, had
> withdrawn her boy not long before from Sandford. She had been told that by
> keeping the boy at a Protestant school she was prolonging her late husband's
> sufferings in Purgatory. Whether this argument in this form was put explicitly
> to my mother I cannot say, but she was certainly aware of its existence.

In fact, when the Roman Catholic Church after several centuries decreed
the nonexistence of limbo, O'Brien was to remark that he knew there was
such a place because his father, and therefore his mother, had been kept in
it by persuasive priests for many years. I don't aim to point out a discrepancy
here—rather to stress the absolute importance of Ireland, and of orthodoxy,
in O'Brien's formation.

O'Brien's immediate ancestors were staunch partisans of Charles Stewart
Parnell, and it is impossible to overstate the importance of Parnell's betrayal,
by the Catholic hierarchy and the Catholic mob, in the makeup of the
Cruiser. That betrayal and abandonment are captured in Joyce's *Portrait of
the Artist as a Young Man* and narrated in O'Brien's *Parnell and His Party*,
but they were probably best evoked by Yeats in his address to the Swedish
Academy on receiving his Nobel Prize in 1925:

> The modern literature of Ireland, and indeed all that stir of thought which
> prepared for the Anglo-Irish war, began when Parnell fell from power in 1891.
> A disillusioned and embittered Ireland turned from parliamentary politics and
> the race began, as I think, to be troubled by that event's long gestation.

A rough beast it was that resulted from this long gestation. As O'Brien
wrote in 1972:

> I live today in a Catholic Twenty-Six County state of which these men [the
> rebels of Easter 1916] are venerated as the founders, although in fact their
> Rising was an attempt to avert the coming into existence of that which they are
> now revered as having founded. Today, many who passionately believe in the

Republic they proclaimed—the Republic for the whole island—are still trying
to win that objective by shooting British soldiers in Northern Ireland.

The relative clumsiness and infelicity of these sentences, so uncommon
with O'Brien, are the consequence of a permanent ambivalence in his thinking, his upbringing, and (it might not be too extravagant to say) his soul.
For him, the forces of nationalism and guerrilla warfare, of the sort that
brought his own country into existence within living memory, are also identified with the cult of martyrdom, violence, and the irrational. This ambivalence is matched by another, which he confided to the readers of his *Writers
and Politics* in 1965. Who can forget the introduction in which he spoke of
capitalist "liberalism" as a habit of thought that made "the rich world yawn
and the poor world sick"? And who could fail to be arrested by the opening
exchange?

> "Are you a socialist?" asked the African leader.
> I said, yes.
> He looked me in the eye. "People have been telling me," he said lightly,
> "that you are a liberal."
> The statement in its context invited a denial. I said nothing.

Yet, reflecting on the exchange, he wrote, less tortuously this time:

> A liberal, incurably, was what I was. Whatever I might argue, I was more
> profoundly attached to liberal concepts of freedom—freedom of speech and of
> the press, academic freedom, independent judgement and independent
> judges—than I was to the idea of a disciplined party mobilising all the forces
> of society for the creation of a social order guaranteeing real freedom for all
> instead of just for a few.

Again, and compulsively, O'Brien attributed his preference for this definition
of freedom to the fact that Ireland had enjoyed so little of it. The pervasive
Irish Church, he wrote, shared "with that of Spain" the distinction of being
"the heart of darkness of the ecumenical movement."

O'Brien's encounter with "the African leader" took place after the disgraceful Western "rescue mission" in the Congo and before the consequent
murder of Patrice Lumumba. Chosen by Dag Hammarskjöld as United
Nations Special Representative for the colony—Hammarskjöld had read and
admired his *Maria Cross*, which examines the extremes of pain and guilt in
Catholic writing—O'Brien took up his post in Elisabethville in June 1961.
He devised—and may even have named—Operation Rumpunch, an effort
to expel the Katangais mercenaries. A later operation, which aimed to end
the secession itself, was not such a hit. O'Brien was accused of exceeding
his mandate and fell victim to the combined pressure of the Belgians, French,

and British. "As a result of the policy of Macmillan's government," O'Brien said after his dismissal, "Great Britain presents in the U.N. the face of Pecksniff and in Katanga the face of Gradgrind." Analogous reflections occur in his play *Murderous Angels*, set in the Congo.* For some years his fury at this business (which like so many other episodes he witnessed at first hand) warred with his liberal misgivings. He gained such a reputation for militancy on the point that *The Observer* wrote, in a characteristic access of liberal cant, that he was "so adamantly keeping silence on Communist excesses that he has done himself and his cause disservice." This was the period marked by his sharp critique of Camus for trying to have it both ways on French "pacification" in Algeria and by stern and beguilingly written speeches and articles on Western imperialism in Rhodesia, Cyprus, and Vietnam. One of those essays, entitled "Varieties of Anti-Communism," could be reprinted today with almost no footnotes.

A decade and a half later, O'Brien was editor in chief of *The Observer* and issuing weekly diatribes against "terrorism," "appeasement," "neutralism," and related transgressions. What explains the difference? Or was there less of a difference than an evolution? Two major things had happened.

Between the murder of Lumumba and his own translation to the redactorial chair, O'Brien had run, successfully at first, as a candidate of the Irish Labour Party. In an anecdote which is memorable in more than one way, he described what the 1969 election in clerical Ireland felt like:

> The Labour Party itself . . . had, fairly recently, taken to itself the designation of *Socialist*, and the distinction between Socialist and Communist is not clear to all Irish minds, and especially not to all Irish clerical minds, especially when they don't want it to be clear. My wife, shortly after this time, heard a priest in Dingle, County Kerry, deliver a sermon on "Communism and Socialism." The priest gave Communism the expected treatment. Then he went on to Socialism. "Socialism," he said, "is worse than Communism. Socialism is a heresy of Communism. Socialists are a Protestant variety of Communists." Not merely Communists, but *Protestant* Communists! Not many votes for Labour in Dingle.

Nineteen sixty-nine was also the year in which repeated Protestant pogroms against the Catholic population of Northern Ireland compelled the deployment of the British troops who remain there to this day (though no longer in the capacity of saviors of the minority). O'Brien's view of this new and improbable turn in events took some time to crystallize, and it was in the course of researching his opinion that he suffered the first kicking that

---

* A UN character in *Murderous Angels* is described as "a troublemaker . . . Clever. Bumptious. Talks too much. The British say he's a communist, but they just mean that he's Irish."

I quoted (it began when a "burly middle-aged Apprentice Boy brushed past me asking: 'Were ye ever in the Congo?' I smiled and he wheeled and came back: 'I wanted ye to know ye've been spotted. It will be safer for you to leave town' ").

That year of 1969 marked the emergence of the limited but ineradicable power of the Provisional IRA—a potent composite of Catholic extremism, populist militia, and Irish myth. This organization and its apologists, and the struggle against both of them, were to turn O'Brien from a reformist in Irish and British politics into a conservative. It's worth noting that in 1969 he already hated the reborn IRA, but chiefly because he suspected that "the CIA will be working the Provisionals" and that other Fenian extremists were "the kind of group a quiet American might well be interested in." These were the judgments of a Parnellite who could still hate the Catholic fanatics for betraying the best of their own cause. They were also the judgments of a man still fixated on Katanga. How long could such a dualism endure?

Not long. Within a few years, O'Brien had become a minister in an Irish coalition government. And not merely a minister, but the Minister of Posts and Telegraphs. In this capacity, he found himself for the first time on the opposite side of the demarcation between censor and writer, cop and protester, peacekeeper and revolutionary. His job involved the strict invigilation of the press and television, to insure that sympathizers of the Provisionals did not succeed in addressing the public directly. It also involved him in a number of threats to his life and property. All of a sudden the old rebel and critic had bodyguards and officials on his side, and heresy to be rooted out. Unlike a number of former nationalist politicians who had found themselves in the same position, O'Brien did not try to run with the hare and hunt with the hounds. He entirely accepted the logic of his position—with honor but, in the opinion of some friends, with slightly too much relish. He became an expert in pointing out that such-and-such a speech, such-and-such a resolution, was "objectively" encouraging terrorism. He delighted in stressing the implacable obstacle that the Protestant Unionists presented to the age-old dream of a united Ireland. He particularly enjoyed taunting the Catholic Church and its party, the mealy-mouthed Fianna Fáil, for the euphemistic way in which they condemned "all" violence while striving to avoid specific references to the IRA or the Republican cause.

These kinds of modifications to the personality and the outlook have a way, as we know from others, of becoming intoxicating. After a while, it came naturally to O'Brien to say things like

The domain of the anarchic and the arbitrary appears to be extending in society generally. To acquiesce in its extension in broadcasting would probably have the effect of accelerating its extension in society.

That was in 1979, which was something of a hinge year for O'Brien. He began to generalize his opinions on Ulster in much the same way as he had once made a touchstone issue of Katanga. There were various symptoms of the change, the most disturbing of which to his admirers was a verbose essay called "Liberty and Terror" (the title obviates the need for any quotation) in the pages of *Encounter*. It was only a decade or so since O'Brien, in his *Encounters with the Culturally Free*, had tossed and gored the Cold War front organization run by Melvin Lasky and Irving Kristol and given them a pasting in the law courts to boot.

It was also in 1979 that the battle for the British colony of Southern Rhodesia, then in the throes of a white-settler rebellion *à la katangaise*, moved to its climax. O'Brien, who had long been a fierce opponent of the Ian Smith regime, began to "evolve" his position. He visited Robert Mugabe, the exiled leader of the black guerrilla struggle, in Mozambique. Mugabe, who had been educated as a Catholic, got off on the wrong foot by asking O'Brien whether he supported "the freedom fighters in your own country." This earned him, and the readers of *The Observer*, a severe lecture about the terrorism of the Provisional IRA. It also earned the Smith regime, then nominally headed by the Protestant bishop Abel Muzorewa, an amazingly indulgent progress report. (Mugabe later told a friend of mine in conversation that he had been joking about the IRA and had really wanted to ask O'Brien about Lumumba.)

As events unfolded, O'Brien had to make a partial recantation of his credulity about the reformist intentions of Ian Smith. But it was clear that his "way of seeing" had undergone a profound change. He had learned to look at the world from the perspective of the foundation seminar, the bullet-proof limousine, and the counterinsurgency technician. He could descry, in the features of a ruling elite, the lineaments of an oppressed minority. The dreary steeples of Fermanagh and Tyrone, occupied provinces of the Protestant Unionist ascendancy, were soon to be superimposed on Southern Africa and the Middle East.

Derry City is a Protestant Holy City . . . a symbol of the spirit of Protestant Ulster. The long siege of Derry by King James's Catholic Army, and its relief by King William's Protestant fleet in 1689, belong with the Battle of the Boyne at the centre of Ulster Protestant iconography and patriotism. The Boyne is a distant image like Jerusalem, a holy place *in partibus infidelium*, a proud memory in a lost land. . . . Northern Ireland itself lives a siege.

(*States of Ireland*, 1972)

I believe that Israel cannot be other than what it is—in the basic sense that Israel is not free to be other than the Jewish state in Palestine, and that the

Jewish state, once in possession of Jerusalem, is not capable of relinquishing that city.

(The Siege, 1986)

So also in Northern Ireland: Orange rallies are generally stolid, casual and good-humored, but the detected presence of a Catholic, presumed hostile, can evoke some latent hysteria and violence; I speak from experience. (The Orange/Afrikaner comparison is quite a fertile one, provided it is not being used just for the stigmatisation, or demonisation, of one community or the other, or both.)

("What Can Become of South Africa?" *The Atlantic*, March 1986)

O'Brien's large, rambling book *The Siege* is the latest flowering of his new style. In this style, which incorporates Ulster as a sort of King Charles's head, polite curiosity extends to all parties, but sympathy is reserved only for the overdogs. I don't propose to review *The Siege* as a historical chronicle but merely to point out how it makes this preference clearly and consistently evident.

The acknowledgments of the book, which run to four pages, do not include a single Arab name. In other words, the putative "besiegers," many hundreds of thousands of whom actually live *within* the citadel against their will,* are not consulted *at all*. This from the man who rightly pointed out the absence of Arabs from the Oran of *The Plague*. The bibliography, which lists two hundred and ninety-six entries, features twenty books or articles written by Arabs and four written by people who might be described as their sympathizers. There is no sign, however, in the text that O'Brien has read any of these books except one—which he quotes, rather revealingly, once. The book is Edward Said's *The Question of Palestine*. O'Brien very briefly states that volume's factual claim that Palestinian Arabs took no part in the Holocaust of the Jews in Europe. Commenting on this, O'Brien adds, as if making the point for the first time against a storm of opposition:

Israelis will accept a part, though only a small part, of this argument. They agree generally that Jews have historically been better, or less badly, treated in Arab and Muslim lands than in Christendom. But Israelis do not accept that Arabs, and Palestinian Arabs in particular, did not sympathise with Nazi Germany and its policy towards the Jews. Not only was the Grand Mufti Hitler's guest in Berlin, while the Holocaust was going on, but he remained the unquestioned leader of the Palestinian Arabs after the defeat of Nazi Germany.

One might ask, "Which Israelis?" of the first sentence, and, "Which Palestinians?" of the last. One might even inquire, unkindly and demagogically,

---

* As, of course, do many nationalist Irish and the actual majority of the population of South Africa.

about the pro-Nazi past of Yitzhak Shamir. Instead, let us compare this paragraph with another one written by O'Brien in the same year:

> This was the late thirties, and the early ideologues of apartheid were influenced to some degree by the language and concepts of contemporary European right-wing authoritarianism—usually in its milder forms. (Though many leading Afrikaner nationalists were "pro-Nazi" during the war, the affinity seems to have been less ideological than a matter of "the enemy of one's enemy" as with other subject people's nationalisms in the same period; compare the "pro-Nazism" of Flemish, Breton and Palestinian nationalists.)

In other words, the Palestinians may be excused, may even be given quotation marks for their "pro-Nazism," but only when it's a question of exonerating the Afrikaners. This is the most vivid single example of O'Brien's overdog world view in operation. It makes it almost but not quite irrelevant to recall that the ideology of the Afrikaner Right was explicitly National Socialist, that the founders of today's National Party were imprisoned for acts of sabotage in the Nazi cause, and that they have run a "master race" system since 1948—the very year that the Palestinians lost their homeland itself. Is this, perhaps, the O'Brien declension of moral equivalence? (Incidentally, there was a time when he would have known how to deal with a person who wrote of "European right-wing authoritarianism—usually in its milder forms.")

If O'Brien now specializes in exonerating the overdog, he is no slouch at blaming the underdog either. Toward the conclusion of *The Siege* he writes:

> By a kind of paradoxical effect often noted in these passages, the main result of the unremitting international efforts to bring about the withdrawal of Israel from the West Bank is probably to speed up that sinister interaction [of "extremists," naturally—C.H.] and to increase the danger to the territory's Arab population.

The *what* international efforts? The unremitting *what* efforts? The unremitting international *what?* The ensuing paragraph is still finer:

> Those in the West who urge that the effort to rule over large numbers of Arabs may eventually destroy Israel itself might do well to note that Meir Kahane is making the same point, while drawing from it an inference radically different from what the Western critics have in mind.

And what's that supposed to mean? It's supposed to mean that, if there is a mass expulsion of Arabs, it will be the fault of those who objected to their being colonized in the first place. No overdog could hope for more deft, more sinuous apologetics.

When it suits him, O'Brien ascribes malign reality to the efforts of malign people. When it does not suit him, he reduces malign reality to a set of unalterable, if regrettable, circumstances. The Israeli–South African revolving door, with quick shifts through the Irish looking glass, is again revealing in this respect.

Take, first, the "necklace." O'Brien knows very well that this and other forms of violence and revenge are very new in the struggle of the South African majority. He is also perfectly aware of the history of the African National Congress and of the long, bitter process by which it was disenfranchised, driven underground, and deprived, along with its huge army of supporters, of any peaceful means of redress. This is ABC. Yet O'Brien does not attribute the sudden arrival of "necklacing" in any way to the long train of oppressions and usurpations suffered by the majority. On the contrary, he sneers at the ANC for being ambivalent in its condemnation of the practice and finally says that the ANC is "a political movement whose sanction, symbol and signature is the burning alive of people in the street." Actually, the sanction, symbol, and signature of the ANC is Nelson Mandela, held in prison for over two decades and still the first choice of most Africans and many whites, Indians, and those of mixed race. But in a twenty-three-page essay in *The Atlantic*, O'Brien mentioned him only once—and that in passing—while devoting great space to the "necklace" and making nine references to the parallels between Northern Ireland and South Africa. The one time in such a long depiction of apartheid that the word "disgusting" is used is in a reference to the academic boycott of the regime—a boycott which O'Brien seems to think it takes courage to break.

In South Africa, then, violent acts are the fault of those among the underdogs who commit them, and all else is cant. But in Israel, acts of repression and discrimination, if they occur, are to be blamed on the circumstances. One of these circumstances, unsurprisingly, is the tendency of underdogs to chafe.

O'Brien quotes the Israeli professor Yehoshua Porath, who says of the Arabs of Israel that "with their numbers they have the power to operate within Israel's democratic political system, to influence its moves, perhaps even disrupt it. (Does anyone recall the tremendous influence that Parnell and Redmond's Irish national party had on parliamentary life in Great Britain in the thirty years prior to World War I?)" Commenting, O'Brien says delightedly that "Professor Porath does not spell out what that comparison implies, so let me do so":

> As Porath and others see, conditions seem in some ways favorable to the emergence in Israel of some kind of Arab Parnell. But such a phenomenon would necessarily have an even far greater [*sic*] explosive impact on Israel than Parnell and Redmond had on Britain. Britain was not surrounded by Irish people, in

overwhelming numbers, hoping not merely for the secession of Ireland but for the destruction of the entire British polity and society.

(Though, it might be fair to add, you would not have known this from Parnell's enemies at the time, who combined to ruin and frame him, and who predicted universal chaos and anarchy if Ireland were to attain self-determination.) What is O'Brien's conclusion from this potentially fertile comparison? Go to the source:

> The day of choice between the Jewish state and the Arab franchise is still some way off, but the nature of the choice can hardly be in doubt.

Here, notice, no judgments are made. If the Arabs must lose their rights as citizens, as O'Brien elsewhere suggests they will—without saying that they shouldn't—then it is nobody's doing and nobody's fault. It's just that the "choice" is somehow ineluctable.

The antecedent of this combination of fatalism with cynicism may lie in O'Brien's lone (or so he thinks) efforts to ward off disorder in Ireland. He made, and makes, repeated use of Sophocles to do so. And as his vision of Antigone has modified, so has he. The following admonitions are taken from a famous talk he gave—in the thick of it again—to the students of Queen's University, Belfast, during the hot autumn of 1968:

> (1) It was Antigone's free decision, *and that alone*, which precipitated the tragedy. Creon's responsibility was the more remote one of having placed this tragic power in the hands of a headstrong child of Oedipus. [italics mine]
> (2) The disabilities of Catholics in Northern Ireland are real, but not overwhelmingly oppressive: is their removal really worth attaining at the risk of precipitating riots, explosions, pogroms, murder? Thus Ismene. But Antigone will not heed such calculations: she is an ethical and religious force, an uncompromising element in our being, as dangerous in her way as Creon, whom she persistently challenges and provokes.
> (3) Without Antigone, we could attain a quieter, more realistic world. The Creons might respect one another's spheres of influence if the instability of idealism were to cease to present, inside their own dominions, a threat to law and order.

It was the Protestant Ulsterman Tom Paulin who pointed out that the last extract had been dropped from the reprinting of the speech in *States of Ireland*. This was because, or so he dryly suggested, the "Loyalist" pogroms had intervened between the giving of the speech and its publication. As Paulin added:

In recommending Ismene's common sense he is really supporting Creon's rule of law. It is as though a future member of Creon's think-tank can be spotted hiding behind the unfortunate Ismene.

That prediction, made in 1980, prefigures O'Brien's increasing willingness to see "status quo" or "backlash" violence as part of the natural order. Ismene, finally, sided with Antigone. Creon's advisers must in the end rely on their own arguments.

The propaganda value of representing politics as a series of "sieges" is largely (I don't say solely) a recruitment of sympathy for embattled *colons* in three loosely related cases of which O'Brien has personal experience. It is an ahistorical, emotional metaphor, which has the effect of translating elites into minorities and absolving them while one's attention is elsewhere. It also leaves out—in all three cases—the truly besieged. By this I don't mean the Catholics of the Six Counties, the Africans of South Africa, or the Arabs of Palestine, all of whom are demonstrably the disadvantaged parties in the present state(s) of affairs. I mean the many brave Ulstermen, Israelis, and South Africans who have, for generations, confronted their own tribes with criticism, opposition, and argument from within. The "besiegers," in O'Brien's weird inversion of things, may suffer from fanaticism and messianism. But can this not also be said of the Broederbond, the Orange Order, and the Gush Emunim? There was a time when the internal dissidents, living in continuous danger and exposed to repeated assault and calumny, would have commanded O'Brien's support. But in all the voluminous sentimentality of his recent books and essays, he has found no space to mention Bram Fischer or Breyten Breytenbach, Meir Pa'il or Boaz Evron, Miriam Daly or David Turnley. The mere mention of I. F. Stone in his acknowledgments to *The Siege* comes with the dull quip "Health Warning there, on this particular subject." Perhaps O'Brien might soon give us an essay entitled "The Quarantine," in which dissidents would be excluded altogether and only the agonies of the potentates would be considered at all. He seemed to be moving in this direction in a December 1985 *New Republic* article which, in a near-parody of the then-regnant Reaganite style, proposed:

If surrender, or partial surrender, to the terrorist organization is excluded, then the only real alternative is to shut up about political solutions and treat the problem entirely as one of security. But even that is now much more difficult as a result of years of "peace processing," including vast international media attention for terrorists, and the encouragement given to known terrorists by international organizations, by many governments, both democratic and non-democratic, and by high spiritual authorities.

That could have been James Burnham on a bad day, or the Committee for the Free World on an average one. But O'Brien is not quite ready, yet, to indulge his taste for low company to that extent. Just as the reactionary crew was closing in on him, avid for a new defector and keen to shine in the reflection of his superior style, O'Brien made a sideways leap. He began to write, consistently and with some verve, against the proxy war waged by the United States on Nicaragua. Careful reading of his article on the question shows a certain consistency with his other contributions. Nicaragua does not properly belong in the "besieged" category that exists in the O'Brien imagination, because it is insurgent. But, then again, it cannot by any device of propaganda be represented credibly as a besieger. And, even in O'Brien's most slippery defense of the conservative elites in Ulster, Israel, and South Africa, there is still the indignant echo of an Irishman opposed to the coercion of small nations.

In fact, his lengthiest essay on the matter, published from his *Atlantic* pulpit in August 1986, took the form of a rebuke to the Nicaraguan Catholic hierarchy. The rebuke was polite and measured, containing none of the abuse or innuendo which O'Brien now reserves for the fellow travelers of besiegers, but it was firm. As he pointed out, in Nicaragua the patron of the opposition, both legal and illegal, is Cardinal Miguel Obando y Bravo. And, despite the fact that Obando displays all the learning and subtlety of a village priest under Vichy, he is a cardinal by the express wish of Pope John Paul II. And John Paul II has one main aim, according to O'Brien:

—to reassert the *magisterium*: the teaching authority and discipline of the Universal Church, under the Successor of Peter.

In other words, to put Central America back under the sway of those who had, before Vatican II, bullyragged O'Brien's widowed mother and pilloried Parnell. Against this, also according to O'Brien:

Putting the thing another way, and invoking the name of another reformer, Managua is a potential Geneva for Latin America.

No need to speculate about the Irish influence on those two *aperçus*; O'Brien while in Managua spent much time interviewing pro-Sandinista Irish missionaries and pointed out with some glee that Irish people had always ignored the Holy Father when it came to contraception. So eager was he to point out the feebleness of Vatican doctrine that he overpraised the callow sacraments of the so-called Church of the Poor and forgot for the moment that he had baited radical Christians in his South Africa article by saying, fatuously:

The invention of apartheid was a major achievement of liberation theology.

O'Brien's teasing is worth a separate essay; he adores to madden radicals by pointing out, for instance, that the Irish Republicans used to support the Boers. But the teasing, like the sober analysis, is all of a piece. The piece is an Irish piece, and it comes from Edmund Burke, whom so many conservative snobs imagine to have been an English gentleman. O'Brien is actually rather more like Burke than like Griboyedov. He once, in introducing an edition of the *Reflections on the Revolution in France*, distinguished three separate Burkean styles:

(1) There is what one might call the Whig manner: rational, perspicacious, businesslike. . . . It is a tone well-adapted to its purpose, which is that of convincing people who have a great deal to lose that certain policies are, and other policies are not, in accordance with their interests.
(2) Burke's second manner might be called Jacobite: both Gothic and pathetic. . . . Once one is aware of this reserve of underlying emotion, even the more prosaic parts of the argument take on a more formidable sonority.
(3) Burke's third manner is a peculiar kind of furious irony. Irony is a marked characteristic of Irish writing; I have argued elsewhere that the Irish predicament, with its striking contrast between pretences and realities, has been unusually favorable to the development of this mode of expression. (Introduction to Burke's *Reflections*, 1969)

O'Brien's early works, especially the essays in *Writers and Politics* and the books on Katanga, Parnell, and Camus, show the first and the third manners in a pleasing apposition. But there was always the trapdoor of the second, waiting to fall open and drop him into a pit of Gothic pathos and sonority. Despite promptings and reminders from his alter ego, the Burke who informs O'Brien today is most often the Burke who dwelt on banal realism and pompously instructed us that "the nature of things is a sturdy adversary." This application of Burke, in its turn, undoubtedly eases the task of telling the besiegers, and reassuring the besieged, that they have no choice: that things must be as they must be. This is why, to put it squarely, it has become less and less of a pleasure to quote O'Brien on anything.

In the end, that shyly expressed preference for "liberal values" over revolution is deceptive. Many people don't have such a choice, and those who do can quite easily find themselves sacrificing the "liberal values" in the battle against revolutionaries. O'Brien won't be the first intellectual to take that route, if he opts for it as he seems to have done. But let him ponder his own verdict on Burke the Irishman:

The contradictions in Burke's position enrich his eloquence, extend its range, deepen its pathos, heighten its fantasy and make possible its strange appeal to "men of liberal temper." On this interpretation, part of his power to penetrate the processes of a revolution derives from a suppressed sympathy with revolution, combined with an intuitive grasp of the subversive possibilities of *counter*-revolutionary propaganda, as affecting the established order in the land of his birth. . . . For him the forces of revolution and the counter-revolution exist not only in the world at large but also within himself.

(*Grand Street,* Spring 1987)

READING TO BORGES

❑

This is my country and it might be yet,
But something came between us and the sun.

As the old man threw off these lines, he turned his blind, smiling face to
me and asked, "Do they still read much Edmund Blunden in England?" I
was unsure of what might give pleasure, but pretty certain in saying that
Blunden was undergoing one of his eclipses. "What a shame," said Jorge
Luis Borges, "but then you still have Chesterton. I used to live in Ken-
sington, you know. What a writer. Such a pity he became a Catholic."

The changes of pace in a conversation with Borges seemed alarming at
the time, but in retrospect showed nothing but one's own nervousness. He
was always searching for a mutually agreeable topic, and seemed at times
to fear that it was he, lonely, sightless, and claustrated, who might be the
dull partner in chat. When he found a subject that would please, he began
to bubble and grin, and even to tease.

I had made my way to Maipu 994, near the Plaza San Martín, and found
apartment 6B after a great deal of discouragement. Argentine government
officials, usually so quick to sing of the splendors of their country, became
curiously *diminuendo* when I asked if Borges was well enough to receive
visitors. "He does not welcome guests, Señor. He does not welcome invi-
tations either. It is better not to trouble him." At last I simply dialed his
number, imagined him working his way across the room as it rang, and was
rewarded with an invitation to call upon him.

This was at the height of General Videla's pogrom against dissent, and I
had already learned that a private telephone conversation in Buenos Aires
was a difficult thing to have. Borges didn't care about this, partly because
he heartily approved of the generals then in power. He gave me the couplet
from Blunden as an instance of his feeling for Juan Perón, the vulgar mobster
who had persecuted him and his family. But we didn't touch upon this until
much later. He wanted to discuss English and Spanish as mediums of literature. "I was speaking Spanish and English before there were any such
languages. Do you know that in Mexico they say, 'I am seeing you' when

they mean, 'I will see you'? I find the translation of the present into the future very ingenious. But when I think of the Bible I think of King James. And most of my reading is in English."

He had a great respect for *Martín Fierro*, the demotic gaucho epic that is the distinctive Argentine ballad. And he had a feeling for the folklore of the country's numerous and futile wars. But he disliked the ornate pageantry that sometimes substituted for tradition in Buenos Aires, "the showy pomp and circumstance—the hypocrisy." His religion, he said, was Presbyterian if anything, and he had some Portuguese Jewish influence in his family. It was this latter aspect that had helped stir the malice of Perón and, though he did not realize it, was the reason for the coolness of General Videla's people as well.

Back to England. "I began to learn Old English when I went blind in 1955, and it helped me to write 'The Library of Babel.' I made a special pilgrimage to Lichfield once, because of Dr. Johnson. But I hated Stratford." "Did you learn Old Norse?" "No, not really, that is—no. But would you read me some Kipling?" "With pleasure." "Then make it 'The Harp Song of the Dane Women.' And please read it slowly. I like to take long, long sips."

> *What is a woman that you forsake her,*
> *And the hearth fire and the home acre,*
> *To go with that old, grey widow-maker* . . .

When I had finished he sat for a while and said, "Kipling was not really appreciated in his own time because all his peers were socialists. Will you come and read me more Kipling tomorrow?" I said yes.

Next day I led him down a spiral staircase on my arm, and took him to lunch. He talked of how reverse and obverse were the same to him, so that infinity was almost banal. He said that he always felt utterly lost when he was dreaming, which was perhaps the source of the recurrent labyrinth in his writing. I asked him why he had always been so polite about Pablo Neruda, and he replied that while he much preferred Gabriel García Már-quez, he didn't want anyone to think that he was jealous of Neruda's Nobel Prize for literature. "Though when you see who has had it—Shaw, Faulkner. Still, I would grab it. I feel greedy." He said later that "not giving me the Nobel Prize is a minor Swedish industry."

I read him lots more Kipling and Chesterton until the time came to part. Could I come back again? Alas, I had to fly to Chile that evening. "Ah, well, if you see General Pinochet, please present him with my compliments. He was good enough once to award me a prize, and I consider him a gentleman." I don't remember what I answered to that, but I do remember that it made a perfect match with the rest of his general conversation. He delighted in saying that the Videla government was one of "gentlemen rather than pimps." He explained to me the precise etymology of the Argentine slang for pimp, which was *canfinflero* or, as he also relished saying, "cunter." Though he was aloof from the Cold War ("Why should we choose between two second-rate countries?") he loathed the idea of the mob and the many-headed. For him, English literature was a respite from all that. "My 'Dr. Brodie's Report' is taken from Swift. And 'Death and the Compass' is like Conan Doyle in 3-D."

Long before war broke out between his homeland and his beloved England (words like "folk" and "kin" recurred in his talk), Borges had seen through the Videla regime. He had signed a public protest about the 15,000 disappeared, which was perhaps the more powerful for having been so belated. He had spoken against the idea of a *macho* war with Chile over the stupid issue of the Beagle Channel. And his poem deploring the Falklands was as ironic and eloquent as anything written in Buenos Aires could afford to be. For a man who told me that "I spend my days alone, in daydreams and the evolution of plots," he was astoundingly alive to "the outside" and peculiarly ready to take risks. I can never hear the sneer about "ivory towers" without reflecting that Borges, who was confined to one by his blindness, managed to make honorable amendments to his cherished point of view.

As I left him, he said he would like to give me a present. I made the usual awkward disclaimers about how he shouldn't think of such a thing but he pressed on and recited a poem which he told me I would not forget. Looking me in the eye, as it were, he said:

> What man has bent o'er his son's sleep, to brood
> How that face shall watch his when cold it lies?
> Or thought, as his own mother kissed his eyes,
> Of what her kiss was when his father wooed?

This remains the only Dante Gabriel Rossetti sonnet I can unfailingly recall.

(*The Spectator*, June 21, 1986)

THE CHORUS AND CASSANDRA

❏

In his imperishable *Treatise on the Art of Political Lying,* published in 1714, Dr. John Arbuthnot laid down a standard for falsifiers and calumniators that has yet to be excelled:

> Detractory or defamatory lies should not be quite opposite to the qualities the person is supposed to have. Thus it will not be found according to the sound rules of pseudology to report of a pious and religious prince that he neglects his devotions and would introduce heresy; but you may report of a merciful prince that he has pardoned a criminal who did not deserve it.

Sixteen years ago I went to the Examination Schools at Oxford University to hear Professor Noam Chomsky deliver the John Locke Lectures. The series was chiefly concerned with modern theories of grammar, syntax, and linguistics, but Chomsky attached a condition which the syndics of the university could not easily decline. He insisted on devoting one entire, self-contained lecture to the American war in Indochina and to the collusion of "academic experts" in an enterprise which was, he maintained, debauching America even as it savaged Vietnam.

Several things intrigued me about the stipulation. First, I liked the way Chomsky separated his political statement from his obligation as a guest lecturer rather than, as was and is the style at Oxford, pretending to objectivity while larding the discourse with heavily sarcastic political "pointers." There was no imported agenda of the kind one got from Hugh Trevor-Roper, Max Beloff, or John Sparrow. Second, I was impressed by his insistence, which was the inverse of the shifty practice of Tory and liberal scholars, that academics could and should have a role in political life but should state their allegiance squarely. It had, after all, been only a few months since Gilbert Ryle had told us, as we clamored about the crushing of Czechoslovakia, "What can we do? We are philosophers, not lifeboat men." That there was *something* wrong with the Rylean bleat I was certain. What it was, I was not sure. Chomsky seemed to suggest that you need not politicize the academy in order to take a stand, but that if you did not take a stand, then you were being silent about a surreptitious politicization of it. To the hundreds of us who broke the habit of many terms and for once attended lectures consistently and on time, he seemed to have a measured, unshakable, but still passionate manner that contrasted rather well with the ardent ultraleft confusion and the creepy conservative evasions that were competing at the time.

Still, Chomsky was unmistakably on the left, though he scorned the sectarians and the know-alls. In those days, also, you could read him everywhere; his name had a kind of cachet. He was interviewed with respect on television and radio, though more often abroad than in America. He was a seminal contributor to *The New York Review of Books*. His predictions about a widening of the Indochina war, and a consequent narrowing of the choices between a Sovietization of the peninsula and an utter devastation of it, now seem almost banal in their accuracy. Nineteen sixty-nine was before Nixon's "madman theory," before Kissinger's "decent interval," before the Christmas bombing, the Church Committee, the "plumbers," and all the rest of it. Tumultuous as it seemed at the time, the period in retrospect appears an age of innocence. The odd thing—and I wonder why it didn't occur to me more forcefully then—was that, the more Chomsky was vindicated, the less he seemed to command "respect." To the extent that I reflected about this at all, I put it down to shifts in fashion ("Chomsky?—a sixties figure"), to the crisis undergone by many superficial antiwar commentators when the American war was succeeded by Spartan regimes (of which more later), and to the fact that Chomsky had started to criticize the Israelis, seldom a prudent course for those seeking the contemplative life.

As "wound healing" went on in American society, and as we were being bidden to a new age where "self-doubt and self-criticism" were things of the past, and just as I was wondering whether one would admire an *individual* who had put self-doubt and self-criticism behind him, Oxford struck back at Noam Chomsky. In the 1983 *Biographical Companion to Modern Thought*, edited by Alan Bullock, there appeared a 550-word entry under Chomsky, Avram Noam. Of these 550 words, the most immediately arresting were those which maintained that he had

> forfeited authority as a political commentator by a series of actions widely
> regarded as ill-judged (repeated polemics minimising the Khmer Rouge atroc-
> ities in Cambodia; endorsement of a book—which Chomsky admitted he had
> not read—that denied the historical reality of the Jewish Holocaust).

The piece was written by Geoffrey Sampson, an academic nonentity who made various other incautious allegations and who later, while engaged in an exchange with my friend Alexander Cockburn [*The Nation*, December

22, 1984, and March 2, 1985], strolled into the propellers and was distributed into such fine particles that he has never been heard from again.

Elsewhere in his entry, Sampson alluded foolishly to "relationships between the academic and political sides of Chomsky's thought," going so far as to say that "Chomsky has sometimes made such links explicit, for instance in arguing that Lockean empiricist philosophy paved the way for imperialism," and concluding lamely that "recently, however, Chomsky has insisted on a rigid separation between the two aspects of his work." This, insofar as it was not a simple-minded non sequitur, I knew to be flatly untrue from my attendance at the John Locke Lectures in 1969. In a 1985 article in *The New Criterion*, Sampson made an equally false claim about threats of legal action against his person from Chomsky, succeeded in convincing only its editor, the too-credulous Hilton Kramer, and the undiscriminating Martin Peretz, of *The New Republic*, of his veracity, was made to apologize by Cockburn, and, as I said, disappeared like breath off a razor blade.

My curiosity was ignited, not at first by the debate over the integrity of the Bullock crib, but by the fact that anything so cavalier and crude had been published at all. Bullock and his deputies are nothing if not respecters of persons. And we live in a world where fact checkers, subeditors, and (except for people like Chomsky, who eschew them on principle) libel lawyers work mightily to protect reputations on both sides of the Atlantic. How came it that Noam Chomsky, among the few Americans of his generation to lay claim to the title of original thinker, could be treated in such an offhand way? As I later found, Chomsky had written to a stoically indifferent Bullock:

> If you would have the time or interest to look into the matter, I would be intrigued to hear your opinion about what the reaction would be under the circumstance that such scurrilous lies were to appear in a biographical dictionary—or were to be published in a book by a reputable publisher such as Oxford or Fontana—about a person who is not known as a political dissident.*

---

* A good question. Looking merely from *G* to *K* in the *Biographical Companion to Modern Thought,* I came across the following references:
Gielgud, Arthur John:
  His popularity with the public was reflected in the long runs given to *Richard of Bordeaux* (1932), *Dear Brutus* (1941) and *A Day by the Sea* (1953).
Goering, Hermann:
  Before 1939 his origins in the regular imperial officer corps had made him the hope of conservative opponents of Nazism inside Germany, a hope which attracted some attention abroad but did not survive his somewhat equivocal role during the phony war period.
Graham, William Franklin ("Billy"):
  His appeal was simple and complicated, he was charming and in no way aggressive except to sin. . . . His last massive campaign was in Korea in 1973 when American prestige in Asia was at its lowest.
Hayek, Friedrich August von:
  Austrian/British economist and political philosopher whose immensely fertile mind has produced nearly 200 separate works, including major contributions to scientific methodology,

All this began to interest me at about the turn of the New Year. In the following weeks, without even trying, I was able to glean the following merely from the journals and papers to which I subscribe in the ordinary way:

As the Khmer Rouge were about to take over, Noam Chomsky wrote that their advent heralded a Cambodian liberation, "a new era of economic development and social justice." (David Horowitz and Peter Collier, *The Washington Post Sunday Magazine,* April 8, 1985)

To justify his assertion that American political science is corrupt (a very serious charge), he [Philip Grant] quotes from Noam Chomsky and other supporters of the North Vietnamese cause in the Vietnam war, who attacked those leaders of political science in America who were either impartial in their attitude to that war or were sympathetic to the cause of South Vietnam. (Professor Maurice Cranston, Letters, *The Times Literary Supplement,* April 5, 1985)

Who among them [leaders of the antiwar movement] has been willing to suggest that the murder of a million or more Cambodians by the Khmer Rouge might have been averted if American military force had not been removed from Indochina? If any of them spoke out this way, I missed it. But I did hear Noam Chomsky seek to prove the Cambodian genocide hadn't happened.
(Fred Barnes, Senior Editor, *The New Republic,* April 29, 1985)

Nor was this all. Without digging very much further, I found that the London *Spectator* had just published an article by Richard West on September 29, 1984, which lustily indicted

---

psychology and the history of ideas. Hayek's name is virtually synonymous with the cause of libertarianism. . . . Honours have been showered on him.

Hook, Sidney:
 As a philosopher, Hook has been concerned primarily with the ways in which values enter into political discourse, rather than with linguistic analysis or the clarification of meanings.

Kerensky, Alexander Feodorovitch:
 The one "strong man" in the provisional governments, he was distinguished for his patriotic refusal to conclude a separate peace with Germany.

Kissinger, Henry Alfred:
 He developed a style of diplomacy that was highly successful on many occasions, most notably the negotiation of the American withdrawal from Vietnam in 1973.

I have not altered the tenor of any of these references, only a few of which in their fatuity or partiality come anywhere close to a discussion of "Modern Thought," and several of which do not even pretend to do so. Like Bullock and his coeditor R. B. Woodings of Oxford Polytechnic, I spent only a few moments in the library in order to uncover this priceless academic trove.

 Incidentally, Sidney Hook referred to "unfortunate accidental loss of life" and to the "unintended consequences of military action" in his own writings on the United States bombing of Vietnam. I did not discover this fact by reading the *Biographical Companion to Modern Thought*.

the Communists and their apologists in the West like the odious Noam Chomsky. When Vietnam invaded Cambodia and let the world see the proof and magnitude of the Khmer Rouge crime, the Chomskys were able to turn to *Sideshow* for an explanation: the Khmer Rouge were the creation of Nixon and Kissinger. The atrocities in Cambodia were used to justify not only the Vietnamese invasion but their remaining as an occupying power.

This comment appeared in a review of *The Quality of Mercy*, which, like *Sideshow*, was written by William Shawcross. On page 55 of *The Quality of Mercy*, which was published in the fall of 1984, appears the following, as an explanation of relative Western indifference toward the Calvary in Cambodia. Of the assumed indifference, Shawcross wrote:

Through 1976 and 1977 and especially in 1978 the Western press's coverage of Cambodia increased. Nonetheless, the issue never reached critical mass. I did not write enough myself. And there was no broadly based campaign of protest in the West as there was, say, over abuses of human rights in Chile.

One reason for this was the skepticism (to use a mild word) displayed by the Western left toward the stories coming out of Democratic Kampuchea. That skepticism was most fervently and frequently expressed by Noam Chomsky, the linguistic philosopher at the Massachusetts Institute of Technology. He asserted that from the moment of the Khmer Rouge victory in 1975 the Western press collaborated with Western and anti-Communist Asian governments, notably Thailand, to produce a "vast and unprecedented" campaign of propaganda against the Khmer Rouge.

It seems that Chomsky is impaled on some kind of inquisitional fork here. He is accused of leaning on Shawcross, who in turn accuses him of culpable complacency, if not outright intellectual complicity. Then there is the bland assertion by the editors of *The New Republic*, on December 24, 1984:

This is also a very old controversy, which Mr. Chomsky has sought to confuse over the years by tossing adjectives like "brazen" and "scurrilous" at critics who recognize both Pol Pot's crimes and the efforts to whitewash the Nazi genocide for what they are.

After reading which, Martin Peretz's flat assertion earlier that Noam Chomsky's views are "quite mad" seems a mere grace note. Reaching for the denunciation of last resort, Peretz yelled that "even in circles which had once revered him, Mr. Chomsky is now seen as a crank and an embarrassment."

As I said, I found all these references with no more effort than it takes to keep up with "the weeklies." And I can count William Shawcross and Richard West among my friends, *The Spectator* and *The Times Literary Supplement* among my employers, David Horowitz and Fred Barnes among my distant nodding acquaintances. No real "research," in other words, was needed to amass these confident citations. But a little work was required to establish a small fact. Not one of the extracts quoted above, whether you take them "in their context" or out of it, contains any approximation to the truth. I lay down my pen and look at what I have just written. Have I the blind spot or have they? Have I discounted enough for my own prejudices? Should I say here that Noam Chomsky once gave a book of mine a very decent review? That I have met him three times and found him sane? All these allowances made, I still maintain that we are in the territory so deftly mapped by Dr. Arbuthnot—and by Ryszard Kapuscinski in *Shah of Shahs*:

> What should one write to ruin an adversary? The best thing is to prove that he is not one of us—the stranger, alien, foreigner. To this end we create the category of the true family. We here, you and I, the authorities, are a true family. We live in unity, among our own kind. We have the same roof over our heads, we sit at the same table, we know how to get along with each other, how to help each other out. Unfortunately, we are not alone.

The gravamen of the bill against Noam Chomsky is this. That, *first*, he did euphemize and minimize the horrors of the Khmer Rouge. That, *second*, he did "endorse" or otherwise recommend a pamphlet or paper that sought to prove the Nazi Holocaust a fiction. That, *third*, he is an enemy of the Jewish state and a friend to footpads and terrorists of every stripe. This is what "everybody knows" about the lonely, derided linguist who no doubt blames America first and is a self-hating Jew into the bargain. Never was an open society better insulated from dissent. In Britain, he would be dismissed as "brilliant but unsound; doesn't know when to stop." In the United States, it takes a little more than that to encompass the destruction of a reputation.

The best procedure must be the tedious one: to take the accusations in order, and to put them at their strongest. Let me arrange them as did Sir Arthur Conan Doyle, with the suspicions uppermost.

THE CASE OF THE CAMBODIAN GENOCIDE

David Horowitz and Peter Collier were wrong, in the syndicated article announcing their joint conversion to neoconservatism, to say that Chomsky hailed the advent of the Khmer Rouge as "a new era of economic development and social justice." The Khmer Rouge took power in 1975. In 1972, Chomsky wrote an introduction to Dr. Malcolm Caldwell's collection of interviews with Prince Norodom Sihanouk. In this introduction, he expressed not the prediction but the pious hope that Sihanouk and his supporters might preserve Cambodia for "a new era of economic development and social justice." You could say that this was naïve of Chomsky, who did not predict the 1973 carpet-bombing campaign or the resultant rise of a primitive, chauvinist guerrilla movement. But any irony here would appear to be at the expense of Horowitz and Collier. And the funny thing is that, if they had the words right, they must have had access to the book. And if they had access to the book . . . Well, many things are forgiven those who see the error of their formerly radical ways.

The Richard West–William Shawcross fork also proves, on investigation, to be blunt in both prongs. Chomsky and Shawcross have this much in common: that they both argue for and demonstrate the connection between the Nixon-Kissinger bombing and derangement of Cambodian society and the nascence of the Khmer Rouge. It is not the case that Chomsky borrowed this idea from Shawcross, however. He first went to press on the point in 1972, seven years before *Sideshow* was published, with an account supplied by the American correspondent Richard Dudman of the *St. Louis Post-Dispatch*. Dudman is one of the few people to have been both a prisoner of the Khmer Rouge and a chronicler of his own detention. His testimony indicated a strong connection between American tactics in the countryside of Cambodia and the recruitment of peasants to the guerrilla side. (Imagine the strain of composing an account that denied such a connection.)

This more or less disposes of West, who has simply got the order of things the wrong way about and added some random insults. The case of Shawcross is more complicated. In his *The Quality of Mercy*, he quotes three full paragraphs apparently from Chomsky's pen, though he does not give a source. The three paragraphs do not express "skepticism" about the massacres in Cambodia, but they do express reservations about some of the accounts of them. They also argue that the advent of the Khmer Rouge should be seen in the historical context of the much less ballyhooed American aerial massacres a few years earlier—a point which the author of *Sideshow* is in a weak position to scorn. Finally, the three paragraphs convey a sardonic attitude toward those who claim that it "took courage" to mention the Khmer Rouge atrocities at all.

But mark the sequel. The three paragraphs as quoted do not appear anywhere. They are rudely carpentered together, without any ellipses to indicate gaps in the attribution, from the "summary" and introduction to volume 1 of *The Political Economy of Human Rights*, which was written by Noam Chomsky and Professor Edward Herman of the Wharton School of Business. The book went to press in 1979, *after* the forcible overthrow of the Pol Pot regime. Thus, even if the paragraphs were quoted and sourced properly, and even if they bore the construction that Shawcross puts on them, they could hardly have contributed to the alleged indifference of civilized opinion "throughout 1976 and 1977 and especially in 1978" or inhibited the issue from reaching "critical mass." Since Shawcross lists the book, with its date, in his bibliography, the discrepancy can hardly be due to ignorance.

As for the gratuitous insinuation about protest over Chile, I can't help recording that one of the anti–Khmer Rouge blockbusters with which the American public *was* regaled came in *TV Guide* (circulation 19 million) in April 1977 and was written by Ernest Lefever. Lefever had earlier told Congress that it should be more "tolerant" of the "mistakes" of the Pinochet regime "in attempting to clear away the devastation of the Allende period." He also wrote, in *The Miami Herald*, of the "remarkable freedom of expression" enjoyed in the new Chile. In 1981, Lefever proved too farouche to secure nomination as Reagan's Under Secretary for Human Rights.

William Shawcross enjoys his reputation for honesty. And so I have had to presume that his book represents his case at its most considered. Why, then, if he has room for three paragraphs "from" Chomsky and Herman, does he not quote the equally accessible sentences, published in *The Nation* on June 25, 1977, where they describe Father François Ponchaud's *Cambodia: Year Zero* as "serious and worth reading," with its "grisly account of what refugees have reported to him about the barbarity of their treatment at the hands of the Khmer Rouge"?

Chomsky and Herman were engaged in the admittedly touchy business of distinguishing evidence from interpretation. They were doing so in the aftermath of a war which had featured tremendous, organized, official lying and many cynical and opportunist "bloodbath" predictions. There was and is no argument about mass murder in Cambodia: there is still argument about whether the number of deaths, and the manner in which they were inflicted, will warrant the use of the term "genocide" or even "autogenocide." Shawcross pays an implicit homage to this distinction, a few pages later, when he admits that Jean Lacouture, in his first "emotional" review of Father Ponchaud, greatly exaggerated the real number of Khmer Rouge executions. These errors, writes Shawcross, "were seized upon by Noam Chomsky, who circulated them widely. In a subsequent issue of *The New York Review*, Lacouture corrected himself. Not all of those who had reported his mea culpa published his corrections. Chomsky used the affair as part of his argument that the media were embarked on an unjustified blitz against the Khmer Rouge."

If this paragraph has any internal coherence—and I have given it in its entirety—it must lead the reader to suppose that Chomsky publicized Lacouture's mea culpa without acknowledging his corrections. But in *The Political Economy of Human Rights* there is an exhaustive presentation of the evolution of Lacouture's position, including both his mea culpa and his corrections and adding some complimentary remarks about his work. Incidentally, Lacouture reduced his own estimate of deaths from "two million" to "thousands or hundreds of thousands." Is this, too, "minimization of atrocities"?

Ironies here accumulate at the expense of Chomsky's accusers. A close analysis of *Problems of Communism* and of the findings of State Department intelligence and many very conservative Asia specialists will yield a figure of deaths in the high hundreds of thousands. Exorbitant figures (i.e. those oscillating between two and three million) are current partly because Radio Moscow and Radio Hanoi now feel free to denounce the Pol Pot forces (which now, incredibly, receive official American recognition) in the most abandoned fashion. Chomsky wrote that, while the Vietnamese invasion and occupation could be understood, it could not be justified. May we imagine what might be said about his complicity with Soviet-bloc propaganda if he were now insisting on the higher figure? For both of these failures to conform, he has been assailed by Leopold Labedz in *Encounter*, who insists on three million as a sort of loyalty test, but, since that magazine shows a distinct reluctance to correct the untruths it publishes—as I can testify from my own experience—its readers have not been exposed to a reply.

Chomsky and Herman wrote that "the record of atrocities in Cambodia is substantial and often gruesome." They even said, "When the facts are in, it may turn out that the more extreme condemnations were in fact correct." The facts are now more or less in, and it turns out that the two independent writers were as close to the truth as most, and closer than some. It may be distasteful, even indecent, to argue over "body counts," whether the bodies are Armenian, Jewish, Cambodian, or (to take a case where Chomsky and Herman were effectively alone in their research and their condemnation) Timorese. But the count must be done, and done seriously, if later generations are not to doubt the whole slaughter on the basis of provable exaggerations or inventions.

Maurice Cranston's letter to *The Times Literary Supplement*, with its unexamined assumption that Chomsky was a partisan of North Vietnam, falls apart with even less examination. In 1970, Chomsky wrote up his tour of the region for *The New York Review of Books* and said:

> It is conceivable that the United States may be able to break the will of the popular movements in the surrounding countries, perhaps even destroy the National Liberation Front of South Vietnam, by employing the vast resources of violence and terror at its disposal. If so, it will create a situation in which, indeed, North Vietnam will necessarily dominate Indochina, for no other viable society will remain.

I think of that article whenever I read wised-up Western newsmen who dwell upon the "ironic" fact that the North Vietnamese, not the NLF, now

hold power in Ho Chi Minh City. It takes real ingenuity to blame this on
the antiwar movement, but, with a little creative amnesia and a large helping
of self-pity for the wounds inflicted by the war (on America), the job can be
plausibly done.

Finally, to Fred Barnes, recruited to *The New Republic* from *The Balti-
more Sun* and *The American Spectator*. I wrote to him on the day that his
article appeared, asking to know where he heard Chomsky say such a thing.
I received no reply until I was able to ask for it in person two months later.
I then asked him to place it in writing. It read as follows:

> I sat next to Noam Chomsky at a seminar at Lippmann House (of the Nieman
> Foundation) of Harvard University in Cambridge, Mass., in 1978. On the matter
> of genocide in Cambodia, the thrust of what he said was that there was no
> evidence of mass murder there. As I recall, he was rather adamant on the point.
> He had, by this time, I believe, written a letter or two to *The New York Review
> of Books* making the same point. Chomsky seemed to believe that tales of
> holocaust in Cambodia were so much propaganda. He said, on another point,
> that there was an effort underway to rewrite the history of the Indochinese
> war—in a way more favorable to the U.S. Perhaps he thought the notion of
> genocide in Cambodia was part of that effort.

Since this meeting took place in the year after Chomsky and Herman had
written their *Nation* article, and in the year when they were preparing *The
Political Economy of Human Rights*, we can probably trust the documented
record at least as much as Mr. Barnes's recollection. And there was no letter
from Chomsky about Cambodia in *The New York Review of Books*. It is
interesting, and perhaps suggestive, that Barnes uses the terms "genocide,"
"holocaust," and "mass murder" as if they were interchangeable. His last
two sentences demonstrate just the sort of cuteness for which his magazine
is becoming famous.

Here is the story, as far as I can trace it, of Chomsky's effort to "minimize"
or "deny" the harvest of the Khmer Rouge. It will be seen that the phony
"credibility" of the charge against him derives from his *lack* of gullibility
about the American mass killings in Indochina (routinely euphemized or
concealed by large sections of the domestic intelligentsia). From this arises
the idea that Chomsky *might* have said such things; was the sort of person
who *could* decline to criticize "the other side"; was a well-known political
extremist. Couple this with the slothful ease of the accusation, the reluctance
of numerous respectable magazines to publish corrections, and the anxiety
of certain authors to prove that they are not unpatriotic dupes, and you have
a scapegoat in the making. Dr. Arbuthnot was right. Nobody would believe that Chomsky advocated a massacre. But they might be brought to
believe that he excused or overlooked one.

THE CASE OF THE NEGATED HOLOCAUST

Here, Dr. Arbuthnot gives way to Ryszard Kapuscinski. The tactic is not to circulate a part-untruth so much as it is to associate the victim with an unpardonable "out group," against which preexisting revulsion and contempt can be mobilized.

My tutor at Oxford was Dr. Steven Lukes, a brilliant and humane man with an equal commitment to scholarship and to liberty. His books on Durkheim, on power, on utopianism, and on Marxism and morality are, as people tend to say, landmarks in their field. He took me as his guest to one of Chomsky's private seminars in that spring of 1969. When, in 1980, he told me that Chomsky had written an introduction to a book by a Nazi apologist, and that the book described the extermination of the Jews as a Zionist lie, I was thunderstruck. Like Noam Chomsky, Steven Lukes is Jewish. Like Chomsky, he was and is much opposed to the usurpation of Israel by the heirs of Jabotinsky. But this seemed incomprehensible. The political rights of hateful persons was one question (rather a vexed one in the British case, where the police and not the courts usually decide who may or may not speak in public), but keeping company with them was quite another. More, it appeared that Chomsky had dignified this character's book with a preface and had not even bothered to read the text he was decorating. I admit that I allowed myself a reflection or two about the potentially harmful effects on Chomsky of his political and personal isolation on the Middle East.

When I began to write this article, I wrote to Lukes at Balliol and asked him to furnish me with the background material to l'affaire Faurisson. I also pursued all the other references in print. I do not read French very well, but I have studied Nadine Fresco's famous article "The Denial of the Dead," adapted in Dissent from Les Temps modernes; Pierre Vidal-Naquet's "A Paper Eichmann?" reprinted in democracy; and Arno J. Mayer's "Explorations" column on the same theme in the same magazine. There is also Paul Berman's article in The Village Voice of June 10, 1981, "Gas Chamber Games: Crackpot History and the Right to Lie," which is a sort of macédoine of the first three.

Let us not waste any time on Robert Faurisson. He is an insanitary figure who maintains contact with neo-Nazi circles and whose "project" is the rehabilitation, in pseudoscholarly form, of the Third Reich. How he came to be appointed in the first place I cannot imagine (from what I have seen his literary criticism is pitiful), but in 1979 he was a teacher in good standing of French literature at the University of Lyons. If, like our own Arthur Butz, who publishes "historical revisionist" garbage from Northwestern University, he had been left to stew in his own sty, we might have heard no more of him. But in that year he published an article entitled " 'The Problem of the Gas Chambers' or 'The Rumor of Auschwitz.' " The whole appeared in

Maurice Bardèche's sheet, *Défense de l'Occident*, and extracts were reprinted in *Le Monde*. Faurisson summarized his conclusions in a supplement:

(1) Hitler's "gas chambers" never existed. (2) The "genocide" (or the "attempted genocide") of the Jews never took place; clearly, Hitler never ordered (nor permitted) that someone be killed for racial or religious reasons. (3) The alleged "gas chambers" and the alleged "genocide" are one and the same lie. (4) This lie, essentially of Zionist origin, permitted a gigantic politico-financial swindle whose principal beneficiary is the State of Israel. (5) The principal victims of this lie and swindle are the Germans and the Palestinians.

The rest of the "supplement" concerned the sinister ways in which the media had prevented these truths from becoming generally known.

I have no idea whether Faurisson hoped to attract unpleasant attention by the publication of this stuff, but the consequences were fairly immediate. His sternist critic, Nadine Fresco, records: "At Lyons, there were displays of antipathy and Faurisson was lightly molested by Jewish students. Consequently, the president of the university chose to suspend his classes." Fresco slightly minimizes (if that is the word I want) the fact that a subsequent suit, brought against Faurisson for "falsification of history" and for "allowing others" to use his work for their own fell purposes, was successful and he was condemned by a French court.

In the early stages of this process, Chomsky received a request, from his friend Serge Thion, that he add his name to a petition upholding Faurisson's right to free expression. This, on standard First Amendment grounds and in company with many others, he did. The resulting uproar, in which he was accused of defending Faurisson's *theses*, led to another request from Thion. Would Chomsky write a statement asserting the right to free speech even in the case of the most loathsome extremist? To this he also assented, pointing out that it was precisely such cases that tested the adherence of a society to such principles and adding in a covering letter that Thion could make what use of it he wished. At this stage, only the conservative Alfred Grosser among French intellectuals had been prepared to say that Faurisson's suspension by the University of Lyons set a bad example of academic courage and independence. Chomsky's pedantic recitation of Voltairean principles would probably have aroused no comment at all had Thion not taken rather promiscuous advantage of the permission to use it as he wished. Without notification to Chomsky, he added the little essay as an *avis* to Faurisson's pretrial *Mémoire en défense*.

Chomsky's seven-page comment received more attention in the international press, as Paul Berman noted, than any other piece of work for which he had been responsible. Let me summarize those reactions, which are still worth quoting and which are still (when occasion demands) being repeated:

Poor Chomsky, innocent victim of a quasi-Pavlovian automatism. Someone mentions "rights"; he signs. Someone says "freedom of speech"; he signs. He goes even further with the famous preface (which is not really a preface, though it strangely resembles one) to Faurisson's *Mémoire en défense*. The press seized on the event, and I leave to others the delicate pleasure of pinpointing the ambiguities and contradictions that run through Chomsky's comments about the preface. But it is important to emphasize that the Faurisson affair is not an issue of legal rights.

(Nadine Fresco, *Dissent*, Fall 1981)

Chomsky—who, breaking with his usual pattern, praised the traditions of American support for civil liberties . . . (Ibid.)

Regrettably, Faurisson's new book has an unconscionable preface by Noam Chomsky that is being used to legitimate Faurisson as a bona-fide scholar of the Holocaust. As an unqualified civil libertarian Chomsky claims—disingenuously—that he has not read the book he is prefacing!

(Arno J. Mayer, *democracy*, April 1981)

Certain people have rallied to Faurisson's defense for reasons of principle. A petition that includes several hundred signatures, among the first those of Noam Chomsky and Alfred Lilienthal, protests against the treatment that Faurisson has received. It implicitly describes his activities as authentic historical research: "Since 1974, he has been conducting extensive independent research into the Holocaust question," and continues by confirming what is not true, namely, that "frightened officials have tried to stop him from further research by denying him access to public libraries and archives." What is scandalous about this petition is that it doesn't for one moment ask whether what Faurisson says is true or false; and it even describes his findings as though they were the result of serious historical research. Of course, it can be contended that everybody has the right to lie and "bear false witness," a right that is inseparable from the liberty of the individual and recognized, in the liberal tradition, as due the accused for his defense. But the right that a "false witness" may claim should not be granted him in the name of truth.

(Pierre Vidal-Naquet, *democracy*, April 1981)

Of these criticisms, the most nearly fair seems to me the one offered by Vidal-Naquet (an early hero of mine because of his book on torture in Algeria). But he is wrong on one factual point. Fresco herself confirmed, and justified, the refusal of certain archivists and documentation centers to permit access to Faurisson. And he is at risk in his distinction between truth and false witness, a distinction which Milton understood better in *Areopagitica* when he argued that the two must be allowed to confront one another if truth is to prevail. There is therefore no obligation, in defending or asserting the right to speak, to pass any comment on the truth or merit of what may be, or is being, said. This is elementary.

Also rather unsafe is the injunction (employed above most crudely by Vidal-Naquet's colleague Arno Mayer) to be careful of the use that may be made of one's remarks or signatures. Elsewhere in the same essay, for example, Vidal-Naquet asserts, "In the case of the genocide of Jews, it is perfectly evident that one of the Jewish ideologies, Zionism, exploits this terrible massacre in a way that is at times quite scandalous." *Scandalous*— the same word that he attaches to Chomsky's signature on a petition. But he supplies the corrective himself—"that an ideology seizes upon a fact does not make this fact inexistent." Precisely. And the "fact" here is that Chomsky defended not Faurisson's work but his right to research and publish it. Vidal-Naquet undoubtedly knows better than to resort to the old Stalinist "aid and comfort" ruse. Where, then, is the core of his objection?

Does this not leave Arno Mayer, also, in some difficulty? The fact that neo-Nazis may have "seized upon" Noam Chomsky's civil-libertarian defense does not, of itself, make that defense invalid. Or, if it does, then by himself seizing upon what they have seized upon, Mayer is "objectively" associating civil-libertarian principles with the Nazis—an unintended compliment that the latter scarcely deserve. Vidal-Naquet's point about Zionism's "exploitation" of the Holocaust could, if cleverly enough ripped from its context, be used to support point (4) in Faurisson's "supplement" above. Who but a malicious falsifier would make such a confusion as to who was in whose *galère?*

I wouldn't accuse any of the critics listed here of deliberate falsification. But it is nevertheless untrue to describe Chomsky's purloined *avis* as "a preface," as Fresco does on almost a dozen occasions and as Mayer does twice. It is also snide, at best, to accuse Chomsky of "breaking with his usual pattern" in praising "the traditions of American support for civil liberty." He has, as a matter of record, upheld these traditions more staunchly than most—speaking up for the right of extremist academics like Rostow, for example, at a time during the Vietnam War when some campuses were too turbulent to accommodate them. It is irrelevant, at least, to do as Fresco also does and mention Voltaire's anti-Semitism. (As absurd a suggestion, in the circumstances, as the vulgar connection between Locke and imperialism.) Would she never quote Voltaire? Finally, she says that no question of legal rights arises because the suit against Faurisson was "private." What difference does that make? An authoritarian law, giving the state the right to pronounce on truth, is an authoritarian law whoever invokes it.

Chomsky can be faulted here on three grounds only. First, for giving a power of attorney to Serge Thion, who seems rather a protean and quick-silvery fellow. Second, for once unguardedly describing Faurisson as "a sort of relatively apolitical liberal." Admittedly, this came in the context of an assertion that Faurisson's opinions were a closed book to him; still, all the more reason not to speculate. The whole point is that Faurisson's opinions are *not* the point. Third, for attempting at the last minute, when he discovered too late that he was being bound into the same volume as a work he had not read, to have his commentary excised. He writes of this that "in the climate of hysteria among Paris intellectuals it would be impossible to distinguish defense of the man's right to express his views from endorsement of these views." Maybe. But Voltairean precepts involve precisely the running of that risk.

This is still nothing to do with "endorsement" and explains the repeated feverish sarcasm with which his critics claim that he had not "even" read the "endorsed" volume. Again, the irony would seem to be at their expense. An unread book is an unendorsed one, unless one assumes that Chomsky would endorse any Holocaust revisionist on principle—an allegation so fantastic that it has not "even" been made. If, by any action or statement, Chomsky had hinted at sympathy for Faurisson's views, I think that we would know about it by now. The recurring attempt, therefore, to bracket him with the century's most heinous movement must be adjudged a smear. And the wider attempt—to classify all critics of Israel as infected or compromised with anti-Semitism—is, of course, itself a trivialization of the Holocaust.

THE CASE OF THE FORGOTTEN WAR

Chomsky's evolving position on the Middle East conflict is the source of much of his unpopularity and (one sometimes suspects) the cause of much of the spite with which he is attacked on other issues. But where are the baying hounds this time? I can offer no lists of critics, no litany of denunciations. Chomsky wrote a book of more than 450 pages that was devoted to the United States and the Lebanese war of 1982, and what do you think? There was barely a squeak.

An unreviewed book is no rare thing in the United States. There is usually some explanation for the nonevent. The author may be obscure, or the subject arcane, or the "issue" dead, or the "issue" too widely covered already. Again, there may be no qualified reviewer in sight, so that, rather than assign the volume to an amateur, the books department may blushfully "pass" on the whole idea. A version of the same procedure is sometimes followed when no reviewer with a big enough "name" is on hand. And there are postal delays, crowded schedules, demands on inelastic space. Everyone remotely connected with "the trade" understands this, even when the rough and the smooth seem to be insufficiently random in their distribution. A good advertising budget has been known to help, but nobody is so coarse as to insinuate that it *determines* anything much.

These well-known vagaries and mutabilities cannot explain why, in the fall of 1983, Chomsky's book *The Fateful Triangle* was treated as if it did not exist. Consider: One of America's best-known Jewish scholars, internationally respected, writes a lengthy, dense, highly documented book about United States policy in the Levant. The book is acidly critical of Israeli policy and of the apparently limitless American self-deception as to its true character. It quotes sources in Hebrew and French as well as in English. It is published at a time when hundreds of United States marines have been killed in Beirut and when the President is wavering in his commitment, which itself threatens to become a major election issue. It is the only book of its scope (we need make no judgment as to depth) to appear in the continental United States. The screens and the headlines are full of approximations and guesses on the subject. Yet, at this unusually fortunate juncture for publication, the following newspapers review it: (1) the *Los Angeles Herald-Examiner*; (2) *The Boston Globe*. In Los Angeles, Chomsky has an admirer who is also a local book reviewer. This man prevails after a struggle. In Boston, Chomsky is a well-known local figure. But that's it. Many months later, after its foal, the *London Review of Books*, has devoted many respectful columns to the book, and after almost every major newspaper and magazine in England, Canada, and Australia has done the same, *The New York Review of Books* publishes a "mixed review." This presumably takes care of the only other possible editorial excuse (itself significant)—that *The Fateful Triangle* was published by a small radical house in Cambridge, Massachusetts, named South End Press.

Paranoia would be inappropriate here. After all, this was not 1973, when the first edition of Chomsky and Herman's *The Political Economy of Human Rights* was suppressed by its own publishers, Warner Communications, for making unpatriotic assertions about United States policy in Indochina and elsewhere. The twenty thousand copies might have been pulped if it were not for a legally binding contract. Instead they were sold to an obscure outfit named MSS Information Corporation, whereupon Warner—which later bid high for the Nixon memoirs—washed its hands of the entire deal and of all responsibility for advertising, promotion, and distribution. Difficult to imagine *that* happening to anyone else of remotely comparable stature, but, as I say, 1983 was different. The book was out, and the foreign-policy intelligentsia had every chance to comment.

I confess that I have no ready explanation for the total eclipse that followed. *The New York Times* had found Chomsky interesting enough to publish two long and pitying articles about the Faurisson business. Other newspapers and magazines seem, as I suppose I have shown, to find him deserving of comment. I therefore rang a selection of literary editors and asked if they could explain their reticence on this occasion.

I began with *The New Republic*, because it is mentioned so often in *The Fateful Triangle* and because its editors had assured me at the time that they would not let the critique go unanswered. Leon Wieseltier, the literary editor, told me jauntily when I inquired:

> The book was sent to reviewers. The first was too disgusted to review it. The second said that he would, and finally didn't, which frequently happens. I see no reason not to assign Chomsky's books for review, because I see no reason for him to be above criticism.

Editors at *The New York Times Book Review* and *The Washington Post Book World* were less ready to be quoted but quite ready to talk. From the *Times* I heard variously, "I think we tuned out on Noam after Vietnam," "It fell through the cracks," and "We never received the book." From the *Post*, I heard that "by the time we got all those letters protesting about not reviewing it, the book wasn't in local bookstores—so we didn't." I also heard that there was some doubt about having received the copy in the first place.

Katha Pollitt, who was literary editor of *The Nation* at this time, told me that there were already too many books about the Middle East, that the "front half" of the magazine devoted plenty of space to the subject, and that she herself preferred to preserve her pages for articles on fiction, poetry, and feminism.

Joe Clark, then books editor at *Dissent*, told me, "My guess is that I didn't feel a very strong desire to review the book." He said he would "have needed an overpowering reason." Clearly, the frequent and scornful mention of *Dissent* in *The Fateful Triangle* did not supply this incentive. For the literary editor of *The New Republic* to say that he sees "no reason for [Chomsky] to be above criticism" is presumably a joke. For him to say that the first invited contributor was "too disgusted" to review the book is not. The first invited reviewer, as I know and as Wieseltier confirmed to me, was Ze'ev Schiff, military correspondent of *Ha'aretz* and coauthor of *Israel's Lebanon War*. "Disgust" is certainly not what he evinced when I spoke to him about the book in the summer of 1984.

A category mistake is involved in the *Post* explanation, unless the editors of that newspaper assume there to be no connection between their failure to review a book and its absence from Washington's bookstores. I like the idea, though, of their not giving in to letters from readers.

The *Times* may perhaps not have received a copy, though South End Press was doing nothing but lobby for its chief title between November and June, and claims to have sent four in all. Radical incompetence allowed for, what is there to prevent an editor from doing what editors do every day and requesting a copy?

Pollitt has a point, and even though the rules of fairness oblige me to be harder on a former colleague, I can't see a way through her candor.

So what it comes down to is this. Life is unfair, and though it does seem odd that such a book is ignored only in its country of origin (and the country whose state policy it attacks), the whole thing is easily explicable. Above all, it is *nobody's fault*. Does this mean that there is no reluctance to hear the bad news about the Middle East? Well, again, and whether or not you believe in "cock-up rather than conspiracy"—a favorite evasion of the soothing commentator—it does seem harder for some people to get an audience than others. Especially hard for the man who, according to Shawcross, enjoyed sufficient sway to confuse or silence the American press over the question of Cambodia.

Whether he is ignored, whether he is libeled, or whether he is subjected to an active campaign of abuse, Chomsky is attacked for things that he is thought to believe, or believed to have said. A lie, it has been written, can travel around the world before truth has even got its shoes on. Merely to list the accusations against Chomsky, whether they are made casually or with deliberation, is a relatively easy task. Showing their unfairness or want of foundation involves expense of ink on a scale which any reader who has got this far will know to his or her cost. Perhaps for this reason, not all the editors who publish matter about Chomsky ever quite get around to publishing his replies. I could write an ancillary article showing this in detail, with his answers either unpublished or unscrupulously abridged. And, of course, a man who writes a lot of letters to the editor soon gets a reputation, like Bellow's Herzog, as a crank, an eccentric, a fanatic. Whereas the absence of a reply is taken as admission of guilt. . . .

Ought I to be "evenhanded" and indicate where I disagree with Chomsky myself? I don't really see why I ought. My differences with him concern things that he does believe and has said. I also dissent from him, quite often, concerning the way in which he says things and on his repeated misuse of the verb "to brutalize." I think he has sometimes been facile about Cold War "moral equivalence" as well. But this is between him and me, or him and any other political opponent or critic who observes the rules of evidence and debate.

For the recurrent way in which this is *not* done, and for the process whereby the complaisant mainstream and the conservative guardians actually *agree not to hear* what is being said about them and their system, we need a word. "Marginalization" is too merely descriptive. "Ghettoization" is too self-pitying. It may come to me.

The contemporary United States expresses the greatest of all paradoxes.

It is at one and the same time a democracy—at any rate a pluralist open society—and an empire. No other country has ever been, or had, both things at once. Or not for long. And there must be some question about the durability of this present coexistence, too. Already spokesmen of the Reagan Administration say plainly that their foreign and military policy is incompatible with the disloyalty and division that stem from a deliberative Congress and an inquisitive press. They laughably exaggerate the reflective capacity of the first and the adversary character of the second, but they have a point. If it is to have the least chance of success, their strategy calls for an imposed national unanimity, a well-cultivated awareness of "enemies within," and a strong draft of amnesia.

The academy and the wealthy new batch of think tanks are awash with people who collude, at least passively, in the process. As C. Wright Mills once wrote:

> Their academic reputations rest, quite largely, upon their academic power: they are the members of the committee; they are on the directing board; they can get you the job, the trip, the research grant. They are a strange new kind of bureaucrat. They are executives of the mind. . . . They could set up a research project or even a school, but I would be surprised, if, now after twenty years of research and teaching and observing and thinking, they could produce a book which told you what they thought was going on in the world, what they thought were the major problems for men of this historical epoch.

Not even Mills, or Chomsky in his "New Mandarins" essay, could have anticipated the world of the Heritage Foundation, of "Kissinger Associates," of numberless power-worshipping, power-seeking magazines and institutes interlocking across the dissemination of culture, priority, information, and opinion. But Mills did write, in 1942:

> When events move very fast and possible worlds swing around them, something happens to the quality of thinking. Some men repeat formulae; some men become reporters. To time observation with thought so as to mate a decent level of abstraction with crucial happenings is a difficult problem.

Noam Chomsky has attempted, as a volunteer, necessarily imperfectly, to shoulder this responsibility at a time of widespread betrayal of it. And it must be an awed attitude to the new style—a willingness to "demonstrate flexibility" in the face of so much pelf and so much cant—that allows so many people to join in ridiculing him for doing so. As a philosophical anarchist, Chomsky might dislike to have it said that he had "done the state some service," but he is a useful citizen in ways that his detractors are emphatically not.

(Grand Street, Autumn 1985)

COMRADE ORWELL

❏

The reputation of George Orwell is secure among those who have never read him, high among those who have read only *Nineteen Eighty-four* or *Animal Farm*, and pretty solid among those who have read his *Collected Essays, Journalism and Letters* for confirmation of their own opinions. The value of his work is debated only by his fellow socialists and anti-imperialists. And even they, by ridiculing or scorning his precepts, pay an unintended compliment to his influence. Orwell's standing approaches that "large, vague renown" which he bestowed on Thomas Carlyle in 1931.

"To have had a part in two revolutions is to have lived to some purpose," wrote Thomas Paine. To have been prescient about both fascism and Stalinism is a possible equivalent, but it is not, in itself, proof that Orwell was a great writer or thinker. Only in the most primitive sense does scarcity define the value of a commodity; prescience is no exception. Orwell has been smothered with cloying approbation by those who would have despised or ignored him when he was alive, and pelted with smug afterthoughts by those who (often unwittingly or reluctantly) shared the same trenches as he did. The present climate threatens to stifle him in one way or the other.

"I knew," said Orwell in 1946 about his early youth, "that I had a facility with words and a power of facing unpleasant facts." Not the ability to face them, but "a power of facing." It's oddly well put. A commissar who realizes that his five-year plan is off target and that the people detest him or laugh at him may be said, in a base manner, to be confronting an unpleasant fact. So, for the matter of that, may a priest with "doubts." The reaction of such people to unpleasant facts is rarely self-critical: they do not have a "power of facing." Their confrontation with the fact takes the form of an evasion; the reaction to the unpleasant discovery is a redoubling of efforts to overcome the obvious. The "unpleasant facts" that Orwell faced were usually the ones that put his own position or preference to the test.

Virtues that Orwell never claimed, such as consistency, are denied to him by the textual sectarians, and patronizing compliments, such as the recurrent "quintessentially English," are fastened upon him by sycophants. In order to drag Orwell out from under this mound of dead dogs, as Carlyle said of his Cromwell, one may as well start with his sworn and stated antagonists:

1. "Orwell seldom wrote about foreigners, except sociologically, and then in a hit-or-miss fashion otherwise unusual to him; he very rarely mentions a foreign writer and has an excessive dislike of foreign words; although he condemns imperialism he dislikes its victims even more."
2. "Orwell's writing life then was from the start an affirmation of unexamined bourgeois values."
3. "Orwell prepared the orthodox political beliefs of a generation."
4. "By viewing the struggle as one between only a few people over the heads of an apathetic mass, Orwell created the conditions for defeat and despair."
5. "Politics was something he observed, albeit as an honest partisan, from the comforts of bookselling, marriage, friendship with other writers (not by any means with the radicals used as material for *The Road to Wigan Pier* and *Homage to Catalonia*, then dropped), dealing with publishers and literary agents."
6. "As far as he considered such matters at all, I think he felt that not to be a product of English history was a sort of moral lapse."
7. "What Orwell said when he wrote for the Ukrainian readers of *Animal Farm* about his alleged commitment to socialism in 1930 is plainly an untruth, made the more reprehensible not only because Stansky and Abrahams show that he had no notion of socialism until much later, but also because we catch him unaware in 1935 'that Hitler intended to carry out the programme of *Mein Kampf.*'"
8. "Is it fantastic to see in Orwell's *Nineteen Eighty-four* the reflection of a feeling that a world in which the pre-1914 British way of life had totally passed away must necessarily be a dehumanized world? And is it altogether wrong to see the inhabitants of *Animal Farm* as having points in common, not merely with Soviet Russians, but also Kipling's lesser breeds generally, as well as with Flory's Burmese who, once the relative decencies of the Raj are gone, must inevitably fall under the obscene domination of their own kind?"
9. "It would be dangerous to blind ourselves to the fact that in the West millions of people may be inclined, in their anguish and fear, to flee from their own responsibility for mankind's destiny and to vent their anger and despair on the giant Bogy-cum-Scapegoat which Orwell's *Nineteen Eighty-four* has done so much to place before their eyes."

All extracts and quotations are, by their very essence, "taken out of context" (what else is an extract or a quotation?). But I do not think that the authors cited above will find themselves or the tendency of their arguments misrepresented. They are, in order, Conor Cruise O'Brien in the *New Statesman* of May 1961, Edward Said in the *New Statesman* of January 1980, Raymond Williams in his *Orwell* of 1971, Williams again, Said again, O'Brien again, Said again, O'Brien once more, and finally, Isaac Deutscher in his 1955 essay "The Mysticism of Cruelty."

It can be seen at once that Orwell is one of those authors who is damned whatever he does. O'Brien, in his rhetorical question 8, does not ask, "Is it reasonable?" (to which the answer would be dubious), or, "Is it interesting?" (to which the answer might be yes). He asks, "Is it fantastic?" to which the answer is, "Certainly." One is forced to ask of O'Brien, Is he as sure of himself as he seems?

Edward Said prefers the non sequitur. Suppose that Orwell's life *had* been one of "comfort," and suppose that we do agree that the less comfortable bits (like the English industrial North and the Catalan front) had been self-inflicted. Suppose that we forget that he did keep up with friends like Jack Common and his former POUM comrades of the Spanish Civil War until the end of his life. We are still supposed to distrust him for his cozy relationship with agents and publishers. It is notorious, and must be known to Professor Said, that *Animal Farm* was published only after strenuous battles with T. S. Eliot at Faber and Faber, who thought it was inopportune, with Jonathan Cape, who thought it unpropitious, and with numerous American houses, one of which (Dial Press) wrote to Orwell that it was "impossible to sell animal stories in the U.S.A." The story of his quarrel with the *New Statesman*, which refused to print his dispatches from Barcelona, though conceding their veracity, is or ought to be well known by Said. One is compelled to ask if there is not some other animus at work. The same suspicion arises when one contemplates O'Brien's liverish remarks in extract 1. What is he *thinking* about when he says that Orwell was scornful of foreign writers and even of foreigners *tout court*? If we discount Orwell's unbroken hostility to British imperialism, a hostility that he kept up at awkward times, such as 1940–45, and if we overlook his seminal essay "Not Counting Niggers," which rebuked those who talked of new world orders while ignoring the coolies, and if we agree to minimize the extent to which racism was a commonplace even among the educated in Orwell's time, we are still left with some evidence. There are the essays in defense of James Joyce, Salvador Dali, and Henry Miller and (admittedly more grudging) the piece on Ezra Pound. There's also a very well crafted article on Joseph Conrad, who was not in vogue at the time. Orwell actually made rather a point of importing and introducing "exotic" authors into his milieus and into the insular and British magazines for which he wrote. His "dislike of foreign words" was a distaste for the very *English* habit of using tags as a show of learning.

What can one say of Raymond Williams? His little book on Orwell is a minor disgrace. It is a warren of contradictions, not all of which can be mitigated by the plea of sloppiness and haste. He writes that *Nineteen Eighty-four* lacks "a substantial society and correspondingly substantial persons." That's poor enough. But elsewhere he denounces the book for "projecting a world that is all too recognizable." What he means, and this at any rate he makes explicit, is that Orwell depicts a brute version of *socialism* as the setting for his nightmare and thus lets down the "progressive" side. Well, imagine how much courage would have been required, in 1949, to base an anti-utopian fiction on Nazism. Such a book might have compelled or commanded near-universal and quite consoling assent. But it would scarcely have outlasted one printing and would not have called upon the "power of facing unpleasant facts." In 1949, socialism was thought, and (mark this) not just by its adherents, to be the wave of the future. In that year, thinkers like Williams were more at ease with that interpretation than they are now. Some of them for good reasons and some of them for bad ones; but any novel designed to make people think had to be, to that extent, *contra mundum*.

Orwell went to the trouble, in insisting that his book was "NOT intended as an attack on Socialism," to capitalize the word *not*. This isn't good enough for his leftist invigilators (or, come to think of it, for his conservative usurpers). The first group evinces a certain unction. Said: "True, he had courage and humanity." O'Brien: "To insist upon the limitations of Orwell's thought is only to establish the limits within which we admire him." Williams: "We are never likely to reach a time when we can do without his frankness, his energy, his willingness to join in." This patronizing stuff betrays a sense of unease. It is an obligatory clearing of the throat before getting down to the real business of blaming Orwell for the Cold War. There is not much doubt that this is, in fact, what they hold against him. The difficulty here is that they object to the same thing about *Nineteen Eighty-four* that Orwell did— which is to say, they are upset by its reception. *Life* magazine said of the book that it would expose "British Laborites" for reveling in austerity, "just as the more fervent New Dealers in the United States often seemed to have the secret hope that the depression mentality of the 1930s, source of their power and excuse for their experiments, would never end." If you want a picture of the future, imagine (to vary Orwell's famous scene) FDR stamping on a human face—forever. This crassness was and is very widespread, and Orwell issued what he termed a *démenti* against it. But one has to marvel at the way in which certain intellectuals will still deliberately muddy cause and effect. It is the clear implication of all four of his senior socialist critics that an author is in some real sense *responsible* for misinterpretations or vulgarizations of his own work. Where this principle would leave Edward Said or Raymond Williams is a matter, perhaps luckily for them, only of conjecture. But notice that when Isaac Deutscher said of *Nineteen Eighty-*

four, "It has only increased and intensified the waves of panic and hate that run through the world and obfuscate innocent minds," he was not so much observing such a process as, if it truly existed, contributing to it. There's something self-destructive as well as self-fulfilling in helping to create an atmosphere which you deplore—what better confirmation could there be of the antisocialist character of a book than that it be subjected to panicky denunciations by socialists? Orwell's careful disclaimer, then, was a small voice drowned in a chorus of apparently opposed but actually collusive propagandists. In a way, that was the pattern of his life.

The question *cui bono* is commonly asked with the intention of oversimplifying. Some reviewers of *Darkness at Noon* noted that Koestler put the Stalinist rationale so persuasively, in the mouth of the interrogator, as to make it convincing. Suppose, what is not unthinkable, that the book had the effect of attracting converts to communism? Would that make Koestler "objectively" an agent of Soviet propaganda? The proposition dissolves in hilarity (though John Strachey took that aspect of the book very seriously). Similarly, in January 1980 Said writes that Orwell turned "to an ideology of the middle-brow 'our way of life' variety, which in the U.S. at least has been dressed up as 'neo-conservatism.' " Exactly three years later, Norman Podhoretz steps forward ("If Orwell Were Alive Today," *Harper's*, January 1983) to take Said up on it and to claim Orwell as a posthumous founder of the Committee for the Free World.

These mutually agreeing images of the man are a serious nuisance and an obstacle to proper appreciation. Orwell stands now where he never wanted or expected to be—almost above reproach. What, or which, are the qualities that we treasure? It might be easiest to begin by admitting what Orwell was not. For one thing, as already stated, he was certainly not consistent. His writings between 1936 and 1940, in particular, show an extraordinary volatility. He veered now toward straight anti-Nazism, now toward anarchism, then pacifism, varieties of *gauchiste* allegiance, and finally (with palpable relief) a decision to support the war effort. Many of his least well guarded statements come from this period—he never actually proposed cooperation with antiwar fascists, and he never quite said that the British Empire was on all fours with the Third Reich (two allegations that have been made against him). But he did flirt with a kind of nihilism because of his fear that another world war would (*a*) be worse than any compromise, and (*b*) be directed by the people who were most responsible for its outbreak. He was not entirely wrong about either of these, especially (*b*), but his friends tended to wince at the letters they were getting.

That specific period of mercurial polemic can be read as a version of larger and more interesting inconsistencies. Orwell was a convinced internationalist but an emotional patriot. He was a convinced democrat and egalitarian, but he often reverted or resorted to snobbery (especially of the intellectual type).

He thought that the United States was an arsenal and ally of democracy, but he suspected its global intentions ("advancing behind a smoke-screen of novelists"), despised its mass cultural output, and never showed the slightest curiosity about it or desire to visit it. He was a materialist and a secularist— particularly hostile to the Roman Catholic heresy—but had a great reverence for tradition and for liturgy. He defended the heterodox and the persecuted, making a special effort for the least popular cases, but was prone to spasms of intolerance. One way of describing him, as well as of valuing him, would be to say that he was a man at war. There was a continual battle between his convictions, which were acquired through experience, and his emotions and temperament, which were those of his background and of his difficult personality. Large works on the famous Orwell–Blair distinction, most of them verbose and speculative, have been written to "explain" this simple point.

Orwell was conscious, at least some of the time, of the paradoxes in his style. He was, if anything, overfond of saying to people that they must *choose*. He chivied and ridiculed the lovers of the middle ground and was often prey to a kind of absolutism, especially before and during World War II. When it was over, in 1945, he wrote in *Through a Glass, Rosily:*

> Whenever A and B are in opposition to each other, anyone who attacks or criticises A is accused of aiding and abetting B.

He added:

> It is a tempting manoeuvre, and I have used it myself more than once, but it is dishonest.

Here, however belatedly, is a recognition and a self-criticism. He may have sensed that the shaft about "aiding and abetting," so often used against himself and his fellow POUM dissidents in Spain, did not properly belong in his quiver. He might at times have relished using this moral blackmail against his old antagonists. At times, as he himself wrote of Swift, he may have been "one of those people who are driven into a sort of perverse Toryism by the follies of the progressive party of the moment." But, when he took an unfair advantage or employed a demagogic style, he knew that he was doing it. Here, I think, is part of the answer to those who blame him for getting a good press from the philistines. Here, also, is part of the secret of his double reputation.

The occasional but still very salient element of nastiness and ill-temper in Orwell's personality and in his prose is something that gives pain to his more herbivorous admirers, such as Irving Howe. Orwell's asides about the "nancy poets" and his sniggers at the giggling, sandal-wearing Quakers are somehow at odds with the interminably reiterated image of his gentleness and decency. But perhaps, if he had been all that gentle and humane, he would not have had the spiteful, necessary energy to go for the hypocrites and trimmers of his day. Certain it is, though, that there are many critics alive and preaching who love him only for his faults.

Most conspicuous among these is Norman Podhoretz. Many conservative exegetes read Orwell as an anti-intellectual, concerned to defend the plain man against mischievous theory. This interpretation of him will never stale as long as there are people who believe simultaneously that (a) "the people" are wiser and more trustworthy than the eggheads and that (b) it takes a really courageous intellectual to summon the nerve to point this out. Such intellectuals generally find themselves elsewhere, or downright opposed, when anything resembling a revolt or movement of real people actually takes place. This mentality defines the modern neoconservatives—the Tories, as Orwell would have called them. In the personification, accurate as well as convenient, of the editor of *Commentary*, they have coated Orwell in sickly and ingratiating matter just as the other lot have heaped him with dead dogs. For example:

1. "The iron relationship Burke saw between revolution and the militarization of a country, each a side of the same coin, is highlighted by Orwell's treatment of Oceania's wars."
2. "[Orwell] was a forerunner of neoconservatism in having been one of the first in a long line of originally left-wing intellectuals who have come to discover more saving political and moral wisdom in the instincts and mores of 'ordinary people' than in the ideas and attitudes of the intelligentsia."
3. "Michels saw what was coming in this respect at the beginning of the century, in the Socialist parties of Europe: in their ever-greater centralization of power and singlemindedness of dreams of use of this power. James Burnham made this fact central in his prescient and largely unappreciated *Managerial Revolution*."

This salad of misrepresentations has neither the venom nor the variety of its *marxisant* counterpart. But it is hardly less opportunistic or inventive. The first and last quotations come from Robert Nisbet, in his essay "*Nineteen Eighty-four* and the Conservative Imagination" (published in *Nineteen Eighty-four Revisited*, edited by Irving Howe). The middle one is from Norman Podhoretz in the *Harper's* article already mentioned.

Podhoretz presents the least difficulty here. His essay claims Orwell for reaction and relishes his attacks on homosexuals and dilettantes. It quotes, with particular savor, his review of Cyril Connolly's *The Rock Pool*, where

Orwell allows himself to abuse those "so called artists who spend on sodomy what they have gained by sponging." It cites, as if it were to be taken literally, Orwell's remark that, "if someone drops a bomb on your mother, go and drop two bombs on his mother." (I should like to read Podhoretz's review of *A Modest Proposal*. It would probably be rich in keen, vicarious approval.) It consciously excerpts and garbles Orwell's piece on the need for European socialist unity in order to give the impression that he was an early supporter of American "peace through strength." For example, as I noted in a letter to *Harper's* (February 1983), on the question of America versus Russia, Podhoretz quotes Orwell as follows:

> It will not do to give the usual quibbling answer, "I refuse to choose." . . . We are no longer strong enough to stand alone and . . . we shall be obliged, in the long run, to subordinate our policy to that of one Great Power or another.

What Orwell had written, in his famous 1947 essay "In Defense of Comrade Zilliacus," was this:

> It will not do to give the usual quibbling answer, "I refuse to choose." In the end the choice may be forced upon us. We are no longer strong enough to stand alone, and if we fail to bring a West European union into being we shall be obliged, in the long run, to subordinate our policy to that of one Great Power or another.

In the same year he wrote:

> In the end, the European peoples may have to accept American domination as a way of avoiding domination by Russia, but they ought to realise, while there is yet time, that there are other possibilities.

Orwell came to the conclusion:

> Therefore a Socialist United States of Europe seems to me the only worthwhile political objective today.

I said earlier that all quotation is necessarily selective and out of context. But there is a sort of tradition that, when length or density of quotation obliges one to omit a few words, the resulting ". . ." should not deprive the reader of anything essential or germane. Podhoretz seems to me, by his inept ellipses, to have broken this compact with his readers in both letter and spirit. All in the name of Orwellian values . . .*

---

* No whit abashed, Mr. Podhoretz preserved these misleading ellipses in his 1987 collection, *The Bloody Crossroads*.

Robert Nisbet is more scrupulous but no more useful. The idea of a genealogy connecting Orwell to Edmund Burke has at least the merit of originality. It also exploits the "large, vague" idea that Orwell is a part of some assumed English tradition. Only by his inspired attribution to Burnham does Nisbet show himself to be altogether deluded. He does not know, or at any rate does not show that he knows, that Orwell was intrigued by Burnham and wrote a long pamphlet on his work. The pamphlet (*James Burnham and the Managerial Revolution*, published by the Socialist Book Centre, London, in 1946) finds Burnham guilty of power worship and distortion, and of a poorly masked admiration of the very "totalitarian" tendencies that he purports to abhor. Since I believe that it is this polemic which, more than any other, marks off Orwell for all time from his reactionary admirers, I'll go on about it a bit.

Most of Orwell's most famous stands were taken on once-controversial issues that have been decided long since—the Spanish Civil War, the Moscow Trials, mass unemployment. Only in his contest with Burnham does Orwell really engage, before his death, with the modern questions that still preoccupy us. (The antagonists were well matched. Burnham liked to combat prevailing orthodoxy, had a pitiless attitude to intellectual compromise, and was an ex-Marxist with a good working knowledge of socialist thought. In fact, when many of our present neoconservatives praise Orwell, it is really Burnham they have in mind.)

Like the Russophobes of the 1980s, Burnham assumed that totalitarianism was more efficient, more determined, and more self-confident than the weakly and self-indulgent form of society known as democracy. He wrote contemptuously of idealism, humanitarianism, and other hypocrisies, which he equated with appeasement and saw as a means of duping the masses. I cannot summarize his opinions better than Orwell did, but I'll "select" one quotation which gives the flavor both of Burnham's book and of Orwell's objection to it:

> Although he reiterates that he is merely setting forth the facts and not stating his own preferences, it is clear that Burnham is fascinated by the spectacle of power, and that his sympathies were with Germany as long as Germany appeared to be winning the war.

This was not because of any special fellow-feeling for Nazism on Burnham's part, but was the result of his conviction that countries like Britain were incurably "decadent." Orwell, who had flirted with this view himself at some points in the immediate prewar period, wrote of Burnham's line, "It is clear that in his mind the idea of 'greatness' is inextricably mixed up with the idea of cruelty and dishonesty."

Burnham borrowed lavishly from Michels and Pareto with his stress on the circulation of elites. (Neither Orwell nor Nisbet, incidentally, mentions the involvement of those two sapients with the later cleansing power of fascism.) In essence, the mentality in both cases contains the same contradiction. The "managerial" dictatorship will be leaner and meaner than flabby, sluggish democracy. But only an open society can allow real recruitment from the lower ranks, even of former dissenters. Burnham saw, eventually, that there was something self-defeating in the hierarchy and obedience of the fascist state. But this did not prevent him from grafting precisely the same attributes onto the Stalinist system and warning of yet another decline of the West in the face of it. Present-day analogues of this mentality would be tedious to enumerate. Or, as Orwell commented:

> It is, therefore, not surprising that Burnham's world-view should often be noticeably close to that of the American imperialists on the one side, or to that of the isolationists on the other. It is a "tough" or "realistic" world-view which fits in with the American form of wish-thinking.

It's interesting, and perhaps important, to notice here that Orwell's critique of Burnham contains the seeds of his *Nineteen Eighty-four*. A few citations should make this clear. In replying to Burnham's opinion that it is only the winning side that can define justice and morals, he writes:

> This implies that literally anything can become right or wrong if the dominant class of the moment so wills it.

Elsewhere he remarks:

> Jack London in *The Iron Heel* (1909) foretold some of the essential features of Fascism, and such books as Wells's *The Sleeper Awakes* (1900), Zamyatin's *We* (1923) and Aldous Huxley's *Brave New World* (1930), all described imaginary worlds in which the special political problems of capitalism had been solved without bringing liberty, equality or true happiness any nearer.

It was also, probably, in reaction to *The Managerial Revolution* that Orwell developed his idea of the trinity of Oceania, Eastasia, and Eurasia. Summarizing Burnham, he says, "The future map of the world, with its three great super-states is, in any case, already settled in its main outlines." He went on to scoff at Burnham's idea that the three would be Japan, Germany, and the United States, because he did not share Burnham's view that the Soviet Union would be defeated any more than he shared his later view that it was invincible. Nonetheless, a thought seems to have been planted. Most appreciations of *Nineteen Eighty-four* understate, if they do not ignore, the way in which permanent superpower conflict is made the necessary condition for the coercion and repression within. The Cold War and its ancillaries such as the "military-industrial complex" and the "permanent war economy" are, in all essentials, *Orwellian* concepts. And Orwell's own repudiation of Burnham prefigures this. It also affords some harmless amusement to the student of Professor Nisbet, who regards militarization as a function only of revolution and who pleads Burnham with apparent innocence as a part of the Orwell tradition.

The most frightening moment in *Darkness at Noon* comes not when Rubashov is interrogated or when he hears of the torture of others, but when he ponders the possibility that "Number One" may after all be right. The worst moment in *Nineteen Eighty-four* is not the cage of rats or the slash of the rubber truncheon, but the moment when Winston decides that he loves Big Brother.

The essence of Orwell's work is a sustained criticism of servility. It is not *what* you think, but *how* you think, that matters. What he noticed about the Moscow Trials, for instance (and long before there was any hard evidence), was the appalling self-abnegation of the "defendants." What he hated about the English class system was the fawning and the acquiescence that it produced among its victims. (The contemptible boy who felt that he deserved to be caned in "Such, Such Were the Joys" is the earliest symptomatic example.) What he disliked in intellectuals—not about intellectuals—was their willingness or readiness to find excuses for power. What he disliked most in prose was euphemism. It is decades now since Czeslaw Milosz wrote *The Captive Mind*, but one sentence there is especially apropos. Describing the Eastern European intelligentsia, Milosz remarked, "Even those who know Orwell only by hearsay are amazed that a writer who had never lived in Russia should have so keen a perception into its life." In some sense, Orwell *knew* what the actual texture of dictatorial collectivism would be. He knew because of a variety of things he had already seen: the toadying of the English boarding school, the smell of the police court, the betrayal of the Spanish Republic, the whining and cadging of the underclass, the impotent sullenness of colonized natives, the lure and horror of war fever, and the special scent given off by the apologist. Others may have had the same experiences, but in our time it was Orwell who knew how to codify his impressions into something resembling a system. He is quoted to the point of annihilation as having said that "good prose is like a window pane," but it might be fairer to say that his own writing resembles a mirror. Anybody looking into it and failing to find some reflected portion of the modern age, or some special personal inhibition about seeing it, is myopic. Many are the Calibans who detest the reflection, and many are the Babbitts who like what they see.

Take Orwell's remark, in the concluding sentence of "The Prevention of Literature":

At present we know only that the imagination, like certain wild animals, will not breed in captivity.

That is a looking glass, not a windowpane. As a transparency, it fails: the imagination has been known to breed in captivity, and no doubt modern zookeepers will coax even the rarest surviving creatures into doing the same. Nonetheless, there is both truth and beauty in the remark. The desecration of literature in Russia—one of its ancestral homes—is an instance. The emigration of genius from Central Europe after 1933 is another. In his pessimistic mood, culminating in *Nineteen Eighty-four*, Orwell seems to have believed in the almost literal truth of his aphorism. But, in his earlier essay on the literary dictatorship of Zhdanov, he was able to see a more hopeful side. A totalitarian society cannot *produce* any imaginative work; it can only *cause* it. Some achievements are quite simply beyond the tyrant but remain, still, within the reach of the individual.

Would Orwell have remained a socialist? It may not be the decisive question, but it is an interesting one. He certainly anticipated most of the sickening disillusionments that have, in the last generation, led socialists to dilute or abandon their faith. To this extent, he was proof against the disillusionments rather than evidence for them. He hated inequality, exploitation, racism, and the bullying of small nations, and he was an early opponent of nuclear weapons and the hardly less menacing idea of nuclear blackmail or "deterrence." He saw how an external threat could be used to police or to intimidate dissent, even in a democracy. The spokesmen for our renovated capitalism, then, can barely claim that their pet system has developed to a point beyond the reach of his pen. Stalinism and its imitators have not striven to prove him wrong either. Cambodia makes his scathing remarks on Auden's "necessary murder" look pallid, while in China and North Korea the cult of Big Brother has far outpaced satire.

There exists a third school of Orwell that argues, more or less, that he would have remained as he was. Bernard Crick, his thorough if uninspiring biographer, is a leading member of it. Irving Howe, the keeper of the keys (it would be hard to call him keeper of the flame) of moderate social democracy, is another. Lionel Trilling, who wrote the best review of *Nineteen Eighty-four* on its publication, also saw in Orwell a confirming, undogmatic, sturdy, and (always that word) "decent" liberal. This opinion is unexceptionable, and those who hold it do not have to resort, as their rivals do, to distortion or caricature. The trouble is simply that they geld Orwell, make him into the sort of chap who should be taught to schoolchildren as a bland and bloodless good example. Stephen Spender evokes this fustian curriculum by his fatuous likening of *Nineteen Eighty-four* to *Erewhon*. Howe rather complacently adds that we will end up with collectivism one way or another—the only question is whether it will be founded "on willing co-operation or on the machine gun." At least he borrows Orwell fairly and accurately here—the trouble is that we are left with an image of Fabian resignation and the prospect of good works.

Orwell detested the machine gun, but he wasn't an enthusiast for "willing cooperation" either. As much as he loathed the will to power, he hated and feared the urge to obey. For Orwell, as for Winstanley, Defoe, Cobbett, and Zola, it is the *lack* of power that corrupts. He is both a founder and member of a modern rebel tradition that, in political writing, comprises Victor Serge and Dwight Macdonald, Albert Camus and Milan Kundera.

(*Grand Street*, Winter 1984)

BLUNT INSTRUMENTS

◻

CAMUS:
Un Copain

❏

Once, in an excess of irritation with his small son Jean, Camus ordered him from the supper table to bed. "Good night, minor writer of no importance," muttered the child as he withdrew. Camus was easily hurt by bad notices and had a long memory for feuds. Sartre was probably right to say of him that "he had a little Algiers roughneck side." But the prickliness and the vanity, which disfigured many of the disputes he conducted in his life, seem more and more irrelevant with the lapse of years. Camus would not fit; every attempt to categorize him left a noticeable penumbra, a jagged outline around the figure. In his labor of love, *Albert Camus: A Biography*, Herbert Lottman has tidied up a great number of old rows and given us a clearer look at Camus's real importance.

For over a decade, argument concerning him has been caught in a boring and artificial dichotomy. There are those who claim to revere him for his apolitical artistry and his deep humanity, while in fact marking him up for his anticommunism. And there are those who reply that he funked the only moral issue which ever touched him personally because he never came out for the Algerian FLN. In many ways, the repetitiveness of these polemics recalls the various posthumous efforts to conscript George Orwell—with whom there are some other suggestive parallels.

For example, Conor Cruise O'Brien manages to suggest (by a very slight elision in his book) that Camus was part of the CIA-sponsored offensive of the Congress for Cultural Freedom. In fact, he adopted the same policy toward that organization as he did to communist front groups. In politics, his friends tended to be of the unorganized Far Left—not unlike Orwell's Catalan revolutionaries. He was always available to help Republican Spain, as he was to intercede for imprisoned Greek communists or victimized Hungarians and Czechs. The stoutest defense of his Nobel Prize—which was elsewhere blurred by Cold War barracking of all kinds—came in the review *Révolution prolétarienne*. The article was entitled "Albert Camus, Un Copain."

The wavering over Algeria, which looks more rather than less damaging nowadays, was certainly less disgraceful than the retreats made by some (such as the French Communist Party) who had less excuse. We know from Lottman that Camus was more engaged than he let on—FLN militants recall that he offered them shelter in his house and that he spoke to them at rallies in Algiers, with fascist settlers baying at the doors. His position and his tactics were far more intricate and complex than have usually been allowed (after all, he left the Algerian Communist Party because it downplayed Arab nationalism). But he certainly did get it wrong, and he did commit himself to statements—like the celebrated one about defending his mother above justice—which made him look a prig. (This famous antithesis between Justice and Mother, like the endlessly recycled Forsterian choice between Friends and Country, is false because it can never really be posed the other way around, and never comes up in "real life.")

Could it be fair to say that he mistook reality in Algeria because he *minded* about it so much? Even O'Brien concedes that Sartre's position, though superior politically, was much easier personally. Camus knew and loved the Algerians; even in the 1930s we find him putting on integrated productions of Malraux's plays in Algiers itself, in the company of two fine old fellow travelers named Bourgeois and Poignant. His errors were not all that rank if one bears his commitment in mind.

Much ridicule has been poured on Camus's idea of the Mediterranean as the civilizing measure of humanity. As a philosophical scheme, it obviously lacks depth, and it clearly finds its counterpart in his personal dislike of Germany and the North. I think it does contain some clues to his Algerian stand—the hope that French and Arab culture might fertilize each other was always accompanied by the insistence that the two peoples should be equal. It was in the beautiful Roman Algerian seaside town of Tipaza that he decided to join the Communist Party; whatever the symbolism here, it most certainly is not colonialist. Likewise, his admiration for Kazantzakis, and even his feeling that fascism and communism were tempered once they got to Italy and Yugoslavia: these may be idealistic but are not *intuitively* inhuman or stupid.

As he eluded classification politically, so Camus kept surprising the critics with his fictions. No sooner had they concluded that he had become formalistic and dry than he hit them between the eyes with *The Fall* (1956). Claude de Freminville, in a letter on the young Camus, concluded that he "continues to *think* despair, even to write it; but he *lives* hope." It was this contrast, which may remind some people of Gramsci's famous "pessimism of the intellect; optimism of the will," that gave rise to much of what is misleadingly called "the Absurd."

Camus had a knack for noticing grotesque things—not just in individuals, but in attitudes. A great deal of it he kept to himself. Lottman has a good example: that of Camus, vanquished in a public exchange with Sartre and Jeanson, taking revenge in his journal by writing, "*Temps modernes.* They admit sin and refuse grace." His lifelong obsession with capital punishment, and his bitter opposition to it in literature and in life, was another source of unhappy reflection. One can surmise his reaction, when proposing a petition against political executions, on being told by Simone de Beauvoir that those were the only sort she *did* believe in. Lottman makes it plain that the guillotining in *The Stranger* is indeed rooted in an experience undergone by Camus's father; the pungent feeling of disgust was not something he could vary from case to case.

All of Camus's involvements were essentially reluctant, which is why he is often remembered with resentment by those to whom politics was the stuff of life. He cannot have been a very *sortable* comrade, and the chapters on his journalistic period, especially with Claude Bourdet on *Combat*, show him to have been a spiky and difficult colleague even when things were going well. Again, there is an echo of Orwell here.

In Britain, the phrase "we are all guilty" is taken by reactionaries as the acme of bleeding-heart leftist doublethink. Camus didn't find it a joke phrase at all, and perhaps, if Britain had endured Nazi occupation, there would be fewer to sneer at it there. He would often, on public platforms, tell the story of the concierge in the Gestapo headquarters, doing her cleaning every morning amid the victims of torture and explaining, "I never pay attention to what my tenants do." His post-Resistance journals contain the entry:

> Temptation to flee and to accept the decadence of one's era. Solitude makes me happy. But feeling also that decadence begins from the moment when one accepts. And one remains—so that man can remain on the heights where he belongs. . . . But nauseous disgust for this dispersion in others.

Lottman has written a brilliant and absorbing book, which supplies new insight simply by including all the light and shade. The detail and the care are extraordinary; further slipshod generalizations about Camus will simply not be tolerable from now on. Now at least we have a clear voice about the importance of liberty and the importance of being concrete about it. Here is what Camus said at a joint rally of French and Spanish trade unionists in 1953:

> If someone takes away your bread, he suppresses your freedom at the same time. But if someone seizes your freedom, rest assured, your bread is threatened, because it no longer depends on you and your struggle, but on the pleasure of a master.

For all the occasional pomposity and introspection, for all the ambiguities over certain personal and political crises, the evidence is that Camus labored in the spirit of that declaration. In *The Exile and the Kingdom,* when Jonas's last message cannot be deciphered as between *solidaire* and *solitaire,* the irony of the two words now seems neither absurd nor self-indulgent, but realistic and necessary.

(New Statesman, July 20, 1979)

BRIDESHEAD REVIEWED

❑

In 1945, shortly after he had completed *Brideshead Revisited,* Evelyn Waugh received a letter from Lady Pansy Lamb. Her name might make her sound like one of Waugh's own less probable creations, but she was a friend and a contemporary and a woman of shrewd taste. She wrote of *Brideshead:*

> But all the richness of your invention, the magical embroideries you fling around your characters cannot make me nostalgic about the world I knew in the 1920s. And yet it was the same world as you describe. . . . Nobody was brilliant, beautiful and rich and the owner of a wonderful house, though some were one or the other. . . . Oxford, too, were Harold Acton and Co really as brilliant as that, or were there wonderful characters I never met? . . . You see English society of the 20s as something baroque and magnificent on its last legs. . . . I fled from it because it seemed prosperous, bourgeois and practical and I believe it still is.

Score one for Lady Pansy. We all see, of course, that she is *right.* Her brisk and knowing style reveals the magic of Sebastian Flyte as an affected sham. And besides, isn't *Brideshead* rather repulsive? In its pages we find the most appalling snobbery, the most rancid sort of Catholicism, commingled with deplorable attitudes toward women, and a sympathy, at times barely concealed, for prewar fascism. Yet the fact remains that Lady Pansy, though she may have had a good memory for the period, did not know what she was talking about.

Brideshead Revisited may appeal to the nostalgic and the reactionary, but not because it idealizes the 1920s. It is written as a hymn of hate toward the entire modern world and the emerging mass society of cleverness and greed. Waugh may have drawn Sebastian Flyte in glowing colors (before consigning him to a signally abject fate), but he did not forget "Boy" Mulcaster, the slob and bully, or Rex Mottram, the moneyed philistine and opportunist. Nor, for the most part, did he glamorize English social relations or English bourgeois mores. In 1945, Waugh felt that a certain world had perished forever. But his recording of it was still markedly less elegiac than might have been expected.

Why, then, does the book continue to fascinate? Everyone has a secret garden, at least in imagination, which they fear has been, or will be, invaded and trampled. By the time of the final desecration of Brideshead Castle by the British army, Waugh has emptied it of all but the most incidental of its original cast. The house and its chapel alone remain—the chapel's lamp providing the only light in the encircling gloom. Waugh himself said later that "the book is about God." So there is more than the secret garden at stake.

I think Waugh aims for, and achieves, quite a different effect. The "sense of loss" he evokes has primarily to do with World War I. When he wrote to a friend that "I should not think six Americans will understand it [*Brideshead*]," he was being more than his usual chauvinist self. He may have meant that the memory of 1914–18 was not really as present or as poignant in the United States. But it is present in *Brideshead*, slyly but unmistakably, from the first episode to the last. Waugh is calling on a common store of English folk memory—well caught in a recent essay by John Keegan in *The New York Review of Books*:

> The close at Shrewsbury at evening, Great Tom tolling over Peck, wickets falling at Fenner's, the shades gathering under the chestnut in Balliol garden quad. Englishmen are still brought up on this sort of imagery, if not directly then by osmosis. Indeed for Englishmen of a certain class it is impossible to escape its effect. It does not, of course, describe an England they inhabit.

Brideshead opens in 1923. At Oxford, the undergraduates are, *ex hypothesi*, too young to have fought in the trenches. Small changes have occurred, including a slight improvement in the standing of women, and as Charles Ryder's servant remarks testily to him:

> "If you ask me, sir, it's all on account of the war. It couldn't have happened but for that." For this was 1923 and for Lunt, as for thousands of others, things could never be the same as they had been in 1914.

(Needless to add here that Lady Pansy would have been right if she had pointed out that "millions" rather than "thousands" would be less elitist.) Charles himself is not untouched—we learn that his mother died while serving with a medical unit in Serbia. Later, describing Charles and Sebastian together in Venice, Waugh has an extraordinary passage, which should be quoted in full:

> The fortnight at Venice passed quickly and sweetly—perhaps too sweetly; I was drowning in honey, stingless. On some days life kept pace with the gondola, as we nosed through the side-canals and the boatman uttered his plaintive musical bird-cry of warning; on other days, with the speed-boat bouncing over the lagoon in a stream of sun-lit foam; it left a confused memory of fierce sunlight on the sands and cool, marble interiors; of water everywhere, lapping on smooth stone, reflected in a dapple of light on painted ceilings; of a night at the Corombona palace such as Byron might have known, and another Byronic night fishing for scampi in the shallows of Chioggia, the phosphorescent wake of the little ship, the lantern swinging in the prow and the net coming up full of weed and sand and floundering fishes; of melon and *prosciutto* on the balcony in the cool of the morning; of hot cheese sandwiches and champagne cocktails at the English bar.
>
> I remember Sebastian looking up at the Colleoni statue and saying, "It's rather sad to think that whatever happens you and I can never possibly get involved in a war."

Soon afterward, Sebastian is a wreck; his charm spoiled and his "epicene" beauty departed. As Waugh says, "The languor of Youth—how unique and quintessential it is! How quickly, how irrecoverably, lost!" I see no reason for Youth with a capital Y in this context unless Waugh intended to remind us of the poems of Wilfred Owen—the "Anthem for Doomed Youth" and all the other verses in which England haltingly came to realize that it had massacred its rising generation a few years before.

That massacre included, in *Brideshead* terms, Sebastian's three uncles. His mother, Lady Marchmain, remains obsessed with their deaths. Mr. Samgrass, the tame and sycophantic historian whom she hires to compose their memorial volume, is also the spy she retains to watch Sebastian at Oxford. She judges all men by the manner in which they measure up to her lost brothers. Sebastian cannot possibly enter the contest with these shades. Especially since his father, too, was lost in the war—in the sense that he went off to battle and never came back, preferring to remain on the Continent with his cynical Italian mistress.

Later in the story, after Sebastian's collapse, Charles Ryder gets melancholy drunk with the boorish Lord Mulcaster. They are both eager to join the upper-crust rabble that in 1926 formed private squads to break the General Strike:

> We went to a number of night clubs. In two years Mulcaster seemed to have attained his simple ambition of being known and liked in such places. At the last of them he and I were kindled by a great flame of patriotism.

"You and I," he said, "were too young to fight in the war. Other chaps fought, millions of them dead. Not us. We'll show them. We'll show the dead chaps we can fight, too."

"That's why I'm here," I said. "Come from overseas, rallying to old country in hour of need."

"Like Australians."

"Like the poor dead Australians."

The boozy bathos of this little scene does not hide the depth of feeling. Indeed, like other English writers of the period, Waugh often preferred to approach the subject by means of allusion. In his magnificent study *The Great War in Modern Memory*, Paul Fussell points out that only in England did the classical tag *Et in Arcadia ego* retain its authentic significance. It means, *not* "And I have dwelt in Arcadia too," but "Even in Arcadia I, Death, hold sway." The whole first section of *Brideshead* is entitled "Et in Arcadia ego." Early in the story, Charles Ryder's rooms at Oxford are embellished with

a human skull lately purchased from the School of Medicine, which, resting in a bowl of roses, formed, at the moment, the chief decoration of my table. It bore the motto *Et in Arcadia ego* inscribed on its forehead.

Fussell also points out, by reference to Siegfried Sassoon and others, the powerful symbolism of the 1914–18 holocaust.

One consequence of all this, if I am right, is that the homosexual undertones of the novel become more comprehensible. I don't think there is much doubt that Waugh means us to understand a love affair between Charles and Sebastian. Again, the context is of doomed youth and of the idea, so essential to the mythology of the Great War, that the summer of 1914 was the most golden and languorous of all:

Now, that summer term with Sebastian, it seemed as though I was being given a brief spell of what I had never known, a happy childhood, and though its toys were silk shirts and liqueurs and cigars and its naughtiness high in the catalogue of grave sins, there was something of nursery freshness about us that fell little short of the joy of innocence.

Wilfred Owen's own homosexual preference was seldom directly evident in his poems (the letters are more explicit). But the cult of youth and beauty, and the influence of A. E. Housman, are both powerful clues. Waugh, writing in 1945, could hardly have been innocent of the suggestions in that last paragraph. It's clear, anyway, that the "grave sin" was not smoking or drinking. So when Anthony Blanche remarks to Sebastian during this time, "My dear, I should like to stick you full of barbed arrows like a p-p-pin-cushion," he doesn't merely remind us once more of martyrdom, but chooses the one that has always had the greatest homosexual appeal—the lissome youth bleeding and transfixed. Owen's dying boy soldiers are not far away in that utterance either. (Nor are Walt Whitman's or Yukio Mishima's.)

It may be that "the book is about God," but there is no real theology in it. Lord Marchmain's deathbed repentance is a sickly farce, embarrassing to serious Catholics. The wrangle over Julia's marriage to the divorced Rex is a mere drawing-room drama, where the fear of "scandal" easily vanquishes any matter of principle. Sebastian's terminus among the monks is a chance result of his own dissipation. The only Catholic with any sort of vocation in the whole lot is little Cordelia, and she volunteers to go and help General Franco. Waugh believed in original sin, all right—he literally personified it in dialogue. For example, Sebastian writes to Charles: "I am in mourning for my lost innocence. It never looked like living. The doctors despaired of it from the start." And his sister Julia says much later:

> "Always the same, like the idiot child carefully nursed, guarded from the world. 'Poor Julia,' they say, 'she can't go out. She's got to take care of her little sin. A pity it ever lived,' they say, 'but it's so strong. Children like that always are. Julia's so good to her little, mad sin.'"

But really, aside from painful constructions like that, *Brideshead* is pretty much free of religiosity. It is not read, nor was it ever read, as a work of devotion or apology. But worse parodies have been made of it. One of them is playing at the moment on PBS.

I expect this series to do very well. British made, and featuring Laurence Olivier and John Gielgud, it trades on a certain image of my country that seems to go down well in America. It is the same image that is catered for by Alistair Cooke in his urbane openings to "Masterpiece Theatre" and by Robert Morley in his plummy promotion of British Airways. A country idyllic, antique, and lovably eccentric, where traditional good manners are upheld at the relatively low cost of an admittedly "outmoded" class system.

The gorgeousness of scenery and setting have been very lovingly done. The hints of upper-class debauchery and high jinks are all there. But there is little subtlety and less tragedy, and none of the feeling of a maimed and bereaved country. The characterization is all wrong, too. Jeremy Irons plays Charles Ryder as a heartbreaker, but Ryder is supposed to be a bit of a stick. (In answer to a query from Nancy Mitford as to how anybody could fall in love with him, Waugh allowed, "He *is* dim.") Sebastian Flyte appears as a second-rate camp individual, instead of the careless but complex figure he cuts in the novel. Anthony Blanche becomes a leering little queen, whereas the book makes plain that he was tough and intelligent as well as sexually versatile. Some of the minor characters are exquisite (Mr. Samgrass is just right, and Gielgud is splendid as Ryder's awful father). But poor adaptation and editing have removed countless nuances that are vitally necessary. (Watch the early scene where Blanche warns Ryder of Sebastian's charm, and then look it up in print.) Finally, beware of the bookstore. Little, Brown has reissued its 1945 edition in a gruesome "book of the series" format. Get the 1960 revised edition if you can.

Brideshead Revisited is not a comedy of social manners or a tract. It is not the intellectual's "Upstairs, Downstairs." It is not a bland celebration of the English country house. It is an imperfect, often awkward, but finally haunting rendition of a national myth. Composed during the last world war, it illuminates the influences, and captures the sense of longing and waste, that had led to it from the previous one.

(*The Nation*, January 23, 1982)

DECIMATION:
The Tenth Man

❏

In his article "The Other Man," Graham Greene described the sensations, partly queasy and partly hilarious, which came over him when he realized that he was being shadowed for life. The existence of a full-time doppelgänger was a cause for some self-congratulation (the sincerest form of flattery), for a touch of unease (What does he *want?*), and for occasional irritation (What if he's a nuisance and people think it's me?). Readers of the essay may have felt that this was just the sort of thing that was meant to happen to Greene. The shadow tended to make more appearances in exotic latitudes, to be shy of cameras and interviews, to be enigmatic when confronted. The full truth about him, one felt, was probably known only in some melancholy brothel or shabby confessional: just the kind of sibling one might have expected.

Now, to Greene's own surprise, he finds that he once wrote a long short story about a man who survived by a desperate act of impersonation. *The Tenth Man* lay in who knows what box or file over the course of four decades. When it was written, Dien Bien Phu had yet to fall; Cuba was still a casino island; Kim Philby, a trusted servant of the Crown. But the pages moldered on. Begun for MGM studios, and composed in a time of exigency, they have been retrieved by that great truffle-hound Anthony Blond, who has done the state some service. I still cannot rid myself of the feeling that this may be a hoax. Take, for example, the following:

> It was horrifying to realize that a man as false as that could sum up so accurately the mind of someone so true. The other way around, he thought, it doesn't work. Truth doesn't teach you to know your fellow man.

Or, from the succeeding page:

> But it was a stranger who replied to his ring: a dark youngish man with the brusque air of a competent and hard-worked craftsman. He packed the sacrament in his bag as a plumber packs his tools. "Is it wet across the fields?" he asked.

Here, surely, are the forgotten entrants in the renowned *New Statesman* competition, where Greene parodies were invited and the master himself came in a pseudonymous third.

Still, whoever actually wrote this book (or film script) certainly knew his business. The action originates in a dank French jail during the Nazi occupation. The prisoners are held as hostages against any act of violence by the Resistance. When a German NCO is slain, the reprisal is predetermined: one man in every ten must die (a surprisingly lenient decision, by the standards of, say, Oradour). The sadomasochistic detail is provided, however, by the Nazi stipulation that the prisoners themselves must cast the lot. Readers of *The Tenth Man* will probably never again employ the word "decimate" in its slack, inexact form.

The alphabet decides the draw, just as a defective watch determines the pace and timing. A reverse order of precedence is hit upon for no good reason, which gives the lead character, Chavel, an illusory feeling of being at the right end of things. The illusion is short-lived.

It's actually quite difficult to sustain tension in a scene where everyone knows what the outcome will be. Greene once wrote of *Brideshead Revisited* that certain decisive episodes, chapter length in memory, turned out to be a mere few paragraphs on rereading. He called it a real test of narrative, and by that test he has succeeded. Had MGM ever made the film, it would have necessitated some intense perspiration close-ups and breath-intakes, with many cutaways to the ticking timepiece. You could surmise that it was genuine Greene a few pages later, when the whole business takes a sudden lurch:

As Voisin said, it wasn't fair. Only Lenôtre took it calmly: he had spent a lifetime in business and he had watched from his stool many a business deal concluded in which the best man did not win.

Voisin has a point. Chavel, the prosperous attorney, wants to cheat the firing squad by offering his whole patrimony to a substitute. And there is a taker, Janvier, who has always wanted to impress his female relations by dying as a rich burgher. . . .

Swallow that, and forget for the moment that it was Dostoevsky who wrote that a condemned man would suffer *anything* rather than keep his appointment. The redeemed Chavel finds himself in a dilemma analogous to that of Raskolnikov. One compromise with death exacts another. Janvier's sister and mother take up their wretched inheritance, the mother ignorant of the price and the sister made miserable by her awareness of it. Can Chavel keep away from his old estate after the Liberation? Not in this script, he can't. And, like Raskolnikov (and Voisin), he has to object: "It isn't fair. This isn't my fault. I didn't ask for two lives—only Janvier's."

For—and by all means suspend your disbelief here—Chavel signs on as an anonymous servitor in his old mansion. Better to serve in heaven than rule in hell? The elements of a Catholic morality tale, at any rate, are all in place. Thérèse, sister of the departed Janvier, is living a Havisham-like existence on her unwanted inheritance and seems to be kept alive only by hatred and desire for vengeance. Chavel, under his newly assumed name of Charlot, feels it his mission to free her from this rancorous obsession. The redeeming power of love is brought into play. And his lawyerly little mind is well evoked as he rehearses the necessary special pleading in a nearby cabbage patch:

> Already the charge against himself had been reduced to a civil case in which he could argue the terms of compensation. He wondered why last night he had despaired—this was no occasion for despair, he told himself, but for hope. He had something to live for, but somewhere at the back of his mind the shadow remained, like a piece of evidence he had deliberately not confided to the court.

A fair depiction of the trials of accidie and the temptations of guilt. And further confirmation that Greene is correct in supposing that he did write it. Not even the *New Statesman* competitors could have easily come up with:

> "Can I have your blessing, father?"
> "Of course." He rubber-stamped the air like a notary and was gone.

Greene has traditionally divided his fiction into "novels" and "entertainments," and it's noticeable that neither definition is awarded to *The Tenth*

Man. There is, at the last, no moral resolution to the story. Nor is there a completely memorable major character like Scobie or Wormald or Dr. Magiot. The final scenes resemble a Wildean or Gilbertian denouement, with people popping up randomly to contribute their individual "twists."

Still, the saving seediness of the protagonists is an authentic Greene touch. Chavel/Charlot can torture himself all he wants, but there is no suggestion that a better man died in his place. The females are dreary; the fellow prisoners appallingly stoic; the sole resistant character is a resentful cripple. French society, sketched against a backdrop of shame and dislocation, is sufficiently bleak to satisfy the most ardent fan. The sole cheerful note is struck rather imperfectly by Carosse, the phony and carpetbagger who typifies the period and who almost spoils Chavel's own imposture by a more inventive one of his own.

The Tenth Man may have been forgotten for decades, but it obviously contributed subliminal "prompts" to other better-known works. Betrayal, mistaken identity, remorse—these are the familiar themes. We learn in the author's introduction that MI5 once proposed to MI6 an official-secrets prosecution on the basis of one of the fantasies here engendered. Who would have been indicted if C had given the go-ahead? Greene or the other man? Men are still told off by numbers, with a continuing search for someone to make up a fourth. We live on the porous boundary between Greeneland and reality.

(*The Times Literary Supplement*, March 15, 1985)

POOR DEAR CYRIL

❑

There is a difference between an epigram and an aphorism. Cyril Connolly, who certainly understood the distinction, seems never to have cared much about it. David Pryce-Jones, who refers to Connolly's style as "aphoristic," seems not to know the difference. An epigram is a witty saying or a deft observation. An aphorism is a concise or clever statement of a truth or a moral. Epigrams, then, are amoral, ephemeral, and often produced purely for effect, while aphorisms have a certain solemnity and preachiness. I think it no insult to Connolly to describe his stuff as, at its best, epigrammatic.

Oscar Wilde, somewhere, makes one of his characters a martyr to the epigram. The man is prepared to ruin his own argument or poison a valuable social occasion for the sake of coining a swift and memorable mot. Connolly seems to have been like that—fatally tempted by the bitchy remark or (if you'll allow me) the momentary shaft. He would jeopardize friendship for gossip and dinner parties for one-liners. This was the destructive obverse, perhaps, of his youthful will to please, his discovery that being amusing and obliging was a hedge against ostracism. "Diverting" might be the word here, with its twin connotations of wit and deflection. For much of his life, Connolly seems to have put off the reckoning by reverting to the skills and artifices of boyhood.

"Boyhood" also seems an appropriate keyword. Connolly's "Theory of Permanent Adolescence" seemed dated a couple of decades ago, with its stress on the retarding and narcissistic effects of public-school mores on English life. But it may have surfaced again, resplendent and reborn, in the half-affectionate cult of the Sloane Rangers and the recent influx of hereditary porkers into the House of Commons. Like Connolly himself, this generation seems doomed and determined to evolve from *joli-laid* into *laid* as fast as can be.

Pryce-Jones remarks quite aptly of Connolly in his book *Cyril Connolly: Journal and Memoir,* that, "with some part of himself, he managed to believe that his head start and his many privileges really had been handicaps." Thus equipped, he fought a long battle against not deprivation but inanition. Decades seem to have gone by, on the evidence of this book, with its hero undergoing a random series of moods, fluxes, deferrals, fads, and lapses. The effect is enervating rather than otherwise, because Connolly's changes of pace and rhythm give no impression of energy, but simply one of restlessness and occasional despair. It would be a chronicle of wasted time if it had not produced some writing of quality, and some worthwhile reflections on the elusive business of friendship.

Connolly rather specialized in epicene yearning and smoldering, as only an adolescent who has been smitten with his peers can yearn and smolder. In a letter to Robert Longden ("Bobbie"), written when he was at Oxford in 1924, he implored:

> Anyhow please don't sleep with Ronnie, he is too tall for you. Smith would be better (this is the page of a letter that one's parents always find). . . . I get awful ποθοσς here, not seeing a soul all day and having a nice bedroom with a fire.

Hero worship, jealousy, the classics—Simon Raven has spun trilogies out of less (without adding the slightly comfy and banal bit about the fire and the bedroom). But the impress of schooldays seems, as it does in Raven's fictional betrayals, to be indelible. By 1939, with air raids and conscription in prospect, Connolly is writing of wartime that "if we're all back at school one must be a prefect." Two major qualities of public-school life seem to have stayed with him despite his effort, in *Enemies of Promise,* to exorcise and ridicule the whole idea. The first was a certain eagerness to truckle and toady to those above or ahead of him: possible patrons like Berenson, Pearsall-Smith, and Nicolson. The second was a marked tendency to shun and scorn, not outcasts (Connolly enjoyed slumming and the demimonde), but the lower orders. On and on he goes about "Jews" and "niggers," and his only qualm about enlisting as a special constable in the General Strike is that he may thereby "lose caste" with his more radical friends. Pryce-Jones's memoir, you may guess, will fit snugly against the more substantial bookend formed by the *Diaries* of Evelyn Waugh.

Reviewing *Enemies of Promise* in *Scrutiny*, Q. D. Leavis frowned upon its "cosy social homogeneity" and claimed to detect "the relation between knowing the right people and getting accepted in advance of production as a literary value." Pryce-Jones regards this as a smear and a caricature of how the "right people" emerge. How does he know? There is a rampart of evidence, much of it thrown up by Mr. Pryce-Jones, to show that Connolly was very careful indeed about the cultivation of contacts and outlets. Mrs. Leavis may have been unkind—Pryce-Jones oddly accuses her of being jealous—but it's rash to assert that she wasn't on to something.

This book takes the form of an unevenly cut sandwich. First is Pryce-Jones's exegesis of Connolly's life and early letters. Then comes a longish and slightly indigestible "journal," spanning the years 1928–37 in the career of "CC" and his pals. Finally, there is a thin slice of eulogy and apologia. The central section is, I find, a bit rebarbative. Peter Quennell and Maurice Bowra and Evelyn Waugh and Anthony Powell and much of Bloomsbury and good old "Sligger" Urquhart, every nickname footnoted and every nuance spelled out in pokerface—do we really need all this again? There's some quite cutting stuff about the *New Statesman*, which I shan't give away, and some fresh glimpses here and there, but it's really another dose of the familiar compound. By which I mean: a dash of the remittance man, some rackety traveling, a tincture of furtive sex (with much sniggering about lesbians), and the business of voyaging long distances the better to fret about some spoiled darling left behind in the Home Counties. Every emotion is either ecstatic or near-suicidal, with the result that both kinds are transitory or shallow. In *The Rock Pool*, one of the best novels of booze and anomie ever written, this mental atmosphere somehow works. Laid out in its original staccato jotting, it cloys very fast. The only really absorbing thing is Connolly's gradual pupation into a heterosexual. Having left school under a cloud—a cloud no bigger than a boy's hand—he comes to see the point of women, even if he does take a long and operatic time about it.

One comes back, or is returned, again and again to the business of "Permanent Adolescence." Pryce-Jones is perceptive about this loom of Connolly's youth, but occasionally very crass. In his reading of Orwell's account of prep-school purgatory ("Such, Such Were the Joys"), he makes two extraordinary and unfair judgments. One, that Orwell did not care about the fate of a rich Russian contemporary—or at least about the fate of that contemporary's father. Second, that Orwell used "albino" as a term of abuse. I challenge anybody to look up the essay and find for Pryce-Jones in this. And if he is dense about Connolly's most famous school friend, how is one to weigh his other opinions?

Amid the longueurs and the repeated sense of being, like Connolly himself, stranded in time, this book does supply the outlines of a portrait. A portrait of a mood rather than an age, and of a manner rather than a personality. It contains one of the most tragic lines I have recently read ("Once married, Cyril was never thin again") and one of the silliest ("Sexually," said Harold Nicolson, "I represent a buffer state"). Parody and teasing are not quite enough, however. They seem to confirm, for Pryce-Jones as well as Connolly, the adage or maxim or apothegm or epigram or even aphorism that those whom the gods wish to destroy they first describe as "promising."

(*New Statesman,* July 22, 1983)

I DARE SAY

❑

The existence of Mr. Reginald Maudling is a thing to marvel at, to ponder of a white night, and, if such is your way, to hoist high as an example. His *Memoir* is, appropriately enough, fat, boring, and dense. It is of interest only insofar as it shows the workings of an instinctively reactionary and commonplace mind. The prose is as primitive as the politics. Here, for instance, is his summary of the Dutschke deportation: "One of the hazards of a Home Secretary is that he is bound to bump into a certain amount of such cases, and the passions that arise are very considerable." No further revelation of that nasty little episode is permitted.

Maudling is, in like manner, evasive and unilluminating about his role in the internment crisis in Ulster. The entire account of his most important political catastrophe takes up three vapid paragraphs, compared with eight devoted to his prep- and public-school days. Your reviewer began to squirm in his chair when the scene moved to Oxford. "Life in Oxford in the mid-1930's was extremely agreeable. It was to some extent over-shadowed by the growing menace of Hitler." It is, I assure you, all as fresh and crisp as that. Sodden, Rotary Club style is the order of the day, and I think the book must have been dictated (probably to the long-suffering Beryl, judging by the number of random tributes to her many qualities). Take, for example, Maudling's reflections on the Real Estate Fund of America:

> One of the great advantages of my business appointments was that they made it possible for me to travel extensively. I think it is of very great value to this country and to the world generally, that both politicians and businessmen should be able to travel widely, and to meet one another. The problem, of course, is one of money.

Just so. As for his relationship with Jerome Hoffman, in case you are interested, he merely says that "for some time after I had resigned the Fund seemed to prosper . . . but then it collapsed along with other funds operating in the same field." He omits Hoffman's record of fraud and his spell in the slammer.

It's conventionally said of Maudling that, although lazy and incompetent, he's really quite cuddly and acceptable. I don't think this is true *at all*. He was once told by his headmaster that he was vain and selfish, and that shot was right on the mark. But he's also a natural authoritarian, sycophantic to the strong and contemptuous of the weak. (The victims of Bloody Sunday, for instance, don't even rate a line here.)

He says of William Armstrong, whom he met at Oxford, "Was there ever a man more clearly destined to become Head of the Treasury?" Was there ever a more fat-headed remark about the worst Head of the Treasury since the war? He says of Suez: "I certainly believe it was a morally correct action." He says of Vietnam that the Americans went "to leave their own blood and treasure there, in defense of what they thought to be right." After resigning over the Poulson affair, he remembers receiving from Henry Kissinger, who had problems of his own, a handwritten letter from the White House, of the most friendly kind. Terrific. The absence of any reflective or critical capacity is astounding—or would be, if we did not have his political record as a reminder.

Even where he makes some shift to be interesting, as he does on the Middle East, he contrives to leave a nasty taste. Despite his buffoonlike asides on Suez, Maudling is rather pro-Arab, and especially pro the fat and rich ones. He records some absorbing visits to the area and says that he is not popular with sensitive Jewish opinion. Then he spoils the whole thing by talking of a "final solution" for Israel—as unhappy and sloppy a phrase as he could have picked. As Thatcher looms, there are plenty of wiseacres to say that the Heath team was more statesmanlike, more in touch, more realistic, and more tolerant. Memory, hold the door. Here is a book that reminds us of what kind of people they were. No impulse for nostalgia need arise. We are well shot of Reggie.

(*New Statesman*, June 30, 1978)

THE MOUTH OF FOOT

❏

In the following passages, who is being assessed by whom?

> It is the superlative ease, the unruffled assurance with which that mind works, which first impresses those who meet him. One can hardly hear the mechanism working at all and yet the results have a perfect precision. Without any sense of strain or pretention, that marvellous instrument absorbs all the arguments presented to it and sifts from them an endless flow of conclusions framed in smooth, yet vibrant English.

Or, in a comparable vein:

> What [he] so valiantly stood for could have saved his country from the Hungry Thirties and the Second World War . . . genius.

The first paragraph is an appreciation of Lord Goodman. The second is a paean to Sir Oswald Mosley. The author in both cases is Michael Foot.

He exhibits here (as he does at much greater length in *Debts of Honour*) the three distinctive traits of his character as author and as politician. These are a deep reverence for the Establishment, especially for its more gamy ornaments; a fascination with certain reactionary rebels; and a prose style which relies on hyperbole for such effect as it can command.

There is a fourth ingredient, only hinted at in the above. It is a pervasive and amusing variety of chauvinist Anglophobia—very highly developed and of an intensity usually found only among Americans.

This ought to make for an enjoyable if not very enlightening read. But it doesn't. The treacly exaggerations start to cloy after a while; it's like eating a whole box of chocolate creams. Swift is "the foremost exponent of lucidity in the English language." Max Aitken "was as handsome as Apollo, as swiftly-moving as Mercury." Isaac Foot "must have been just about the happiest man who ever lived." Randolph Churchill "set the Thames, the Hudson, the Tiber or the Danube on fire with his boiling intoxicant invective." There is no subtlety, no light or shade. Everybody has got to be larger than life.

Foot was apprenticed to flattery at the court of Beaverbrook and learned his trade well. The longest essay in this collection of profiles and memoirs concerns the old monster himself. He would not be able to claim that Foot did not take him at his own valuation. Apparently Beaverbrook favored the "rumbustious, marauding private enterprise system which had enabled him to become a multi- or as he would call it, a Maxi-millionaire." And which enabled him to keep Foot (and to a more parsimonious extent, *Tribune*) in fair old style. Luckily, Beaverbrook was quite nice if you really knew him, as well as "a volcano of laughter which went on erupting till the end."

This rebarbative style is more of a trudge when it is used to praise a good man than when it is employed to whitewash a villain. Ignazio Silone was a very great writer and a very fine comrade. But he was not "the New Machiavelli" and didn't pretend to be. Bertrand Russell was and remains an inspiration in philosophy and politics. But who really regards him as a "Philosopher Englishman"? And how many takers for the following estimate?

> He became one of the chief glories of our nation and people, and I defy anyone who loves the English language and the English heritage to think of him without a glow of patriotism.

What the hell, one is moved to inquire, has *that* got to do with it? It might be truer to say that Russell would resent very much any attempt to annex him and his thought in such a way. A man who gave so much of himself to other countries, and who was so opposed to the crappy orthodoxies of British arrogance, cannot be captured in lines and thoughts like Foot's. Not that Foot's admiration for Russell is feigned. I should say that most of his essay on Tom Paine was inspired by a piece Russell wrote in 1934—except that Foot inserts a factual error about Jefferson that Russell did not make.

This tendency to hero worship results in some very bizarre formulations. Say what you like about Disraeli ("the Good Tory"), it is difficult to recognize anything "Byronic" in his career or in his novels. Yet that is the precise epithet Foot selects for him. There is a great deal yet to be learned about Robert Blatchford, but it will not be found out by calling him "just about the best writer of books about books there ever was." For one thing, such praise is meaningless. For another thing, it elides the obvious about Blatchford—his miserable declension from an affected socialism to an unaffected racialism and insularity. Perhaps Foot finds the reminiscence an uncomfortable one.

The obverse of Foot's credulity about people and institutions (who now remembers his slavishly adoring biography of Harold Wilson?) is an unattractive streak of sentiment. He manages to enlist a kind of sympathy when he writes about H. N. Brailsford or about Vicky. Even though the Brailsford essay is clotted with overwriting ("glorious," "imperishable," etcetera), one can see that Foot does not *need* to strain for effect on this occasion. The subject matter tells its own story.

But all the rest is rambling and bluff. Apparently Sarah Churchill, "given her magnificent head," could have salvaged England in the reign of Queen Anne. Apparently "the magnanimous English Left, led as usual by the Irish," came to the rescue of Jonathan Swift. These reworkings have at least the merit of improbability (especially in the latter case, coming as it does from the Orangemen's best friend—the man who dealt them a new hand to buy Callaghan an extra month).

I don't think that Foot can ever have blotted out a line. The collection is much harder to read than it must have been to write. Did he, for instance, really mean to say the following about his poor wife?

> The room of her own, the room where she works when she is not cooking, gardening, shopping, cleaning, making beds, entertaining and the rest, is a feminist temple, a shrine dedicated to the cause of women's rights.

If this is one of Foot's arch bits of self-mockery, I think we should be told. When a man can write about Beaverbrook that "I loved him, not merely as a friend but as a second father," one needs a stone of some sort to separate parody from the real thing.

The point about hero worship is not that you may be worshipping the wrong hero. It is that you surrender your reason and suspend your critical faculties. Foot's book on Aneurin Bevan, though written with much greater care than the present collection, is a disappointment because it makes its subject into a devotional figure and thus greatly exaggerates his real importance in our time. Issues like Churchill's conduct of the war, Tito's treatment of political opposition, or the Russian invasion of Hungary are shaped in a procrustean fashion to fit Bevan's own role. The book cannot be read (unlike, say, Isaac Deutscher's biography of Trotsky) as a guide to the period in which the central figure operated.

Still less do any of these portraits fulfill that necessary function. Once you start calling Beaverbrook a "buccaneer," it is only a short while before you find you have written this:

> The military vision of Churchill and his chief advisers was still fixed on other and lesser objectives and it was Beaverbrook who, within the Cabinet, seized and sustained the initiative to turn the national energies along the road of commonsense.

Eh? Does Foot read his articles through when he's finished?

Foot is never happier than when writing about World War II. It is a favorite theme in his contemporary speeches as well. He seems to remember a period of social harmony, democratic impulse, and social innovation. His famous polemic *Guilty Men* (which he penned under the nom de guerre of Cato) has an account of Dunkirk that could have come from the *Boy's Own Paper*. Such an attitude, which might have made agitational sense in wartime, has more than outlived its usefulness. I remember hearing Foot invoke the spirit of Dunkirk in the Commons on the night Labour lost the vote of confidence in 1979; it was ghastly to hear the titters of the Tories and to see the embarrassment on the Labour benches.

In 1940, also, it might have been permissible for a socialist to write as if Britain did not have an empire (though Orwell, for one, kept insisting that the subject be remembered). Foot contrives to daub his portrait of Beaverbrook as if the man had never been an imperialist at all. He does have the grace to recall "Max" at the time of Munich, but only to mention it as an aberration. For the rest, this beautiful friendship, and its seminal role in Our Island Story, is preserved and mummified forever in scented prose. It seems almost unkind to disturb it now.

Foot is a charming old ham in one way, and one should not be surprised at his liking for fellow hams. He has given plenty of harmless pleasure to hopeful audiences in his time. Some say that his present attachment to the most flagrant conservatism is the result of a "mellowing" process. Others talk darkly of a "sellout." But, as far as can be discerned, Foot is quite right to claim consistency in his own record.

He has never been otherwise than a poseur, moving smoothly, for instance, from the Campaign for Nuclear Disarmament into Callaghan's Inner Cabinet on the Cruise missiles and back into irrelevant pacifist attitudes. Like Disraeli, he is a quick-change artist. The objection comes when he dresses up this act as socialism and thus disfigures a good idea. (Just as he here proposes Disraeli as a radical—because he once gave a civil audience to that old fraud and chauvinist H. M. Hyndman.)

In his brief essay on Vicky's enduring cartoons, Foot asks the reader, "And, if he had lived, which of us would have escaped the lash?" Good question. I believe that there does exist a link between Foot's gullibility as a person, his credulity as a profile writer, and his disqualifications as a politician. The same weakness of character that makes him fawn in print makes him a conformist in politics. The same glutinous style (he even writes of the acid Defoe that "the truth he had bottled up within himself for so long poured out in golden spate") has its analogue in the gross sentimentality which marks his public speaking.

A good test is this: listen to a Foot speech, whether made on a party conference platform or in the House of Commons. Mark the dewy response it sometimes gets. Then grab a copy of Hansard or the conference report and *read* the thing. Full of evasions, crammed with corny special pleading, usually rounded off with an appeal for unity, and generally couched, behind its rhetorical mask, in terms of strict political orthodoxy. A classic case is his defense of Mrs. Gandhi's merciless Emergency, where a crude and reactionary political maneuver was defended by Foot as an inheritance from the splendid days of Congress, and a necessary insurance against "destabilisation."

Another relationship exists in the matter of detail. Whether he is writing about Tom Paine or justifying the last Labour government's breaking of the firemen's strike, Foot likes to deal in sweeping generalities. He once echoed Lamb's toast to Hazlitt, "Confusion to Mathematics," by proposing the toast "Confusion to Economics." How predictable, then, that he would become the stout defender of the most dismally conventional economic policy when he got anywhere near power. And how regrettable, when discussing Tom Paine, that he should say, with habitual absolutism, that Jefferson "never wavered" in his high opinion of Paine. It is important, in any evaluation of Paine's American years, to recall the coldness that did interrupt his relationship with Jefferson.

These details matter. In Britain, it is pretty easy to get a reputation as a radical. The standard of our politicians is such that, when they prove literate at all, they are hailed as Romantics, Renaissance men, Revivalists. The timing of this book could not have been more fortunate; we shall be able to examine both vainglorious claims at once.

The best interim obituary may be that written about Foot's hero Disraeli by Lady Gwendolen Cecil:

> He was always making use of convictions that he did not share, pursuing objects which he could not own, manoeuvring his party into alliances which though unobjectionable from his own standpoint were discreditable and indefensible from theirs. It was an atmosphere of pervading falseness which involved his party as well as himself.

(*New Statesman*, November 14, 1980)

BORN-AGAIN CONFORMIST

❑

I

Anglo-American commentary on "culture and society" has sometimes been infiltrated by writers who believe they are Orwell but who think like Babbitt. Norman Podhoretz, for example, is to Manhattan what Bernard Levin has become to London's commuter belt—a born-again conformist with some interesting disorders of the ego. If this seems an excessive way to begin a consideration of a "serious" writer, then recall what Alfred Kazin wrote in his essay on the brave days of Podhoretz's own magazine *Commentary:*

> There is real madness to modern governments, modern war, modern moneymaking, advertising, science and entertainment; this madness has been translated by many a Jewish writer into the country they live in, the time that offers them everything but hope. In a time of intoxicating prosperity, it has been natural for the Jewish writer to see how superficial society can be, how pretentious, atrocious, unstable—and comic.

There is the measure of Podhoretz's betrayal. Kazin was writing in 1966. One year later, Podhoretz published *Making It,* a drooling libation to the bitch-goddess success, in which he made his peace with intoxicating prosperity and abandoned the crisp, even lucid style of his earliest critical writings. *Making It* was an awful book all right, but it did have certain attractive qualities of the chutzpah sort—a kind of eagerness and a wideness of the eyes.

In *Breaking Ranks,* the eyes have narrowed appreciably. Podhoretz here makes his peace with modern government, modern war, and modern moneymaking. Robert Lekachman has described the jacket photograph as "the spitting image of a central banker age 70 who has just plunged his country into a depression for its own good." I think it more closely resembles a man about to unload some underwater real estate. Podhoretz sets down, in the wretchedly affected form of an open letter to his son, the experience of personal assimilation and adjustment, the business of growing up out of "radicalism." Like many letters nowadays, this one gives the impression of having been typed rather than written. It is a torment to read, but it does offer some clues to the mind-set of the neoconservative—more especially the insecure, name-dropping, self-obsessed, and slipshod variety.

The first and most obvious thing to say about Podhoretz is that he is an ex-radical in the same way that Richard Nixon is an ex-President. He never had any real claim on the noble title. His boldest ever essay was "My Negro Problem," written in 1963, when he advocated planned miscegenation in a style offensively glib. This qualification does not restrain him from a tremendous exhibition of self-regard as the man who single-handedly defied the "Left Establishment."

While it is true that New York publishing has had a febrile tendency to the radical chic (and a parallel tendency to overreact to the egregious Podhoretz, thus confirming him in his conviction of martyrdom), you would not find our Norman querying the local narcissism for an instant. It is indeed, for him, the very breath of life. It's no exaggeration to say that his review of the reviews of *Making It* gets more space than Vietnam, desegregation, nuclear weaponry, environmentalism, and Watergate all put together. But this is not the chief failure of proportion and perspective. If Manhattan is the navel of the world, and if it groans under a *marxisant* dictatorship, then what does that make Norman? Why, Pasternak and Solzhenitsyn combined— what else?

Should this sound like an overstatement, try the following as an example. Podhoretz has already made the straight-faced claims that "*Making It* did more than fly in the face of the radical party line" and that it made him "a traitor to [his] class." Then Norman Mailer dumped on the book too. Listen:

> The fact that Norman Mailer—a founding father and patron saint of the "Left Establishment" and, though not perhaps quite so brave as he thought he was, much less cowardly in this respect than most—should have felt himself forced into a maneuver like this was all the proof anyone could have needed that the "terror" had become pervasive and efficient enough to make strong men quake and to leave no one feeling safe.

Sic. This preposterous extract gives a representative flavor of Podhoretz's clichéd and dismal style, as well as of his insulting manner. To compare his salon bust-up with the reality of Stalinist terror—leave alone the reality of McCarthyite persecution about which *Commentary* was always so equivocal—makes the paranoia of F. R. Leavis (Podhoretz's old supervisor) seem like mildness itself.

But if only that were all. Just as *Making It* dropped the name of Leavis whenever possible, so *Breaking Ranks* is larded with references to Lionel Trilling. Trilling was an authentic defender of the "reasonable" and the "moderate," in a fashion Podhoretz tries in vain to emulate. He is prayed in aid, often in ways he might not have admitted, throughout these pages. Only once is he abused—for advising Podhoretz not to publish *Making It* in the first place. Suddenly, sycophancy is replaced by its twin brother of spite:

> I did not understand until much later, and then only in the light of how Trilling would conduct himself in the coming years, how telling a sign it was of his own failure of nerve.

Everything, then, is defined in relation to Podhoretz. He has all the third-rater's loathing for those people better equipped to face high tasks and principles. Gnawed (if we are to be charitable) by this sense of his own paucity, he's driven to a series of ungenerous and inaccurate sketches. On Noam Chomsky:

Far from reciprocating the support he had received from the American government, Chomsky was later to issue a bitter denunciation of his fellow-intellectuals for being pro-American, though unlike him, many he denounced had never received any government grants.

On Irving Howe:

Yet in view of the fact that the socialism to which he was committed had no discernible content, I began to think that his stubborn loyalty to the word, as well as the idea, came out of the same primitive loyalty that made so many Jews go on calling themselves Jews.

On A. J. Muste:

Whatever else Muste exuded, he looked and talked even less like a winner than [Norman] Thomas.

On Jason Epstein:

Jason felt trapped by the life. I felt trapped by the ideas. Together we made a team.

In the sense that he is incapable of representing an opposing viewpoint, Podhoretz does not really qualify as an intellectual at all. The patronizing and low-rent level of those (typical) quotations is depressed still further by Norman's other dirty little habit. He throws off names (Delmore Schwartz, Hannah Arendt, Philip Rahv) as if to suggest—never quite claiming—that they somehow associated themselves with the author.

As a result, everything Podhoretz does or says is on the record. One imagines him tooling off to keep a luncheon appointment with a publisher and mentally intoning, "It was on March 12, 1976, that Podhoretz went to have lunch at Harper & Row . . ." But he gets nervous at the absence of witnesses, and makes them up, too.

So it seems that *Making It* was not a catharsis. Nor did its title intend any saving irony. Podhoretz really *is* like that: the child was father to the man. His latest autobiography of an autobiography has the piss and vinegar of the original—only it's gone sour. Even the self-deprecation is now conceited. This finds its corollary, as do his cheap portraits of American radicals, in a certain power-worshipping trait.

For not everyone is insulted here. Lyndon Johnson is held up as a model President, combining agrarian shrewdness with a capacity as "one of the great senators of modern times." Daniel Moynihan, of course, can do no wrong (Podhoretz even tells one of his jokes *twice* in his excitement—a joke, moreover, which he would surely denounce as snobbish radicalism if told by anyone else). He weaves in some slightly ambiguous toadying to the Kennedy family. Leslie Fiedler is described in a rather otiose way as "the wildly brilliant literary critic." There's also some posturing around the idea that Podhoretz "knows" England and can synthesize its finest into the pages of his magazine:

> There were, for example, R. H. S. Crossman, C. A. R. Crosland and Denis Healey—all future cabinet ministers and all talented intellectuals by any definition of that term (they were all, by the way, past or future contributors to *Commentary* as well).

Talented and intellectual. Better still:

> Machines and factories—those "dark Satanic mills" which as William Blake had said as far back as the late eighteenth century were ruining "England's green and pleasant land."

Oh, *that* Blake.

After all this, it's just a weary duty to record that Podhoretz thinks Vietnam was no more than "a mistake" (and never confronts the case of those he slanders for taking the harder view). Or that he only mentions Kissinger once, to accuse him of being too tender-minded in dealing with the OPEC nations. Or that he feels that "the underlying belief of American radicalism in the 1960s was that all the sufferings of the human heart were caused and could therefore be cured by laws and kings." Like all reactionaries who think that they are against the stream, and who appear to believe in his case that American power is controlled by *The New York Review of Books*, Podhoretz winds up mouthing mainstream commonplaces under the illusion that he is saying the unsayable.

One need not be a "liberal" to object to his desecration of that ambivalent but honorable term. He doesn't even seem to know what he's talking about. On page 117, he speaks slightingly of "the liberal idea that any and all technological advances were to be welcomed." Later he records and overstates Trilling's view that the whole literary tradition (and ipso facto a goodish bit of what Podhoretz defines as liberalism) stands in opposition to industrialism and the industrial revolution. It doesn't matter so much that both statements are misleading as it does that they do not cohere. Podhoretz, once again, is chewing more than he bites off.

His "book" concludes with a hail of badly aimed shafts at the sexual-minority movements. This is no more than a grace note to the crashing chords of nonsense and venom that have gone before. Podhoretz, the man who says, "in 1970, shortly after my growing doubts about radicalism had coalesced and come to a head in a conviction so blazing that it ignited an all-out offensive against the Movement"—this same Podhoretz ends up whining about contraception and homosexuality. *Commentary* was once flatteringly termed an organ of the "military-intellectual complex." To criticize its editor in his own terms would be to echo Kazin's phrasing—superficial, pretentious, atrocious, unstable, and (unconsciously) comic.

(New Statesman, March 21, 1980)

II

On January 13, 1898, Georges Clemenceau's Paris newspaper, *L'Aurore*, published an article over the name of Emile Zola. In it, Zola denounced the military, political, judicial, and clerical hierarchies of France. He excoriated the cynicism and the brutishness of those who had condemned Captain Alfred Dreyfus, and he made it plain that their actions were infected with, and motivated by, anti-Jewish bigotry. The article compelled the retrial of Dreyfus and led to his eventual acquittal and reinstatement. It also changed France more than any polemic had done since Voltaire or Marx. In 1945, when Charles Maurras, the spiritual leader of French fascism, was convicted of collaborating with the Nazis, he denounced the verdict as "the revenge of Dreyfus."

Looked at in one way, the Dreyfus case was historic and encouraging because it was the first occasion on which a European country divided itself passionately on the question of justice for a Jew. Dreyfus was victimized, but also vindicated. The legions of the Catholic Church and the other anti-Semitic rabble were beaten. Theodor Herzl, who witnessed the Christian mobs calling for the death of Jews, drew the equal and opposite conclusion. He was sufficiently affected to conclude that Jews would never be safe in Europe, and from his reaction to the Dreyfus case we can date the birth of modern Zionism.

Zola's germinal article was entitled *"J'Accuse."* In an article in the September 1982 issue of *Commentary* (written before the Beirut massacres), Norman Podhoretz felt morally and personally secure enough to appropriate the title for his own purpose. He argued, or at any rate asserted, that the outraged response to the Israeli invasion of Lebanon could be compared to the anti-Dreyfus frenzy. In short, he accused the critics of Sharon and Begin of being anti-Semitic.

That is an old argument, and anybody who has ever written critically about Israel can testify to its force. Anti-Semites are usually but not invariably anti-Zionist. Some critics of Israel are anti-Semitic. Some Jews regard Zionism as a blasphemous assault on the teachings of their religion. Some Zionists were pro-fascist (like Begin's mentor, Jabotinsky). Some Nazis were even sympathetic to Zionism. The author of the Balfour Declaration, Arthur Balfour, disliked very much the prospect of Jewish immigration to Britain and spoke hotly of the "dual loyalty" problems it would create. The leading opponent of the Balfour Declaration in the Cabinet, Edwin Montague, was also its only Jew. He described Zionism as "anti-Semitic in result."

Taken singly, these examples may be mere ironies. Taken together, they show that there is no necessary—no logical—identity between anti-Israeli (or anti-Begin) views and anti-Jewish ones. Anti-Semites are people who dislike Jews *because they are Jews*. Moreover, they dislike them for reasons not merely of complexion or physique or supposed inferiority, but for reasons having to do with religion, history, secrecy, mysticism, blood, soil, and gold. Given the "right" circumstances, such a prejudice can and does become murderous and unappeasable. To be accused of harboring it, therefore, is no joke.

Curiously, Podhoretz does not actually accuse anyone of harboring it. He plants a few innuendoes against individuals, but he isn't enough of a Zola to deal in plain words or to offer any evidence. Apparently, the new wave of anti-Semitism in America has no active anti-Semites in it. This certainly distinguishes it from its historical predecessors and must come as something of a relief to anybody who has studied or experienced previous periods of pogrom or intolerance. (In Poland in 1968, there was an anti-Jewish purge mounted under an anti-Zionist guise. Nobody was in any doubt as to the identity of those responsible, and their leader, General Mieczyslaw Moczar, is notorious to this day.)

The nearest Podhoretz comes to a definition is this:

> For example, whereas the possibility of a future threat to its borders was (rightly in my opinion) deemed a sufficient justification by the United States under John F. Kennedy to go to the brink of war in the Cuban missile crisis of 1962, the immense caches of arms discovered in PLO dumps in Southern Lebanon have not persuaded many of the very people who participated in or applauded Kennedy's decision that the Israelis were at least equally justified in taking action against the PLO in Lebanon.
>
> Criticism of Israel based on a double standard deserves to be called anti-Semitic.

This argument has a long way to go before it is even half-baked. But it is revealing stuff, all the same. Apparently, if you supported Kennedy over Cuba and you don't support Begin and Sharon over Lebanon, you are a Jew-baiter. Well. What if (like many Jews) you opposed Kennedy and support Sharon? What if (like any sane person) you opposed Kennedy's readiness to destroy the human race in his undeclared war on Castro and now oppose Sharon?

Podhoretz does admit what has become obvious: that "loose or promis-

cuous use of the term anti-Semitism can only rob it of force and meaning."
As if sensing the swamp of gibberish that is opening at his feet, he adds
generously: "Conversely, criticisms of Israel based on universally applied
principles and tempered by a sense of balance in the distribution of blame
cannot and should not be stigmatized as anti-Semitic, however mistaken or
dangerous to Israel one might consider them to be."

Responses to the mass killings at the Shatila and Sabra camps are, it might
be thought, as nearly in conformity with those criteria as it is possible to
be. The Israeli army occupied West Beirut, in defiance of an earlier agreement, on the pretext of securing law and order. It admits that it permitted
the Phalangist troops to enter the camps. It cannot claim, having armed and
trained the Phalange for years, not to know of its views on Palestinians.

Then came the flares, the bulldozers, and the rest. Here, surely, is a case
that *by any standards* would expose the army responsible to criticism. Armed
with Podhoretz's own criteria, I wondered what he would say about it.

On September 24, he surfaced in *The Washington Post* to assert that those
making a fuss about Shatila were anti-Semitic. This must mark a new low.
Apart from abandoning his own rather lax standard of what is permissible
in the criticism of Israel, Podhoretz is defaming, as bigots or self-haters,
many of the most eminent Jews in Israel and the United States. We don't
yet have a term for this prejudice.

There are two remaining ironies in Podhoretz's article. In seeking to excuse
and minimize the massacre, he resurrects the old argument about the Palestinians being the authors of their own destruction. By having armed men
in their midst, so runs this view, they invite death from the skies or murder
by night. (There don't seem to have been any guerrillas to defend Shatila
or Sabra, but that is beside the point.) I hope, very sincerely, that Podhoretz's
logic (which is also official Israeli logic) is never used against the Jewish
settlers in the West Bank. These people, who are opposed by the Arab
inhabitants not because they are Jews but because they are settlers, have
made their homes and enclaves into armed camps with the help of the ever-
considerate Sharon. Should the world shrug if someday civilians are massacred there?

Podhoretz wrote very warmly in his *Commentary* article of Menachem
Milson, then head of the occupation authority in the West Bank. He spoke
of Milson's distinction between the PLO and the Palestinians. He said,
sardonically, that "the PLO and its apologists have naturally done everything
in their power to sabotage and discredit Milson." But it took more than that
to get him out of office. It took Sharon. Milson, a hard-liner and a writer
for *Commentary*, resigned his post over the Shatila/Sabra affair. Podhoretz,
writing after that extraordinary piece of news, talks as if Milson, too, were
a victim of anti-Semitic paranoia. No theoretical reductio ad absurdum could
be more crushing. Even William Buckley, leader and teacher of the Amer-

ican Phalange, was forced to tell Podhoretz in two public epistles that his cry of anti-Semitism was not intellectually reputable.

On one point, though, Podhoretz is right. It is indecent and illiterate to compare Israel to Nazi Germany. But not all those who do this can possibly be ill-intentioned. Rabbi Arnold Wolf, former Jewish chaplain at Yale, said of Shatila, "It's Babi Yar all over again and this time we're not innocent." The rabbi was obviously reaching for a standard of cruelty and horror that matched the crime. But he's still wrong: Babi Yar was part of a process of literal genocide. "Genocide," along with "Final Solution" and "Holocaust," is a term not to be lightly used for propaganda. By the same token, it is wrong for the Israeli government to speak of the Palestinians as neo-Nazis and for Israeli apologists to invoke the Holocaust against every criticism. If the moral chaos exists, it is partly because of Israeli special pleading. Podhoretz should also object to that, but he doesn't.

No honest person would be the loser if the morally blackmailing argument of "anti-Semitism" were dropped from the discourse. Any fool can tell a real anti-Semite a mile off. Any fool can see that the Phalangists are in the same tradition as the persecutors of Dreyfus. Any fool can see that Begin uses the memory of the Holocaust to muffle his own guilt. But it takes a real fool to confuse the editor of *Commentary* with Emile Zola. Who the hell does Podhoretz think he is?

(*The Nation*, October 9, 1982)

THE TROUBLE
WITH HENRY

❑

I

When I had finished digesting *The White House Years*, I was so replete with its mendacity and conceit that I took a vow. I swore that I would never read another work by Henry Kissinger until the publication of his prison letters. But the old prayer "O Lord, Let Mine Enemy Write a Book" has proved too strong not to be answered once again.

How does one review a book like *Years of Upheaval* for a magazine like *The Nation*? After all, our readers have been battered by a revelation or two in their time. It would be insulting to "reveal" to them that Kissinger lies about his part in the Nixon bugging scandal and otiose to inform them that he still cannot face the truth about the bombing of Cambodia and the subversion of Chile. I suppose one might resort, in the light of Seymour Hersh's excellent forensic material, to some discussion of Kissinger's complicity with Nixon's anti-Semitism. If I interviewed the king of Saudi Arabia, and he droned on about "Jewish traitors," and I replied, "Well, your majesty, there are Jews and Jews," would I get respectful reviews from people named Max Frankel and Stanley Hoffmann?

So let's get the obvious out of the way, and the power-worshipping reviewers along with it. This entire book is predicated on an enormous and conscious falsehood. Kissinger (or HAK, as he calls himself in photograph captions) would have us believe that he was constructing an intelligent and imaginative foreign policy, which was haltered and finally crippled by an extraneous force. It's as if HAK were plowing a harmless furrow and was hit by lightning out of a clear sky. Hersh's material shows that Kissinger was implicated not only in the actual violations that became known as Watergate but in the power plays overseas that made the illegal invigilations "necessary." Q.E.D. Kissinger lies. What does this prove except that we have credulous book critics?

So we need not waste time exploding HAK's apologia. It is, like the policy on which it was based, autodestructive. The volume repays study all the same. It contains, for instance, the following *aperçu:*

> Hanoi and Washington had inflicted grievous wounds on each other; theirs were physical, ours psychological and thus perhaps harder to heal.

And this:

> Our immediate task was to stop the war; to remove nuclear weapons from *Greece* while Turkey invaded Cyprus would eliminate all restraints on Turkish military action. I also feared that if we once withdrew nuclear weapons we might never be able to return them—setting a dangerous precedent.

And this:

> No nuclear weapon has ever been used in modern wartime conditions.

What have we here? What we have is an appalling moral deafness. And a species of doublethink whereby the "wounds" of Washington and Hanoi can be equated, whereby the country that *ceases* to harbor nuclear weapons becomes "dangerous," and whereby the obliteration of Hiroshima and Nagasaki can be simply forgotten. Many people on the left become embarrassed by talk of morality; they prefer to insist that it is policies and institutions, not individuals and personalities, that really "count." Now, it is probably true that the policies Kissinger followed and the leaders he served demanded a robotic and ruthless operative. But, on the evidence of this horrible book, the specific character of HAK did make a life-and-death difference to thousands of people.

The thing is so badly written that the eye often slides over the atrocities (how on earth could Stanley Hoffmann praise the style?). Take this small but useful example. During the October 1973 war in the Middle East, the Portuguese government was reluctant to let its airfields be used for the resupply of Israel:

> I had therefore drafted a Presidential letter of unusual abruptness to Portuguese Prime Minister Marcelo Caetano that refused military equipment and threatened to leave Portugal to its fate in a hostile world. By the middle of Saturday afternoon, the Portuguese gave us unconditional transit rights at Lajes airbase.

There you have it—the relish in bullying and the implication, always present in the book, that you have to play hardball in this world if you want results. But there is no mention of the client status of the Portuguese dictatorship elsewhere, no mention of the colonial wars it was fighting with HAK's support, and no mention *at all* of the Portuguese revolution that took place the following year. So, when he comes to describe his tussle with Congress over intervention in Angola, HAK has abolished all the complexity of recent history by simple elision.

There is only one occasion when HAK admits the prime importance of local factors and allows that the internal life of a nation is more than the sum of its links to the United States. That is when he seeks to wriggle off the hook about Chile. He would prefer us to think of the coup as something spontaneously generated by endogenous conditions. (He also asks us to believe that Allende committed suicide.) As usual, he achieves his effect by a combination of omission—there's nothing on the famous "make the economy scream" meeting—and special pleading. He also stretches the definition of euphemism by admitting that, after Pinochet took power, "rumors of torture were widespread." Just read the sentence twice—you will have done more than the editors of this book or most of its reviewers have done.

You can, of course, agree with *The New Republic*, whose reviewer was Walter Laqueur. As he puts it in his worldly way, "It's an all too well-established fact that prolonged government service . . . usually has a debilitating effect on a person's ability to write." Passing over the matter of Laqueur's own fluency, and forgetting the stylistic contributions of, say, Churchill, Talleyrand, Trotsky, and de Gaulle, and bearing in mind that Laqueur makes this point in order to praise Kissinger's writing ability, I beg to differ. It is not politics and good writing that do not mix. It is the great mass of lies and crimes, moldering undigested at HAK's core, that makes his style so evasive and convoluted. Hardest to take are the moments of cracker-barrel philosophy that punctuate the narrative: "It is easy to go with the tide; more difficult to judge where the tide is going." Lots of that kind of thing.

Very occasionally, there is a moment of genuine revelation and interest. Usually, these occur when HAK is trying to justify himself. The following, for instance, is a useful account of the real logic of the Nixon foreign policy:

> Détente helped rather than hurt the American defense effort. Before the word détente was even known in America the Congress cut $40 billion from the defense budgets of Nixon's first term; even so dedicated a supporter of American strength as Senator Henry M. Jackson publicly advocated small defense cuts and a "prudent defense posture." After the signing of SALT I, our defense budget increased and the Nixon and Ford administrations put through the strategic weapons (the MX missile, B-1 bomber, cruise missiles, Trident submarines, and more advanced warheads) that even a decade later are the backbone . . .

Etcetera, etcetera. I imagine that paragraph, at least, will be read with consuming interest in Moscow.

This book is a dishonest account of a period in which America's internal politics were debauched (it was the legal system, not the "liberals," that did in Nixon) and its foreign policy became synonymous with dictatorship and aggression. Reading it *really* made me feel sick. There's a lot of talk these days, much of it flatulent, about various "hangovers" of the 1960s. There are a lot of things about the 1960s that I don't miss. But, to judge by the reception accorded this volume, one thing we seem to have lost is the ability to be shocked—morally shocked—by politicians. There has been a dulling of the nerve of outrage. This encourages Kissinger, in the supreme arrogance with which he closes his book, actually to pose the question of whether he was too good for us. Get hold of *Years of Upheaval*. It deserves, as we say in the trade, the widest possible audience. In its pages, and in the parallel text which Seymour Hersh is supplying, you can see the character of the real totalitarians. The men who frame and blackmail their domestic opponents and murder their foreign ones. The men who believe that nuclear warfare is justified and guerrilla warfare is not.

(*The Nation*, June 5, 1982)

II

A favorite anodyne, and a plausible last resort for dubious characters in tight corners, is the one that runs, "Well, I think we should concentrate on issues rather than personalities." Usually, this defense is employed by people who have spent entire careers projecting their own, or somebody else's, "personality" and who are faced with the uneasy realization that the poor candidate has become threadbare or been caught out. Skeptics and freethinkers, sickened by overemphasis on image and public relations, often fall for this baited line. But a moment's thought will show that personalities *do* matter, in politics no less than in any other field. The German elections of 1933 were the last occasion on which all Germans were allowed a free vote. It would be hard to maintain that the voting was not—well—a trifle personalized. The victorious candidate was, to be sure, the instrument of greater forces than the mere individual. Nonetheless . . .

All this ought to be obvious, but I've made the point in its grossest form in order to draw attention to a surprising fact. For several years, the foreign policy of the United States was, by any definition, the unique and individual province of Henry Kissinger. Probably never before, and certainly never since, has a secretary of state been so untrammeled in the exercise of office and power.

In *The Price of Power*, Seymour Hersh has written a book which says in effect that the secretary was a moral and political catastrophe, interested principally in pleasing one of the most sordid Presidents on record. Yet the critic who complains that Hersh's book is a personal vendetta will be the very same critic who says that Kissinger "brought peace" in Vietnam or "made the opening" to China. Those who claim belief in exceptional statesmen should accept that such statesmen are responsible for the logical and probable, not to say the intentional, consequences of their actions. But with Henry the K and his defenders, one encounters the same species of fawning credulity as is apparent in a certain school of Churchill chroniclers. When he was great, he was a titan. When he was a fool or a knave, it was due to uncontrollable or unforeseeable tides. We have Thomas Carlyle to thank for some of this, but I suspect that good old power worship and sycophancy still play their substantial part.

A classic example here is supplied by Norman Podhoretz, editor of the unmissable *Commentary*. Podhoretz spent some years decrying our hero as a man who was naïve about the Russians, gullible about the Third World, and slippery when it came to Israel. Yet in June 1982, in his landmark essay "Kissinger Reconsidered," he approached as nearly as he ever will to humility. "One of the great works of our time," he said (twice) about *Years of Upheaval*, Kissinger's second volume of memoirs. "High intellectual distinction," "writing of the highest order"; one could go on—and Norman did. No diplomacy ever ventured by the shuttling Doctor was half so skillful as his diplomacy with the press and with a certain coterie of scribes in particular.

Hersh has written his book in conscious opposition to the hagiographic version, and is unapologetic about having done so. When I watched him on

"Nightline" in June 1983, being faced with a squad of inquisitors, some of whom I knew to have been at Kissinger's sixtieth birthday party a few days before, I could scarcely fault him for his abrasive derision. There are many well-placed people who regard Kissinger as somehow occupying a position *above politics* and who view an attack upon him as profane or even unpatriotic. Even if he were as great a man as they think he is, or as he thinks he is, this would be an unwholesome state of affairs.

What does Hersh allege? He says that Kissinger was personally involved in riveting dictatorship onto Greece and Chile. He says that Kissinger was not just complicit in the bugging and lawlessness of Watergate, but actually an instigator of it. He says that Kissinger indulged Nixon's foul-mouthed anti-Semitism and drunken crisis management while sniggering about the latter to more "polished" friends. He says that Kissinger winked at the Pakistani near-genocide in Bangladesh in order to win favor with Peking—and thereby drove the Indian government to seek an alliance with Moscow. He says that Kissinger prolonged the war in Indochina, at some cost, to a point where only he and his master could settle it and take the credit. He says (the slightest of his charges but the one that has received the most media attention) that Kissinger sold himself to two masters in the 1968 election and was prepared to take the lower bidder as long as it was the victorious candidate.

The above allegations have this to be said for them: they are all true. They will survive, and in most cases have survived, any amount of checking and corroboration. So will some others that I can think of but that Hersh has no room for, such as Kissinger's direct collusion in the dismemberment of Cyprus in 1974. Even his admirers at *Commentary* allow that he was conned, during the SALT talks, into thinking that the Soviets were more anxious for a deal than they really were. Which error led him to the madness of the MIRV, and thus to a superpower pact that was cynical without being effective—the worst of both worlds. No doubt Kissinger thought, as many such men before him have thought, that ruthless men would understand one another. That is a near-infallible sign of a naïve person.

Kissinger's defenders, I notice, tend to scorn vulgar detail. The history books, they are fond of saying, will vindicate him as the man who brought disengagement from Vietnam, contact with China, and understanding with the Soviet Union. Their argument, with its suggestive reliance on the all-forgiving "long view," is not as null as it can be made to look. Kissinger was associated continually with policies that resemble that triad. "Well, Mr. President," he told Nixon on October 12, 1972, "it looks like we've got three out of three"—signifying China, SALT, and peace in Vietnam.

Yet the two men had only the simulacra of these achievements. And if one had called for any of them in 1968—the year in which, to coin a phrase,

Henry "took off"—one would have had no deadlier antagonist than Kissinger himself. His magic, and, to an extent, that of Richard Nixon, is to be able to say that certain things are wrong unless *they* do them, and to make sure that such things are undoable by anyone else. The Hersh passages on the Vietnam peace talks in 1968 are an excellent case in point, if rather horrid to reflect upon. He shows that Kissinger urged Thieu of South Vietnam to hang tight for a better deal from the Republicans—thus consummating a power play of Henry's own and making him indispensable to the incoming Administration. And Hersh shows how Kissinger in office was ready to dump Thieu, and even ready to contemplate killing him, when he continued to stand awkwardly in the way of the White House plan to evacuate Vietnam on cosmetic terms. The intervening months and years cost—well, you know what they cost.

Norman Podhoretz says that Kissinger has "a judicious respect for even the least powerful of nations and the sensitivity of an anthropologist to the distinctive features and beauties of even the least imposing of cultures." He also says that Kissinger's "easy willingness to tell stories at his own expense is the surest mark of a supreme self-confidence." Now, on the first point we know that Kissinger described Bangladesh as an "international basket case" a few months after it achieved an appallingly hard-won independence that he had tried to abort. We know that he told the ambassador of Cyprus to Washington that his president, Archbishop Makarios, was "too big a man for so small an island"—and this just before a fascist coup against Makarios of which Kissinger had direct foreknowledge. We know that he said of Chile that its people were too irresponsible to be allowed to choose their own president, and we know (with even more detail supplied by Hersh) what he did to Chile when it flouted his wishes. We know that he endorsed Nixon's plan to bomb the Palestinians in their Jordanian havens in September 1970, a decision that, as Hersh shows, was only averted by the timely disobedience of Melvin Laird. These fastidious attitudes toward "the least imposing of cultures" would be enough for most men.

As for his "easy willingness to tell stories at his own expense," I may convict myself of lacking humor when I say that I can't see it. I have read, in his memoirs, the frequent references to a faux pas on his own part—usually at some baroque occasion in Saudi Arabia or Eastern Europe. But such stories are designed to suggest a pleasing lack of formality on the part of the teller. Self-critical, Kissinger is not. Whenever anything goes wrong, and plenty of things did toward the end of his term, he blames it on the "tragedy" of Watergate, which left the United States fatally disabled in leadership. This, coming from Kissinger, is an unusually feeble excuse. He was not tripped up, in his selfless international jet-setting, by the hubris and nemesis of Richard Nixon. He was caught in the same web of intrigue and deceit that he and his chosen boss had helped to spin. For him to claim Watergate as something exogenous, a deus ex machina that spoiled his diplomacy, is in other words a vulgar three-card trick. A man who compares himself freely to Archimedes, looking for a spot from which to move the world, should not always say, when things go awry, that it is somebody else's fault.

Hersh, though, does tell a story at Kissinger's expense, but I doubt that the Doctor will find it all that amusing. In September 1970, at about the time when he was urging that the Sixth Fleet be used to plaster the Palestinians (and just imagine how much nearer that would have brought a peace agreement), Kissinger charged into the office of H. R. Haldeman. He bore with him a folder of the now-traditional aerial-reconnaissance photographs which depicted various structures on the island of Cuba. "It's a Cuban seaport, Haldeman, and these pictures show the Cubans are building soccer fields. . . . These soccer fields could mean war, Bob." Haldeman inquired for more details of the Doctor's signs and portents. "Cubans play *baseball*. Russians play *soccer*." From this meeting, Kissinger cranked up the United States to a condition approaching full alert, until even Nixon realized that it was a false alarm. Unrepentant in his memoirs, Kissinger himself says that "in my eyes this stamped it indelibly as a Russian base, since as an old soccer fan I knew Cubans played no soccer." They do, of course, very enthusiastically. The World Cup is a big event in Cuba, and any visitor can testify to the popularity of the game. I'm retelling the story at such length because it illustrates several things about Kissinger that often escape comment. First, his singular faith in his own judgment, and his peremptory way with subordinates. Second, his love of crisis and drama—one might almost say his need for these things. Third, his ingratiating pseudodemotic style ("as an old soccer fan," forsooth). Finally, his ignorance. Cuba, it seems, joins that roster of less imposing cultures, a nearby country of which he knows nothing.

One may need silver bullets to fell a reputation like Kissinger's. Hersh's book is not, I'm bound to say, written in an outstanding silvery fashion. But its dense and difficult pages do contain the material for a revision of the most inflated career of our day. People like Kissinger behave as if they have a franchise on the world. The least (and, alas, usually the most) one can do is examine their qualifications for ownership. This, Hersh has done. I'm driven to the reviewer's cliché of simple recommendation: If you don't take my word for it, get and read the book.

One returns, after closing it, to the matter of personality. Kissinger posed as a man of detachment and impartiality, but he was always committed to the sustenance, and dependent on the patronage, of Richard Nixon. He affected a lofty and long-run view of affairs but dabbled ceaselessly in short-term backstairs pettiness. He scorned the "tender-minded" critics of his designs and praised toughness, but he failed in all his jousts with people tougher than himself. The vengeance he exacted on weaker opponents, at home and abroad, is a matter of record and, thanks to Hersh, of well-documented record. Is there anybody who will say, carefully and specifically, that they know of a country or a good cause that is better off for Kissinger's attentions?

(*Inquiry*, September 1983)

III

The more I think about it, the more convinced I am that Henry Kissinger's most signal achievement is to have got everyone to call him "Doctor." There are literally millions of Ph.D.'s and second-rate academics in the United States, but he is the only one below the rank of professor to have managed to pull off this trick. And to pull it off, furthermore, without getting himself called "Doctor Death" all over the place—a nickname which would suit him much more than it does the good physician Owen.

There are three Mr. Kissingers. The first we know through Seymour Hersh and William Shawcross, and through the testimony of his former aides. This man is a power worshipper and a sycophant. He bugs his friends' telephones; he arranges for governments to fall and for "difficult" politicians to disappear. You can find his spoor in Bangladesh, in Chile, in Cambodia, in Vietnam, and in the slimy trail leading to the corridors of the Watergate building. This man is good at being somewhere else when things go wrong and very good at taking credit for things like "the opening to China," which would have occurred years previously were it not for the opposition of people like Nixon and himself.

The second Mr. Kissinger is a feature of the chat show and the rubber-chicken speaking circuit. For vast fees, he will send a vicarious thrill through an audience of Rotarians and their wives. I have seen the act a few times now, and it was on about the third occasion that I noticed the penchant for other people's nervous laughter that is his stock-in-trade. He understands the pornographic appeal of power, secrecy, and the control over life and death. He is very good at hinting at his familiarity with these things.

The third Mr. Kissinger, and, I'm very much afraid, the one under review, is the aforesaid second-rate academic. This Mr. Kissinger is the old hand at the think tank; the after-dinner guest at the mediocre foreign-affairs circle; the pundit of the opinion page and the member of the commission of inquiry. In *Observations: Selected Speeches and Essays, 1982–1984*, we encounter intoxicating topics like "A New Approach to Arms Control" and "Issues Before the Atlantic Alliance." Solemnity, turgidity, and bureaucratese are the norms. Triteness is all. Cop this, for example, from the essay "Mr. Shultz Goes to China" (January 1983):

> To the Chinese, Americans often appear unstable and slightly frivolous. To Americans, the Chinese occasionally present themselves as either inscrutable or uncommunicative.

You don't say. The urge to write "swell" in the margin of this book came over me at least three times in every chapter. It came over me, for instance, in the opening paragraph of "The Crisis in the Gulf" (1982):

> The governments of the Gulf face a fourfold threat: Shiite radicalism, Moslem fundamentalism, Iranian revolutionary agitation, Soviet imperialism.

That sentence is as well thought out as it is grammatical. The first three "folds" are actually triple invocations of the same fold, the fourth is standard-issue rhetoric, and there is no mention of the oil price, the presence of large Palestinian diaspora populations, the American weapons industry, or the pressure for political and social modernization. But then, logical encapsulation is not Mr. Kissinger's strong suit. In "A Plan to Reshape NATO" (1984), we encounter the following *aperçu*:

> Too many seek to position themselves somewhere between the superpowers—the first step toward psychological neutralism. Thus Europe's schizophrenia: a fear that the United States might not be prepared to risk its own population on a nuclear defense of Europe, coupled with the anxiety that America might drag Europe into an unwanted conflict by clumsy handling of Third World issues or East-West relations.

There are more than syntactical problems with that passage. First, many countries actually *are* "somewhere between the superpowers"—a position the discomfort of which Kissinger has no means of understanding. Second, having identified *America* as being in two minds (which it is), he awards the condition of "schizophrenia" to—the Europeans! Whence cometh this man's reputation for ruthless clarity?

Occasional nuggets of interest protrude from the sludge of cliché and self-regard. We learn that Mr. Kissinger approaches South Africa from the per-spective of "a well-disposed outsider." We discover that he thinks that the Suez invasion was okay, and Eisenhower and Dulles were wrong in opposing it. We are favored with the information that the Soviet Union is behind the upheaval in Central America. These nasty revelations are barely enough to keep one going, however, through prose like this peroration, unloaded on an audience of bankers in Washington in 1984:

> All great achievements were a vision before they were a reality. There are many in this room better qualified to fill in the many blanks for an overall design.

My major point is that the world needs new arrangements. A burst of creativity is needed to eliminate our dangers and fulfil our promise.

Swell. I hated every minute it took to read this book, but I think it may have been worthwhile. On pages 93–110 of the American edition, there appears an interview that Mr. Kissinger gave to the editors of *The Economist* in 1982. It is called "After Lebanon: A Conversation." The questions are unbelievably tough. He is asked, for instance, "Do you see still, after recent events, an opportunity for progress in the Middle East?" After that, the questioning gets perceptibly easier. The recorded interjections are of a toadying, collusive kind that make a Reagan press conference seem like hardball. So I think I have worked out what it is that allows the Kissinger reputation to survive. He has lied to Congress, he has betrayed his colleagues, and he has seen all his famous "mediation" efforts come to naught. But when it comes to the press, his diplomacy is unrivaled. Flatter the hacks, and you need never dine alone.

(*Literary Review*, September 1985)

FALSE START

❏

The accepted categories of British politics show a stubborn resistance to redefinition. For the most part we continue to judge actions by reputations instead of reputations by actions. Thus, the prime minister is repeatedly and tiresomely identified as "a monetarist," despite the profligacy of her Treasury. Thus, the leader of the Opposition is lazily identified as a socialist, despite his evident distaste for anything more than mild *dirigisme* laced with insularity. Most oddly of all, the Social Democratic Party, which is consecrated to the preservation of British politics and institutions in their postwar centrist pattern, is believed to be bent on "breaking the mold."

In this Lilliputian world, which is chiefly written about by correspondents and practitioners who have every interest in keeping the clichés alive, it is only exceptionally that a genuine political book is written or, indeed, read. There was a time when social democrats freely quoted Edward Bernstein and even Anthony Crosland, while more traditional socialists would riposte with R. H. Tawney, G. D. H. Cole, and (when they dared) Karl Marx himself. The Conservatives, who usually feel less need of ideological reinforcement, had Hayek or Oakeshott and, since the collapse of Heath, have made halfhearted gestures at their disinterment. Generally, though, empiricism was good enough for our grandfathers and might be expected to outlive intellectual fads in our own time.

The need for the programmatic book is still felt most keenly on the left of center. This may be why, at first glance, two books by William Rodgers (*The Politics of Change*) and Michael Meacher (*Socialism with a Human Face: The Political Economy of Britain in the 1980s*) exhibit so many superficial resemblances. Both have portentous titles. Both are designed to plug present-day gaps in the political front. Both give the impression of having been written on the intercity trains to their authors' respective northern constituencies. Both bear the heavy impress of a mentor (Gaitskell for Rodgers and Benn for Meacher). Both are written with a practiced eye for sudden shifts in public opinion.

Of the two men, I should unhesitatingly nominate Rodgers as the more successful in this respect. He has really learned how to get away with things, and that learning is his main—one might as well say his sole—political skill. Imagine the grave nodding among the lobby correspondents as he intones the following in his introduction:

> But how many Labour politicians regularly include in a public speech a ringing declaration of faith in a mixed economy? How many argue the role of profits in the private sector? The conventional wisdom inhibits. Some matters are better not talked about—or mentioned only in whispers. Similarly, it is strange that Conservative Ministers should feel uncomfortable about discussions with the TUC when a third of all trade unionists lately voted Conservative and the TUC is a major influence on industry and the economy. It is strange that the CBI—representing most of British industry, including the public sector—should not have easy and informal relations with most Labour Members of Parliament.

Here we have the familiar, something-for-everyone paragraph that has come to typify the prose style of the Social Democrats. It reminds one of nothing so much as the old Wilson-Heath duet, when exhortations to "both sides of industry" were the staple. Yet Rodgers apparently regards it as an act of supreme political courage and iconoclasm to echo these hackneyed sentiments.

Note also the question-begging. Either the TUC is a force for torpor and waste in the national economy (as the SDP really maintains) or it is not. (The fact that many trade unionists vote Conservative is neither here nor there—nor is it "lately," but a steady factor in the last dozen or so general elections.) Of course it is a "major influence on industry and the economy." Rodgers adores the obvious. But he prefers the safe ground of calling for dialogue rather than taking a position on the outcome. Fair enough—except that he is calling for a party which will dispense with "fudging and mudging."

Still, a kind of evenhandedness has served Rodgers well in the past, and he guesses, probably correctly, that it is this old ingredient of politics, rather than any fresh departure, which commends the SDP to the voters of today. He is thus extremely careful to avoid sharp questions even when he has to raise them. For example, he lays a little more stress than is modest on his twenty years as an MP and minister. Most of those years were spent on defense and foreign policy. Indeed, it was his disagreement with Labour's revived tendency to unilateralism that in large measure caused his defection. Yet the book contains practically nothing on nuclear weapons as a defense policy, and less than nothing on foreign affairs. Hidden away in a banal rumination on the trials of ministerial and civil existence, we find the following:

> What became known as the Chevaline programme for the improvement of Polaris missiles (eventually costing the taxpayer £1,000 million) was not explained to the House of Commons until (in a Statement on 24 January 1981) it had been completed. The Defence White Paper of 1975 had said of Polaris, "We shall maintain its effectiveness." Subsequently, as Minister of State for Defence, I was instructed to say that the Government was "up-dating" Polaris, although not going in for "a new generation" of nuclear weapons. There was no question, for example, of "MIRV-ing." It is impossible to believe that those towards whom secrecy was justified, in particular the Soviet Union, failed to put two-and-two together or would have been wiser had the costs of the programme been revealed. A Member of Parliament with normal access to Washington defence gossip could also have made a shrewd guess at what was happening. Why, then, was Parliament not told?

Is he asking us or telling us? He's certainly not recommending anything. What he reveals, evidently without intention, is his own familiarity with coterie politics and his habituation to what he would no doubt call, with his gift of phrase, the corridors of power. These, evidently, are where he intends to roam, come what may. I rate this book as the least amusing of the many SDP volumes—less weighty even than David Owen's and much less hilarious than Shirley Williams's. In terms of pith, it ranks with Jaroslav Hašek's famous manifesto "The Party of Moderate Progress Within Bounds of the Law."

Michael Meacher has tasted office but not power and feels that the loss is ours as much as his. He writes with infinitely more energy and conviction than Rodgers, and his nerve of outrage has not been hopelessly dulled, as has that of his rival. On the very first page appears the telltale "agonized reappraisal," and this tone is maintained fairly steadily throughout. What one gets, in return for persistent and sometimes trudging reading, is a thoughtful and useful book.

Where William Rodgers spends a few self-regarding pages on the difference between being a "social democrat" and a "democratic socialist," Meacher spends much of his time arguing for a personal but defensible definition of what socialism is in the first place. The ingredients are on first reading rather short of a surprise: planning, harnessed to protectionism, in order to maximize employment, aim for equality, and reduce dependence on overseas exploitation. These are standard Bennite themes; all one can add is that the section on planning in this book is very detailed and involves many tiers of "planning agreement" and economic-sector analysis. "Useful for the specialist" might be the best judgment here. But the chief interest of the book, and I suspect its chief motivation, is the argument about political democracy and individual liberty.

Meacher is perfectly well aware that most people are not socialists because most people are suspicious of, or hostile to, the extent of bureaucracy, conformity, and mediocrity that socialism seems to necessitate. He takes this point on the chin and nearly floors himself in the process. A whole chapter, very dense and passionate, is given over to the question "Does a Socialist Society Already Exist?" Meacher prints a little chart which "rates" five putative socialist regimes under seven socialist headings. The Soviet Union passes only one test, which oddly enough is "real full employment." Yugoslavia comes out as "political democracy with individual freedom." Despite these absurdities, and the sophomoric way in which they are laid out, it does emerge gradually that Meacher's ideal was the Dubček experiment in reformist socialism. This is a humane and reasonable conclusion, if rather an unexciting one. At any rate, the chapter shows more grappling with hard issues than anything in *The Politics of Change*. Behind Meacher's eagerly flashing Fabian spectacles, a brain and a conscience are striving to engage.

Socialism with a Human Face suffers, however, from being poorly written. The following passage is not untypical:

> After all, in the last analysis, what is life for? Man, even capitalist man, cannot live by material things alone. Yet at present he is severely starved of moral or spiritual values by the sheer unbalanced weight of materialistic propaganda grossly distorting the value system of society in the economic interests of the capitalist Establishment. Both the religious side of man and the secular construct of the welfare state, each of them motivated by aspirations which transcend the self, have been downplayed by the selfish forces of materialism, and a counterrevolution is urgently needed if Western man is to rise above the distortion of his present unidimensional mould.

We can see what he means here (the Marcusian echo makes me feel ten years younger), but only because the ideas expressed are so trite.

Britain's politicians may be Lilliputian, but the problems they face are

Brobdingnagian. Probably the greatest is the issue of democracy itself. Meacher, at least, has the sense of the overweening power of the state and the permanent bureaucracy. His chapters on this topic, which are well researched and presented, are better than the callow use of the phrase "capitalist Establishment" might suggest. He has some persuasive evidence that the Treasury and its political allies have used IMF power and pressures on sterling purely to win internal battles and preserve a sort of state within the state. This, not reselection of MPs, is the real threat to the oft-invoked sovereignty of Parliament.

Some of Britain's problems are too large for either Rodgers or Meacher to face. The relationship with its Irish neighbors is ignored. The arms race is merely touched upon. British readers who are black or brown will not find that they worried either distinguished MP very much. But at least *Socialism with a Human Face* can be criticized for failing at various points. *The Politics of Change* should be criticized for not trying at all.

(*The Times Literary Supplement*, June 25, 1982)

EARACHE

❑

Diana McLellan is precisely the sort of British journalist I left London to get away from. The Fleet Street gossip column is a hideous invention, at once bullying and sycophantic. Under the pretense of daring exposure and rapier wit lurks a horrid conformism and a lust for easy targets. As for the style necessitated by this kind of journalism, it is typically arch, gushing, and repetitive. Unfunny euphemisms ("confirmed bachelor" for homosexual) are thought of as subversive coinage. The mighty and the famous occasionally use such columns to take revenge on their friends by means of leaks. But for the most part the scandal page is a banal conveyor belt for received ideas, old gags, and witch hunts against the deviant. The really bad gossip writers aren't even reactionary—just boring. McLellan is a soupy blend of both.

What on earth, one is moved to inquire, does *The Washington Post* want with one of these exhibits? The paper has cut down the appearances of "Ear" to four a week, as if to say that it doesn't really endorse this shop-soiled survivor of the defunct *Washington Star*, but the comparative rarity of the column's appearance only makes it look worse. Perhaps Ben Bradlee thinks that McLellan has that elusive Brit cachet? But, no, that can't be right.

Here is a ripe sample from *Ear on Washington: A Chrestomathy of Scandal, Rumor, and Gossip Among the Capital's Elite*—what some have called a wickedly mischievous love-it-or-hate-it-you-must-read-it anthology:

"I see you wear a hearing aid too, senator."
"Oh, well, yes. But it's not because I'm hard of hearing, just helps filter out background noise in the hearing rooms."
"Oh, really? What kind is it?"
"Let's see. Exactly 4:30."

I wish I had a dollar for every year that has elapsed since I first heard that joke. McLellan attributes it to Senator Charles Percy, which is odd since, for a gossip columnist, she uses blind attributions ("one aide") more than most—almost as often as she employs the word "darling."

That habit by itself gives the lie to her claim to fearlessness. (In truth, I have seldom met a gossip columnist who wasn't a coward.) You can search through this entire collection of cultured pearls without finding a single real gem, a single item that would embarrass anybody rich, famous, or powerful. The only tales that are even faintly waspish concern members of the Carter hick entourage, now safely removed from pelf and power. On their own, these are no funnier than the labored gags about ham-fisted servants that used to appear in *Punch*. (As I had feared, the antique story about gauche dinner guests drinking from their fingerbowls appears here more than once.)

Then there's the pseudoknowing style of writing. Give ear to this:

It is very poor form in Washington to use your host's bed for any purpose other than storing outer clothing. Even a rather hip D.C. crowd was enraged on going to the bedroom of one chic political journalist to retrieve their coats. They found them buried beneath an amorous New York journalist and his then current belle.

Everything is wrong with that paragraph. The first sentence tells you what the last sentence (I refuse to call it a punch line) is going to be. "Rather hip," "chic," "amorous," and "belle" are not naughty or clever; they are tired affectations. And what's the point of the tale if McLellan doesn't identify the New York journalist? (*I* know, but *The Nation* is for family reading, not sleazy revelations.)

On almost every page there is either a breathtaking "so what" story or a whiskered and recycled curio. The line about the man who gets his lab sample back with a note warning that his horse may have diabetes cracked many a grin during the Depression. It's hardly any better when it's (allegedly) quoting Walter Mondale on Billy Carter's beer.

Diana McLellan is a sort of sad omnivore. All jokes are funny, all gossip is "scandal," anything involving people she's heard of is a revelation about the private lives of the stratospheric. But she has no sorting process. The only "scoop" she ever got—the bugging of Blair House—turned out to be a turkey. She lacks the most basic attribute of a gossip writer—a posture of antagonism. Here she is, revealingly, on the denizens of her Washington beat:

> The great show rolls on. The players make us mad, they make us laugh, they make us cheer and cringe and blow razzberries and pay taxes.
> They've got an awful lot of guts.
> I salute them.

She does *what*? Here we are in the Washington of Ronnie and Nancy, with crass vulgarity and foolishness abounding on every side, and *The Washington Post* has a gossip column that is, by its own admission, *perfectly innocuous!* Alexander Pope described this kind of courtier coverage very well:

> *Willing to wound and yet afraid to strike*
> *Just hint a fault, and hesitate dislike.*
> *Alike reserved to blame, or to commend,*
> *A timorous foe, and a suspicious friend.*

McLellan, with a style and a column that grow more ingratiating and desperate every week, is certainly not going to risk offending the supply-side high society. Her reputation, then, is the only really mysterious thing about her.

(*The Nation*, September 11, 1982)

SOMETHING FOR EVERYBODY

❏

Something terrible seems to happen to David Cornwell (alias John le Carré) every time he leaves England or, to be generous, every time he leaves northern or eastern Europe. Give him a drizzle-sodden English prep school, a gentleman's club in London, a high table at Oxford, a windswept beach or a dripping forest "somewhere in Germany," and he can make a show of things. What he must curb is his yearning for the exotic East, or for anything that doesn't fit the prescribed European categories of the freezing Cold War. *The Honourable Schoolboy*, which relied so much on Hong Kong, was a failure partially mitigated by some doses of colonial British ambience. With *The Little Drummer Girl*, John le Carré has finally found the point where he is quite definitely out of his depth.

If this novel were a film (and it reads like the result of a script conference with a greedy agent), it would be the sort of movie that one views only on airplanes. The characters are all either clichéd or impossible, the scenery banal, and the moral dilemmas bogus. There are egregious errors of fact and continuity, and the effort to sustain tension sags into such longueurs that it would have any discerning customer tearing off his earphones and—which I've always thought the airlines bank on—calling hoarsely for an expensive drink.

Despite its excessive length, the book is alarmingly easy to summarize in point of plot. The Israeli secret service badly desires the death of a certain Palestinian guerrilla. They feel they need two things in order to encompass this objective. The first, of course, is a girl, who must be simultaneously gullible and plausible—both of these to a degree which tries the imagination. The second is the cooperation of various intelligence officers in other countries—principally Britain and West Germany. It goes without saying that neither the girl nor the other agents should ever know precisely what it is they are being asked to do, but that they should do it anyway. Only the glacially intelligent men from Mossad, plus of course Mr. le Carré himself, are ever privy to what is going on. And sometimes even they, especially Mr. le Carré, seem uncertain as well.

The Little Drummer Girl has been inexplicably praised by some reviewers, and no more explicably decried by others, for its sympathetic presentation of the Palestinians. In practice, le Carré deals in stereotypes which, when they are not boring, manage to be insulting to both sides in the Palestine conflict. Thus, Israelis are shirt-sleeved and grizzled, their occasional doubts dissolved with wry humor and ruthless, lethal dedication. The Palestinians are chaotic, colorful, sexually exuberant, but liable to turn rancidly nasty at any moment. Since this is 1983, it is of course understood that they both share a tender feeling for their mutual, twice-promised homeland. Le Carré has adapted various speeches and pamphlets into unimpressive dialogue, with persons babbling on at great length uninterrupted, in order to show that he has read both sides and is "evenhanded." But when he strays far beyond the cuttings library, he is lost. He has one of his Palestinian protagonists traveling from Beirut to Istanbul and over the land border to Greece. He does it all (before he is daringly kidnapped by the relentlessly vigilant, etcetera, etcetera) on a Cypriot diplomatic passport. Turkey is the only government in the world that does not recognize the Republic of Cyprus. A Cypriot passport (most of all a diplomatic one) is a means of getting unwelcome attention in Turkey. Then le Carré has the Mossad team receive a telex message from the Israeli Embassy in Athens. There have not been, since 1948, full diplomatic relations between Israel and Greece. Both of the above examples are extant controversies in the region. They are not trifling by any standard, and certainly not in the case of an author much touted for his mastery of detail.

The slipshod approach to politics and ideas in this book is not at all offset by its characterization. "Suspension of disbelief" may be a necessary faculty in a theatergoer, but modern fiction is supposed to carry a certain conviction to its readers and consumers. In the central person of Charlie, the young British actress conscripted by the Israelis to act as bait for their target (he uses the analogy of goat and tiger as if he had thought of it himself), le Carré has invented a figure who is simply and literally incredible. Everything about her is implausible at best; she has no real identity or motivation, and it therefore makes no sense for the Israelis (who can command both qualities with ease) to employ her. She is expected to play the part of widow to a man she never met, and we are expected to believe that this man's family or friends never really knew him. Le Carré here is impartially insulting the intelligence of the Israelis and the Palestinians, as well as that of his readers. Huge swaths of narrative are taken up with Charlie's internal monologues and hysterical conversations:

> She put her knuckles in her mouth and discovered she was weeping. He came and sat beside her on the bed, and she waited for him to put his arm around her or offer more wise arguments or simply take her, which was what she would have liked best, but he did nothing of the kind. He was content to let her mourn, until gradually she had the illusion that he had somehow caught her up, and they were mourning together. More than any words could have done, his silence seemed to mitigate what they had to do. For an age, they stayed that way, side by side, till she allowed her choking to give way to a deep, exhausted sigh. But he still did not move—not towards her, not away from her.
>
> "Jose," she whispered hopelessly taking his hand once more. "Who the hell are you? What do you *feel* inside all those barbed wire entanglements?"

This is rubbish. Not only is it written at the level of pulp romance fiction, but it clearly disqualifies the girl for the role in which "Jose" (her pet name for the Mossad agent Joseph) is supposed to be molding her. (Another silly slip occurs at about this point. Charlie, who has earlier shown herself as a deft spouter of modish anti-Zionist propaganda, says that she has never heard of Deir Yassin.)

Perhaps half-aware of his cardboard or contradictory characters, and even of his extreme unfamiliarity with the region or the issues, le Carré spends some time trying to set out the symbols and totems of the conflict. Here again, cliché lies in wait for him. The Israelis pay visits to the Holocaust museum at Yad Vashem in order to strengthen their resolve. The Arabs get a bow in their direction with a description of what must be the hideous Kiryat Arba settlement in Hebron. A punch line is made out of the unsurprising fact that a Palestinian woman has a biochemistry degree from an American university. Something, in fact, for everybody. I was especially pleased to find, on page 328, the oldest and stalest line of all: the one that appears in the first story of every journalist on his first trip to the region—the one that reads, "from crackling loudspeakers wailed the *muezzin*, summoning the faithful to prayer."

At only one point does le Carré catch and sustain any really intriguing or vivid dialogue or insight. The meeting between the Mossad and the British secret service is very well done indeed and reminds one of how he got his reputation. The Brits are instinctive anti-Semites who have learned to "respect" Israeli cunning, and the Israelis are tough guys who expect nothing better from the Gentiles who once hunted them under the Mandate. But this is home ground for our author, and he obviously felt safer on it.

Finally, I'm moved to protest at le Carré's creation of Professor Minkel, the bumbling Israeli academic who protests at the maltreatment of Arabs and is, by what le Carré no doubt considers an irony, made into a pawn of the Mossad. The whole is a poorly crafted caricature of Professor Israel Shahak, a man whose ceaseless work for human rights should not be cheapened in this way. Le Carré has used him lazily as the basis for an unconvincing figure, and then got bored and thrown him away. That, in effect, is what he has done here with the whole drama and struggle of the Middle East.

(*Literary Review*, July 1983)

SAME, ONLY MORE SO

❑

Against stupidity, as we know, the gods themselves labor in vain. The study of history is replete with idiocy; not the idiocy of the simple-minded but the elaborate crassness of those who set out to deceive themselves. Santayana remarked somewhere that fanaticism consisted in redoubling your efforts when you had forgotten your aims, and the examples of Custer, Haig (Sir Douglas), and George III are known to every schoolboy. It's no coincidence that most of the famous citations of foolishness are military. Not only does war give immense latitude to the stupid and the blinkered, it also passes verdicts in rather a swift and summary manner.

Barbara Tuchman's book *The March of Folly* considers epic folly from the standpoint of a contented liberal. Having reviewed the question, Why were the Trojans so gullible about that horse? Ms. Tuchman surveys three other self-destructive episodes. She writes about the Renaissance secession; about the British and their brilliant provocation of pro-independence feeling among the American colonists; about the United States and its heroic attachment to illusions about Vietnam. These three evidently deserve their place in any anthology of the higher loopiness.

Ms. Tuchman writes in rather a lofty manner, as if what she had to say was laughably obvious. Sometimes, indeed, it is. "Folly's appearance is independent of era or locality; it is timeless and universal, although the habits and beliefs of a particular time and place determine the form it takes." Well, yes, I think we can all agree about that. In less tautologous form, she instructs us that, "Shorn of his tremendous curled peruke, high heels and ermine, the Sun King was a man subject to misjudgment, error and impulse—like you and me." No argument there either, though it would be equally true to say that His Majesty was fiasco-prone even when *not* shorn of his tremendous curled peruke and other garnishings. Ms. Tuchman is the doyenne of the middle-brow American talk circuit, and some of her archness and triteness in this role has been allowed to infect her prose.

The recurring failure of ruling classes to act in their own apparent best interests is, from a Marxist point of view, a worthwhile conundrum. Marx himself was very intrigued by the role of accident and by the blinding effects of ideology, and E. H. Carr in *What Is History?* made use of Montesquieu's famous dictum, "If a particular cause, like the accidental result of a battle, has ruined a state, there was a general cause which made the downfall of this state ensue from a single battle."

As often as not, the crisis of a system is provoked by something which only a few people consider significant at the time. The Trojan case is too imbricated with divine interference to make a good paradigm, and you can't have Christianity without schism, so Ms. Tuchman's first two examples are a little unsatisfying. But she can show without difficulty that the British Crown was willfully deaf on the question of taxation in the Americas and could probably have dissuaded Washington and his confreres from a step which, until the very last, they were most reluctant to take. She can "prove" that one American President after another allowed himself to be deceived about the state of affairs in Vietnam, on several occasions, for instance, insisting that pessimistic reports be redrafted for purposes of unity and consolation.

The explanation employed by American pop psychologists in such cases is that of "cognitive dissonance." Ms. Tuchman writes of this diagnosis with some respect. Cognitive dissonance is the ability (she terms it the tendency) "to suppress, gloss over, water down or 'waffle' issues which would produce conflict or 'psychological pain' within an organization." "An unconscious alteration in the estimate of probabilities" is, in the jargon, the result. The average person, realizing the capacity for self-sustaining illusion in his or her daily life, may begin to sympathize with rulers who practice the same trickery on themselves. Only human, after all, "like you and me." That is just what is wrong with the theory, and with much of Ms. Tuchman's narrative. American presidents and other mighty figures are often rather tough-minded. They never seem to develop the illusion that they can abolish poverty and privilege, nor do they fall prey to fantasies about universal justice. They are perfectly well aware of the self-interest of their backers and themselves. It is precisely by acting upon it that they create disaster and ruin. This could be because their interest does not reflect the general interest—a possibility that Ms. Tuchman, with all her fondness for paradox, never canvasses.

America went into Vietnam with its eyes relatively open, and with the intention of supplanting a French colonial empire. As it happened, the Indochinese people had outgrown foreign rule by 1954 at the latest, and Vietnam was where—and how—the United States found this out. Here we see Montesquieu's relation between an accidental and a general cause, rather than Ms. Tuchman's speculative stuff about presidents trying to look good in front of their advisers. She's not wrong about the political shenanigans involved (in fact she summarizes them very well), but she sees an irony in American conduct where none exists. Her conclusion—the very acme of spurious evenhandedness—is: "Perhaps the greatest folly was Hanoi's—to fight so steadfastly for thirty years for a cause that became a brutal tyranny when it was won." This is too fatuous for words. Either Hanoi communism is brutal and tyrannical or it is not, and, if it is, then it did not "become" so in 1975. And how are the Vietnamese supposed to have duped themselves into resisting an alien partition and occupation? This is not even good journalism, let alone good history.

Ms. Tuchman's book belongs several shelves below her earlier work on General Stilwell in China, and many shelves below Isaac Deutscher's *Ironies of History*. I'm impelled, finally, to one ad hominem reflection. If ever there was an example of a nation creating a disaster for itself, and screening out the discordant voices within, it is Israel under the new leadership of the Revisionist movement. Watching it is like viewing a film of which one has already seen the end. In the United States, where historians and moralists commingle as opinion makers, this matter is debated almost daily. Among the loudest voices which damn all criticism of Israeli policy as made in bad faith is—but endings are the prerogative of historians with hindsight.

(*New Statesman*, July 20, 1984)

BETTER OFF WITHOUT

❏

Contrary to all interpretations, from liberal to Stalinist, Karl Marx did not believe that religion was the opium of the people. What he did say, in his *Critique of Hegel's Philosophy of Right*, was this:

> Religious distress is at the same time the expression of real distress and the protest against real distress. Religion is the sigh of the oppressed creature, the heart of the heartless world, just as it is the spirit of a spiritless situation. It is the opium of the people. The demand to give up the illusions about its conditions is the demand to give up a condition that needs illusions. Criticism has plucked the imaginary flowers from the chain, not so that men will wear the chain without any fantasy or consolation, but so that they will break the chain and cull the living flower.

This makes it plain even on the most cursory reading that Marx had a serious understanding of religious belief. He was anticlerical and, especially in his writings on the civil war in France, he denounced the cynical way in which the ruling order deceived its subjects by means of a Christianity in which it did not itself believe. But, unlike many of his radical contemporaries, he did not hold that religion could be legislated away. Nor did he believe that mere advances in social or economic emancipation would make the supernatural redundant.

Michael Harrington's excellent study of this question, *The Politics at God's Funeral*, confirms the wisdom of the authentic Marxist approach, against the vulgarizations of those who have succeeded him. Left to themselves, most thinking people have opted for a view that is in effect agnostic. Once the Church loses its monopoly and becomes just another competitor in the battle of ideas, it loses everything else that makes for the domination of faith. Science has easily undone the creationists (who have been only a joke in this generation), but it has also demolished the assumptions about man's place in the universe that are necessary to sustain religion. Even those who still describe themselves as believers are living with doubts and compromises that would have been seen as unthinkably heretical only a few decades ago. Real, old-fashioned visceral faith is now found only in those countries where it is persecuted.

Still, as G. K. Chesterton once put it, when people cease to believe in God, they do not believe in nothing—but rather believe in anything. It's not easy to regard agnosticism or atheism as naturally coextensive with progress when one surveys the wasteland of capitalist materialism, the sinister credulity of "cult" members, or the hysterical adulation heaped on mortal leaders in parts of the communist world. Chesterton was an unscrupulous Roman Catholic apologist, but he had a point. Michael Harrington, who has honestly lost his faith—but is, I'm sorry to say, still nostalgic for it—wants to lay God decently to rest in order that we may mourn him properly and then see where we stand. As he puts it:

> A strident, anti-clerical atheism is as dated and irrelevant as the intransigent anti-modernism of Pope Pius IX. Even more to the point, atheist and agnostic humanists should be as appalled by *de facto* atheism in late capitalist society as should people of religious faith. It is a thoughtless, normless, selfish, hedonistic individualism.

I believe that I am right in identifying this as a statement of belief on Harrington's part. He has not lost his reverence for the religious life (recall his writings on Dorothy Day and the *Catholic Worker*), and he wants to preserve Christian values in a secular movement of community. This makes it the more interesting that, in one of his few mistakes, he confuses Hegel's term *Aufhebung*. He renders it, in his appendix on Kant, as meaning "the culmination, the completion."

In fact, *Aufhebung* means, and was used by Hegel and Marx to mean, the *transcendence* of an idea or a system of ideas. In order to retain Christian values (whatever they may be) while rejecting religious authority or the religious explanation of reality, one must reject Christianity itself. Socialism may be, as Harrington would like to argue, the "culmination" of those values as well as of the Enlightenment. But it has to start by understanding religion, as Marx did, the better to vanquish it.

Nor can one so easily say, as Harrington does, that the old anticlerical battles are quite over. Whenever Western reactionaries are in a tight corner, they proclaim to be defending "Christian civilization." The child martyrs of the Iranian army, drafted before their teens, are told by their mullahs that an Iraqi bullet will send them to Paradise. The Polish workers were enjoined by their spiritual leaders to spend their spare time on their knees. What sort of advice was that?

The list runs on—anybody who has seen an Israeli election knows that the mere mention of the holy places of Hebron or Jerusalem is enough to still the doubters and divide the dissidents. And everybody knows that the "Christian Democratic" parties of Europe have a reserve strength of religious iconography they deploy when they think nobody is looking. We are not as far out of the medieval woods as some suppose.

Harrington's book, nonetheless, is lucid enough to supply the material for its own criticism. He begins with an exposition of Kant, Hegel, and the French philosophes. He shows that all attempts to marry new discovery and new thought with existing religion only drove the two further apart. He stresses the way in which philosophers before Marx considered themselves a privileged group and thought that skepticism was permissible in their own cases but dangerous and subversive if allowed to permeate the people. He rightly compares Marx to Prometheus. But Prometheus could not assume that the gods were necessarily benign.

This is difficult terrain. There are, obviously, millions of people who cannot bear the idea that the heavens are empty, that God is dead, and that we are alone. There are also secular radicals who feel a bit queasy at the idea. And there are people who do not believe that God is dead because they never believed that he was alive in the first place. Most irritating of all, there are still people on the left who say feebly that, "after all, there are so many 'progressive' church people. Look at the Maryknolls or Archbishop Romero." This is usually said by those who are not themselves religious but who feel that religion is good enough for other people—usually other people in the Third World. It is just as trite and unoriginal as the view that the shameful papal concordat with fascism "proves" the reactionary character of Catholicism.

Harrington is actually very adroit in his discussion of the religious and mystical element in modern tyranny. He shows that the Nazis, though they made opportunistic use of the conservative churches, were also hostile to Christianity and sought to replace it with bogus pagan rituals. While the Stalinists, publicly committed to atheism, called upon old traditions of Russian orthodoxy as well as the "God-seekers" and "God-builders" whom Lenin had almost driven out of the Bolshevik Party. Lunacharsky, Gorki, and others who tried to synthesize Marxism with Christianity cannot have intended that their ideas would become a synthesis of orthodoxy and Stalinism symbolized by the gruesome Lenin mausoleum. Still less can they have intended that the mausoleum would help legitimize the exorbitant and grandiose cult of Stalin himself. Harrington does not say so, but the Stalin cult was less of a blasphemy on Eastern Christianity than it was on Bolshevik materialism, however vulgar. Why else would the Soviet regime still take such care to maintain a tame Orthodox Church with its very own archbishop? What we have to face as an enemy is not any particular religion but the slavish, credulous mentality upon which all religious and superstitious movements feed.

After publishing *The Future of Illusion*, Freud began to doubt that its optimistic predictions would be vindicated. He hoped that people would gradually, as it were, "grow out" of the need for faith and subjection. The appalling mixture of modernism in technology and antiquity in superstition—which drove Freud from Vienna and which might be the ideal definition of totalitarianism—made him wonder if he might not have been too sanguine.

Wilhelm Reich, Freud's disciple (about whom Harrington is too easily dismissive), argued that the Left did not know how to speak to people except in arid, bread-and-butter terms. His work on repression and mass psychology was designed to undercut the Nazi appeal and to dilute the materialism of Marxism. It collapsed into eccentricity and foolishness, but it was an important try. It anticipated much of the radical spirituality of our own time. It also recalled missionary Christianity, which often maintained that, by codifying and ritualizing primitive magic, it civilized paganism and witchcraft. A fair claim, but one that reminds us that man made God in his own image and not the other way around.

Can man, unassisted by God, make himself in a new image? Harrington believes it can be done and that "men and women of faith and anti-faith should, in the secular realm at least, stop fighting one another and begin to work together to introduce moral dimensions into economic and social debate and decision."

As the conclusion to a fairly rigorous book, that strikes me as a very insipid one. It could have been part of some bland ecumenical exhortation or some trendy encyclical. Neither believers nor unbelievers need to give up anything if they want to join the battle for socialism. But, if the religious promise is good or true, then there is no absolute need for socialism, and therefore the believer must always be joining in spite of his or her beliefs. That the two schools should "stop fighting" is, fortunately, impossible. If it were possible, it would not be desirable.

In a country like the United States, where religion and religiosity are everywhere and where elements on left and right claim divine authority, atheists and humanists need to be more assertive rather than less. I'm thinking here of the prevalence of pathetic oxymorons like "Liberty Baptist" or "Liberation Theology."

In his masterly book *The Class Struggle in the Ancient Greek World*, G. M. de Ste. Croix shows that there is no evidence that Christianity ever improved the lot or the morals of any people—and a great deal of evidence the other way. Its holy texts are the warrant for slavery, genocide, monarchy, and patriarchy, and, even more important, for servility and acquiescence in the face of those things. The apologetic "modern Christian" who argues faintly that of course the Bible isn't meant to be taken literally is saying that it isn't the word of God. He is, thereby, revising his faith out of existence. If the religious have so few real convictions left, why are socialists supposed to defer to their insights? Michael Harrington has ably summarized the evidence for the death of God. He should now start to "transcend" his grief for the departed.

(*In These Times*, November 16–22, 1983)

FROM HERE
TO DEMOCRACY

❑

When Henry Adams wrote his fictional satire on Washington life in 1880, he entitled it *Democracy*. It pleased him, perfect snob that he was, to associate the world of shenanigans and mediocrity with a political idea for which he felt disdain. He issued the book anonymously, hoping that the vulgar public would make the wrong guess about its authorship, and hoping particularly that they would attribute it to his friend John Hay.

If Joan Didion had published her *Democracy* anonymously (a remote contingency, in view of the fact that she inserts herself as a character in its early stages) and had invited us to guess at its provenance, how would one proceed? Take, for example, the opening of chapter 12:

> See it this way.
> See the sun rise that Wednesday morning in 1975 the way Jack Lovett saw it.
> From the operations room at the Honolulu airport.
> The warm rain down on the runways.
> The smell of jet fuel.

Obviously, the writer of this is a student with some, but not many, course credits in Hemingway. Perhaps majoring in *The Sun Also Rises*. But wait. What about this section, toward the close of part 2?

> Which was when Adlai said maybe she heard she could score there.
> Which was when Inez slapped Adlai.
> Which was when Harry said keep your hands off my son.
> But Dad, Adlai kept saying in the silence that followed. But Dad. Mom.
> *Aloha oe.*

Here, surely, we can trace the undigested influence of Kurt Vonnegut? But these purely textual interrogations are inadequate, in themselves, to the task of inference. What does the book, taken as a whole, reveal about its author? We may intuit that the author is nervous, edgy, alive to the nuances of menace even in the most banal situation. We can detect, and acknowledge, a sort of thwarted perfectionism—a concern with getting an atmosphere *right* and a nagging anxiety that this ambition has not been quite fulfilled ("Aerialists know that to look down is to fall. Writers know it too"). This writer must be introspective, even self-doubting. The cuticles, perhaps, a little gnawed.

There are clues, too, in the references to parts of the West Coast and to midtown Manhattan. Why, for instance, do Harry and Inez identify themselves as living, not on Central Park, but at 135 Central Park West? That fine building actually houses Mick Jagger, Carly Simon, Whitney Ellsworth, and the splendid and gracious hostess Jean Stein, at one of whose soirees I once met, briefly, a tense and frail woman wearing dark glasses. She had recently published an account of what it felt like to be very insecure indeed about being an American in El Salvador. Yes, I think I would have guessed that the author of *Democracy* was Joan Didion.

Her novel (*Democracy* is handily subtitled "A Novel") has thirty chapters and is unevenly divided into three parts. There are two trinities in the action also. One is a triangle of the time-honored kind, between the heroine Inez Christian, her conceited husband Harry Victor—who thinks he is good enough to be President—and her lover, the sinister, hard-boiled Jack Lovett, who broods on the decline of the West and does his poor best to arrest it. The second triangle is one of location: *Democracy* is set in Hawaii, in Saigon (though we never actually go there except in reported speech), and in the bi-coastal world of American movers and brokers. The context is that of a family crisis—hard to summarize but involving murder and a runaway daughter—which is uneasily synchronized with the collapse of America's "commitment" to Vietnam.

The staccato organization and the style of the novel make it both easy and difficult to read. One is reminded of the rapid crosscutting that Hollywood, a Didion haunt, has imposed on modern narrative. Effort must be expended in turning back pages for brief and testing refresher courses. But the effort is often worthwhile. If you valued Ms. Didion as herself in *The White Album*, you will like Inez Christian's internalized reflections, and if you recall her essay "In the Islands" from that collection, you will have a rough map by which to read *Democracy*.

Hawaii, least typical of all American states, offers an angular perspective. It refracts, into mainland American life, happenings from the Pacific and Indochina. Pearl Harbor is there. James Jones chose Schofield, Hawaii (a place-name which sums up the combination of the exotic and the quotidian), as the setting of *From Here to Eternity*. Jones had his Robert E. Lee Prewitt, the exemplary "grunt," and Ms. Didion has her Jack Lovett. Lovett is the best evoked of her characters, and we've all met him somewhere:

> All nations, to Jack Lovett, were "actors," specifically "state actors" (non-state actors were the real wild cards here, but in Jack Lovett's extensive experience the average non-state actor was less interested in laser mirrors than in M-16s, AK-47s, FN-FALS, the everyday implements of short-view power, and when the inductive leap to the long view was made it would probably be straight to weapons-grade uranium), and he viewed such actors abstractly, as friendly or unfriendly, committed or uncommitted; as assemblies of armaments on a large board. Asia was ten thousand tanks here, three hundred Phantoms there. The heart of Africa was an enrichment facility.

This is a deft portrayal, showing (correctly) how noisy the "quiet" American can often be. It also, at its close, has a (presumably) intentional echo of Conrad. Ms. Didion tells us in "In the Islands" that she came to maturity holding before herself the example of, among others, Axel Heyst in *Victory*. Her recent work has been preoccupied with the question of why, in this American century, the world is so inhospitable to Americans. Even when, as in her *Salvador*, she overdramatizes this, she still recognizes and conveys it in a way that few of her contemporaries can. There are, she seems quakingly to suggest, certain latitudes and sweltering interiors where Mr. Kurtz, or his American analogue, should just not venture. This is a daunting thought, and one which is utterly antithetical to the prevailing temper of raucous bullishness in the United States. But those body bags which Didion saw coming into Honolulu airport in the early 1970s are with her still—and are present in these pages. As a result, there are no more winners in *Democracy* than there were in *Victory*.

The brittle, febrile style of the novel may be intended to match its message, if "message" is not too assertive a word. The tone, if so, is subtly wrong for the purpose. Preferable is the way in which Didion boldly records the robust American speech of Lovett and of the worldly fixer Billy Dillion, a friend of the family ("A major operator, your brother-in-law. I said, Dick, get your ass over to Anderson, the last I heard the Strategic Air Command still had a route to Honolulu").

In the background, which advances and recedes, are Pacific nuclear tests, real-estate criminals, political opportunists of every stripe, and endangered American innocents who force the weary professionals to clean up after them. In a perhaps unconscious concession to the time, Ms. Didion makes all her liberals into platitudinous poltroons. It's not absolutely clear whether she thinks, with some part of herself, that Americans are too good for this harsh, ungrateful world or too ill equipped for it. Inez, for example, finally moves to Asia and "ceases to claim the American exemption." Her junkie daughter is preferred, by her maker, to her pompously radical brother. These loose ends may be part of the fray in Didion's own warp and woof. *The White Album* found her in the Royal Hawaiian Hotel in Honolulu, fretting about tidal waves and confessing that "I have trouble making certain connections." In *Democracy*, she briskly discards a whole agenda of questions about the personality of her characters, saying that they are "suggestive details in the setting, but the setting is for another novel." That could very well be.

(*The Times Literary Supplement*, September 14, 1984)

UMBERTO UMBERTO

❏

Jorge Luis Borges, the blind Argentine novelist and ex-librarian, is perhaps the most complex and imaginative literary craftsman alive today. A few years ago, he published a story about an infinite library: a labyrinth of books and shelves that "existed" in a shifting continuum of space and time.

Umberto Eco, the Italian semiotician, has constructed a fourteenth-century Italian abbey, the center of which is a labyrinthine library organized on mystical, recondite principles. The guardian of this library's secret is a blind savant named Jorge of Burgos.

It is tricks and allusions of this kind that have made *The Name of the Rose* into a success on so many levels. It has generated enough interest to justify the publication of a *Postscript*, in which the author explains himself by raising more questions than he cares to answer. *The Name of the Rose* can be read for diversion, as a thriller or a historical romance. It can also be mined for various guessing games (even the meaning of the title is opaque), for stylistic insights and linguistic conceits. A knowledge of Latin and some grounding in the history of schism and medieval philosophy are useful but not essential.

The novel's central character, William of Baskerville (Eco likes Conan Doyle as well as Borges), is a rationalist and a logician who is compelled to argue within the framework of Christian orthodoxy. He enters the abbey as an outsider, charged with an investigation into murder and backsliding. The entire narrative is based upon his method and his personality—there is scarcely a scene that he does not command.

As an Englishman, imbued with Roger Bacon's love of scientific inquiry and Peter Abelard's attachment to logical procedure, he is distrusted at once by the more superstitious and dogmatic elements within the abbey. Moreover, as a former inquisitor who resigned his post in disgust, he has given proof of his willingness to tolerate heterodoxy and even—the key word in the novel—heresy. It becomes impossible for him to confine his inquiry to the narrow course proposed by the authorities.

The narrator, a young and credulous monk named Adso, plays the part of a prompter in a Socratic dialogue, feeding lines and questions to the master. He notices early on that William possesses "curiosity, but at the beginning I knew little of this virtue, which I thought, rather, a passion of the covetous spirit." It is also the case, reflects Adso, "that in those dark times a wise man had to believe things that were in contradiction among themselves."

In "those dark times" the emperor and the pope were sworn foes, who might make peace at any moment to combine against another enemy. Varying Christian factions maneuvered against one another. And for "the simple," God and the devil were everyday presences. So, too, was the impending Apocalypse, signs of which were detected on every hand. But the doctrinal center of the Church was also unstable, and yesterday's imperative could well go into tomorrow's discard. When the pope is rumored to be reconsidering the existence of the fiery pit: "Lord Jesus, assist us! Jerome cried. And what will we tell sinners, then, if we cannot threaten them with an immediate hell the moment they are dead?"

The difficulty is, evidently, that small heresies—even William's vice of "curiosity"—will inevitably lead to bigger ones. The least challenge to the edifice of the faith must therefore be avoided, or crushed. In this instance, the faith is enshrined by the *Aedificium*: the library. Here, as the abbot puts it, may be found "the very word of God, as he dictated it to the prophets and the apostles, as the fathers preached it without changing a syllable."

But someone is moving through the abbey and the library, and murdering its devout servants at the rate of one a day. The order and method of dispatch is designed to suggest a prefiguration—even an enactment—of the Apocalypse. One by flood, one by blood, one by poison: the last days are being inexorably counted off. It takes William of Baskerville some little time to realize that this panic-inducing sequence is a brilliant feint and that the false trail is intended to lead away from the mysterious library.

The conclusion (which I'll leave as obscure as I can) has also been prefigured in the text. Jorge of Burgos is determined that no pre-Christian enlightenment be allowed or tolerated. Once you concede that humanity possessed numerous truths and values before the Bible, you may as well admit that Christianity is just another religion. And this would endanger more than just the spiritual hierarchy. The work of Greek and Jewish predecessors, then, must be kept hidden from profane "curiosity."

In the metaphorical, allegorical conflict between William and Jorge, their recurring dispute concerns Aristotle, who taught that laughter is a cathartic and vivacious thing. It is precisely because of this passage in the *Poetics* that Jorge opposes Aristotle so viciously:

> Laughter frees the villein from fear of the Devil, because in the feast of fools the Devil also appears poor and foolish, and therefore controllable. But this book could teach that freeing oneself of the fear of the Devil is wisdom. When he laughs, as the wine gurgles in his throat, the villein feels he is master, because he has overturned his position with respect to his lord; but this book could teach learned men the clever and, from that moment, illustrious artifices that could legitimize the reversal.

One could go on (and Eco does, for pages). But the point is made. There are secrets that the vulgar multitude *must not know*. "The license of the plebeians must be restrained and humiliated, and intimidated by sternness."

Even William's friends counsel him: "Mortify your intelligence, learn to weep over the wounds of the Lord, throw away your books." There is, naturally, more than pure theology at stake. Abbeys and monasteries did not only hold monopolies of learning and education; they were centers of economic, political, and even military strength. They exerted immense influence over the market and were the possessors ("in trust," of course) of extraordinary wealth.

Indeed, there is a striking modernism about *The Name of the Rose*, often missed by those who look for mere analogies in it. At one point, Adso asks the ignorant monk Salvatore why a fundamentalist Christian sect, the Shepherds, has decided to turn on the Jews:

> He explained to me that all his life preachers had told him the Jews were the enemies of Christianity and accumulated possessions that had been denied the Christian poor. I asked, however, whether it was not also true that lords and bishops accumulated possessions through tithes, so that the Shepherds were not fighting their true enemies. He replied that when your true enemies are too strong, you have to choose weaker enemies. I reflected that this is why the simple are so called. Only the powerful always know with great clarity who their true enemies are.

The climate of repression and denial is very well evoked; it is obviously the source from which many of the terrors and delusions in the abbey derive. Those who brood on the imminence of Armageddon, with its visions of dreadful woman-beasts, or who employ it to frighten others, are prey to awful fears themselves. Eco writes as far as possible as if he were a denizen of the fourteenth century, but only by the most lurid imaginations of the Apocalypse (perhaps easier now than in any intervening epoch) can he recreate the holy terror by which Jorge of Burgos conceals his real purpose.

Jorge's real purpose, by preventing access to a lost book of Aristotle, is to prevent Adso from asking the question he is eventually forced to ask:

> But how can a necessary being exist totally polluted with the possible? What difference is there, then, between God and primigenial chaos? Isn't affirming God's absolute omnipotence and His absolute freedom with regard to his own choices tantamount to demonstrating that God does not exist?

Eco's *Postscript to The Name of the Rose* both confirms and questions this interpretation. He allows that any reader can find more in the book than its author intended. He suggests that many of his own themes and repetitions are subconscious or accidental (my own use of the word "curiosity" falls into this category). But, despite his playful attitude to serious textual criticisms, he insists that the reader submit to certain demands and disciplines:

> If somebody wanted to enter the abbey and live there for seven days, he had to accept the abbey's own pace. If he could not, he would never manage to read the whole book. Therefore those first hundred pages are like a penance or an initiation, and if someone does not like them, so much the worse for him. He can stay at the foot of the hill.

Elsewhere, Eco's *Postscript* is less satisfying, as when he says that his characters (Jorge in particular) have written their own parts and that a cosmology, once created, will determine the rhythm and the outcome of a novel. But his insights at least balance his frivolities, and when he jokes about readers mistaking modern texts for medieval ones, and vice versa, he is being acute:

> If a character of mine, comparing two medieval ideas, produces a third, more modern idea, he is doing exactly what culture did; and if nobody has ever written what he says, someone, however confusedly, should surely have begun to think it.

(*In These Times*, January 30–February 5, 1985)

BLUNT INSTRUMENTS

❑

I have never been able, except in my lazier moments, to employ the word *predictable* as a term of abuse. Nor has the expression *knee-jerk* ever struck me as a witty way of denigrating a set of strongly held convictions. The pseudoscientific word *Pavlovian* (which is often used by mistake to describe a nonconditioned reflex) is even less help. It is favored by the sort of sage who describes as "schizophrenic" someone who is of two minds about where to eat lunch. Such sages will also describe as "paranoid" or "conspiracy-theorist" anyone who believes that the CIA hired the Mafia to kill Fidel Castro or that the FBI sent notes to Martin Luther King, Jr., urging him to commit suicide.

Speaking purely for myself, I should be alarmed if my knee failed to respond to certain stimuli. It would warn me of a loss of nerve. I have written in the past year about the MX missile, constructive engagement, the confirmation of Edwin Meese and other *grand guignol* episodes. Naturally I hope that my arguments were original, but I would be depressed to think that anyone who knew me or my stuff could not easily have "predicted" the line I would take.

In the charmed circle of neoliberal and neoconservative journalism, however, "unpredictability" is the special emblem and certificate of self-congratulation. To be able to bray that "as a liberal, I say bomb the shit out of them" is to have achieved that eye-catching, versatile marketability that is so beloved of editors and talk-show hosts. As a lifelong socialist, I say don't let's bomb the shit out of them. See what I mean? It lacks the sex appeal, somehow. Predictable as hell.

Picture, then, if you will, the unusual difficulties faced by Charles Krauthammer, newest of the neocon mini-windbags. He has the arduous job, in an arduous time, of being an unpredictable conformist. He has the no less demanding task of making this pose appear original and, more, of making it appear courageous. At a time when the polity (as he might well choose to call it) is showing signs of Will fatigue, it can't be easy to write an attack on the United Nations or Albania or Qaddafi *and* make it seem like a lone, fearless affirmation. An average week of reading *The Washington Post* op-ed page already exposes me to appearances from George Will, William F. Buckley, Jr., Jeane Kirkpatrick, Norman Podhoretz, Emmett Tyrrell, Joseph Kraft, Rowland Evans and Robert Novak, and Stephen Rosenfeld. Clearly its editors felt that a radical new voice was needed when they turned to the blazing, impatient talents on offer in *The New Republic*—and selected Krauthammer. I dare say *Time* felt the same way when it followed suit. We live in a period when a chat show that includes Morton Kondracke considers that it has filled the liberal slot.

Of Krauthammer's book, *Cutting Edges: Making Sense of the Eighties,* with its right little, trite little title, George Will has already written that it comes from "the best new, young writer on public affairs. It is only a matter of time, and not much time, before the adjectives 'new' and 'young' will be put aside." I don't doubt it. There's certainly nothing new or young here. And it's only a matter of reading the book to make one realize that the other adjective will be not so much put aside as stuffed elsewhere.

In common with most but not all of his conservative columnist colleagues, Krauthammer does not write very well, reason very well, or know very much about anything. In common with them, too, he holds the "unpredictable" view that the United States is far too modest and retiring as a world power. In common with them, finally, he thinks that it takes an exercise of moral strength to point this out.

Do I shrink from giving an example that encapsulates all these shortcomings? I do not so shrink. Here's a paragraph, recycled from a Krauthammer column in *The New Republic:*

> In the 1984 Democratic campaign, the principal disagreement over Central America was whether the United States should station twenty advisers in Honduras (Walter Mondale's position) or zero (Gary Hart's). On Angola, El Salvador, Grenada, Lebanon and Nicaragua, the Democratic position has involved some variety of disengagement: talks, aid, sanctions, diplomacy—first. In practice this invariably means—only. Force is ruled out, effectively if not explicitly.

Scrutinizing this clumsily written passage, one is struck by the following:

1. Charles Krauthammer used to work as a speechwriter for the ridiculous Mondale. Ordinarily, he underlines this bit of his résumé in order to show that he is a former bleeding heart, knows the score, has been an insider, has seen the light, has lost his faith and therefore found his reason—all the familiar or predictable panoply of the careerist defector.

2. To have known and worked for Mondale, and to have kept a reasonably attentive eye on the press during the 1984 election, is presumably to know that Mondale publicly called for a quarantine of Nicaragua. A quarantine is an armed blockade.

3. Ronald Reagan's military excursions to Beirut, Grenada, the Honduran border, and elsewhere all received the sanctification of the House and Senate Democratic leadership. So it might be said that nobody wanting to make a case for the Democrats as appeasement-sodden buffoons could have argued it in a more unlettered, sly, and misleading manner.

Can it be that Krauthammer enjoys coveted space, and Establishment affection, more because of this manner than in spite of it? The suspicion cannot be groundless. This man actually began a column, in 1985, by telling that antique story about Calvin Coolidge and Dorothy Parker as if he had minted it himself. He believes, or at any rate he writes, that "the death of Senator Henry Jackson has left an empty stillness at the center of American politics." That would be pardonable, if corny, in an obituary piece, but it introduces a rather unexciting reflection on the fate of Cold War liberalism which omits to mention that Jackson's clones (Elliott Abrams, Richard Perle, Kirkpatrick, and other of Krauthammer's favorites) are all over the place.

In a slim field, my nomination for the most memorable and emblematic quotation would go to his view that "the great moral dilemmas of American foreign policy arise when the pursuit of security and the pursuit of democracy clash. *Contra* aid is not such a case. That is Cruz's message. Is anyone listening?" That was in *The Washington Post*—this year. It contains everything that has made Krauthammer a figure. Cliché ("moral dilemma," "pursuit"). False antithesis ("security" versus "democracy"). Pomposity (Hubert Humphrey posing as Winston Churchill in the sonorous periods of the sentencing). Banality (Arturo Cruz original at this late date?). Last and as usual, the parroting of the Reaganite party line, written as if by a lonely, ignored dissident (*Listening?* They're fighting a war for him). This is affectation, poorly executed.

In this entire salad of emissions, I could find no "cutting edges" and nothing that qualified as "against the stream" of the regnant orthodoxy. And, as a regular reader of Krauthammer, I can recall only two columns of his that I have admired. One was about the birth of his son Daniel. The other was about the absurdity and implausibility of the Star Wars project. Neither of those articles appears here—the first because it came too late to include and the second because it was Krauthammer's only moment of dissent and misgiving, and, what with one thing and another, he would rather forget it. I think I could have predicted that.

(*The Nation,* November 16, 1985)

THE BLOOD NEVER DRIES

❏

When the Chartist leader Ernest Jones first heard the boast that the British Empire was one on which the sun never set, he riposted, "And on which the blood never dries." Among the chief beauties of George MacDonald Fraser's Flashman narratives is their taste for imperial gore. Those who have followed the old braggart through his previous campaigns will remember the suicide charge of the 21st Lancers at Balaklava (in which he took part by accident), the butchery in the Khyber Pass, and the sanguinary revenge taken upon the Indian mutineers. Who can forget, also, the moment when the slave ship *Balliol College* tossed its human cargo over the side to escape arrest and detection?

Surrounded as he is by heaps of cadavers, Flashman is no Victorian Rambo. He is the perfect illustration of Dr. Arnold's precept that a bully is always a coward. Beneath his magnificent whiskers and medaled chest, there is an abject, scheming poltroon, who whimpers with fear at the sound of the foe and falls over himself to betray friends and colleagues. Anything is thinkable if it preserves him with a whole skin. The very qualities which got him expelled from Tom Brown's Rugby School—deceit, cruelty, and funk—fit him admirably as a man to take credit for the sacrifices of others.

With this episode, he is whirled up in the hellish carnage of the Taiping Revolt. In this, the bloodiest civil war in human history, China convulsed itself in an attempt to throw off the "foreign devils." Great Britain's prized opium trade—the greatest narcotics scandal of all time—was at stake. Human life was not so much cheap as barely reckoned at all. Flashman goes through the whole blood-bolted affair with his bowels like water, but he never loses his faculty for description. If you like this sort of thing, then Flashy's your man:

> When the guns haven't come up, and your cavalry's checked by close country or *tutti-putti*, and you're waiting in the hot, dusty hush for the faint rumble of *impi* or *harka* over the skyline and *know* they're twenty to your one—well, that's when you realize that it all hangs on that double line of yokels and town scruff with their fifty rounds a man and an Enfield bayonet. Kitchener himself may have placed 'em just so, with D'Israeli's sanction, *The Times'* blessing, and the Queen waving 'em good-bye—but now it's *their* grip on the stock, and *their* eye on the backsight, and if *they* break, you're done. Haven't I stood shivering behind 'em often enough, wishing I could steal a horse from somewhere?

This passage from *Flashman and the Dragon* gives the flavor of Fraser's historical sense (notice how he makes a point of the reactionary gentry's rendition of Disraeli) as well as his talent for bathos—from Sir Henry Newbolt to Schweik in one move. Not only are the Flashman books extremely funny, but they give meticulous care to authenticity. You can, between guffaws, learn from them.

There is a chapter in this book which I would select from a strong field as being exemplary. It recounts Lord Elgin's decision in 1860 to raze the Summer Palace at Peking, and it depicts the manner in which the order was carried out. The Summer Palace was not just a building. It was a gorgeous landscaped park of over two hundred temples and great houses. Contemporary accounts of it and its contents show it to have been the summit of Manchu taste and civilization, perhaps unequaled in history. Fraser, through Flashman, shows how Elgin came to his conclusion (revenge for the hideous treatment of British and French prisoners) and why he pressed on (to show the Chinese that the Son of Heaven, their emperor, was a fake). The pages which describe the actual desecration—while Elgin read Darwin and Trollope in his tent—are vivid, moving, and awful. They promote Fraser well out of the thriller class and into the ranks of historical novelists.

There is lots more, of course. We meet the cultivated Sir Garnet Wolseley, the original for "the Very Model of a Modern Major-General." F. T. Ward, the Yankee adventurer, is excellently well drawn. Flashman himself, who had been showing worrying signs of conscience in recent books, is back in midseason form. His powers of description have not deserted him ("Her skipper was one Witherspoon, of Greenock, a lean pessimist with a cast in his eye and a voice like coals being delivered"), and neither has his Stakhanovite tumescence. Old addicts will mainline *Flashman and the Dragon*. New addicts are to be envied. The words *Albion Perfide* will never sound alien again.

(The Washington Post Book World, May 4, 1986)

STYLE SECTION

❑

Hitchens had been in Washington four years, working for a magazine that might have been published on Pluto for all the clout it had. "Screw you," he would quip wryly to himself as hostesses failed to catch his eye and as movers and shakers in Georgetown and Foggy Bottom looked wildly over his shoulder upon introduction. He'd been meditating revenge ever since a taxi driver had failed to recognize his catastrophically unfashionable address, and the canker of rancor had eaten deeper as he was successively excluded from the Gridiron Club, a decent table at the White House correspondents' dinner, and—final indignities came in pairs—from the Z list at the Reagan inaugural ball and the A list at "The McLaughlin Group" advertisers' buffet.

A novel. That would show them. One of those through-the-fly-button, fly-on-the-wall novels. A novel with short, staccato sentences. Often with no verbs in them. The sort that are harder to read than they are to write (the sentences, that is).

What was necessary for success? The people didn't actually have to be characters. The Brit diplomat, for example, could be "Sir Rodney, terminally boring, from a well-known and titled family, and as rich as he was dull." The ambitious Secretary of State would, of course, be a "crusty old" figure. Color of hair? "White." Style of hair? "A mane." Type of tie? "Bow." Eyes? "Silver blue changing to steely gray." Nose? "Beaked." This kind of stuff practically wrote itself. A woman at the Soviet Embassy could be—why not?—"a short, stocky woman with an enormous chest, a rather heavy mustache, a mole on the end of her nose, and her mousy gray-brown hair pulled back in a bun."

The President, of course, would present more of a problem. You had to *have* a President, but people could tell them apart even when they had no human characteristics at all. Why not a decent, avuncular type whose good intentions were thwarted by crafty, self-seeking advisers? Not easy to believe in, admittedly, but at least a type that hadn't featured lately. Perhaps— yes—perhaps an unsuspected health problem that would get the old turkey out of the picture at the midway point. Then a drama of succession. The Vice President catapulted into the Oval Office. No need for verbs at all. The heartbeat factor.

What of sex? Try as you will, you always end up writing for men here. Hitchens collapsed into the conventions with a relief he had not suspected in himself before. Sara Adabelle Grey, the Southern darling married to the Vice President, was to find herself First Lady in a rush. Meanwhile, she was "ravishing" (several times in about six pages), "glamorous," and "fabulous." Her husband would have to make do with "distinguished" until a better word came along, which it never did. Should he have a kink? By all means. And what a kink! (He thought oral sex was overrated.) Allison Sterling, ace reporter and goddaughter to the stricken President, was "elegant, confident, and untouchable." His thesaurus in ribbons, Hitchens invented one other grande dame, Edwina Able-Smith, voracious mate to the stuffed-shirt Brit. She had "had affairs with half the richest, most powerful and famous men in the world," but she was too exhausting to appear at all after the second chapter.

The women needed men—boy, did they need men—but all they got was Desmond Shaw. Shaw was a hard-drinking Boston-Irish reporter who had a way with him. "His curly black hair was disheveled; his Burberry had the requisite stains and rips ('bullet holes'); his shirt collar was unbuttoned; his tie was loosened and there was a tiny spot on it." He had a deep voice, an occasional brogue, a smile that flattened females like pancakes; and he would do anything for a story except master English prose. There had never been an actual journalist with all these characteristics (though there had been plenty with the last one), but Hitchens knew what the public expected, and was no snob.

For more than five hundred pages, the novel turned on Des and his triflings with these two women. Whenever Hitchens introduced a new twist to the tale, he was careful to honor the forerunners of the trade. Georgetown hostesses said "divine" a lot, and also "darling." Women, when confronted with sexual innuendo, "blushed" or "flushed" or "felt the blood rush to their faces." That happened on pages 69, 77, 118, 139, 147, 149, 165, and 167 (three times). He had never seen a woman in Washington blush in this way, any more than he had seen people get drunk on one or two glasses of wine, but he knew the rules. In the fiction of the nation's capital, a bottle of hock is a bacchanalia, and half a bottle of hock at lunchtime is a debauch. An odd rule, to be sure. But not made to be broken. (Hitchens himself must have spilled about a bottle a day just getting the glass to his lips.)

Other conventions proved more troublesome and several times threatened to clog the narrative utterly. Journalism in Washington is notoriously syco-phantic. "Respectful" would be a euphemism for the behavior of reporters in the presence of the powerful. Still, for dramatic purposes, there is sup-posed to be something called an "adversary" relationship. He had dared to cast one reporter as being literally in bed with the President's wife. Did he dare show the whole press corps in bed with the presidency? He would lunch alone for the rest of his life if he did that. With a moan of shame, he found that he had written the following paragraph about a "Meet the Press" TV show. Intrepid Allison was questioning the White House Chief of Staff:

> During the campaign you were always fighting or reported to be fighting with somebody. Since you've been in the White House, there has hardly been a week when you weren't engaged in some form of combat with some colleague or staffer. . . . Do you think there is something about you which provokes these kinds of reports, and in the end, is this kind of behavior really helpful to your President?
>
> The reporter next to her gasped under his breath. "Heavy stuff . . ."

Actually, for the toadying atmosphere of 1986, this *was* quite heavy. But still he felt that he might be observing bipartisan idiocy a little too formally.

On, on—that was the answer. Reading over what he had typed, he felt a certain sense of achievement. There were some things that needed tidying, some rough edges. He noticed that he had typed, to introduce a long passage, the words, "It was a coincidence that Sonny Sterling and Sadie Grey had the same birthday." Well, what the hell else could it have been? A con-spiracy? He made a note to revise, but he never did. Then there was Allison recalling to herself, while sipping a kir, her first night of shame. " 'Now' was all he said. She didn't have time to tell him she was a virgin." What if she *had* had time? What did time have to do with it? Ah, well.

Hitchens was still nagged as he blotted the last page and wondered about movie rights. The title was good—no question. But had he avoided controversy enough, or too much? Why had nothing *happened?* Why were none of the subplots ever resolved? Why did they just disappear? He guessed that this was Washington. Anyway, too much substance and you got called an advocacy journalist.

When he heard that a leading Washington lady had beaten him to the entire formula, he was crushed out of shape. It showed that no journalist had a monopoly on ingenuity. It also meant another address where the doorman wouldn't know him.

(*The Boston Sunday Globe*, August 3, 1986)

MUGGED BY REALITY

❑

When *The Bonfire of the Vanities* was still a glint in its maker's eye, I heard the maker himself describe its intended scope as Dickensian. When pudding came to proof, the only Dickensian thing about this capacious entertainment was its serialization, episode by episode, in a monthly magazine. And, when even the readers of *Rolling Stone* forbore to ask for more, the pudding was withdrawn from the public subscription and a new recipe contrived. The final concoction is diverting, deceptively light and various, with a distinct aftertaste. Only the other week, Mayor Ed Koch of New York was angrily heckled by black citizens of Harlem as he tried to smirk his way agreeably through a commemoration of Martin Luther King, Jr. In the course of the next day, I heard more than a dozen people remark that this event was a vindication of the opening chapter of *The Bonfire of the Vanities*, wherein the mayor is thoroughly Mau Mau-ed (*and* pelted with mayonnaise). More recently, having taken an ill-advised wrong turn off the West Side Highway above 110th Street, I was impressed at the instant, uneasy jokes made by fellow passengers about the scene in *Bonfire* where a missed exit spells ruin.

In some fashion, then, Wolfe has proved his continuing ability to touch a nerve in the general subconscious. *The Bonfire of the Vanities* treats of reticence-inducing subjects like class envy, racial hatred, vaulting ambition, and hectic greed. It scorns those who try to emulsify these basic questions. At its mid-point, and rather obviously, it introduces Poe himself, via *The*

Masque of the Red Death, to show that not even Prospero can purchase immunity. The slight but definite tug of nastiness in the underlay of the text is probably necessary to qualify it as a romp through modern manners.

One thing that distinguishes this novel from the Dickensian is the relative ease with which it can be summarized. A rich and spoiled Wall Streeter named Sherman McCoy, who is innocuous rather than innocent, can hardly credit his luck in the possession of a sumptuous Park Avenue spread, a fashionable wife and adorable daughter, a lubricious mistress and a franchise upon life in general. Driving the lubricious one into town for an off-the-record soirée, he takes a wrong turn from the airport and commits the moral equivalent of a hit-and-run in the smoldering wasteland of the Bronx. A confederacy of hypocrites—the opportunist public prosecutor, the demagogic black "community" leader, the shameless Brit journalist, the ambitious attorney—combines to dismember him. Butchered to make a New York holiday, McCoy is condemned to the filthy pit of the city's nether regions, where the hideous words "criminal justice" have become oxymoronic.

The telling of this rather banal unsuccess story allows Wolfe to do some very accomplished eavesdropping. He excels at the nuances of pseudery, making clever use of the undoubted fact that, in New York society, there is no shame, no infamy, but only celebrity. At an early show-off dinner given by Leon and Inez Bavardage, McCoy fails to shine. At a dinner thrown by Silvio and Kate di Ducci after his exposure, much is made of him. Wolfe, however, cannot resist ramming home his tiny point. He compels poor Sherman to say, on the way home with his wife: "It's perverse, isn't it? Two weeks ago, when we were at the Bavardages, these same people froze me out. Now I'm smeared—*smeared!*—across every newspaper and they can't get enough of me."

This is a clunker of a nudge. We'd *noticed* that, thanks all the same! Wolfe's fondness for italics and exclamation marks is indulged to the full in this book, and I would defend it because it helps to capture the way New Yorkers *talk*. But his aptitude for names is rather hit-and-miss. Leon and Inez Bavardage are good, the di Duccis less so, Lord Gutt and Lord Buffing feeble. Nunnally Voyd, the ambivalent mid-Atlantic novelist, is just about O.K. The descriptions of place settings, fad food, décor and snob accessories come rapidly and acutely enough. If anything, Wolfe is a little *too* good at that kind of detail. Very often, he will identify or stigmatize one of his creations simply by a telling or withering register of the brand of loafers or make of briefcase. His emphasis on the "designer" aspect of today's chic saves him a good deal in the way of characterization. His obsessively *knowledgeable* touch also makes one wonder whether he really feels contempt for this sort of affectation.

The underclass and its boiling, pointless, vicious life is always "the other" in *The Bonfire*. There is a brilliantly witty and unsettling depiction of the

Bronx courthouse and its environs, which introduces Judge Myron Kovitsky, "the warrior of Masada," as he faces down a vanload of snarling felons. This highly promising early scene is not built upon. In fact, it merely inaugurates a whole series of unbuttoned sequences in which ethnicity among cops, lawyers, and defendants is paramount. As in John Gregory Dunne's *Red White and Blue*, the new bluntness about such matters is presented with defiant insouciance. No doubt, this candor is refreshing to many. I lost count of the number of times that Wolfe employed animal noises to represent human ones when venturing across the tracks. His fabled ear has evidently not lost its cunning.

Upon one ethnic stereotype, however, Wolfe plays a genuinely unfashionable hand. He writes with some mordancy about the English exiles of Manhattan, expressing an educated dislike for members of that inexplicably popular minority. They turn out here to be chiefly spongers and queens, posturing for their supper and then sniggering at the vulgarity and gullibility of their hosts. Much American Anglophobia is rather ill-informed and fails to draw the requisite blood. Wolfe knows better. Here is Peter Fallow, Brit-on-the-make who is suffering himself to be bought a costly lunch by a source: "Fallow stopped listening. There was no way Vogel could be deflected from his course. He was irony-proof." Other passages, too lengthy for quotation, establish Wolfe as unsettlingly *au courant* with the freeloaders from the Old Country.

An insight of the stricken McCoy's which Wolfe likes enough to repeat is that: "A liberal is a conservative who's been arrested." This makes a neat but obvious inversion of Irving Kristol's likable remark that "a neoconservative is a liberal who's been mugged by reality." That gag more or less opened the Reagan era—guilt-free; hostile to self-criticism; impatient with the sickly platitudes of reform and "compassion." And this is, in every line and trope, a Reagan-era novel. It foreshadows rather than anticipates the collapse of the Wall Street commodity fiesta. It depicts a society of narcissism and debauch, where everything is on sale and where Thomas Hobbes has been thoroughly internalized. The characters in Wolfe's world indeed know the price of everything and the value of nothing. Yet the total effect is not so much a satire on these *mores* as it is an expression of them. Reading Wolfe, you could suppose that New York City over the past decade had seen the victimization of the rich by the poor, the white by the black. The only figures who are actually painted as responsible for their actions are the bigmouth tribunes of Harlem and the Bronx. All the others, reprehensible and avaricious as they may be, are the mere playthings of circumstance. The chaotic ending, which is fictionally very weak and overwrought, takes the form of a vile mob scene in which the dominant emotion is *Exterminate All the Brutes!*

The city argot is well-caught, the social absurdities are lovingly etched, and there is the best description of an Englishman awakening to a primordial hangover since *Lucky Jim*. But the people are mostly representatives, who strut and fret their moment. And when Wolfe decides to mingle with the luckless and the downtrodden, he does so in the person of Mistah Kurtz rather than Mr. Pickwick.

(*The Times Literary Supplement*, March 18–24, 1988)

DATELINES

NICARAGUA LIBRE

❑

Toward the close of his *Memoirs of a Revolutionary*, Victor Serge contemplated the fate of the "socialist experiment." Faced with a miserable Mexican exile and oppressed by the spread of totalitarian ideas, he reflected on the ideas of the betrayed Russian revolution and wrote:

> It is often said that "the germ of all Stalinism was in Bolshevism at its beginning." Well, I have no objection. Only, Bolshevism also contained many other germs—a mass of other germs—and those who lived through the enthusiasm of the first years of the first victorious revolution ought not to forget it. To judge the living man by the death germs which the autopsy reveals in a corpse—and which he may have carried in him since his birth—is this very sensible?

I went to Nicaragua, as I had gone to Cuba, Angola, Zimbabwe, Grenada, and other such *focos*, not as a tourist of revolution but as a very amateur biochemist. How were the bacilli doing? Which were becoming the dominant strain? In other words, would Nicaragua turn into another frowsty barracks socialism, replete with compulsory enthusiasm and affirming only the right to agree?

I tried deliberately to screen out all the pseudointellectual special pleading about "double standards" with which my hometown of Washington is awash. In that town, the conservatives (who do not believe that there are laws of history) believe that the law of history is that all revolutions evolve into totalitarianism. For them, Nicaragua is a macho test of Western "will" versus cretinous appeasement. The liberals change the subject by talking of human rights in the here and now, and by arguing in rather a wheedling manner that the business community in Managua is still free and we mustn't "drive them into the arms of Moscow." The Left, or what remains of it, has a tendency to change the subject too. Surely Nicaragua is better than the abattoir states of El Salvador and Guatemala, which enjoy American imperial patronage? If there are "problems," do they not result from blockade, sabotage, and the hiring of mercenary thugs by the CIA? And anyway (raising the voice a little), what right have Western commentators to pass judgment on the struggling poor who are trying to cancel generations of underdevelopment? It is both striking and depressing to see the three main "schools" still frozen in their Bay of Pigs or Tonkin Gulf attitudes. A tribute, anyway, to the persistence of ideology and tradition.

I don't affect to be above this battle (and I still think that the Left comes out best of the three). But I was looking for the worst and was determined not to come away saying things like: "You have to remember the specific conditions." The Sandinistas make large claims for a revolution in liberty, for socialism with a human face, for a new kind of American state, for the fusion of the best in the two opposing world systems. This time, they seem to say, will be different. It didn't seem patronizing to take them up on it.

They don't tell you what an extraordinarily beautiful country it is. Managua, of course, is a famous hell-hole, combining the worst of the Third World and the tackiest of the New, with its sprawling barrios (where Reagan's sanctions will tighten already exiguous belts) and its crass, nasty Hotel Intercontinental. In between—nothing much. Until the FSLN cleared the earthquake rubble from 1972, there were the beginnings of an urban jungle in the real sense. Lianas and creepers were spreading everywhere, and along with them the exciting prospect of snakes, parrots, and pumas in midtown. How like Macondo that would have been, and what stirring copy.

In the interior, though, ravishing Castilian architecture, cool colonial verandas and courtyards, mountain resorts, lava plains, riotous jungles and forests. Nicaragua is a caesura between the Atlantic and the Pacific; built on an earthquake fault and precarious to a degree. The great volcano at Masaya, with its enormous crater full of swirling green parrots, makes such a hypnotic inhaling noise that the Spanish conquerors put up a huge cross to ward off the breath of the Evil One. Miraculous virgins have appeared recently in this land, and the most frantic rumors are small change. The only calm spots are to be found on the shores of the giant inland ocean of Lake Nicaragua. Here Pablo Antonio Cuadra wrote his *Songs of Cifar and the Sweet Sea*, which represents the lake as the Aegean of his Odyssey, and here the fishermen do their millennial stuff. Here, also, various American adventurers of the last century planned to build the first isthmian canal and to recruit Nicaragua as a slave state into the Union. Not far from the lake and the volcano is Monimbo, an Indian town where, in legend and in fact, the insurrection against Somoza and the Americans began.

Nicaragua is a country where writers have always been impelled into politics, or exile, or both. Rubén Darío had to leave the stifling backwardness of the country in order to conduct his experiments in modernism. Sergio Ramírez spent much of his life as a Berliner. The poet Rigoberto López could see no future at all, and killed the elder Somoza in what he must have known was a suicide attack. The last Somoza had such utter contempt (per-haps as a result) for the literary and intellectual life of the country that he helped to fuse the intelligentsia into a unanimous front against his rule. But, with his dynasty abolished, the unifying effect has disappeared also. Taking the writers of Nicaragua as the specially sensitive register of the country's affairs, I spent most of my time talking to two men, former friends and still mutual admirers, who exemplify the depth and the intensity of the breach in the Nicaraguan revolution.

Sergio Ramírez is the nation's leading novelist and one of the few non-uniformed members of the Sandinista directorate. He serves as vice-presi-dent to Daniel Ortega and was the founder of Los Doce (the Group of Twelve), which mobilized civilian and intellectual support for the revolution. His novel *Te dió miedo la sangre?* is published in English as *To Bury Our Fathers*, because the translation ("Were You Scared of the Blood?") sounded too much like a thriller.

Pablo Antonio Cuadra is a poet known well beyond the confines of his own country. He publishes the review *El Pez y la serpiente* ("The Fish and the Snake") and edits the literary supplement of the right-wing anti-Sandinista news sheet *La Prensa*. A disillusioned ex-supporter of the Somoza family, he counts himself a supporter of the 1979 "Triumph," which he now regards as a revolution betrayed.

Sergio Ramírez was acting president on the night that I saw him, because Daniel Ortega had winged off to Moscow. Our five-hour conversation was punctuated only three times—twice by calls from Ortega and once by an earth tremor which first removed and then replaced the smiles on the faces of the guards. I, who knew no better, decided to take their relative insou-ciance at face value. Ramírez, on the other hand, sprang to his feet and ordered the doors thrown open. In an earthquake zone, you are ever ready for the moment when you may have to stand under the lintel. Also, a door temporarily shut can become a door permanently jammed.

Our discussion was bounded by these two analogies. Like every Sandi-nista, Ramírez expects that one day the *yanquis* will bring the roof in by invasion. And, like most visitors, I wanted to know whether "temporary expedients" like censorship, informing, and conscription would harden into a permanent system.

It was not the first time, evidently, that Ramírez had been confronted by the second line of questioning. Considering that he was speaking on the record as acting president, in a week when the White House had announced economic sanctions, he displayed considerable candor and skepticism about the course of the revolution. So, sometimes, does Fidel Castro (who also likes late-night sessions with foreign guests). So I tried my best to be unimpressed.

Before the "Triumph" there were many discussions about writing and culture. We felt that we might have the first opportunity to test ourselves in a society where writers have always had a role. But there was a temptation to develop a "line"—and I call it temptation because of the old idea that art should "serve." We knew of the negative experiences of other socialist and Third World countries. But we decided on a policy of complete creative freedom.

At our first assembly of writers in the National Palace, I made, and later published, a speech. I warned that we don't need a recipe or a line. I don't mind experiments by our "workshop" poets, though there is a risk of doggerel. The result of an individual's intimate work, though, must not be despised.

One sees what he means about the workshop poets. I came across a stanza by Carlos Galan Pena of the Police Complex Workshop, who writes to his beloved Lily:

> *You and I are the Revolution*
> *and I am filled with my work*
> *and you spend hours and hours*
> *. . . in the Office of Propaganda.*

The best that can be said here is that Ernesto Cardenal's Ministry of Culture is encouraging people who have never thought of themselves as writers before.

I ask Ramírez about the dismal state of writing in Cuba and the persecution of authors like Heberto Padilla. He responds rather cautiously that it is "necessary to be present" in a revolution and that those who defect have in essence surrendered. But he says that Padilla is "not a bad poet—and there are rights which everyone involved in criticism must have." For the first five years of the revolutionary government, says Ramírez, he himself did not write at all for fear of producing politicized or didactic prose.

I suggest to him that there is an axiomatic connection between writing and pluralism, and mention Orwell's remark about the imagination, like certain wild animals, being unable to breed in captivity. I've always thought that the observation has its weaknesses, because of the long tradition of clandestine and "opposition" literature, but that it definitely expresses a truth. Ramírez agrees with enthusiasm. "We don't censor the cultural section of *La Prensa,*" he claims (incidentally admitting that they do censor the rest of it). He shows a knowledgeable admiration for Milan Kundera and says that he cannot blame him for choosing exile over military occupation. But he criticizes him as "simplistic—totalitarianism doesn't come only from the East."

To Bury Our Fathers deals with two generations of Nicaraguan life under the ancien régime. Ramírez claims that every incident in it actually took place, at least in the sense that oral history has established certain episodes as having "actually happened." Nicaragua is a country alive with myths and rumors. The brain of its greatest poet, Rubén Darío, for instance, has gone missing. Its dimensions were reputedly enormous; a "fact" which greatly impressed the provincial minds of the time. Possession of the preserved cerebellum seemed important, but somehow it got mislaid, and every now and then a fresh piece of gossip about its whereabouts goes humming on its rounds. And nobody knows where Sandino is buried. His body was interred hugger-mugger by the American-trained Somocistas who betrayed and murdered him. Strenuous, fruitless efforts have been made to locate his grave (which may well be under the runway of the Managua airport), but perhaps it's a relief that no embalming of that corpse will ever take place.

In many ways, rumor and myth are the enemies of the Sandinistas. The CIA manual that was written for the right-wing terrorists is obviously strong on such matters as assassination, the use of local criminal networks, and the techniques of economic sabotage. But it also places a heavy accent on the spreading of slander and alarm. Stories about Sandinista orgies or the nationalization of the family are staples. And, whether you believe the Graham Greene or the Mario Vargas Llosa version, there is the Virgin of Cuapa.

Cuapa is a nothing town in Chontales province, where on May 8, 1981, a local sacristan named Bernardo found himself in conversation with the Virgin Mary. In a succession of appearances, she told him that "Nicaragua has suffered a great deal since the earthquake and, if you do not change, Nicaragua will continue to suffer and you will hasten the coming of the Third World War." Our Lady showed a shrewd grasp of contemporary politics when she described the Sandinistas as "atheists and communists, which is why I have come to help the Nicaraguans. They have not kept their promises. If you ignore what I ask, communism will spread throughout America."

This is higher than the usual standard of the Christian Democratic miracle. In its pedantic toeing of the State Department line (especially the artful bit about the FSLN not keeping its promises), it outdoes Fatima in 1917 or the repeated counterrevolutionary uses of the blood of San Gennaro. Despite official downplayings and denunciation of "bourgeois Mariolatry" by the liberation-theology faction, the Virgin of Cuapa, in some sense, lives. She is a decisive weapon in the campaign to get peasants to join a Vendée run by their former masters.

Ramírez, who describes his whole literary endeavor as a conscious struggle against the seductive, fantastical influence of Gabriel García Márquez, smilingly says that "as a writer, of course, I believe in the Virgin of Cuapa." But the Sandinistas possess what they consider to be a more potent icon. There is nobody in Nicaragua who dares oppose the spirit of Augusto César Sandino. Even his former enemies pay homage to him in their pamphlets and broadcasts, and one presumes that they would not bother to counterfeit a bankrupt currency. Disgruntled stall-holders who dislike the regime will tell you that, in spite of everything, they feel prouder to be Nicaraguan these days. One is, in vulgar terminology, either a Sandinista or—one of Sandino's favorite expletives—a *vendepatria*: seller of the country. In conversation, Ramírez discloses how this mythology, too, can make you a captive.

I had asked him what he thought to be his government's greatest mistake. He replied that I was drawing on a large repertoire, but he chose to illustrate his answer by way of an episode from his forthcoming book about Julio Cortázar:

> On the day that we took over the American-owned mines on the Atlantic coast, Julio was with us. I wanted to show him what we had found. There were files on every worker. One, for example, was the file of a man who had labored there from 1951 until one week before "the Triumph." He was listed as having been fired. Under the heading "Cause for Dismissal" was the entry "killed in an accident." I can show this surreal file and many others like it. They would sack dead workers in order to avoid paying compensation. And we also captured the records of the "personal tax" that the owners paid to Somoza in order to get away with it. His regime had a *carnal, sensual* relationship with the United States.
>
> The mines themselves were worthless—another piece in the Somoza museum of horrors. The machinery was useless; fit only to be worked by the cheapest labor. Nationalizing gained us nothing. But we did it to show that an era had ended. It was an act of love as much as hatred. Maybe it was a mistake.

In Chile and Argentina, he says, the middle and upper classes are a real social force, powerfully organized and with a real presence. In Nicaragua, they are a mere shadow thrown by foreign influence, an "appendage of the United States." *Vendepatrias*, in fact? "I don't like such simplistic phrases."

Oh, doesn't he? Pablo Antonio Cuadra sits in his dingy office at *La Prensa literaria*, talking about his old friend Sergio Ramírez (*"un buen hombre de letras"*) and saying that anti-Americanism is a local contagion. The hemisphere, admittedly, is dominated by the United States, but there is too much inclination to blame the *yanquis* for everything. "And radicalization is like the lianas in the jungle—it swallows you up. Sergio should be writing, not trying to be a politician. The FSLN have thrown away the revolution— the most magnificent moment that Nicaragua ever had." Cuadra is prepared to say that the situation is actually worse than it was ten years ago under Somoza—"if you omit his last few weeks of terror and bombing," when he ordered his own capital strafed from the air.

I ask Cuadra what his attitude would be to a United States invasion. This, he says, is "a horrible question. The Americans might negate even the original revolution. But to imitate the Soviet Union is the most macabre thing of all." More macabre than a Somocista restoration? "Sí. It is more difficult to remove."

Cuadra is not a particularly expert political commentator—as I said earlier, there was a time when he professed a nationalistic enthusiasm for the Somoza dynasty, and he has that worst of qualifications in a revolution: the reputation of being a late joiner. Toward the end of the Somoza terror, he wrote a defense of Ramírez's literary faction Los Doce, which got him into hot water. *La Prensa* is a vulgar, sensational, superstitious, right-wing propaganda sheet, which publishes lies and distortions on a scale that even Western diplomats find embarrassing. Cuadra's name, under the sonorous title of "Don Pablo Antonio," appears on the masthead as its director, together with that of Jaime Chamorro. The Sandinista party paper *Barricada* used to be edited by Carlos Chamorro, his brother. *Nuevo diario,* the other leftist daily, is edited by Xavier Chamorro, another family member. Chamorro, Chamorro, and Chamorro. . . .

In spite of his links to the shabby politics of the main paper, Cuadra's defense of his own section, *La Prensa literaria,* is soundly based. I ask him whether there is not something inescapably political about Latin American contemporary writers—Neruda, Fuentes, Márquez, Cortázar, Vargas Llosa, even Borges? Is this automatically unhealthy? Not at all, he replies. Every one of us has been politicized, and life itself *(la vida)* is political. But very few of these writers have mixed their literary work with their politics— except for Neruda, whose downfall as a writer it was. Even Márquez keeps his polemics in a separate compartment. It is, in other words, not politics but politicization that must be avoided.

To Ramírez's claim that the first assembly of Nicaraguan writers repudiated a "line" or a "recipe," Cuadra replies that he remembers it well. "Cortázar was there and so was I. There were great proclamations about artistic freedom from Sergio and Ernesto Cardenal. I even had Cuban friends who said that this might have a good influence in Havana. But within a year, *Ventana* was publishing Fidel Castro's notorious speech to the intellectuals, saying that "within the Revolution, complete freedom; against the Revolution, none." *Ventana* is the Sandinistas' literary and cultural magazine. I suddenly recall Ramírez saying that it was "boring." It is edited by Daniel Ortega's wife.

Ramírez says that Cuadra is a great poet who doesn't understand revolution. Cuadra says that Ramírez is a great novelist who has become intoxicated by politics. Ramírez and Cardenal say that restrictions on liberty result from the exigencies of war and blockade, and from the threat of invasion. Cuadra says that they result from a dogmatic, ideological tendency inherent in the FSLN. Ramírez says that Nicaragua will not become "like Bulgaria." Cuadra grants that so far there is no imposed socialist realism, but says that many of his contributors are asking to be published anonymously and that there is a general tendency toward "the correct."

It is possible to conclude rather glibly that both men are right and that Nicaragua is becoming a hybrid or a compromise. Mario Vargas Llosa, for example, takes the view that the Sandinistas will become like the ruling party in Mexico, the so-called Institutional Revolutionary Party, which retains the lion's share of power and patronage without acquiring a total monopoly. This sort of diagnosis treats a very volatile present as somehow static. Ramírez doesn't want conformity and Cuadra doesn't want the forcible reimposition of right-wing dictatorship. Both men may be optimists.

In spite of the brave and, I believe, genuine aspirations of Sergio Ramírez, there are symptoms of an encroaching orthodoxy in Nicaragua. During our conversations, for example, he used the terms "one-party society" and "closed society" as synonymous. Today's Nicaragua is, at least in the cities, a multiparty *society*. The posters and emblems of the Conservatives (who really are conservative) and the Liberals (who really are not liberal) are everywhere. Likewise those of the Communists (who really are communist). But it is a one-party *state*. All the power worth having belongs to the FSLN; the broadcasting station and the armed forces are both officially called "Sandinista." In foreign policy, despite some anomalies, the "line" is pretty solidly Warsaw Pact–oriented. And, in cultural matters, a sort of dull utilitarianism is creeping in. Even Ramírez is not proof against it. Denial of newsprint to the opposition, for example, is due to "the rationing of scarce resources." The unavailability of books and magazines, except from the East, is due to "the lack of foreign exchange." There is an important half-truth in these claims. But they are just the sort of euphemisms that led, through many false dawns, to the Zhdanovization of culture in Cuba.

The Sandinistas say that they welcome honest criticism, and I did notice that they were irritated by Western sycophancy, of which there is a plentiful supply from some of their visitors. So I'm happy to have a "concrete" test to apply. On April 6, 1984, Father Ernesto Cardenal wrote to his friend Lawrence Ferlinghetti from the Ministry of Culture, promising that censorship of opposition newspapers would end the following month when the elections began. It didn't. Father Cardenal is a devout Catholic and was a friend of Thomas Merton (two qualifications he shares with Pablo Antonio Cuadra). These facts are often cited, by observers like Graham Greene, as proof of the good Father's commitment to freedom and pluralism. Why not as proof of his readiness to believe anything—like his wide-eyed admiration of the austere absence of materialism among the Cubans?

In numerous respects, the Sandinista revolution *is* its own justification. Despite some exaggerated claims, the achievements in social welfare and education are spectacular and moving. So is the fact that, after a half-century and more of tutelage, the country is no longer a ditto to the wishes of the United States. But the only way to justify the gradual emergence of a party-state is by continual reference to the neighboring fascisms and the menace of imperialist invasion. And I would rather leave that job to the cadres of sincere, credulous, self-sacrificing American youth who are everywhere to be found in Nicaragua. ("Look, man, the people care more about full bellies than about freedom in the abstract.") Their motive is generally religious, and likewise their method of argument. I have seen this movie before, most recently in Grenada, where Maurice Bishop abolished such independent media as there were and then had no means of appealing to the people when his own turn came.

The contortions and ambiguities of the Left are familiar. What about those of the Right? Pablo Antonio Cuadra told me, almost visibly squirming, that the worst thing the CIA had ever done was to finance and train the Somocista terrorists in the north. It seems that counterrevolutions consume their children too—nobody who has seen the Contras' work can doubt that they would emulate Guatemala and El Salvador if they got the chance. And regimes like that are just as hard to remove as Stalinist ones. In addition, they don't even claim to be trying to raise the economic "floor" on which most people have to live the one life that is allowed to them.

This is why no conversation with a Sandinista lasts for more than a few minutes before coming up against the name of Salvador Allende. By murdering him, and by collapsing Chilean society into a dictatorship, Kissinger and his confreres educated a whole generation of Latin American radicals. Pluralism is now seen by many of them as a trap or a snare; an invitation to make yourself vulnerable; a none-too-subtle suggestion of suicide. Stand in the middle of the road, and you get run down. Did not Sandino surrender to his murderers and under a safe-conduct? The fact that this argument can lead to disastrous conclusions (as it did with Maurice Bishop, who used it all the time) does not diminish its force or its relevance.

And the Nicaraguan opposition does not believe in democracy. Its leaders will tell you so. The cardinal dislikes the revolution because it promises free education and teaches Darwin in the schools ("atheist indoctrination"). The rightist parties, and most of the centrist ones, are mostly organized around one caudillo and say openly that they would be happy to come to power by force or with the aid of a foreign power. Most deplorable in many ways are the American liberals, who have now voted to aid the Contras in the hope of avoiding the accusation of "appeasement" from Ronald Reagan. These people never thought of Central America as "critical" when it was a sweltering, superficially tranquil serfdom. To deem a country worthy of your attention—possibly, of your military attention—only when it explodes from misery and neglect: this is the highest and most callous form of irresponsibility. North American *bien-pensants* have more to apologize for than they can ever realize. As Victor Serge put it:

> A feeble logic, whose finger beckons us to the dark spectacle of the Stalinist Soviet Union, affirms the bankruptcy of Bolshevism, followed by that of Socialism. . . . Have you forgotten the other bankruptcies? What was Christianity

doing in the various catastrophes of society? What became of Liberalism? What has Conservatism produced, in either its enlightened or its reactionary form? If we are indeed honestly to weigh out the bankruptcy of ideology, we shall have a long task ahead of us. And nothing is finished yet.

What, then, of the bacilli? The healthy ones are still alive and still circulating. As Ramírez said to me, "Without the confrontation with the United States, we could put Nicaragua under a glass bell and experiment in freedom." And, as Cuadra told me, without some of the pressure from abroad, things might be proceeding further along the Castroite path. Both men are still free to speak, and both of their futures will be significant monitors. The critical, forensic finding seems to me to be this: Nicaragua has logged six years of revolutionary government after half a century of the Somozas and more than a century of humiliating colonial subordination. It has done so with hardly any vengeance or massacre—capital punishment has been abolished, and some Sandinistas now say they wish they *had* shot the Somocista Old Guard instead of releasing it to reincarnate in Honduras and Miami. It has not avoided all the mistakes and crimes of previous revolutions, but it has at least made a self-conscious effort to do so. The Stalinist bacilli are at work all right, but they do not predominate as yet, and there is nothing that says they have to. Perhaps one should beware, anyway, of biological analogies. On the shirts and badges of the American "advisers" in Honduras is a monogram that predates Marx and Lenin, and, probably accidentally, has an echo of an earlier Crusade. Emblazoned with a skull and crossbones, it reads: Kill 'Em All—Let God Sort 'Em Out!

(*Granta* 16, 1985)

THE CATHOUSE
AND THE CROSS

❏

THE CATHOUSE

Gloria César's is open for business behind a fortified door off the Avenida Roosevelt in San Salvador. The guard on the door is surly and torpid, the crone who brings the meanly poured drinks is unsmiling and pretends not to have heard of a Cuba Libre, the moneyed Salvadoran men at the bar do not give newcomers any grin of complicity. When the joint is plunged into candlelight by a blackout from a guerrilla bomb attack, there is no blitz humor on offer. Our little party—made up of one randy American, one undecided American, and my purely anthropological self—does not get the "number one Johnny" treatment that Americans in Saigon or Bangkok were and are accustomed to. Yet this sourness and reserve has nothing in it of national pride. It is a compound of the simultaneous servility and resentment that this country's Establishment has had to internalize.

"For the first time in the history of U.S. foreign aid, the level of U.S. aid now exceeds a country's own contribution to its budget. . . . U.S. funding for fiscal year 1987 stands at $608 million, equal to 105 percent of El Salvador's $582 million contribution to its own most recent budget." So runs a recent report to Congress. You can read the same relationship on the faces of the army public-relations men, the soldiers at the checkpoints, and the management of Gloria César's. It is the expression worn by people who know that their paymasters are slightly ashamed of them. They need the North American subvention. But they don't need the attention that comes with it—the fact finders, the journalists, the missionaries, the troublemakers. These little groups make about an inch of difference in the vast design that is being scrawled across the country. Yet it is in that inch that many, many Salvadorans live—and die.

One of the younger whores comes to our table and demurely accepts a drink. She doesn't in the least mind submitting to a few questions, despite glares from the other girls. In El Salvador, she says, little shame attaches to her profession. Too many women have to resort to it, for *la vida*. She herself does it to support three children. And, if there is no shame, how does the children's father feel? She doesn't know, she says, quite where her husband is.

It isn't possible, in El Salvador, to make any further inquiry. The man might be working in the United States, or he might have moved to another province. But a banal discussion about *la vida* can too swiftly become a harrowing revelation about *la muerte*. In every conversation there lurks the memory and the present reality of terror. You do not need a very vivid imagination to detect a whiff of "the unmentionable odor of death." And imagination receives continual, incongruous promptings. There is a buzzard surplus in this country, for instance. Many a gallows joke is made when these circling beauties, elegant from a distance, are spotted. After one grueling interview with a survivor, I was jolted to see a cinema advertising the film *Los Muchachos perdidos*. A few blocks away was another cinema, this time featuring an imported nerd movie under the translation *La Universidad del desorden*. Was I being solemn in thinking at once of the National University, closed by an army massacre, and of ORDEN, the old acronym for the death squads? I must have had the Lost Boys somewhere in mind when I was arrested for a full minute by the illuminated sign of a Chinese restaurant near the cathedral. There were the neon words CHAP SUEY. The implications seemed impossibly macabre.

It must be unhealthy to keep returning to the subject of the death squads and to the site of El Playón, the gulch on the outskirts of town where the bodies were dumped, with all the flagrant, hysterical pride in display that a lunatic might take in exposing himself, by some of the more primitive recipients of American aid. Obviously, it's unwholesome to keep on about that. And of course it's morbid to dwell upon the disappeared, who were denied even the dignity of a last appearance at El Playón. It isn't for nothing that the Hotel Camino Real hosts Dale Carnegie conferences, or that Jimmy Swaggart opens a large office and rents the local football stadium. What El Salvador needs is to put the past behind it and to break with the sickly introspection that comes with bereavement. The embassy of the world's greatest amnesiac is on hand, replete with every manifestation of uplift and goodwill, to urge a concentration on the future. Its employees and representatives are celebrated for their attitude to bygones, which, they affirm, should be bygones.

There are two means by which a nightmare like the Salvadoran massacres can be assimilated and forgiven, if not forgotten. The first is by a full investigation and hearing, which can requite the victims and punish the murderers and the torturers. This was the road taken by the Argentine authorities when they established the Nunca Más ("Never Again") Commission in 1983.

And the second is a concerted effort at denial, euphemism, and evasion. In this option, the perpetrators agree to forgive themselves and to leave the forgetting to others. This was the method adopted by the Salvadoran ruling class—in 1932. The best condensed description of the events of that year may be found in Jeane Kirkpatrick's celebrated book *Dictatorships and Double Standards*:

> General Maximiliano Hernández Martínez, who governed El Salvador from 1931 to 1944, had been Minister of War in the cabinet of President Arturo Araújo when there occurred widespread uprisings said to be the work of Communist agitators. General Hernández Martínez then staged a coup and ruthlessly suppressed the disorders—wiping out all those who participated, hunting down their leaders. It is sometimes said that 30,000 persons lost their lives in the process. To many Salvadorans the violence of this repression seems less important than the fact of restored order and the thirteen years of civil peace that ensued. The traditionalist death squads that pursue revolutionary activists and leaders in contemporary El Salvador call themselves Hernández Martínez brigades, seeking thereby to place themselves in El Salvador's political tradition and communicate their purposes.

This tradition and these purposes have, it must be said, been communicated extremely well. A few days after a fresh paroxysm of murders had taken place in the city, I sat talking with Ricardo Stein, one of the country's few Jewish intellectuals and a development worker who has the faculty of commanding respect among all political factions. I put to him the obvious journalistic question of the hour: Were the traditionalists starting up again in earnest? He answered laconically that he suspected otherwise. "The carnage," as he called it, had made its point. "The carnage" had terrified those it had not killed. "The carnage," he said in a striking phrase, had had "a pedagogic effect." All that was necessary these days was an occasional well-chosen reminder.

In Chile in 1973, journalists and deputies loyal to the Allende government started to receive anonymous postcards in their mail. The cards bore the single inscription *Djakarta*. Many of the recipients threw the cards away, unaware of the intended hieroglyphic purpose. Chile had no memory of massacre and torture; it was not until later in the year that the supporters of *Unidad Popular* realized that their local traditionalists had been studying the Indonesia of 1965.

When billets-doux started arriving from the Hernández Martínez brigades in 1979 or so, no Salvadoran had any difficulty in recognizing the traditionalist code. A body that has once felt the current will twitch at the sight of the cattle prod. It may or may not be coincidence that the most commonly cited figure for the carnage of 1932 is the same—thirty thousand—as the estimated toll of 1982. During the latter carnage, many reporters and diplomats wrote as if covering the irrational. This campaign of death, it seemed, had no shame. Were there no wiser heads? Didn't they know how it *looked?* How it *played?* This was naïve. The traditionalists were well aware of their audience, and well rehearsed for their performance, too. And who were the squeamish going to call? The police?

I don't think it quite hit me until I went to call on María Julia Hernández, the stout, cheerful, stoic woman who runs the farcically overstretched human-rights office at the archbishopric. In her battered quarters, daily swamped by petitioners, we were discussing the case of two campesinos who had turned up, beaten to death and with the initials of a leftist party scrawled on their chests. Some people, said María Julia, had claimed that this was a common rural crime masked as a political one. She herself was not of this opinion. The killing bore the signature of *los escuadrones de la muerte*—the traditionalists. How, I inquired, did she decipher this signature? Well, the deaths had taken place at a time of night when civilians have to be off the roads. And there was a barracks very near the scene of the crime. The local people had said . . . As she accumulated the circumstances, I realized that the nearer the forces of law and order, the more experience had taught her to look for an official culprit. So, add one more condition for the proper investigation and assimilation of a trauma of mass murder. In order to be summed up and dealt with, *it must stop*. The Salvadoran murder mill has not stopped. It has only, for pedagogic purposes, taken to grinding a little more slowly.

Induction can give one the same reeling sensation. The Reagan Administration says that traditionalist murder must cease, or at any rate decline noticeably, before military aid can be given. Oliver North and other officers testify before Congress that "pressure" has been employed to reduce traditionalist murder. The only people Oliver North or Ronald Reagan can "pressure" are the armed forces of El Salvador. Traditionalist murder then declines noticeably. Yet nobody is ever convicted of, or charged with, a traditionalist murder. Military aid from the United States thereupon rises to a level of nearly $2 million a day. You can state these unchallenged facts in any order you please, and what they say is this: in return for admitting publicly and generally to the murder of thirty thousand civilians, the traditionalist armed forces are rewarded with $608 million per annum. As at Gloria César's, this transaction is one that degrades both parties while leaving them both, in contrasting ways, temporarily better off.

The traditionalists in El Salvador were actually more adventurous in the 1980s than they had been in the 1930s. In the 1930s, the targets were mainly peasants and those of Indian provenance, the latter ceasing to be a feature in several provinces. And after the slaughter, the newspapers and records of the period were destroyed, removed even from libraries and museums. (The illiterate, it must have been assumed, had already got the point.)

In the 1980s, the carnage was flaunted in the face of what is sometimes called the international community. There seemed to be a certain relish in the idea that nobody was safe. The archbishop of San Salvador shot down at the service of Mass; four American nuns raped and murdered; two conservative American trade-union officials shot to death in the San Salvador Sheraton coffee shop. But if it hadn't been that bad, would the perpetrators have earned so much American aid?

"Class" in El Salvador, as one rapidly discovers, means two different things. It means class all right, as we might find it in a Marxist primer. There they all are: the superexploited land-hungry peasants, the strike-hardened proletarians of the foreign-owned factory belt, and the fifty percent or so chronically unemployed. Then we have the underdeveloped middle class, which seems to produce revolutionary doctors, lawyers, and poets in some profusion. And—yes—the upper class as scripted by Buñuel. On an ordinary day, perhaps two dozen pages of *El Diario de hoy*, one of the capital's few surviving newspapers and an arm of Roberto d'Aubuisson's ARENA party, are consecrated to *la vida social*. The lights must never go down. The music must always play. You may go to the Paradise restaurant in the chic Zona Rosa and see the alligator-infested shirts and the terminally bejeweled women. As far as I could discern, the specialty of the *casa* was *always* lobster thermidor, as if any other crustacean would be a sign of appeasement and weakness. I had to pass a conspicuously armed guard to get at it, all the same. In the *rincón* across the road, a huge picture of Franco adorns the back wall, together with an illuminated panel giving his last testament to the people of Spain.

The other declension of the word class is derived from the Spanish word *tanda*, which means a class at the military academy. It's as well to know about military gradations because El Salvador is, as used to be said of Prussia, not a country that has an army but an army that has a country. For generations, long before the Russian and Cuban revolutions, the national product was usurped and annexed by a military caste with no external enemies and no raison d'être save enrichment and perpetuation. In the Casa Presidencial is a vast portrait of the founder of the Salvadoran army. He clutches a scroll of paper which reads: "The Republic shall live as long as the army shall live." Every position taken in domestic politics depends on some interpretation of that claim, which certainly implies the menacing and weird notion of an army actually outliving its host.

A vignette of the predatory character of this class was supplied by the 1986 case of the army kidnapping ring. A number of Salvadoran businessmen found themselves taken hostage and held for ransom by Leninist guerrillas, and they parted with millions in American dollars to save their own hides. Their ire was great when they discovered that the "guerrillas" were actually senior officers in the armed forces. The standing of the victims was high enough to secure that rare thing—a judicial inquiry. And a startling confession by one of the members of the extortion racket led to the direct implication of Lieutenant Colonel Roberto Mauricio Staben, along with a number of graduates of his "class." Himself no mean traditionalist (he used to mount guard over El Playón), Staben flatly refused to report for questioning even when summoned by a military commission. Three witnesses against him thereupon expired in prison. The American Embassy was moved to issue a statement deploring this turn of events and noting that the said witnesses "may have had valuable information that could have shed more light on the case." But in spite of testimony against him by Isidro López Sibrian, who happens to be the prime suspect in the murder of the two American trade unionists, Lieutenant Colonel Staben stayed free. It would be misleading to say that he went unpunished. He has since been reinstated to the command of the elite American-trained Arce Battalion, which spearheads the counterinsurgency campaign in the area of San Miguel. Staben's associates are known as the *tandona,* or big class. They are—Colonel Mauricio Vargas, Colonel Emilio Ponce, and the rest—the recipients of American medals and Fort Benning grooming. They stand to inherit command and control of the Salvadoran armed forces. For its mild and short-lived expression of distaste over this affair, the American Embassy was attacked on the front page of *El Diario de hoy* for "intervening in the internal affairs of the country." It is that hilarious coda which breathes with the unmistakable ambience of Gloria César's.

THE CROSS

I had another opportunity to experience the pedagogic effect of fear while traveling on a cross-country bus from San Miguel. The windscreen of the vehicle was covered with cheap religious decals and adorned with a big sign that proclaimed, with conspicuous absence of humility, ¡ES GLORIOSO SER CRISTIANO! Splendid to be a God-botherer, is it, I muttered as the bus was pulled to the side of the road and the passengers began to cross themselves. Every hand at once flew to the pocket containing the *cédula,* the life-saving ID card available only to those who can prove they have swelled voter turnout and thus defied the guerrillas. As I lined up with the men on the edge of a ditch, I found the smiles were the worst. The placatory ones on the faces of the passengers, that is, and the beaming ones of the soldiers. It was unpleasant to be a prisoner of their forced bonhomie. It was humiliating to have to fake a grin of one's own in return. The traditionalists are at their most menacing when they are most polite.

I like my Christianity straight, as in this instance: a false comfort to the poor and a morality for the forces of order. All the traditionalists are fanatical

Catholics, of course, in the Franco style. Here and in Nicaragua and Guatemala, they often call themselves the Warriors of Christ and inscribe mysterious icons on their banners and insignia. They all rally to the Virgin of Cuapa—Our Lady of the Contras. Like their Phalangist cousins, they make useful reinforcements.

When Marcel Neidergang wrote his famous report "The Twenty Latin Americas" for *Le Monde* at the close of the sixties, he found that the continent was dominated by a quartet of forces: the army, the Church, the Americans, and the Left. The first and the third used to be able to defeat or to neutralize the fourth with the help or at least the indulgence of the second. But some years after the end of the Second Vatican Council, the bishops of the region met in Medellín, Colombia, and began to change their reactionary tune. It became possible to speak from the pulpit about oppression, to organize "Christian base communities," and to stress something called "the preferential option of the poor." Out of this crucible came the oxymoron of "liberation theology."

For all its secular sacraments and jolly ecumenicism, and its manifestation of "witness" and piety, liberation theology rested just as heavily upon credulity as did the traditional stuff. Some of its "interfaith" manifestations in the United States were barely to be distinguished from consciousness-raising cults or from Salvation Army proselytizing in generations before. But in El Salvador, it has to be acknowledged, the blood of the martyrs has again been the seed of the Church. Liberation theology in this country has been consecrated.

One of the first of the post-Medellín experiments took place in the parish of Aguilares, near San Salvador, under the patronage of the Jesuit Father Rutilio Grande. For his efforts to organize dignity for the campesinos, he was murdered by the traditionalists in March 1977.

Two other landmarks in the history of the repression are provided by the fate of religious people. In March 1980, Archbishop Oscar Romero was shot through the heart as he raised the host at Mass. A few days earlier, he had appealed to Salvadoran soldiers to disobey unjust orders. His murder was arranged by a holy alliance of the traditionalists: Major Roberto d'Aubuisson, Colonel Ricardo Lau, and Mario Alarcón Sandoval. D'Aubuisson, the leader of the Salvadoran Right, was at that time appearing on national television, flourishing the CIA files on local dissidents. Lau is a former Somoza guard officer, the founding head of "security" for the Nicaraguan Contras. Sandoval is the leader of the "White Hand" death-squad movement in Guatemala and was a guest at Ronald Reagan's inauguration. Romero's murder was commissioned by d'Aubuisson and contracted to Lau; its perpetrators were sheltered by Sandoval.

Then, in December 1980, four American religious were butchered. A collector's item here is the *Report to the Secretary of State* by William

Bowdler and William Rogers. The secretary of state in question, the devout Catholic General Alexander Haig, had given it as his opinion that the women were leftists who had been trying to run a roadblock. The report left him to answer why it was, in that case, that "all four women had been shot in the head. The face of one had been destroyed. The underwear of three was found separately. Bloody bandanas were also found in the grave." As the two U.S. officials also reported, the local justice of the peace had been forced to make a hugger-mugger interment, with his secretary, "following procedures they said had become standard at the direction of the security services. They told the Ambassador that two or three such informal burials of unidentified bodies occurred every week."

This, then, was the relationship of forces between Catholics, in a tiny country named for the Savior, at the moment at which I attended a Mass in a refugee camp. It was on a Sunday afternoon, in a miserable barrio outside the capital. The inhabitants had been evicted from the region of the Guazapa volcano in a punitive military sweep grotesquely entitled Operation Phoenix. The very first person I met was a Franciscan nun from Iowa, who told me that every family in the encampment had lost at least one member and that the women still cringed whenever soldiers came near. I sat through the service of the eucharist, which was conducted, as it happened, by the Jesuit who had succeeded Father Rutilio Grande. I was reasonably unmoved by his popular style, by the guitar music, and by his practice of passing the microphone around for communicants to give their views on the day's text (the Parable of the Talents). I had to shake myself a bit when the congregation sang, by heart, the "Corrido a Monseñor Romero" from the official hymnal of the archbishopric. Its penultimate verse runs:

> Al pueblo le queda claro
> Que tu muerte no fue aislada
> Fue acción del imperialismo
> Junto con la Fuerza Armada

> [It's clear to the people
> That your death was not an isolated event
> You can say it was the result of imperialism
> Joined with the armed forces.]

Then came the kiss of peace, which if I had had time to reflect upon it would have led me out of the crowd and into the trees for a cigarette. Instead, and without warning, I found my hands being taken by ragged strangers, and the word *paz* intoned. A lifetime of Protestant reserve and later atheist conviction seemed compromised by my smile. But it was not the sort of smile I had been obliged to affect on the road from San Miguel. Nor, and much more to the point, were these people's smiles feigned. Their bishop —the one prelate who had ever cared about them—had been foully murdered. So had the good priest Rutilio Grande. That Franciscan from Iowa— who was I to patronize her for her "good works"? It was women of her type who had gone to the province of Chalatenango and been found, in that most dangerous province, in the obscene circumstances relayed with such tact to the uncaring Alexander Haig. The case for a little modesty seemed very strong.

As the Mass broke up and night came on, I noticed a middle-aged European standing apart. He had been seated in a place for honored guests and, although dressed for safari, had the curious, offputtingly childish look that one often sees in those who have led the priestly life. Introduction established him as Hans Küng, down here on a visit from his Texas teaching retreat. In earnest tones, he inquired if I thought the United States had major economic interests in El Salvador, and whether these might explain its commitment to the country's bizarre social arrangements. I replied that El Salvador's problem was that nobody much needed its meager produce, and that even its delicious coffee was part of a mounting glut. The United States, I averred, needed to inflict a defeat upon Leninism, to show itself and others that revolution was not inevitable.

"Well, if it is Leninism they are against," said Küng, "then I am with them. Leninism is terrible. I have seen too much of it. Did you read *The New York Times* recently, where they said that the real Russian revolution was a liberal one, and that Lenin made a coup against it?" I hadn't read that *New York Times*, but I had heard the argument. And Lenin comes up a lot in El Salvador, as he tends to do in all class wars. He may never have heard of El Salvador, but a lot of Salvadorans have heard of him and taken up quite firm positions for and against. The best oral history of the 1932 massacre ("Oral history," said a Salvadoran academic bitterly, "is the only history we are allowed") comes from Miguel Mármol, who survived it. Miguel Mármol lay wounded under a pile of his friends' corpses and shammed death. He went on to found and lead the Salvadoran workers' movement, instilling Leninist precepts at every opportunity. We owe his memoirs to the poet Roque Dalton, a Leninist romantic who transcribed them, in Prague of all places, in the 1960s. From this painful account one can learn, among other things, how very hesitantly and belatedly the Salvadoran communists decided on armed struggle.

Roque Dalton was brave and ironic and talented. He seems to have been precisely the sort of young militant whom it is said that the revolution will devour first. Asking for trouble, one sees in retrospect, was his poem "On Headaches":

To be a communist is a beautiful thing,
though it causes many headaches.

And the problem with the communist headache
is, we assume, historical:
it will not cede to analgesic tablets
but only to the realization of Paradise on earth.
That's the way it is.

Under capitalism our head aches
and is torn from us.
In the struggle for the Revolution
the head is a delayed action bomb.

Under socialist construction
we plan the headache
Which does not minimize it, quite the contrary.

Communism, among other things, will be
an aspirin the size of the sun.

Asking for trouble. In his famous essay in *Dissent* in the winter of 1982, the Mexican writer Gabriel Zaid took the case of Roque Dalton as his metaphor for the dogmatism and fratricide that infect the Salvadoran revolution. Dalton was murdered in 1975, on suspicion of being a CIA (and, oddly enough, a Cuban) agent, by the leadership of the People's Revolutionary Army (ERP), whose commander, Joaquín Villalobos, remains one of the main chieftains of the Salvadoran guerrillas. Zaid went for the heavily sarcastic in his account of the death:

> Roque Dalton was slain by a comrade who beat him at the use of his own arguments, in an internal power struggle. Terrible enough; neither the most thorough accord between thought and action, nor the most absolute and unconditional surrender, nor even taking to the mountains, strapping on arms and offering himself up to kill the Chief of Police saved Dalton from the final spit in the face at his death; accused by his comrades as a bourgeois. Just as if he'd remained a writer signing manifestos and eating three meals a day.
>   In the discourse of reason, the winner is the one with reason. In the discourse of guns, the winner's the one with the gun.

New readers should not begin here. Zaid is a veteran who is confidently repeating an old and well-tried lesson. His closing epigrams may be a touch glib (reason doesn't always win even in a rational discourse, and, in the discourse of guns, surely the winner is *one of* those with the gun?), but he is sure in his general import, which is: a Salvadoran revolution would transform the country into another dreary Sparta. The favorite slogan of the Salvadoran left is "If Nicaragua won, El Salvador will win!" Ricardo Stein pointed out to me that there are two unintended pedagogic effects of this battle cry. First, many of the Salvadoran middle class would not choose to exchange the oligarchy for a Sandinista system. Second, if Nicaragua won, then Nicaragua was immediately subjected to a long war of murder and attrition by the United States. How many people will have the stomach to endure a war of liberation and a long war of defense? And what would happen to liberty along the way? The Dalton affair suggests that the attitude of the guerrilla leadership would not be a sentimental one. (Just to show that they, too, study the dialectic, the U.S. Embassy in San Salvador passed out hundreds of copies of the Zaid article during the height of the traditionalist frenzy in 1982.)

Well, if this is the choice, then let us not forget who posed it. The shock of the Cuban revolution was enough, after 1960, for the United States to embrace limited reformism through the Alliance for Progress. Its showcase politician in those days was Eduardo Frei rather than Augusto Pinochet. Unfortunately, in El Salvador the "reform" bit got left out. The counter-revolution bit did not. The founder of the traditionalist movement in the country was General José Alberto Medrano, who set up ORDEN—the rural paramilitary death squad and informer network—and ANSESAL, the national political police. In a 1984 interview, he said proudly that "ORDEN and ANSESAL grew out of the State Department, the CIA and the Green Berets during the time of Kennedy." We will never know how many thousands of peasants lost their lives to this initiative, which kept the country as a miserable, sweltering backwater until the "reformist" coup of 1979. And the reformist coup of 1979 led directly to the terror mounted by the Treasury Police, the National Guard, and the National Police—all of them trained and equipped and protected by the United States. Thus, the record of liberal reformism in El Salvador actually inverts Lenin's admonition by following the pattern of one step forward and two steps back. And it wasn't the Leninists who opened "the discourse of guns."

The brute fact is that there would have been no reform at all if it were not for the force exerted by the Farabundo Martí Liberation Front—itself named for an early victim of the traditionalists. Despite numerous inducements to do so, the public leaders of Salvadoran social democracy will not disown the FMLN. And, though the Americans and their allies are almost certainly strong enough to prevent the FMLN from winning, they are not strong enough to enact half the reforms the FMLN proposes and thus cannot rob the *frente* of its claim to have saved the honor of the country.

As the mass in that refugee camp was dispersing, I spoke to the Jesuit about what I refuse to call his flock. He told me of the open contempt with which they viewed the Duarte government and its pretended new face for the old system. He spoke with warmth about the prolonging of the war. But surely, I said, it takes two sides to fight a war. Isn't your congregation just sick of the fighting? Aren't the people indifferent as between the two sides? The priest looked at me pityingly. "These people," he replied, "are not neutral *in the least*." If they can resist the temptations of moral equivalence, then so can I.

(*Grand Street*, Spring 1988)

HOBBES IN THE LEVANT

❏

Abu Jihad is an Arab name meaning "father of Jihad." Jihad means "holy war." As a choice of nom de guerre, then, it suggests a very serious fellow. And Khalil al-Wazir, the man who affects it, is indeed deputy commander of Al Fatah. I spent an evening in his flat in Beirut last week (in an area of the town since pounded to rubble), discussing the chances of an Israeli invasion. I suspect him of rather liking the impression he produces on visitors. He receives them in the bosom of his very large and happy family. Jihad himself, the eldest son, turns out to be a polite, plumpish, and cheerful youth with a serious interest in politics. Much time is spent in recounting the sorrows of the clan: the exile from Ramleh in 1948, the wretched years in the Gaza Strip, the indignities visited upon relatives, the second exile, and the gradual burgeoning of the Palestinian revolution. Tea is brought, hands are pressed, cheeks are pinched. Presiding over all is the jovial paterfamilias, as if to say, "What, me a terrorist?"

Yet, when the talk turns to the impending attack, the atmosphere alters. I mention the extreme vulnerability of the Palestinian forces in the south. "Look," he says, "I remember when the Israelis invaded in 1978. General Mordechai Gur was publicly criticized in Israel for not being harder and tougher, and for not seizing Tyre and Sidon. He replied that he didn't want to risk his men against fighters who *wanted* to die. So maybe they will kill all our forces there—but we will be back again. See for yourself. . . ."

Miles to the south, in Sidon, I carried a dog-eared Hachette guide to Lebanon, published in the early fifties. Describing the town, the battered volume had this to say: "Like most of the ancient Phoenician cities, it is built on a promontory faced by an island. It is surrounded by pleasant gardens where oranges, lemons, bananas, medlars, apricots and almonds are successfully grown. It has some 40,000 inhabitants including 15,000 Palestinian refugees."

Three decades later, that laconic charming description would need a few amendments. The lush crops rot on the ground because thousands of cultivators long ago fled from Israeli bombardment to live, in doubtful security, in the filthy bidonvilles of Beirut. The old buildings and streets are charred and furrowed with the evidence of previous raids. For the surviving inhabitants, Phantoms and Mirages long ago became reality.

The Palestinians who remain there, not just from the 1948 exodus but from many subsequent ones, were as insouciant about the prospect of an invasion as their deputy commander. The only sign of nervousness was a blank refusal to permit a visit to Beaufort Castle, off limits to the press since 1978. In the event, this shrug at the inevitable has proven militarily deceptive. The Israelis in 1978 were satisfied with driving the PLO forces northward—with forcing them to fold their tents and flee. This time, they have tried to encircle and destroy as many trained Palestinians as possible. Mr. Begin may claim that the object is to create a twenty-five–mile strip between his northern border and the Palestinian positions in order to protect the Galilee. But it's more revealing to attend to General Sharon, who has been saying in public for weeks that the objective must be the physical destruction of the guerrillas and their infrastructure. By this means, he hopes to buy five years of peace and perhaps to drive the Palestinians into their designated Transjordanian "home."

So much is becoming clear from the hourly and daily bulletins. But travel a little farther south from Sidon and Tyre, and you come to the border of Major Haddad's ministate: a strip six miles wide garrisoned by a rough militia and armed and victualed by Israel. Here can be seen one of the outlines of the emerging partition of Lebanon. Paradoxical as it may appear, there is now a tacit agreement between Israel and Syria on spheres of influence. Ever since Joseph Sisco's 1978 shuttle from Damascus to Jerusalem, it has been understood that Syria holds eastern Lebanon and the vital Bekaa Valley (historic route of invasion thrusts toward Damascus), while Israel controls the southern zone and exercises the right to blitz the Palestinians without Syrian reprisal. There are advantages to both sides in this makeshift, unspoken deal. The principal advantage is that it neutralizes and quarantines the PLO—neutralizes it militarily from the point of view of Israel, and quarantines it politically from the point of view of Syria. Neither party wishes to see a really independent Palestinian state, though Syria is hampered by having to pretend that it does. This explains the refusal (rather than the reluctance) of Syrian forces to engage Israel during the crucial first few days, even in Beirut airspace. There may be, for the sake of honor, some slight breaking of lances. But the keystone state in the "Arab front of steadfastness and confrontation" will be sitting this one out.

Numerous considerations, however, make the arrangement precarious. American annoyance at Israel's unilateral annexation of the Golan Heights stemmed from a fear that it would destabilize the unwritten accord by touching Syrian territory. Abu Jihad said rather sarcastically that many Arab countries want to "protect" the Palestinians—to monopolize and manipulate them. And currently the Syrians are feeling rather frisky because of the humiliation of their Iraqi foes by the Iranians. They may take revenge on American policy in some more indirect way as a salve to Arab pride. Philip Habib, who must fill the shoes of Mr. Sisco, represent Mr. Reagan, conciliate the Israelis, and appease the Arab League, will find his brow getting dewy before he wings gratefully home. The Fahd plan for a Palestinian ministate, so named after Crown Prince Fahd of Saudi Arabia, was still somewhere near the table a few weeks ago and commanded a certain amount of State Department support. It must be reckoned among the terminal casualties of the Israeli invasion.

Two areas of Lebanon remain outside the "spheres of influence" compromise. Beirut may be full of Syrian soldiery directing traffic and manning roadblocks, but it is otherwise still the Hobbesian city of the war of all against all. During my stay, the nights were being made late by the gun battle between supporters of Iran and partisans of Iraq. They hardly broke off when Israeli sonic booms rattled windows. On any other night, it might be any other group. The city has become a free port for every kind of militia and faction. The French embassy was blown up, and nobody knew whom to blame because there were so many obvious candidates. A secretary at the British embassy was raped and told to deliver a warning to the embassy, and speculation was only slightly more concentrated. In a few months a general election is due, and a selection by the subsequent parliament of a new president. A poll taken by the excellent Beirut magazine *Monday Morning* found that there were only ninety-two surviving MPs out of the proper complement of ninety-nine. Of those interviewed, only five were imprudent enough to state the name of the presidential candidate they were backing.

The other region of Lebanon which escapes inclusion in the Syrian-Israeli accord is the Christian belt north of Beirut, which has its own access to the sea and its own relative autonomy. The Christians both need partition and reject it. They ruled the country for so long that they cannot ever fully acknowledge the end of their own dominion. But mastery in a kind of Crusader ghetto may be the best they can now achieve. To get to their capital of Jounieh, you have to cross the appalling central belt of Beirut, where for street after street and block after block everything is scorched and desolate. This was the business and banking quarter—Beirut is one of the few cities where a civil war has been fought in the opulent areas rather than in the suburbs and shanty towns. Remember the Battle of the Holiday Inn.

When you reach Jounieh, you can see where the banks and the businesses have gone. The place is full of semi-chic and pseudo-French effects, with new building and investment in evidence everywhere. The militia of the Phalange Party is always on view, and is much better groomed than its Syrian or Palestinian counterparts. The craggy face of Pierre Gemayel, the old fascist leader who has now ceded power to his two sons, glares from large hoardings like some forgotten patriot of the Fourth Republic. In every palpable way, you have entered another country. Here, sympathy for Israel is widespread, but it's unlikely to take, as it once did, the shape of a formal military alliance. As long as the Christians stay well out of regional politics, the Syrians are inclined to leave them alone. Christian spokesmen say privately that the Americans have told them this is a smart policy.

So Lebanon will continue to exist on the map, and Beirut will continue to be a *place d'armes* for every quarrel in the region. But gradually Greater Syria is living up to its dream of recovering lost territory, and Greater Israel is asserting its sovereignty too. In between are the Palestinians, now loved by almost nobody. I would very much like to know who shot Ambassador Argov. Usually, these things turn out to have been done by the Al Fatah renegade Abu Nidal, who used to operate from Baghdad in his campaign against the "sellout" leadership of Yasir Arafat. He has now moved his headquarters to Damascus in the course of the Byzantine feud between the two capitals. You can start to believe anything after a week or two in Beirut, so I will say no more except that I hope Mr. Argov will recover and will consider himself properly avenged.

(*The Spectator*, June 12, 1982)

DEAD MEN ON LEAVE

❑

In early March 1976, I sat in a bare office in Baghdad, contemplating my good fortune. Across the desk from me was the lean and striking figure of Masen Sabry al-Banna, leader of the renegade extremist faction of Al Fatah and a man sought for murder and conspiracy by both the Israelis and the PLO. He didn't give many interviews, and there was no decent extant photograph of him (the one since circulated in books about the "terror network" seems to me to be of the wrong man). Under his nom de guerre of Abu Nidal, he had set himself against any attempt at binational or inter-communal accord over the Palestine issue. By way of opening proceedings, he had just invited me to visit one of his camps and perhaps to undergo a little training. How could one refuse without risking a change of mood, or, at least, the termination of the interview? My lucky assignation was turning sour.

Things got worse as our talk progressed. He took my declining of his offer quite calmly, but then shifted mercurially in his approach. Did I, he wanted to know, ever meet Said Hammami? Hammami was then the PLO envoy in London, who had, in a celebrated article in *The Times*, advocated mutual recognition between Israel and the Palestinians. I knew him and liked him and agreed with him. "Tell him," said Abu Nidal, "to be careful. We do not tolerate traitors." I delivered this billet-doux back in London, and Said shrugged. He had been threatened before, but saw no alternative to an "open-door" policy. A few months later, a man walked through his open door and shot him dead. Abu Nidal "claimed credit," as the argot has it, for the deed.

Still, the idea of a dignified composition of the quarrel between the Zionist movement and the Palestine national movement did not die with Said. The most zealous exponent of the principle was Dr. Issam Sartawi. His own story was a very instructive one. Born in Acre under the Mandate, he ended his education as a heart surgeon in Ohio. After the shattering events of 1967, he returned to the Middle East and to his family—now displaced to Amman, Jordan. Like many other young Palestinians of the time, he joined a radical combatant group and fought to erase the stain of defeat. It was this experience which led him, in his own words, to see things differently:

> Perhaps the most dramatic evolution in contemporary Palestinian thinking is that moment when Palestinians started looking into the question of the existence of Israel. For me, it came in 1968 after the battle at Karameh [where PLO forces engaged Israeli armor directly for the first time]. It enabled me for the first time to see Israel. Prior to that, when I closed my eyes to escape from the misery of non-nationhood, I could only escape to the Palestine of my dreams, to the Palestine of my childhood fancy, to the open spaces, to the green meadows. I really, truly did not see the new Palestine, the Israeli Palestine with its avalanche of immigrants, the destruction of those green, peaceful meadows, the rise of the skyscrapers, the growth of the megalopolis. . . . It raised in my mind Article Six of our National Covenant, because Article Six said only those Jews who came before the Zionist invasion will stay in Palestine. I remember what went through my mind: Who do we send away? The Polish Jew who came in 1919? It was at this point that it dawned on me that we have to seek justice for our people without inflicting any suffering on others.

This interview was given to a friend of mine only a few months after the Palestinians had been hounded out of Beirut. At the time, Dr. Sartawi was still Yasir Arafat's envoy to Western Europe, establishing warm contacts with Bruno Kreisky of Austria, Willy Brandt, Andreas Papandreou, and others. He even set up a meeting in Tunis between Arafat and three senior Israeli doves, including reserve general Mattiyahu Peled. He did not, in short, confine his peaceful rhetoric solely to sessions with Western correspondents.

He had, after three assassination attempts from Abu Nidal's gunmen, become slightly insouciant about the likelihood of his death. But his real disappointment came in February at Algiers, when Arafat forbade him to defend his "recognition" policy from the platform of the Palestine National Council. He resigned from the PNC the next day, criticizing the official view that the siege of Beirut had "objectively" been a victory for the Palestinians, commenting sardonically that many more victories like that would see the leadership meeting in Fiji.

Abu Nidal must have smiled at that observation. It was his group which had shot the Israeli ambassador to London, Shlomo Argov, and thus given General Sharon his green light or red rag for the assault. Things, from his point of view, were going nicely. The conditions for compromise were being physically destroyed. It only remained to stop the mouth of Dr. Sartawi himself. (At the Lisbon conference where Sartawi was murdered, it was Shimon Peres of the Israeli Labor Party who kept him from the microphone.)

All in all, it's been a pitiful year for those who hope for a solution short of colonization, annexation, or irredentism. In July, three senior Jewish figures, with the encouragement of Issam Sartawi, signed what became known as the Paris Declaration. Pierre Mendès France, Nahum Goldmann, and Philip Klutznick called for Palestinian independence, mutual recognition between the two contending parties, and direct negotiations. They were, of course, snubbed and ignored by the Begin government—despite the fact that Nahum Goldmann had nearly been the president of Israel and was certainly the most distinguished living Zionist. Since the statement was signed and published, both Mendès France and Nahum Goldmann have died, and Issam Sartawi has been murdered. Israeli dissent is being swamped in a sea of chauvinism, but any future Palestinian advocate of self-criticism will have to consider himself a dead man on leave.

(*The Spectator*, April 16, 1983)

A MORNING WITH
RABBI KAHANE

❏

I wouldn't say that a morning spent with Rabbi Meir Kahane was exactly an enlightening experience, but it was certainly an educational one. Kahane possesses a horrid energy. Over the past year he has survived numerous clumsy attempts to silence him and to circumscribe his party. These measures have included a stupid bureaucratic challenge to his U.S. passport, a pretty obvious ban by Israeli television and radio, and a bill against racism in the Knesset that was so diluted by the religious and right-wing parties that Kahane voted for it. On all this harassment Kahane thrives, enjoying the controversy and addressing rallies five nights of the week.

The annual survey of Israeli opinion, which is carefully carried out by the magazine *Monitin*, was published in May. It showed that only 46 percent of the population found the views of Kahane and his Kach Party "totally unacceptable." Of the remainder, 23 percent found the Kach program "mistaken in general but partly right"; 17 percent found it correct in general but partly wrong; and 6 percent agreed with Kahane outright. (In the last election, Kahane gained a parliamentary seat with 1.2 percent of the vote.) The writer of the *Monitin* report, Eliyahu Hassin, concludes that the political message of Kach is "supported in full or partially by 23 percent of the adult Jewish population, spread among all social groups." This, he says, "we must assume is the scope of potential support for Israeli fascism, which need not necessarily be represented in the future only by a dubious rabbi of American origins and a gang of revolting hooligans."

In conversation, the object of all this obloquy does not rave or babble. His madness lies only in his logic, which is cool and vicious. He, too, distinguishes Kahane from Kahanism. "I get the applause," he says, "when I tell them, 'I say what you think.' " There is clearly a latent audience for his view that "the Arab problem and the Sabbath problem are the same."

"Judaism is a totality and can never recognize the separation of synagogue and state," he says. "We need a state based on Judaism; a Jewish state and not a state of Jews."

Now, it is a fact that, despite a torrent of criticism and outrage from liberal Zionists in Israel and America, Kahane has never been condemned or disowned by the rabbinate. I can't test his claim, made to me in conversation, that the Orthodox leadership has privately assured him of its sympathy. That is the sort of thing that demagogues say. But one cannot fail to notice the utter silence of the chief rabbis about his proposal for mass expulsion of Arabs and enforced conformity for Jews. And because Kach is a religious party, it can easily make nonsense of any "bill against racism" by quoting the relevant sections of Holy Writ.

A lurid manifestation of Kahanism without Kahane was proffered just before I met the man himself by Rabbi Shmuel Derlich. Rabbi Derlich is the Israeli army's chief chaplain in Judea and Samaria, and had sent the troops in his area a thousand-word pastoral letter in which he urged them to apply the biblical injunction to exterminate the Amalekites to the last man, woman, and child. The letter went unremarked until it was challenged by the army's chief education officer, who demanded to know Rabbi Derlich's working definition of Amalekite. The rabbi disingenuously replied that the Germans would be a good latter-day example. So he had only been urging the Israeli soldiers to kill all Germans—a people conspicuous by their absence from the Bible and from the West Bank of the Jordan River. The matter was referred to the Judge Advocate General, who ruled that Derlich had committed no offense. This was also the view of no less than forty military chaplains who came to his support in public.

Kahane is, if anything, more moderate. He told me with unblinking seriousness that he did not think there were any Amalekites these days, adding that of course if there were, the commandment to extirpate them would be valid. While I reeled from this, he hurried on to say that Kach did not want to kill the Palestinians, only to make them clear out from Eretz Israel. They may stay on two conditions: either they convert, according to *halakhah* (Jewish law) and with no Reform or Conservative nonsense; or they abandon all civil rights and remain as hewers of wood and drawers of water. (The actual words of his proposed law stipulate that "a foreign resident must accept the burden of taxes and servitude.")

It's been pointed out often enough that Kahane-type scriptural propaganda is racist and potentially genocidal so far as it concerns the Arabs. But it occurred to me as we talked that before he could get at the Arabs, he would have to settle accounts with many, many Jews. He agreed to this as soon as I raised it, claiming that his left-wing enemies wanted a civil war in Israel and would get it if they refused to accept the verdict of the people. I should have asked him how this tallied with his view that "Zionism and Western-style democracy are in direct contradiction."

Read Kahane's writings on the Jews. Here is his depiction of American Jewish life today:

> The massive, gaudy mausoleums that dot the landscape of every Jewish suburb. The temples. The temples whose senior rabbi is the caterer. The temples that perform human sacrifice rites each Sabbath morning, and they call it the Bar Mitzvah . . . the Bar Mitzvah, that obscene cult of ostentatiousness, the ultimate in Jewish status-seeking, where materialism runs amok in the guise of religion, where drunks and half-dressed women dance and give praise to the Lord, with African dances, American tunes and universal abominations.

This rather makes "Hymietown" pale. You should also read Kahane on "the loving Jewish mother who took off her golden nose rings and made a golden calf which she worships avidly" and "the Jewish father whose values are those of the garment center and the race track." The man is an Arab-hater, and he has that in common with a large and growing number of Israelis and gentile Americans. But he is also—and at last one finds a proper and apposite use for this amorphous term—a self-hating Jew.

(*The Nation*, August 16–23, 1986)

GOING HOME WITH
KIM DAE JUNG

❑

Kim Dae Jung could have spent his sixties living comfortably in Virginia, where I met him first. He might have been publishing a newspaper for the Korean-American community or perhaps leading a nominal South Korean "government in exile." He might have spent his later years giving college lectures, as he had been doing since his arrival in the United States in 1982, and accepting annual human-rights awards. He would have been a significant but not unexceptional figure in those New York and Washington intellectual circles where people congregate who, for political reasons, cannot live in their own countries.

But Kim Dae Jung is a rare man. What makes him exceptional is not his politics or ideas, which are moderate and democratic, but the fact that he would not compromise his principles to preserve his personal safety in America. With flimsy assurances from the Seoul government and the Reagan Administration, Kim went home and took his stand. As far as he could see, there was no alternative.

"I really think," said Kim, "that if you had not come with me, I would not now be sitting here in my home." He was paying this quiet compliment, in his small house in Seoul, to a number of Americans who had accompanied him back to Korea. Events in the streets and lanes outside seemed to bear him out. The area had been sealed off—as the saying goes—by sentry boxes and guard posts. Making a courtesy call required at least two inspections by hefty guards from the Korean Central Intelligence Agency (KCIA), backed up a short distance off by trucks full of riot police and soldiers. While I was in the house, there was yet another unpleasant confrontation as these guardians of the peace refused entry to a pair of clergymen, a Roman Catholic for Kim and a Methodist for his wife, thereby dashing the hope of a Sunday ecumenical service. The explanation for the ban—that the two priests were *Korean* and therefore were excluded under the terms of Kim's house arrest—

only underlined the contempt displayed by the regime of General Chun Doo Hwan for its own people.

I talked a fair bit to Kim Dae Jung in the weeks and days before he left the safety of America to take the risk of rejoining his people. I talked to him as we flew over the Pacific to Tokyo, and on the final leg to Seoul itself, with Mount Fuji receding beneath us. He seldom expressed concern for his own safety, changing the subject whenever it came up. But he did talk about the *other* reception he might get—the reception by the people of Seoul. He had heard, he told me, that there might be fifty thousand or more people to welcome him at the airport. Was I mistaken, or did he seem a touch worried? Exile, imprisonment, age (he's sixty-one), a decade-long ban on the mention of his name: might all these have conspired to make people forget him?

Of all the allegations thrown at Kim recently by the Chun regime— "revolutionary," "communist," and other epithets—only one had stung him. That was the suggestion, which is also carefully spread by American officials when they think they are speaking off the record, that Kim Dae Jung is passé. "Passé," he would repeat angrily, his brow wrinkled, "passé?"

In 1983, when Kim was on a fellowship at Harvard, he had lunch with Benigno Aquino (we have often spoken of the meeting). Aquino told Kim, in effect, that he was going home because exile led to impotence, to becoming passé. Many things could be borne, but not that. Particularly not by two men who were both barred by the stroke of a dictator's pen from becoming president of their respective countries. (In spite of the widespread fraud in the 1971 elections, Kim got forty-six percent of the popular vote.)

But if Kim was a little worried over what kind of welcome to expect from his fellow Koreans, the South Korean regime was far more concerned than he. In anticipation of his arrival, all public transportation to the airport was closed for the entire day. Yet, at the airport, and all the way into town, there were throngs of people. By my count, at least half of them would have been in their teens when Kim first ran for president and a good number of them would have been younger. And all of them had walked. They must have been determined, too, because side streets leading to the poorer districts and quarters were blocked by teams of leather-helmeted men, and the stink of tear gas (that special essence of dictatorship) was pervasive.

I learned later from a leading Presbyterian clergyman, the Reverend Moon Ik Hwan, that congregations burst into spontaneous applause whenever Kim's name was mentioned. Forbidden to quote him or refer to him directly, candidates for the heavily circumscribed opposition New Korea Democratic Party drew vast crowds and huge ovations for veiled references to him. (This was the party that became legitimate only three months prior to the February 1985 election, in which it burst upon the scene as the leading opposition group in Korea's National Assembly.)

Identified by some scouts as having been on Kim's plane, my American friends and I were mobbed in the friendliest way: beseeched for information and gossip. A Japanese newspaper with a picture of Kim's forbidden features was torn from our hands and passed frenziedly through the crowd. How was he? Most of all, and most urgently, *where* was he?

These last questions were embarrassingly hard to answer. The phalanx formed by Representatives Ed Feighan of Ohio and Thomas Foglietta of Pennsylvania; Jimmy Carter's El Salvador ambassador, Robert White; and Pat Derian, Carter's Assistant Secretary of State for Human Rights, had been kicked, punched, and shoved out of the way by a pack of KCIA professionals. It may have looked like a mere scuffle on television, but from close up it was very chilling. A premeditated "wedge" attack split Kim's immediate party from the press, then split him and his wife from the other supporters, and finally whisked him away from his four chosen escorts and into an elevator. Kim, who walks with a stick as a result of a KCIA assassination attempt in 1971, when a truck ran his car off the road and killed three people in the car behind his, was in no position to resist. As I was trying to get into a better viewing position, I was seized and thrust down a moving stairway. At the bottom I found an agitated U.S. Embassy official demanding to know what the Christ was going on.

He might well have asked. As Kim Dae Jung said, "No one ever dared challenge the will of the nation as brazenly as Chun did, and no one ever rose to power by such a bloody and cruel path." Yet, observed Kim in 1983, "It is the feeling of the Korean people that the United States has never supported a Korean government as strongly as it is currently backing the Chun Doo Hwan regime and that this support is the umbilical cord which keeps the Chun regime afloat."

Even before we left Washington, we had been treated to a statement by Elliott Abrams, who holds the paradoxical title of Assistant Secretary of State for Human Rights and Humanitarian Affairs. He told everybody who would listen that Kim Dae Jung was in danger only from the North Koreans, who might kill him in order to sow dissension in General Chun's otherwise untroubled Eden. This statement was incredible in two ways. First, it ignored the two occasions on which the KCIA was caught in the very act of trying to murder Kim. Second, it gave Chun's police license *in advance* to blame any mishap on the communists. Not even Ferdinand Marcos, who tried to pin Benigno Aquino's death on the Philippine Communist Party, had had such a green light from the Reagan Administration.

Further impetus was provided to Chun by the Heritage Foundation, Reagan's think tank of choice, which selected the week of Kim's departure to describe the Korean leader as a troublemaker and to praise the stability conferred on South Korea by the military dictatorship. Ambassador Richard "Dixie" Walker, Reagan's appointee in Seoul, is close to the Heritage Foundation and was among the twenty-one ambassadors who signed a letter last fall endorsing the reelection of Jesse Helms. Any KCIA man worth his salt and able to review evidence and place bets would have concluded that the agreement between the State Department and the Korean Foreign Ministry that Kim's return would be "trouble-free" could be overidden. The State Department could be overridden by the conservatives who really determine White House policy, and the Korean Foreign Ministry by the usual dictates of "security." It was a case of like speaking to like—or nodding to like—with no conspiracy required. Even so, Dixie Walker became angry and pompous when he saw the bad press he got from the U.S. journalists who had been at the airport. He blustered about the "internal affairs" of South Korea, as if no visitors from the U.S.A. other than those who had accompanied Kim had ever gotten involved there. "This country," he said, "is not an American colony."

Oh, but it is.

In President Chun Doo Hwan's long mercenary past, his success came in always putting the baser interests of the United States above the best interests of Koreans. He first achieved notice in Vietnam, commanding the 29th Regiment of the White Horse Division, a detachment of soldiers that tortured the very few prisoners it took. In May 1980, while still Acting Director of the KCIA, Chun had to deal with a popular revolt in the city of Kwangju, which is in Kim Dae Jung's home region of South Cholla. No reputable source puts the death toll from that "pacification" at under a thousand, and many estimates are closer to two thousand.

As in Vietnam, General Chun had American "back-up" in Kwangju. A U.S. general is always at the top of the South Korean military's co-command structure; his permission is required for any significant movement of troops within the country. In 1980, the commander was General John Wickham, who approved Chun's use of paratroopers against the civilian uprising in Kwangju and then issued statements saying that Korea was not yet ready for democracy. Thus encouraged, Chun blamed Kim Dae Jung for the uprising and had him sentenced to death. Intense international pressure was needed to secure his release on medical grounds in 1982. The sentence was commuted to twenty years and then suspended, but it is still in effect.

The Korea of Generals Wickham and Chun will never be "ready" for the democracy they fear so much. But the Korean people are more than ready for it, as they proved once again in the February 1985 election. They were promised democracy at the end of the long and brutal Japanese occupation, in 1945. Instead, not having been even a minor combatant country in World War II, they got military occupation by the United States and the Soviet Union. Then, in the south, they got the outrageous dictator Syngman Rhee, who was finally swept from office by a bloody rising in 1960.

After one year of tentative but decent civilian rule by Chang Myon (whose official spokesperson was Kim Dae Jung), the Koreans were subjected to another rightist coup and eighteen bitter years of Park Chung Hee. Official texts refer to events of that era as "the malpractices of the past accruing from a prolonged one-man rule" (the echo of classic Stalinist apology is presumably unintentional). General Park died in October 1979 at the hands of his own secret police chief—there has not yet been a peaceful or democratic transfer of power in this "stable client state"—but the "Korean spring" that followed his death was brief. Kim Dae Jung, in his first appearance since his detention began in 1972, spoke to huge and receptive crowds, but the risk of free elections was considered too great by the real masters of the country, and perhaps also by their mentors in Washington.

Too much of the press comment after the airport incident tended to focus on the wounded amour propre of the accompanying Americans. This was not the fault of the media, because the ambassador chose to characterize the event in a way that could only prolong the controversy. But that ought not to obscure the crucial matter, which is the fate of Kim Dae Jung and the collusion of the United States with those who disfigure his country.

Given that South Korea is sown with perhaps two hundred fifty American nuclear warheads, and given that the United States is committed by forty thousand troops to going to war for South Korea at a moment's notice, the proper concern *is* with the internal affairs of this tripwire country. Yet Korea receives almost no mention in the American press. There is still no national monument in the United States to the dead of the Korean War. Nor is there—aside from a few revisionist works by I. F. Stone and Bruce Cumings—any literature of any depth or merit about the American commitment there.

Even a short visit to the country can illustrate the sheer scale of that commitment. I attended a briefing given by the very affable General M. G. Ellis at the headquarters of the U.S. Eighth Army at Yongsan. The usual slide-and-pointer show was on offer, showing truthfully enough that North Korea spends a crippling proportion of its surplus on weapons. But the general was able to show an "imbalance" only by restricting the map of forces to the Korean peninsula, although the Eighth Army is in fact deployed far more widely. As is customary, he refused to discuss the presence of nuclear weapons. And, under questioning, he admitted that the North Korean leader Kim Il Sung, presented as a Russian stooge in the slide show, was in fact maintaining a balancing act between the Soviet Union and China.

The real point was made by accident later the same day, when I visited the DMZ at Panmunjom. Here, too, it is Americans who give the orders and who patrol and police the perimeter. My guide, who was stationed at the *M*A*S*H*-like Camp Kitty Hawk, at the foremost extent of the American line (motto: Out in Front of Them All), pointed to the famous tree where American officers were slain by North Koreans wielding axes in an "incident" in 1976, as they were supervising an attempt to lop off the branches and clear a view of a nearby American outpost.

"When we came back to finish that tree trimming," said my escort with pride, "there were six hundred martial-arts experts in the woods. We had a fleet of B-52s flying to and fro south of the border. South Korean and U.S. forces were both on full alert. And we had the USS *Midway* right off the coast. Most expensive tree trimming in history." Reassuring for the tree trimmers, I suppose, but the idea of going on full alert for a disputed poplar is one to give anybody, however anticommunist, pause for thought.

Kim Dae Jung is as anticommunist a politician as you could meet in a day's march. He was nearly killed by the North Koreans in the war, kept fairly quiet about his opposition to Korean troops in Vietnam, sets great store by his contacts with the Christian Democratic International, and repeatedly gives West Germany as his example of the model society. Why, then, is he considered to be such a dangerous person? The answer to that question probably lies in the origins of the South Korean state.

The Republic of Korea, or ROK, began by claiming to be the rightful government of the whole of Korea. This claim was immediately met by a counterproclamation, to the same effect, from the Democratic People's Republic of Korea, or North Korea. These positions set the stage for the incredibly destructive war between 1950 and 1953, which left the partition line very much where it had been drawn in 1948. But it did not settle the question of legitimacy.

The ROK armed forces and high command remained indelibly compromised by the collaboration of their senior cadres with the Japanese occupier and by their continued dependence on American arms and aid. This problem of puppetry—as it might be defined—remains acutely sensitive. The regime, despite its monopoly on force, feels insecure and has never been able (even to the small extent once achieved by Marcos in the Philippines or Suharto in Indonesia) to demonstrate a popular mandate. Faced as it is by the world's most regimented and leader-oriented communist state, Chun & Co. must regard this failure as a large one.

This would explain the marked chauvinism with which the regime attacks Kim Dae Jung, calling him "a Westernized Christian." This also explains the astonishing rudeness and demagogy with which it received his American friends, telling the populace through a controlled press that "American" interference in Korean internal affairs could not be tolerated. And this explains the hysteria with which it greets his mildly expressed challenge to Chun's right to rule.

There is a dirty secret at the root of South Korea's economic and political "miracles," and the repression of that secret has created a neurotic system, one that seems compelled to bite the hand that feeds it. An oligarchy that is parasitic on America grows enraged when it is criticized as such and appeals to anti-Americanism. An oligarchy that resorts to official hatred of the Japanese was obliged to rely on Japanese collusion to cover up its 1973 kidnapping of Kim from his Tokyo hotel. The names of the kidnappers were well known and are on file with the Tokyo police. But the Japanese government apparently cares more for good relations with a docile South Korea than it does for democracy. So the Seoul authorities find themselves, to their suppressed rage, depending on a version of Japan's discredited Greater East Asian Co-Prosperity Sphere.

Kim is amazingly restrained in his approach to this thicket of contradictions. He never resorts to anti-Japanese rhetoric, though his grievances against the Japanese authorities are genuine. He never goes in for cheap anti-Americanism, though he has been betrayed by the American government and though there is undoubtedly an audience in Korea for propaganda of that kind. He never overstates his case against the South Korean regime, saying even after the squalid scene at the airport that, although he could feel pain and bruises, he could not swear that they had been inflicted by any one cop. At the slight risk of sounding sentimental, I would observe that history is very often made, even if only by accident, by men and women who draw a line beyond which they will not be pushed. It was a privilege to fly home with one such man.

(*Mother Jones*, May 1985)

LIBERTÉ À LA POLONAISE

❏

If the police in Poland ever feel the necessity to enter and search the home of a citizen, Polish law obliges them to have an impartial witness present while the weighty duty is discharged. A man in Warsaw who has been prominent in opposition circles for years told me that the most recent inspection of his books and papers had been fairly routine, but that he and the cops had haggled for almost an hour over who the impartial person should be. It is always nice to have a metaphor when attempting to describe a situation rather than an event, and in Poland at the moment the problem is very much one of who can hold the ring. The poet Miron Bialoszewski once wrote:

> *The elect are few*
> *Everybody in the last resort*
> *Elects only himself.*

Poland has a non-elected government and a self-appointed opposition. It is, as a matter of fact, the only communist country with any permanent semi-public and quasi-legal opposition at all. The coexistence between the two may not last very long, but if it did, it might spare the country one of the huge and violent lurches—1956, 1968, or 1970—by which it has managed to alter course since the war. As it is, the state dare not crush its critics and many Party officials would probably like to use them as a means of finding out what the population thinks. But nor can it really tolerate them, however scrupulously they keep their activities and petitions within the law. In addition to which, Gomulka made the mistake of forcing so many bright Poles into exile after 1968 that there is now a fairly flourishing network of international contacts and publications in existence, and the task of imposing silence would be a tough one.

Sitting in the same recently searched flat with my new friend—his name is Jacek Kuron and he is an ex-Marxist dissident with a prison record for political activity—I learned a certain amount about the inches of leeway within which critical activity is carried on. At regular intervals his telephone would ring, and "spontaneous" abuse would be anonymously delivered. There was a death threat, too, which had started at a countdown of a hundred days and stood at 65 to go on the day I was there. This left him unmoved. He kept returning to the main subject of political conversation in Warsaw, which is the trial of workers involved in food-price riots last summer. These disturbances, in which Communist Party property and several stretches of railway line were severely damaged, led to the rescinding of the price rises, the deaths of some rioters, and the imposition of a collective charge on all those known to have been involved in the protest. As a result, money has been collected, bulletins issued, lawyers approached, and petitions launched. The latest and most ambitious plan is to lobby the Sejm—Poland's Parliament—for an inquiry into the conduct of the police and militia. All this has been going on, harassed certainly but not halted, for several months.

A feature of the abuse to which Kuron was subjected, and an index of the nervousness of the atmosphere (and the authorities), is anti-Semitism. Things are not as bad as they were in 1968 (when the "cosmopolitan" origins of student leaders were sneered at in the newspapers). But they are nasty. One man who wrote an insulting letter to Kuron by registered mail sent another letter by hand saying that the anti-Semitic innuendos in the first one had been dictated to him in a police station. Nobody to whom I told this story (unprovable by me firsthand though I saw the letters) seemed a bit surprised. It is, of course, an utterly deranged method of dealing with dissent; first because Kuron himself is *not* Jewish, and second because much of the vulgar postwar anti-Semitism in Poland originates in the fact that so many of the Communist Party apparat *were*. For a communist government to use, or tolerate the use of, a racial prejudice which has been used against itself is a kind of cynicism which suggests more than temporary unease.

Indeed, cynicism is a common currency. Although many of the Committee to Defend the Workers (K.O.R.) are ex-members of the Polish Socialist Party (and, interestingly, mention the fact in the short biographies they have produced), the general boredom with political rhetoric goes incredibly deep. True, the dissidents set great store by the support of Western Communist and Socialist parties. But they are careful to de-emphasize politics when approaching Polish public opinion. One girl who worked as a sympathizer of the Committee told me that she found herself believing things she knew not to be true or reasonable, just because the government media kept telling her the opposite. Kuron himself, whose prison sentence was largely incurred for a near-Trotskyist critique of the ruling party in the sixties, said rather sadly that he did not feel the next wave of popular opposition would be very socialist in character because the very word had been brought into disrepute by the authorities.

The treatment of news, ideas, and information is, indeed, revealingly bad. Bad, for the obvious reason that it is monotone and boring. Revealing, because any intelligent Pole can get the book or paper he requires, listen to the radio, or correspond with friends abroad. It takes a little effort and, in the case of Radio Free Europe, a little skepticism, but it can be done and the government knows it. Why, then, does it persist in acting as if it did not? It almost suggests that those in charge of propaganda do not care whether they are believed or not. One example. Everybody knew that the much hailed Corvalán release in exchange for Bukovsky was due to a deal and not to the trumpeted "international solidarity." Another example. The second shipyard strike at Stettin in 1971 was virtually provoked by workers reading in the Party paper that they had volunteered to work longer hours in the interest of production. How could the editor have imagined anybody believing him? There were promises of more press freedom at the start of the Gierek administration, but these have receded.

Sometimes the papers behave like an extension of the police force. Recently, visiting and domiciled Polish dissidents in London were called on by the Special Branch and asked if they intended any protest against the visit of Prime Minister Jaroszewicz. (This is routine in the case of state visits to London and probably ought not to be as much taken for granted as it is.) The newspaper *Zycie Warszawy* then reported on its front page that Adam Michnik and others had been held by the British police for anti-British activities, defining anti-British as anti-Polish and linking the two with the spirit of international cooperation. Michnik is quite well known in Poland as a historian and political activist. He proposes to return there soon. The falsity of the report will become obvious to all. It is hardly surprising that the Polish government lacks sympathy and understanding among the intelligentsia.

It is quite impossible to gauge the likelihood of the upsurge that some people have gleefully or gloomily predicted. The only certain thing is that opposition has become markedly more bold at all levels, and police methods more jumpy. People are arrested and released again very quickly, as if minds were changing every minute. Interference with the distribution of the K.O.R. communiqués is sporadic and random. The international telephone system is a great boon, and so is the internal one. Workers are prepared to go on strike, and to sign open petitions for the rehiring of sacked employees. Students are prepared to collect money and organize other forms of support and discussion. There is also the prestige of the Church, which publicly criticizes the violations of human rights, without falling into the trap of Cardinal Mindszenty's rabid reactionary line. Indeed, its record on anti-Semitism is better than that of many Western Catholic leaderships. (Again on the press, Cardinal Wyszynski made a strong statement on repression in his Christmas sermon, in a country not much less than 90-percent Catholic, and there was not a word of it reported.)

When I spoke to Adam Michnik, he was guardedly optimistic. The long Spanish struggle for liberty had impressed him very much by its determination and its solidarity. He felt that there were ways of enlarging the area of pluralism in the here and now, but that there was always the possibility of an outright conflict with no real winners. As for socialism, he favored it in spite of its discredit. "After all, freedom and democracy are words that have been discredited by governments as well, but we do not abandon them. The real struggle for us is for citizens to cease being the property of the state." There must be a fair number of Polish and Russian bureaucrats who wish they did not own this particular troublesome freehold.

(*New Statesman*, January 14, 1977)

CONVERSATION WITH DJILAS

❏

The victimization of Milovan Djilas is the outstanding blot on Tito's claim
to sturdy independence within the communist world. A revolution which
cannot deal honorably with its own historians, which forbids them to publish
in their own country and then traduces them as unpatriotic when they publish
abroad, is in some important sense deformed. When I saw him in June 1977,
Djilas was resigned to obscurity in his native heath. Not only was he forbidden to sell his political work in Yugoslavia and subjected to various limitations on his movements in and out of the country, but he also found
himself prohibited from marketing his translation of *Paradise Lost* into Serbo-
Croat. And, as he remarked ruefully, there is no other translation which
could serve in its stead. Party leaderships commonly distrust and dislike the
heretic more than they detest the common enemy, but the streak of peasant
vengeance which has been vented on Djilas has deprived young Yugoslavs
of the chance to find out where they really came from.

Because, with his new book *Wartime*, Djilas has undertaken to describe
the birth of a nation. Total war came early to Yugoslavia, made all the more
terrible by the fact that the Nazi invaders considered their victims to be
racially inferior. This license to kill led to such atrocity, and such resistance,
that by the end Churchill and Stalin were vying for the favors of the communist leadership. The fact that both scrounging imperial paws were severely
bitten goes to show something that is still true—and still denied by impe-
rialists of all hues. Put simply, whole peoples do not wage bitter struggles
for liberation in order to become the creatures of another power. Yugoslavia
was really the first country in this century to prove that point, and to uphold
it in the face of the travesty socialism of other lands "liberated" by the Red
Army alone.

The scope and intensity of *Wartime* is such as to defy paraphrase. For
example, here is Djilas recording an incident in the hideous winter of 1943:

> The Italians in the little town surrendered, and we took over the outer forti-
> fications. All the Italian troops—the entire Third Battalion of the 259th Regiment
> of the Murge division—were put to death. We put into effect the conditions

they had rejected, and vented our bitterness. Only the drivers were spared—
to help transport the munitions and the wounded. Many corpses were tossed
into the Rama river. Several got caught among the logs, and I shared with our
officers a malicious joy at the thought of Italian officers on the bridges and
embankments of Mostar stricken with horror at the sight of the Neretva choked
with the corpses of their soldiers.

It seems useful to quote this at length because it shows total callousness:
such prisoners as are spared are specifically described as being spared for
the performance of menial tasks. Also because Djilas does not just describe
the gloating of others at the deed, but specifically includes his own
schadenfreude.

Unlike all previous Balkan hostilities, the fight of the Yugoslav partisans
was not just for national emancipation but for a parallel social revolution.
Thus it was a civil war as well, and some of Djilas's most effective passages
describe the cruelty and coldness of the battle between Tito's men and the
pro-fascist forces and their collaborators. If anything had been missing from
the description of total war, this last dimension supplied it. It also, and of
necessity, internationalized the conflict. Tito and Djilas looked to Moscow
as the motherland of all oppressed classes and nations. Djilas sets down here,
as he has in a different context elsewhere, his initial misgivings about the
great despot. Stalin in these pages radiates cynicism and cunning, and another feature which is less often remarked: he did not seem to care what
even his most devoted foreign admirers thought of him. This glimpse of
untrammeled, arrogant, *pure* power is valuable even if it is not surprising
in retrospect. One has to imagine a man like Djilas, who has fought the
Wehrmacht for scorched earth over several years, has lost almost all his
family and many of his friends, has fought not in somebody else's country
but in his very own, and who then takes a precarious airplane flight to
discover disgust in Moscow. The sequence of events makes up a genuine
fragment of twentieth-century experience.

Eurocommunism these days is presented as a bland and sophisticated
business. There is the Gucci socialism of Enrico Berlinguer or the *petit-
commerçant* compromise of Georges Marchais, both redolent of the main
chance but both partially sanctified by the resistance records of the parties
concerned. Djilas is one of those uncomfortable presences who remind us
of the pioneers and of the utter ruthlessness required in order to have a
revolution and to preserve it. He concludes:

Revolutions are justified as acts of life, acts of living. Their idealization is a
cover-up for the egotism and love of power of the new revolutionary masters.
But efforts to restore pre-revolutionary forms are even more meaningless and
unrealistic. I sensed all of this even then. But choice does not depend only on

one's personal outlook but also on reality. With my present outlook, I would not have been able to do what I had done then.

There is a testament of ambiguity worth having, from a man who knows. When I saw Djilas last, he had not degenerated into cynicism. He described himself as a democratic socialist ("Please, *not* a social democrat. They want to reform capitalism; I want to reform communism"). So I asked him whom he admired. The answer was swift and provocative. "If you mean current thinkers, I most admire von Hayek and Karl Popper." *Hayek?* "Yes, though I cannot agree with him about property." It seemed at first sight like *Hamlet* without the prince, but when one of the leaders of the revolution has to keep his mouth shut, and when the right to hold an opinion is more important than what opinions you hold, perhaps it isn't so surprising. After *Wartime*, it would be difficult to be surprised by anything.

(*New Statesman*, September 9, 1977)

A SENSE OF MISSION:
The Raj Quartet

❏

The approach to Bombay over the Arabian Sea is both more and less stirring when made by Air-India than when taken as a passage on the P&O Line. You miss the commerce of Port Said, the charms of the Canal, and the stunning heat of Steamer Point at Aden. But, if you are lucky enough to arrive in early evening, you see the gorgeous Bombay waterfront from the air. It reveals itself as a string of pointed brilliants along a fine and curvaceous corniche. "See—we are calling it Queen Victoria's necklace," said my Indian neighbor with more pride than irony. Once on the ground, the first-time visitor has an Aladdin's cave of choice. There is the Gateway to India, a grandiose arched monument to the visit of Their Majesties King George and Queen Mary in 1911. Beside it stands the Taj Hotel, one of the finest in the Orient and a place of resort which was, in colonial times, what Shepheards was to Cairo or Raffles to Singapore. A boat ride from the steps will take you to the Island of the Elephants, to inspect the cave art of prehistory. In the other direction, a horse-drawn taxi will deposit you at a respectful distance from the Towers of Silence, where the Parsees expose their dead to the reverent and efficient vultures. Many of the inhabitants of this ancient quarter are recent arrivals from Iran, where the new Islamic Republic has no time for their rare and exclusive beliefs. It was in Bombay, too, that Mohammed Ali Jinnah was born, practiced law, and began to conceive of the first modern state to be consecrated to Islam. He wanted to name it for the provinces of Punjab, Afghanistan, Kashmir, and Sind. The acronym Pakistan, thus happily formed in the Urdu tongue, means "Land of the Pure."

Behind the imposing British-built law courts, railway station, museum, and civil-service buildings, there is as fine a stew of misery and deprivation as you could wish to find. This area of the city sends its envoys up to the corniche, each one accredited with the appropriate sores, deformities, and amputations. I used to think that the story of "organized begging"—of urchin godfathers and ghetto Fagins—was a callous invention by British tourists who wanted to rationalize their own parsimony. It isn't. Offer a parched and filthy child a sandwich and a glass of milk after he's followed you along the street pointing at his stomach and his open mouth, and see what happens. He looks almost terrified. He must furnish the handful of coins at the end of the day, or woe will betide him.

All this is temporarily eclipsed for me, however, by an incident on my very first day. I have come to write a film script for the BBC, so I am met by an English travel agent and a driver. The agent is a veteran; parchment-colored and carefully dressed; one of those who "stayed on" after independence instead of legging it to Kenya, to Rhodesia, or to Cheltenham. He smokes and so do I, so I offer him an English cigarette ("from home," as he puts it) and pass the packet in front of the Indian driver. The driver takes one, too, and stores it somewhere. I'm at once aware of a certain "as it were" in the atmosphere. As soon as the driver has left us, my protector says, in a moderately avuncular way, "Look, old boy, you're new here. A word of advice. It doesn't do to be too chummy. Only encourages them."

I ought really to be angry or impatient. But I am delighted. So it *is* true! They really *did* talk like that. Here is a direct, anthropological link with a past that seems, over a mere forty years, to have receded into antiquity. The tones of the Raj, so often caricatured and lampooned, still have their continuity. Except that, today, their proprietor would not care to employ them in front of the driver.

My grandfather was a ranker in the Indian army, and his retirement bungalow was named for the hill station of Coonoor. Gurkha kukris and a bound history of the Mutiny were the centerpieces of its decoration, together with a scattering of ivory elephants and a Benares brass tray as if ready for a round of Kim's game. My father's naval and military club was hung with prints, more than half of them commemorating battles like Chillianwallah or Gandamack—bloody shows in which the outnumbered British (how few there always were, in truth as well as in legend) fought off the gaudy warriors of the Mahrattas or kept watch on the hopeless defiles of the Khyber Pass.

One grew up knowing about it. Today, in every English town there is at least one restaurant called the Star of India, and in London the mixture of Bengali, Gujerati, Punjabi, and Tamil recipes has produced one of the world's finest cuisines—a staple for lower-income Brits as well as, at its most exalted, a luxury and an indulgence. Sikh temples and Pakistani mosques have broken the near-monopoly of the Church of England; men with turbans and women in saris are a common sight, though, as in their home country, they are too often relegated to sweepers' jobs. In everyday language there is an Indian presence in the vernacular, ranging from innocuous words like *veranda*, *bungalow*, and *gymkhana* to more ominous ones such as *juggernaut*, *goon*, and *thug*. The Raj is all around us, still.

If English history divides into the imperial and the postimperial, then the only really important date in the transition is 1948, when the subcontinent became simultaneously partitioned and independent. India was not just the Jewel in the Crown; she was the crown. All other imperial commitments— in Egypt, Mesopotamia, Aden, Cyprus, Somalia, and elsewhere—were undertaken with the idea of safeguarding or shortening the route to India. Even the Cape of Good Hope was seen as a staging post to Bombay. Once India had "gone," you could predict with certainty that the rest would wither. There was no point. No one had the heart or the stomach to keep them up. For many English people, the shock has never worn off. As they look back on India, the British feel that odd and stirring mixture of guilt and pride that is the essence of the postimperial. Paul Scott's quadrilogy is without competitors in the skill with which it distills this essence further into literature.*

These antinomies—of pride and guilt in having "civilized" India and exploited the Indians—have their ancestry in the Victorian era. The two greatest historical commentators of the period both expressed themselves vividly on India and "the Indian Question." One way of introducing Scott's achievement is to compare and contrast the writings of Marx and Macaulay.

When Ernest Jones, the Chartist leader, first heard the imperialist phrase about the dominion "on which the sun never sets," he added scornfully, "and on which the blood never dries." Marx and Macaulay would have found the first phrase fatuous but the second simplistic. Even when I was a stripling, English schoolchildren were still being taught, and sometimes made to learn by heart, Macaulay's famous encomium to British rule in the East. He enthralled the House of Commons, on July 10, 1833, with a long and majestic defense of the India Bill, the *locus classicus* (for once the term is unaffected) of what lesser Britons could hardly have articulated for themselves. What he articulated was the sense of mission. India before the advent of the East India Company had been, he declared, "the rapid succession of Alarics and Attilas passing over the defenceless empire." With this brisk dismissal of past millennia, Macaulay went on to evoke the British engagement in "a great, a stupendous process—the reconstruction of a decomposed society." He stressed the unselfish optimism with which this project was being executed:

I observe with reverence and delight the honourable poverty which is the evidence of a rectitude firmly maintained amidst strong temptations. I rejoice to see my countrymen, after ruling millions of subjects . . . return to their native land with no more than a decent competence.

* The four books in *The Raj Quartet* are *The Jewel in the Crown*, *The Day of the Scorpion*, *The Towers of Silence*, and *A Division of the Spoils*.

This was certainly the self-image in which the servants of the East India Company were wont to bask. But, as Macaulay wrote to his sister, Lady Hannah Trevelyan, on August 17 of the same year:

> I must live; I can live only by my pen, and it is absolutely impossible for any man to write enough to procure him a decent subsistence, and at the same time to take an active part in politics. I have never made more than two hundred pounds a year by my pen. I could not support myself in comfort on less than five hundred, and I shall in all probability have many others to support. The prospects of our family are, if possible, darker than ever.

However, there was a gleam of light in this Stygian prospect—the offer of a post as Law Member in India. As he went on:

> The salary is ten thousand pounds a year. I am assured by persons who know Calcutta intimately and have themselves mixed in the highest circles and held the highest offices at that Presidency, that I may live in splendour there for five thousand a year, and may save the rest of the salary with the accruing interest. I may therefore hope to return to England, at only thirty-nine, in the full vigour of life, with a fortune of thirty thousand pounds. A larger fortune I never desired.

He got the job a year later and did indeed return from Calcutta with something more than "a decent competence." We are all the richer for it, so it might seem churlish to draw attention to this example of the higher British hypocrisy. There was, at any rate, something of magnificence about it.

The striking thing about Karl Marx's view of the matter is not its hostility to that of Macaulay but its similarity. In a penetrating series of articles in the *New York Daily Tribune*, published in 1853, he naturally excoriated the greed and the callousness of the British system of extraction. But, in a passage that almost recalls Macaulay on "Alarics and Attilas," he wrote:

> Sickening as it must be to human feeling to witness those myriads of industrious, patriarchal and inoffensive social organizations disorganized and dissolved into their units, thrown into a sea of woes, and their individual members losing at the same time their ancient form of civilisation and their hereditary means of subsistence, we must not forget that these idyllic village communities, inoffensive though they may appear, had always been the solid foundation of Oriental despotism, that they restrained the human mind within the smallest possible compass, making it the unresisting tool of superstition, enslaving it beneath traditional rules, depriving it of all grandeur and historical energies. . . .
>
> We must not forget that this stagnatory, undignified and vegetative life, that this passive sort of existence, evoked on the other hand, in contradistinction, wild, aimless, unbounded forces of destruction and rendered murder itself a religious rite in Hindustan.

We must not forget that these little communities were contaminated by distinctions of caste and by slavery, that they subjected man to external circumstances instead of elevating man to the sovereign of circumstances, that they transformed a self-developing social state into never-changing natural destiny, and thus brought about a brutalising worship of nature, exhibiting its degradation in the fact that man, the sovereign of nature, fell down on his knees in adoration of Hanuman, the monkey, and Sabbala, the cow.

In a very candid and blunt fashion, Marx affirmed that "the British were the first conquerors superior, and therefore inaccessible, to Hindu civilisation." Not content to treat India as a mere satrapy, they had penetrated down to village level in pursuit of gain, and their introduction of cotton-milling machinery and of a network of railways had begun the transformation of the country even though, as one governor general reported in the year that Macaulay took up his post, "The misery hardly finds a parallel in the history of commerce. The bones of the cotton-weavers are bleaching the plains of India."

Marx identified five tendencies, all of them derived from British dominion, which gave promise of making India what it had never been before—a country in its own right. The first was "political unity . . . more consolidated and extending further than ever it did under the Great Moguls"; a unity which was to be "strengthened and extended by the electric telegraph." Second was the existence of a "native army," disciplined and owing allegiance to a central power. Third was "the free press, introduced for the first time into Asiatic society." Fourth was the creation, however grudgingly, of a stratum of educated Indians, "endowed with the requirements for government and imbued with European science." Finally, and rather obviously, comes "regular and rapid communication with Europe" through steamships. All of these developments, given time to mature, would enable Indians to transcend the colonial power which had, for its own purposes, conferred the benefits.

I haven't the least idea whether Paul Scott (who died in 1979) ever read these tentative but prescient articles. His *Quartet*, nevertheless, illustrates their point to an extraordinary degree. By the time that we are introduced to his characters, British and Indian, and to their context, it has become obvious that India has outgrown Britain. "We don't rule this country any more," says the resentful policeman Ronald Merrick to the thoughtful Sarah Layton. "We preside over it." Only the most myopic and farcical characters in these four novels fail to see that this is true. Of those who *do* see it, each achieves the realization in a different way and with differing degrees of good grace. But the novels are unique in their genre, in taking the end of Empire as imminent, or for granted, from the very first page.

In the four successive novels, though, the British as a class are still reclining on their credit without fully realizing that a term has been set to it. "Political unity," especially in contrast to the venality and instability of the Moguls, is endlessly celebrated as the justification for Empire. So is the wonder of the electric telegraph and the railway. The "native army," in the shape of the Pankot Rifles and the Muzzafirabad Guides, is practically the raison d'être of the British military caste, the existence of an Indian host under the British flag affording the most adamant proof of the durability of their "mission." Hari Kumar, in his Anglicized incarnation as Harry Coomer, exemplifies both the "free press" and the emergence of the educated governing class. He is so English and sophisticated that he irritates even the non-public-school Brits (like Ronald Merrick). When he has annoyed so many of them as to make himself unemployable, he finds a job on one of the local papers—the Mayapore *Gazette*. Though the British censor the paper in time of emergency, they can never quite bring themselves to close it down.

As World War II begins, the authorities are becoming queasily aware that even their favorite Indians are turning against them. There is passive resistance when the viceroy declares war on the Axis, on behalf of India, without even the pretense of consulting the Indian National Congress. Passive resistance turns to riot and mayhem when the leaders of the Congress Party are arrested for urging noncooperation with the war effort. In the course of this disorder, the British find that it is the most advanced and refined Indians who are the political leaven. Worse still, there are rumors from the war front with Japan. It seems that soldiers and officers of the Indian army have deserted and joined the enemy, preferring even Hirohito to continued British rule. Of what avail are the telegraphs and the railway networks when the natives have become convinced that theirs is to be the last unfree generation?

In almost every chapter of the quadrilogy there is some reference, however slanting, to one or other of two historical events. The first is "Bibighar" and the second is "Jallianwallah," or Amritsar. Bibighar is the name of the public garden where Daphne Manners, an awkward, gentle, decent English girl, is set upon by a gang and raped during the "disturbances" above. The injustice which results from this outrage, and the perverted motives of those who perpetrate and perpetuate the injustice, is the nemesis of the whole *Quartet*. It is the single incident that binds all the characters, and all the action, together. "Bibighar" happens also to be the name of the place in Cawnpore where English women and children were done to death by the sepoy mutineers of 1857. "Jallianwallah," in apparent contrast, was the bazaar district of Amritsar where, on April 13, 1919, General Dyer gave the order to fire on a protesting crowd, killing over three hundred and maiming over one thousand Indians.

These two "incidents" became part of the British imperial psyche. The Bibighar massacre at Cawnpore was essential in providing a righteous justification for the crushing of the Indian Mutiny—a crushing that was not without its own sadistic aspect, with prisoners blown from the mouths of cannon and others flogged nearly to death. (Marx and Macaulay both, incidentally, agreed that the British were justified in suppressing a revolt aimed at the restoration of the Mogul system. It was the events of 1857 that decided the British to replace the East India Company with direct rule by the Crown—a conspicuous "advance.")

Amritsar/Jallianwallah was more complex. Officially, General Dyer's action was condemned. But the view of most of the colonial Establishment, who clubbed together for an appeal fund in his name, was that he was an honest soldier betrayed by the usual pusillanimous bureaucrats. Mabel Layton, the honorable military widow in Scott's narrative, risks ostracism by sending her subscription instead to the families of the massacred Indians. Toward the end of her life, when she talks in her sleep and appears to be asking for someone named "Gillian Waller," nobody can make out her ramblings.

It's not too much to say that these two symbols form the counterpoint of *The Raj Quartet*. On the one hand is the fear—in part a guilty fear—of treachery, mutiny, and insurrection; of burning and pillage in which even one's own servants cannot be trusted. On the other is the fear of having to break that trust oneself; of casting aside the pretense of consent and paternalism and ruling by terror and force. The persistence of these two complementary nightmares says a good deal about the imperial frame of mind.

Scott works on this counterpoint in a long, clever section entitled "Civil and Military," in which he gives two accounts of the same Indian uprising in 1942. The first is by Brigadier A. V. Reid, author of the unpublished memoir "A Simple Life." The second is by Robin White of the Indian Civil Service. Reid is one of those brilliantly uncomprehending fellows who just haven't got the point about the end of Empire and who are inclined to "leave all that to the politicians" while they "get on with the job in hand." For him, law is law and order is order. Like Dyer, he can make history only by accident. White sets him off perfectly by saying:

> I honestly believe that the Indian is emotionally predisposed against violence. That would explain the hysteria that usually marks his surrender to it. He then goes beyond all ordinary bounds, like someone gone mad because he's destroying his own faith as well. We on the other hand are emotionally disposed *towards* violence, and have to work hard at keeping ourselves in order. Which is why at the beginning of our wars we've always experienced a feeling of relief and said things like, "Now we know where we stand."

Having caught, with such economy, the British attitude to fighting (We didn't start it but we can finish it. . . . We lose every battle but the last), White also makes the following dry observations:

I would take as my premiss that the Indians wanted to be free, and that we also wished this, but that they had wanted to be free for just that much longer than we had felt or agreed that they should be; that given this situation the conflict arose partly as a result of the lack of synchronisation of the timing of the two wishes but also because this, in time, developed into a lack of synchronisation of the wishes themselves.

This must be Scott speaking. In 1857, the British *knew* they were right, and may have been. In 1919, they had to bellow that they were right in order to drown out the suspicion that they might be wrong. By 1942, the only justification for remaining in India was, at least ostensibly, the defeat of the Japanese. But, by then, Indians had lost interest in all justifications, however righteous. The simplicity of Gandhi's slogan—Quit India!—was ideal in its pith and pungency. Unfortunately, he also added (as his admirers tend to forget) that the British should leave India "to God or to anarchy," which was a false antithesis in view of what lay ahead, as well as a very permissive view of Japanese imperialism.

This is the point at which to introduce Scott's second main theme. Even while the British were thumping their chests about preserving India, they were preparing to amputate and dismember it. *The Raj Quartet* foreshadows and prefigures partition from its earliest chapters. Hari Kumar writes, as Harry Coomer, to his old friend from public-school days in England, Colin Lindsey. The year is 1940, and young Lindsey is back from Dunkirk:

I think there's no doubt that in the last twenty years—whether intentionally or not—the English *have* succeeded in dividing and ruling, and the kind of conversation I hear at these social functions I attend—Guides recruitment, Jumble Sales, mixed cricket matches (usually rained off and ending with a bunfight in a series of tents invisibly marked Europeans Only and Other Races)—makes me realise the extent to which the English now seem to depend upon the divisions in Indian political opinion perpetuating their own rule at least until after the war, if not for some time beyond it. They are saying openly that it is "no good leaving the bloody country because there's no Indian party representative enough to hand it over to." They prefer Muslims to Hindus (because of the closer affinity that exists between God and Allah than exists between God and the Brahma), are constitutionally predisposed to Indian princes, emotionally affected by the thought of untouchables, and mad keen about the peasants who look upon any Raj as God. . . . But isn't two hundred years long enough to unify? They accept credit for all the improvements they've made. But can you claim credit for one without accepting blame for the other? Who, for instance, five years ago, had ever heard of the concept of Pakistan—the separate Muslim state? I can't believe that Pakistan will ever become a reality, but if it does it will be because the English prevaricated long enough to allow a favoured religious minority to seize a political opportunity.

Kumar has seen the irony, one that encompasses his own position. The British are now negating their very own justification for being in India and are allying themselves with exactly the forces of feudalism, of faction, and of superstition which it was their original mission to depose. But, with the coming of the Japanese threat, there is one last excuse. Even the liberal Brits, like the selfless and dotty missionary Edwina Crane, take down their pictures of Gandhi. With characteristic sympathy, Scott portrays their hopeless position too:

> The upright oblong patch of pale distemper, all that was left to Miss Crane of the Mahatma's spectacled, smiling image, the image of a man she had put her faith in which she had now transferred to Mr Nehru and Mr Rajagopalachari who obviously understood the different degrees of tyranny men could exercise and, if there had to be a preference, probably preferred to live a little while longer with the imperial degree in order not only to avoid submitting to but to resist the totalitarian. Looking at Clancy and Barrett and imagining in their place a couple of indoctrinated storm-troopers or ancestor-worshippers, whose hope of heaven lay in death in battle, she knew which she herself preferred.

Which is finely wrought stuff, but which does not prevent Miss Crane and Miss Daphne Manners from being coarsely handled when the Indians rebel against their actual oppressors. The point is that Britain's right to decide these questions of preference and degree is no longer acknowledged *even when*, or perhaps *especially when*, the British themselves may have a point. This is Robin White's paradox about timing and synchronization. Scott illustrates the problem by showing how Edwina Crane and Daphne Manners are made the excuse for reprisal by the very type of Englishman they least admire. In this apparent contradiction, of humane argument being made the license for an inhumane policy, Scott catches the end of Empire. It is the cultivated Hari who is framed for the assault on Daphne, and framed by men who loathe his educated bearing and detest the thought of interracial "carrying-on." The whole contradiction is put, with ferocious understatement, in the early chapters of *The Towers of Silence*:

> If you look in places like Ranpur for evidence of things these island people left behind which were of value, you might choose any one of several of the public works and installations as visible proof of them: the roads and railways and telegraphs for a modern system of communication, the High Court for a sophisticated code of civil and criminal law, the college for education to university standard, the State Legislature for democratic government, the Secretariat for a civil service made in the complex image of that in Whitehall; the clubs for a pattern of urbane and civilised behaviour, the messes and barracks for an ideal of military service to the mother country. These were bequeathed, undoubtedly; these and the language and the humpy graves in the English cemetery of St

Luke's in the oldest part of the cantonment, many of whose headstones record an early death, a cutting off before the prime or in the prime, with all that this suggests in the way of unfinished business.

But it is not these things which most impress the stranger on his journey into the civil lines, into the old city itself. . . . What impresses him is something for which there is no memorial but which all these things collectively bear witness to: the fact that here in Ranpur, and in places like Ranpur, the British came to the end of themselves as they were.

Here is the elegiac echo of the annual Remembrance Day service ("And some there are who have no memorial"). Here, also, we can find a reminiscence of Macaulay ("the prime or in the prime" sits well with the "full vigour of life" with which he hoped to enjoy his spoils) and more than an echo of Marx, who saw that the imperial edifice was built to change but not to last. He did not anticipate, as he celebrated the technical and administrative innovations of the British, that they would lose to a man who revered the spinning wheel and the stifling village culture.

The British began by raping and plundering India, then developed a sentimental conscience about it, only then conceived of themselves as "civilizers." At the start, an officer was supposed to be the father of his native troops—thus the concept of "Man Bap," which carried with it the responsibility to die for them if need arose. One of Scott's officers actually does live up to this code, expending his life in a pointless attempt to retrieve some deserters. But the image that remains is that of his brother officers, who never even put on their shoes without first rapping them on the floor for fear of scorpions. By the very end, they were full of pretended astonishment and hurt at the base ingratitude of their subjects. As Brecht once put it:

> And even in Atlantis of the legend,
> The night the seas rushed in—
> The drowning men still bellowed for their slaves.

Like E. M. Forster, Scott saw the ways in which illustrations of sex and character could bring these dilemmas alive. His most scrupulously drawn figures are sometimes the ones who take up the least apparent space. Among these, the brave and gawky Daphne Manners is the most salient. She realizes quickly, even from her protected background, that the sex thing and the race thing have a kind of sickly connection:

I thought that the whole bloody affair of us in India had reached flash point. It was bound to, because it was based on a violation. Perhaps at one time there was a moral as well as a physical force at work. But the moral thing had gone sour. Has gone sour. Our faces reflect the sourness. The women look worse than the men because consciousness of physical superiority is unnatural to us. A white man in India can feel physically superior without unsexing himself. But what happens to a woman if she tells herself that ninety-nine per cent of the men she sees are not men at all, but creatures of an inferior species whose colour is their main distinguishing mark? What happens when you unsex a nation, treat it like a nation of eunuchs? Because that's what we've done, isn't it?

The matter of "character," always so decisive in a colonial enterprise, is given great prominence by Scott's narrative. Daphne's aunt, Lady Ethel Manners, is by her rank and station invulnerable to the climbers and the bigots who infest the British community. Nobody can accuse her, the widow of a governor, of being low in moral fiber. So, when she says

> the creation of Pakistan is our crowning failure. I can't bear it. They should never have got rid of Wavell. Our only justification for two hundred years of power was unification. But we've divided one composite nation into two and everyone at home goes round saying what a swell the new Viceroy is for getting it all sorted out so quickly——

she is hard to contradict.

Scott disliked hypocrisy, and his novels are pitiless about self-deception. He even admires those who are honest in their prejudices and prepared to take risks for them. Ronald Merrick, the chip-on-the-shoulder cop who proposes to Daphne and who frames Kumar, has no time for Daphne's agonies of embarrassment for the gelded Indian male:

> That's the oldest trick in the game, to say colour doesn't matter. It does matter. It's basic. It matters like hell.

Mohammed Ali Kasim, the Muslim Congress activist who knows that Congress is becoming a Hindu sectarian movement but who will not betray his party to the British and spends the war in prison, is another man who gets points for character. He tears a strip off his own son for defecting from the Indian army to the Japanese—not just because it was a politically repulsive act but because it involved the breaking of an oath and the betrayal of friends. The son, of course, opts for Pakistan when the time comes.

Scott's *Quartet* is the only work in English, moreover, which is serious or thoughtful about Subhas Chandra Bose. The neglected and forgotten hero of Bengali resistance to British rule, Bose became the leader of the pro-Japanese deserters during World War II. Streets and squares in Calcutta are still named for him, setting a puzzle for those who believe that India was liberated by Gandhian nonviolence. The figure of Gandhi emerges from Scott's pages in his full and deserved colors: as ambiguous and evasive, and as prepared to compromise with violence only when he could plausibly disown it. The British colonialists seldom appreciated this point, and the English and American liberals never. Scott clearly favors the Indian side but sees no occasion to romanticize it or to conceal the real cost of its victory. This enables him to hold out the realistic promise of genuine friendship between Indians and Englishmen, and to name its price, which was the abolition of hypocrisy and condescension. The condition for that, in turn, was the realization that the glory had departed.

This realization was, in its literal sense, unavailable to Forster. When he was visiting India, and later writing about it, there seemed every likelihood that the Raj would endure for many generations to come. This is one of the many contrasts between his work and that of Scott. The two have been much compared lately, because of the renewed interest in India generated by Richard Attenborough's hagiography of Gandhi and because both *A Passage to India* and *The Jewel in the Crown* have been adapted for the screen.

The prospects for the film version of Forster's masterpiece look dire, if the reported remarks of its director, David Lean, are anything to go by. "As far as I'm aware," he says, "nobody has yet succeeded in putting India on the screen" (*The Times* of London). Too bad for Mrinal Sen and Satyajit Ray. Then he reveals, in an interview with *The Observer*, that

> Forster was a bit anti-English, anti-Raj and so on. I suppose it's a tricky thing to say, but I'm not so much. I intend to keep the balance more. I don't believe all the English were a lot of idiots. Forster rather made them so. . . . I've cut out that bit at the trial where they try to take over the court.
>
> As for Aziz, there's a hell of a lot of Indian in him. They're marvellous people but maddening sometimes, you know. . . . He's a goose. But he's warm and you like him awfully. I don't mean that in a derogatory way—things just happen to him. He can't help it. And Miss Quested . . . well, she's a bit of a prig and a bore in the book, you know. I've changed her, made her more sympathetic. Forster wasn't always very good with women.
>
> One other thing. I've got rid of that "Not yet, not yet" bit. You know, when the Quit India stuff comes up, and we have the passage about driving us into the sea? Forster experts have always said it was important, but the Fielding-Aziz relationship was not sustained by those sorts of things. . . . Anyway, I see it as a personal not a political story.

One rubs the eyes at such a find. What a trove of pristine, boneheaded artifacts! Beside this Compleat Philistine, my Bombay guide is a poet and a dreamer. There is no sense of mission here, no risk taking. Nor yet any grandiose engagement with India. All that is left is a banal sense of superiority and a desire "to keep the balance more." Add the distinctly inexpensive remark about Forster and women, and you have the whole tepid, vulgar mixture at the right temperature.

It's almost enough to coerce one into agreement with Salman Rushdie, the clever author of *Midnight's Children* and *Shame*, who has emerged as a sort of professional scourge of the postcolonial stereotype. But he fails, with his slightly obvious sarcasm, to wipe the foolish smirk of complacency off the face of David Lean. And, in the course of his essay "Outside the Whale," he also attempts a great injustice against Scott;

> The rape of Daphne Manners in the Bibighar Gardens derives just as plainly from Forster's *Passage to India* [*sic*]. . . . Where Forster's scene in the Marabar caves retains its ambiguity and mystery, Scott gives us not one rape but a gang assault, and one perpetrated, what is more, by peasants. Smelly persons of the worst sort. So class as well as sex is violated; Daphne gets the works. It is useless, I'm sure, to suggest that if a rape must be used as the metaphor of the Indo-British connection, then surely, in the interests of accuracy, it should be the rape of an Indian woman by one or more Englishmen of whatever class. . . . Not even Forster dared write about such a crime. So much more evocative to conjure up white society's fear of the darkie, of big brown cocks.

This is so crude as to seem intentionally unfair. It is hopelessly wrong, for a start, in point of the action. What happens to Daphne Manners in the Bibighar is that she is observed, *making love to her Indian boyfriend Hari*, by a gang of louts who she later says (partly to protect Hari, and partly in order to prevent a court hearing) could well have been British soldiers in disguise. How much more different could she be from the spoiled, vapid Adela Quested (made "more sympathetic" by Lean), who only aborts her hysterical frame-up by a last-minute failure of nerve. Not to be too dogmatic about it, Adela is not raped and Aziz is not punished; Daphne is raped, though not by Hari, and Hari is punished.

Indeed, the whole drama of Scott's *Quartet* is that the wrong people are arraigned and viciously punished, for a crime that is not imaginary, by the supposedly civilizing and impartial British. More, that even those who know the circumstances are unable to alter the process. The gradual realization of this injustice, and of its varied implications, is what gives the four books their unity and provides a nexus between the disparate characters. Hari Kumar is himself sexually assaulted by Merrick in the course of his inter-rogation. Does Rushdie say that "not even" Forster would dare to describe *that?* If not, what is the force of his point? As for the "big brown cock" factor, surely Rushdie knows that the British were not especially paranoid on this point (at least not in India). And Daphne seems hardly to have been afraid of the idea at all. One senses a gallery being played to here.

Scott actually uses his rape and its aftermath as a metaphor of divide and rule. The Hindu boys who are flogged, fondled, and framed by the British are also given beef disguised as mutton by their Muslim jailers. The ramifications of this blasphemy (which recalls the British-sponsored dietary violations leading to the 1857 Mutiny) would not be attempted by an author who sought merely to counterfeit Forster.

Yet it is true, in a more generous sense than the one intended by Rushdie, that Scott is in debt to *A Passage to India*. I think that the debt is handsomely paid and that the lines which connect the two works are not plagiaristic but form authentic continuity and descent. Some phrases, for instance, are common to both. "Bridge Party" occurs in both Forster and in *The Day of the Scorpion*. It means not a card game, but an official, sponsored mingling of English hosts and Indian guests. It conjures up appalling scenes of obligatory hospitality and contrived politeness, but it was obviously common colonial argot and therefore available to both authors.

Like Scott, Forster was preoccupied by the Amritsar massacre, which actually occurred between the time of his trip and publication of the novel. Phrases such as "He wanted to flog every native that he saw," "Call in the troops and clear the bazaars," "They ought to crawl" were all inserted as evocations of precisely what General Dyer had actually ordered. It has even been speculated that the name of Aziz's counsel, Amritrao, is intended to recall the Jallianwallah massacre to the inner ear.

In the case of Amritsar, it was the rough treatment of the missionary Marcella Sherwood which brought out the beast in General Dyer and made him command the floggings and the shootings, as well as issue the order that all Indians traverse the street where it happened on their hands and knees. Edwina Crane, the missionary lady who is ill used by the rioters in *The Jewel in the Crown*, is told by their leader that he will not rape her because he would not "waste his strength and manhood on such a dried up old bag of bones." Daphne, too, is unmistakably depicted as plain and awkward. This must owe something to the famous court scene in *A Passage to India* where the prosecutor, Mr. McBryde, gives his opinion that the dark-skinned desire the fair, but never vice versa. An anonymous interjector says, to the horror of the British, "Even when the lady is so uglier than the gentleman?" Alas, what he says is true and undeniable.

Those who employ rape as a literary metaphor for dominion must remember not to take it too far out of its sexual context. Forster and Scott bear this in mind, whereas I think Rushdie overlooks the obvious. Turton, the Collector of the District, remarks in *A Passage to India*, "After all, it's our women who make everything more difficult out here." He implies that they will ask naïve questions about justice, besides making themselves vulnerable to unpleasantness. In his portrayals of Sarah and the Layton family, as well as in his careful depiction of Daphne, Scott is faithful both to Forster and to history on this point.

The political context of *The Raj Quartet* is strikingly more modern than that of *A Passage to India*, but here again Scott has borrowed in order to build. He actually sets himself to answer the question that Forster poses on his penultimate page, where Aziz exclaims, while he and Fielding ride past a statue of Hanuman the monkey:

> "Clear out, all you Turtons and Burtons. We wanted to know you ten years back—now it's too late. If we see you and sit on your committees, it's for political reasons, don't make any mistake. . . . Clear out, clear out, I say. Why are we put to so much suffering? We used to blame you, now we blame ourselves, we grow wiser. Until England is in difficulties we keep silent, but in the next European war—aha, aha! Then is our time." . . .
>
> "Who do you want instead of the English? The Japanese?" jeered Fielding.

The "jeered" there is perfect—Fielding fancies he has asked a clever and unanswerable question. Scott has now managed to answer it.

For a book published in 1924, that was not a bad prefiguration. So many of its themes are taken up in the *Quartet*—the restless feminines, the English distrust of the educated class in which they are supposed to take pride, the paltriness of their justice when their own caste is threatened—that it must be said to stand on Forster's shoulders. Where is the shame in that? Scott took the English experience in India up to the conclusion that Forster could only anticipate. In the course of doing so, he created some imperishable moments and characters which, if read with the honesty with which they are written, make all the pathetic efforts at "Raj revisionism" superfluous. He also, in describing how "the British came to the end of themselves as they were," made a point that is easily overlooked. In its postimperial mode, Britain is often described by reformers as "living on borrowed time." For all its attempt at conveying a sense of urgency, the phrase has rather a comfortable ring to it, redolent of some dowager in Brighton with expensive ailments and an income from a principal which, however depleted, will nonetheless last her time. The achievement of Scott is to have shown how much of that "borrowed time" belonged to other people.

(Grand Street, Winter 1985)

IN THE ERA OF GOOD FEELINGS

❑

LIES, ALL LIES

❏

This week I got my copy of *Quotations From Chairman Ron*, a handy, fresh compendium of Reagan howlers that was put together by Morton Mintz. Mintz is an excellent reporter for *The Washington Post*, and his effort goes right up on my shelf, taking an honored place next to *Reagan for Beginners*, by David Smith and Melinda Gebbie; *There He Goes Again: Ronald Reagan's Reign of Error*, by Mark Green and Gail MacColl; and *Reagan Speaks*, by Paul D. Erickson. In this corner of my library, I can readily put my hand on almost every damn-fool remark, cretinous simplification, historical false-hood, fatuous self-contradiction, "deniable" racist innuendo, pig-ignorant anecdote, sly misrepresentation, and senile discourtesy ever uttered by the village idiot now in occupation of 1600 Pennsylvania Avenue. This little retrieval system is, you might think, enough for my simple needs as a columnist. And yet, and yet . . . With the unappeasable dissatisfaction that is the mark of my kind, I crave just one more book. It could be fat or it could be slim, but it would have to say what the volumes above do not say. It would not dwell on Reagan the klutz or Reagan the ignoramus. It would make the point that hasn't been made in six years of fixed press conferences and stage-managed interviews. Ronald Wilson Reagan is not (just) a hapless blooper merchant. He is a conscious, habitual liar.

Even the reporters who cover the President, and who get together to submit the regular "Reaganism of the Week" that adorns the bottom of Lou Cannon's column in *The Washington Post* every Monday, are a trifle shy about what stares them in the face. Cannon himself, who has seen more of the man than most, has gone no further than to say, "More disquieting than Reagan's performance or prospects on specific issues is a growing suspicion that the President has only passing acquaintance with some of the most important decisions of his Administration." That hardly counts even as a euphemism. In fact, the whole concept of a "Reaganism" is an affectionate collusion with the notion of a genial oldster who's a bit out of his depth. The White House managers can live with that idea. Why, it even attracts sympathy. Many voters of all ages are sure *they* would fluff if they had to make speeches, meet foreign potentates, and face the allegedly adversary press.

But there is a difference between a lie and a slip, and you don't have to be a Boy Scout to notice it. On November 29, 1983, Reagan told Israeli Prime Minister Yitzhak Shamir that he himself had assisted in the liberation of the Nazi death camps. On February 15, 1984, he repeated this claim to Simon Wiesenthal. On March 3, 1984, Cannon wrote a column confirming that both Shamir and Wiesenthal had heard the preposterous claim. Shamir had even retailed the story to the Israeli Cabinet, an incident corroborated by the Cabinet Secretary, Dan Meridor. In *The Nation* for March 4, 1985, Alexander Cockburn made some pithy comments on the claim in the light of Bitburg. Just after his column went to press, Reagan told a group of foreign journalists: "Yes, I know all about things that happened in that war. I was in uniform for four years myself." Even the minor detail is a lie here: Reagan's war service was notoriously confined to the First Motion Picture Unit of the Army Air Corps at the Hal Roach studios in Hollywood, where he never donned a uniform.

Now, it is one thing to say you took the cliffs in Normandy when you were throwing up in a landing craft a hundred yards from the beach. In the American Legion posts that display Reagan's grinning photograph, feats like that (and amazing feats of valor in Indochina) are boozily exhaled every night of the week. And, ever since *Henry V*, it's been allowed and expected of the veteran that "He'll remember, with advantages, what deeds he did that day." But Reagan's boast to Shamir and Wiesenthal is not the pardonable "embellishment" (Cannon's term) of an old fart long past his best. It is an insult to the victims whose moral credit he is trying to appropriate. It is an insult to those who did risk their lives. And it is a lie. In fact, given the certainty of detection, it almost counts as a pathological lie. According to some experts, pathological liars will pass a polygraph test because they don't know the difference between truth and falsehood. If only Reagan would submit as willingly to the polygraph machine as to urinalysis. But there are clear limits to his willingness to share in the tribulations he imposes on others.

If you bear the Shamir distinction in mind, it becomes easier to read the numerous blooper anthologies. Reagan may not know the difference between Bolivia and Brazil, and may get a laugh for not knowing, while many in the audience secretly think, "Who's counting?" That might be written off as a blunder. But to say that South Africa "has stood beside us in every war we've ever fought" is not to mistake South Africa for France, say; it is to make a false claim and hope that nobody notices. Which is to say, it is to lie. To say that "North and South Vietnam had been, previous to colonization, two different countries" is to show a fantastic, almost incredible, ignorance and stupidity. To claim that he has just had a message "from Pope John Paul, urging us to continue our efforts in Central America" is to lie.

I don't want to seem pompous by insisting on this distinction, but it is an important one. And liberals and satirists have often overlooked it. Of course, some politicians are know-nothings and vaguely proud of the fact. But the Reagan presidency has been a sort of experiment in the limits of mendacity, made even more objectionable by its presentation as "wing-and-prayer" inspired amateurism.

Don't be discouraged from getting Morton Mintz's book. But don't fall for the forgiving "Saturday Night Live" version of Reagan as a bumbling dotard. He's a dotard all right, and a bumbler too. But liars don't merit the indulgence that is reserved for dotards and bumblers. How can you tell when he's lying and when he's just making it up? No easy answer here. A rule of thumb is that when he's lying, his lips move.

(The Nation, September 20, 1986)

THE MEESE FACTOR

❑

In October 1975, the staff of the Watergate special prosecutor released its final report. Prominent among the recommendations was the following:

> The President should not nominate, and the Senate should not confirm, as Attorney General or as any other appointee in high Department of Justice posts, a person who has served as the President's campaign manager or in a similar high-level campaign role. . . . A campaign manager seeks support for his candidate and necessarily incurs obligations to political leaders and other individuals through wide geographic areas.

If only the liabilities incurred by Edwin Meese were merely geographic in their scope. He has shown, in his contriving a tax exemption for the racialist degree-mill Bob Jones University, that his loyalty is to the Republican Party platform rather than to the body of law and precedent. He has proved, in his correspondence with Reagan crony Lyn Nofziger regarding the desegregation of schools in Washington State, that his right ear is cocked to the voices of his fellow time-servers. He has also shown, in his December 1983 comment about poor people's preference for soup kitchens and in his description of the American Civil Liberties Union as a "criminals' lobby," that his other ear is as deaf as a stump.

Unfortunately, it is not these considerations that will obstruct his confirmation as Attorney General of the United States. When the Senate Judiciary Committee meets next month for what the White House and the Republican majority regard as a pushover hearing, they will have to confront three serious contradictions in the bluff testimony Meese gave before the committee last March. These were not recognized at the time. Nor were they emphasized sufficiently in the report of independent counsel Jacob A. Stein. They are:

1. *The Barrack Factor*. On March 5, 1984, Thomas Barrack, a real-estate developer, told the Senate Judiciary Committee that although he had helped sell Meese's house in La Mesa, California (putting $83,000 of his own money into the deal), and had later secured a government post, he "had never had a meeting in Mr. Meese's office" between the two events. In a testimony richly larded with "I cannot recall" and "at that point in time," this assertion was one of the few that Barrack made unambiguously. He added, "Did Mr. Meese ever talk to me about a job? Absolutely not."

Buried in the turgid and evasive text of the Stein report is clear proof that Barrack met at least three times with Meese between the house sale and his appointment as Deputy Under Secretary of the Interior. He met Meese in Washington on September 8, 1982, one week after the sale. Stein records a letter concerning that meeting, in which Barrack thanks Meese for his "counsel and encouragement." Barrack maintains that this refers to a discussion about the possibility of his moving to New York, a city about which Meese knows nothing. He justifies the remark by "reference to a discussion with Mr. Meese of the problems involved in moving a family from the West Coast to the East, and Mr. Meese's assurances that the move was not a difficult one." Barrack was never asked why he would discuss his moving plans with Meese or what he proposed to do on the East Coast. Meese, says the Stein report, "had no recollection of Mr. Barrack's September 8 visit to his office until he found and reviewed the letter in his files."

One month later, on November 9, Barrack dined with Meese and his wife at the 1789 Restaurant in Georgetown. That very afternoon, he had met with Transportation Secretary Drew Lewis and Housing and Urban Development Secretary Samuel Pierce. Next day, he was due to see Interior Secretary James Watt and Energy Secretary Donald Hodel. This blissful round was to culminate on November 11 with an appointment with Commerce Secretary Malcolm Baldrige. Two weeks previously, E. Pendleton James, former Director of Personnel at the White House and another principal in the La Mesa house sale, had written to each of the above, urging that Barrack's talents be recognized, adding, "I should mention that Ed Meese knows Tom and I'm sure also would endorse my strong support."

Barrack and the Meeses maintain that they endured a dinner between these two hectic rounds of meetings without ever alluding to the vulgar subject of a job for "Tom." They supposedly preserved the same reticence over Thanksgiving, which the Meeses passed agreeably enough at the Barrack ranch in Santa Barbara. As the Stein report noncommittally puts it:

> Mr. Barrack had by this time accepted the position of Deputy Undersecretary of Interior and was planning to begin his work in Washington on December 1, about one week later. He stated that he instructed his staff at the ranch not to mention this fact in the Meeses' presence.

He told the *help* but not Meese? Why would the help bring the question up? On December 2, 1982, the day after he assumed his duties at Interior, Barrack went to Meese's birthday party at Meese's house. Again, it seems that he was too delicate to mention his own good fortune to the President's chief counsel, a man keenly interested in appointments.

In light of all this, Meese's earlier sworn testimony to the Judiciary Committee, and Barrack's too, seems to hover just on the safe side of perjury. But, on one point, Meese can be said to have told the plain truth. The move from the West Coast to the East is, if you approach it in the right style, "not a difficult one." This brings us to . . .

2. *The Transition Trust.* On March 1, 1983, Meese replied to Judiciary Committee Chairman Strom Thurmond's indulgent question about the sacrifices he had made to serve his President by mentioning "the unanticipated expense of moving to Washington, D.C., none of which was reimbursed by the government." The next day, under equally soft questioning from Senator Orrin Hatch, Meese phrased the matter in a similar but not identical way:

> HATCH: And in addition to that, if I understand it, you had to pay all of your moving expenses as well?
> MEESE: That is right.
> HATCH: And all of the costs of bringing your family back here as well?
> MEESE: Yes, Senator.
> HATCH: And that all came out of your own pocket?
> MEESE: Yes, sir.

Facts can be dreary as hell, but, as the Stein report shows, Meese received $10,000 for "moving expenses" from the Presidential Transition Trust. On Trust check number 1069, made out to Edwin Meese, the words "moving expenses" are crossed out and the words "consulting fees" inked in. It's not even clear whether Meese declared this income or had another of his nagging bouts of amnesia.

Again, this nifty little adjustment was unknown to the Judiciary Committee at the time of its hearings. So was the inelegant little shuffle that I'll call . . .

3. *The Promotion*. Did Meese pull strings to gain promotion to full colonel in the Army Reserve in 1983? Like the staunch soldier that he is, Meese prefers to blame the brass for his rapid rise through the ranks. At his confirmation hearings he boldly claimed that he was "a victim of the Army's bad judgment." In fact, the promotion presents another example of his failure to distinguish between public and private interest. And it underlines, once more, his lack of veracity on the stand.

On November 1, 1982, the army's Deputy Chief of Staff for Personnel, Lieutenant General Max Thurman, wrote a memorandum to the Chief of Staff, General Edward C. Meyer. The memo stated that "constructive credit" for a course in national-security management qualifying Meese for promotion to colonel could be granted only at the request of Meese or his commanding officer (General Thomas Turnage, director of the Selective Service System). Such a request had to be approved by General William Berkman, chief of the Army Reserve. General Thurman's memo advised against such approval, since Meese was taking the requisite course by correspondence and had not yet completed it. Generals Turnage and Berkman overruled Thurman, effectively raising Meese to full colonel. Turnage is described in the Stein report as "an acquaintance and former associate of Mr. Meese from California, who had been designated (though not yet confirmed) as director of the Selective Service System." Stein points out too that, very shortly after, General Berkman was nominated for a second four-year term as chief of the Army Reserve.

General Thurman's memorandum recommending against Meese's promotion was passed to Secretary of the Army John Marsh, who forwarded it to Meese. Meese says that he doesn't recall seeing it, but Stein records statements by Defense Secretary Caspar Weinberger and by Marsh in which they recall the memo and say that Meese urged them to reappoint General Berkman.

Meese told the Judiciary Committee that he had no knowledge of any army concern about his appointment receiving special treatment. Either he is lying or Secretaries Marsh and Weinberger are.

The contradictions in the three areas discussed above have not been put to Meese for explanation thus far. They should be. The matters are not trivial. But all one can find is complicity among the Republicans and resignation among the Democrats. The following Democrats sit on the Senate Judiciary Committee: Max Baucus, Joseph Biden, Robert Byrd, Dennis DeConcini, Howell Heflin, Edward Kennedy, Patrick Leahy, and Howard Metzenbaum.

I telephoned all their offices last week. Leahy's staff told me that the senator was too busy wondering whether he could "rank" on Intelligence or Agriculture and feared that a new controversy over Meese would be "seen as counterproductive." Biden's people assured me that "most senators were off campaigning" when the Stein report came out. Heflin's office said: "It's too early—the members have not focused. It's the same nomination." Still others refused to comment or spoke of the psychological effect of the Reagan victory or said "in terms of" or "with regards to" all the time. Kennedy was on his way to Ethiopia when I called his office, but in his last statement on the matter he said, prematurely, that the Stein report had cleared Meese of any suspicion of impropriety and that such "questions" as remained were about civil and human rights. As we went to press, Common Cause issued an analysis of the Stein report which, though it did not correlate Stein's evidence with the transcript of the committee hearings, found against Meese on ethical grounds. Media attention to this was slight.

Only from Howard Metzenbaum's office has there been any sign of an understanding that this is the next Attorney General we're talking about. Now the Reaganites are going around Washington telling all who will listen that Metzenbaum made the HUAC enemies list back in 1954. Meese will probably have "no recollection" of that little gambit either.

One of three things could now happen. The President may, as he should, blushingly withdraw Meese from nomination. The Judiciary Committee or the full Senate may vote him down. Or, in the lazy belief that they asked all the right questions the first time, the ten Republicans and eight Democrats on the committee may nod into office, as "the People's Attorney" and the nation's chief law officer, a man who has already shown that he cannot recognize a conflict of interest when it bites him in the leg.

(*The Nation*, December 29, 1984–January 5, 1985)

THE FIDDLER'S ELBOW

❏

Everybody remembers the case Sherlock Holmes cracked because of a dog that did *not* bark in the night. The case of Raymond Donovan, still Secretary of Labor, puts me in mind of that old tale. To read about him is to have the sensation of treading on the place in the dark where the top stair ought to be. There's a strong feeling of something missing, of something that ought to be there and isn't. There's also a pungent sense of something that ought *not* to be there, and is.

The best way I can express this is to say that if Donovan were now nominated as Secretary of Labor, he wouldn't make it. When he passed his Senate confirmation hearings, several crucial things had *not* happened.

1. Frederick Furino had *not* been murdered. Furino, a friend of the deceased mobster Salvatore Briguglio, was given a lie-detector test in April 1982. The test was designed to prove or disprove his claim that Donovan and Briguglio were complete strangers. Furino flunked. A few weeks later, he was found shot dead and crammed into the trunk of a car.

2. Nathan Masselli had *not* been murdered. He was the son of William Masselli, a former subcontractor of Donovan's Schiavone Construction Company. Masselli Senior, a convicted Mafia criminal, had been moved to a Manhattan jail for the convenience of special prosecutor Leon Silverman, who was then pursuing his second inquiry. It seems, from Silverman's second report, that William Masselli was eventually *not* questioned. His son, however, was shot dead in the Bronx on August 28, immediately after paying a visit to his incarcerated father. James Shalleck, head of the homicide bureau in the Bronx DA's office, refused in court to deny a link between the murder, which he called an execution, and the Donovan investigation.

3. The serious suggestion that Donovan was involved with the Teamsters union election fund had *not* surfaced.

4. The FBI had *not* revealed all it knew about Donovan and his contacts. To quote the *Supplemental Report of the Committee on Labor and Human Resources*, issued months after that committee had found him above reproach:

> During Mr. Silverman's investigation it was determined that certain information was contained in the files of the F.B.I.'s Newark field office which did not appear to have been furnished to the Senate Committee on Labor and Human Resources or the Special Prosecutor.

The paragraph's smarmy euphemisms join "insufficient credible evidence" as part of the weasel talk that dominates the official handling of the case.

Donovan, who laughably claims to be the only victim of the inquiry, is in fact the beneficiary of a Catch-22. The witnesses are not "credible" because they are criminals, or because they need protection, or because they are informants in other cases. That is why 66 of 111 pages of Silverman's second report are deleted. But if the witnesses were "credible," they would not be caught up with the Sicilian business community. And it is precisely Donovan's contacts with the SBC that are the issue.

Donovan is also the beneficiary of a further anomaly. The FBI gave as the reason for the deletions, and the reason for its general coyness about releasing evidence, the excuse that disclosure could jeopardize "the source of the conversation and the ongoing FBI investigation." That is a catchall and coverall, rather like "national security." It did not prevent the FBI from eventually revealing some of the material it had inexplicably held back. But it does prevent us from finding out quite how often Donovan's name comes up in SBC circles. So, for the Secretary to rave about charges from "nameless accusers" is hubris. Would he really rather that the names were made public?

Finally, Donovan is the beneficiary of a most unusual special prosecutor. If I am ever on trial and have anything to fear, I shall hope to be prosecuted by Leon Silverman. In him, the milk of human kindness runs free and uncongealed. Donovan told the Senate that neither he nor his company had ever done business with Philip Moscato, a man apparently well known in SBC gatherings. Silverman's subsequent investigation established that Schiavone Construction had done some thousands of dollars' worth of business with Moscato. This discrepancy was attributed to a lapse of memory. Silverman did, however, astonish some onlookers by saying after the Masselli murder that if a third investigation is needed, he is "willing to accept such an appointment." As the man said, it's steady work.

Now comes the question: Why does the President endure this? If it is because of his famous loyalty to his friends, as his defenders in Washington suggest, then why did he fire Richard Allen for mislaying a few grand? Allen, though in every way a creep, was actually acquitted in an investigation, which is more than Donovan can claim. But he got the boot. Donovan is even less qualified for his job than Allen was for his. He is a laughingstock in his department. His only political achievement has been to raise money for the President's election chest by holding Sinatra concerts at his unimprovably named Fiddler's Elbow country club. As Senator Donald Riegle put it during the confirmation hearings, "If this nominee were a person of towering reputation and stature in this field over a number of years, I would give that considerable weight. That is not the case here." Senator Riegle was worried about SBC penetration in high places. So should we all be. The Teamsters union, after all, got one of its men on the Reagan transition team even as he was actually being sued by the Department of Labor. It has in the past seated its nominees in government. Donovan might perhaps now survive a trial, but the FBI would be unlikely to tell the court, as it told the Senate in January 1981, that he is "a loyal American whose character, reputation and associates are beyond approach [sic]."

The misprint in the record is endearing. Indeed, some of Donovan's associates are unapproachable in the worst way. But Silverman was mandated only to see if the evidence would warrant prosecution. He could not recommend whether Donovan should or should not remain in the Cabinet. On that, the verdict is already in.

(The Nation, October 2, 1982)

THE OLD BOY

❑

An Oxford professor meets a former Ph.D. student and courteously inquires what he's working on these days. "I'm writing a book," says the other, "on the survival of the class system in America."

"Really, how fascinating. I didn't think they had a class system in America."

"Nobody does. That's how it survives."

As long as this joke (if it is a joke) has any point, it will be futile to dismiss Marx as "irrelevant." The centenary of his death, celebrated with smugness or indifference in most quarters (*The New York Times* spent itself in a snigger about the old story of his bastard child), should remind people how much they owe the old man every time they discuss civilization and its surprisingly numerous discontents. Like Molière's too-much-quoted Monsieur Jourdain, who discovered to his pleasant astonishment that he had been speaking prose all his life, many people who dismiss Marx as a "determinist" and an "economic materialist" or as the grandpapa of Stalinism are actually using his lines all the time.

The core of Marxist thought, and the reason for its stubborn survival, is the enduring conflict between the *forces* and the *relations* of production. The genius of the capitalist system lies in its inventive and creative nature—in its scorn for tradition, custom, and fetish. The menace of that same system occurs when it erects, by apparently voluntary labor, a thing beyond the control of its creators. To take a currently salient example, the "environment" is not the gift of entrepreneurs, risk takers, or investors. It is the common, inherited property of humanity. Yet, as Marx put it:

> At the same place that mankind masters nature, man seems to become enslaved to other men or to his own infamy. Even the pure light of science seems unable to shine but on the dark background of ignorance. And our invention and progress seem to result in endowing material forces with intellectual life, and in stultifying human life into a material force.

Who, living under the wings of the nuclear state and experiencing the pressure of conformity, can dismiss that as a nineteenth-century observation?

Again, it's only a short while since characters like Daniel Bell and Sidney Hook were writing as if they had understood Marx better than he had himself. They pointed to the apparent abandonment of "alienation" in the canonical texts and with much gravity alleged that the poor had not got poorer. This half-formed critique was intended to challenge the labor theory of value. But it took no account of Marx's seminal work (commonly known as the *Grundrisse* or *Foundation*), in which a clear distinction is made between "labor" and "labor power." Thus, the term *exploitation* need not mean starvation and misery—though in much of the capitalist world it still does. It signifies the extent to which the skills and abilities of those without capital are appropriated by those with it.

> Although every capitalist demands that workers should save, he means only his own workers, because they relate to him as workers. By no means does this apply to the remainder of workers, because they relate to him as consumers. In spite of all the pious talk of frugality he therefore searches for all possible ways of stimulating them to consume, by making his commodities more attractive and by filling their ears with babble about new needs.

Remind you of anything? Don't overlook the coda, the sting in the tail:

> It is precisely this side of the relationship between capital and labor which is an essential civilizing force and on which the historic justification—but also the contemporary power—of capital is based.

Marx's paradox, then, is the love hate attitude he manifests toward the achievements of the bourgeoisie. That distinguished class has never produced or paid anyone who could sing its praises as he did. On its own, this elementary observation demolishes the pseudoscholastic view that Marx was a "determinist" or a banal proponent of the idea that economics decides everything. It is, in our day as in his, the apologists of the existing order who argue that economic logic justifies their own position. Marx wrote, and believed, that

> history does nothing; it does not possess immense riches, it does not fight battles. . . . It is not "history" which uses men as a means of achieving—as if it were an individual person—its own ends.

Yet, for all his insight into the innovative and ingenious character of capital, Marx also understood the destructive and destabilizing path it might take. He may never have imagined the horrors of World War I and fascism when he diagnosed the ills of class society, but he realized that capital was suspicious of its own claims about the market system and the "freedom" that it supposedly allowed. As he pointed out, the abolition of competition in favor of monopoly, when it occurred among businesses, would only intensify competition among workers. Does such an idea seem antiquated in the decade of the disposable employee?

When people talk of "the economy" as an organic unity, untrammeled by class, by interest, and by special holdings, they convict themselves of ignorance and of not having read Marx. When they say that Marx was the patron of the Warsaw Pact, they convict themselves of not having read his famous assault on Hegel. Bureaucracy is not the resolution of social conflict but the result of it, he wrote. Militarism is the forcible resolution of that contradiction. Let Prussia be Prussia.

Socialism was an idea before Marx. Democracy was an idea before Marx. Social revolution was an idea before Marx. What he argued was that you can't have any of the above until you are ready for them, and that you can't have one without the others:

> The materialist doctrine concerning the changing of circumstances and upbringing forgets that circumstances are made by men and that the educator must himself be educated.

(*The Nation*, April 2, 1983)

AGAINST THE CONTRAS

❑

Just what kind of government is the Reagan Administration trying to bring to power in Managua? Alas, neither the Administration nor its critics seem to have the vaguest idea.

The Administration's critics are at an increasing disadvantage. Opponents of what is still bizarrely called a "covert" war, they tend to argue in rather oblique, even evasive ways. You hear them say that Nicaragua does not really matter to the United States—a dubious argument for anyone who claims to be an internationalist. They plead that Nicaragua is not all that radical—another slightly shamefaced defense and one that finds little echo in Managua itself. Other critics suggest that the policy "won't work"—an unprovable assumption given the many triumphs of counterrevolution in the hemisphere.

Finally, there is the analogy of the Bay of Pigs. It is used as if everybody agreed on its meaning. Actually, the meaning is often nebulous. In the Third World, the Bay of Pigs is a synonym for aggression. In the United States, it is a synonym for fiasco and embarrassment. When North American liberals warn against "another Bay of Pigs," what do they mean? No more aggressions, or no more botched ones?

Shortly after the original Bay of Pigs, President Kennedy was speaking with Clayton Fritchey, who was then with Adlai Stevenson's staff at the United Nations. There had been many inquests and recriminations, and nobody had come out of them very well. Fritchey surprised his President by remarking, "It could have been worse." Kennedy asked how. After all, the United States had been spared almost no humiliation. "It might," replied Fritchey, "have succeeded."

He was right, of course. Washington was very fortunate in the incompetence of its covert-action specialists and the brutal stupidity of its Cuban mercenaries. If they had won, captured Havana, and perhaps killed Fidel Castro and Che Guevara, they would have been faced with the awesome task of governing a resentful and defiant Cuba. The cost, in every sense, to the United States would have been extremely heavy. The cost to Cuba would have been heavier yet. And it might still be felt today—just as the calamitous consequences of the successful intervention in Guatemala in 1954 are still being felt.

If the Reagan Administration has a plan for Nicaragua after the Sandinistas have been overthrown, it has not made that plan public. Nobody seems to have the courage or the foresight to inquire. What, for instance, would the leaders of the Contras, or counterrevolutionaries, fighting in the north of the country consider a victory? Are they committed to holding free elections? (If so, as mostly onetime supporters of the former dictator, Anastasio Somoza, they have a funny way of showing it.) What is their opinion on land redistribution or on the Sandinistas' literacy program? One suspects that they have not been asked these questions by their trainers and paymasters. As long as they undertake to break relations with Cuba and the Soviet Union, they are deemed by Washington to have a fully rounded political program. How they propose to govern the Nicaraguan people, apart from by the gun, is not discussed.

The debate on the Boland–Zablocki bill, which would cut off United States aid to the Contras, ought to be widened to include these questions. It is absurd for the Administration to contend that it is not seeking the overthrow of the Managua government—for what else can be inferred from the fitting out of an army of invasion? Certainly, the Contras make it plain that they seek to seize state power. Unlike Edén Pastora, who is fighting the government in southern Nicaragua and was a Sandinista himself, they do not even pay lip service to the original objectives of the Nicaraguan revolution. How much money will they want before they are done? How many guns? What promises have been made to them and by them?

Ten years ago, a secret United States stratagem did succeed in removing a leftist government in Chile. Indeed, the murder of the reformist Salvador Allende did a great deal to sow distrust of pluralism among Latin American radicals. If the United States conservatives who so detested Allende had known what his successor, General Augusto Pinochet, would be like and how threadbare and disgraced his regime would be in ten years, would they have applauded so loudly in 1973?

The Reagan Administration will obviously carry on arming and paying the Nicaraguan Contras whatever Congress decides. We should dread the possibility of their "success." It would be in the best interests of the United States and of Nicaragua if these mercenaries were soundly and finally defeated.

(*The New York Times*, July 27, 1983)

CONFLICT OF INTEREST

❏

Touching this "debategate" business, it is possible that the Reagan Administration, which has the luck of the devil himself, can live forever with the howling discrepancy between William Casey's poor memory and James Baker's clear evidence. But it's also possible that there will have to be some kind of hearing. If so, I'd be inclined to put my money on Casey. He is no stranger to hearings and has emerged scatheless from more inquiries than Spiro Agnew. It's hard to see how this lazy and indulgent Congress can hope to be a match for a man who has made conflict of interest into a way of life.

"Conflict of interest," as understood by the Reaganites, is more a term of art than a term of abuse. Take, for instance, the brief autobiography that Casey submitted to his confirmation hearing before the Senate Intelligence Committee in January 1981. Its final paragraph, headed "Publications," reads as follows:

Tax Sheltered Investments; Lawyer's Desk Book; Forms of Business Agreements; Accounting Desk Book; Tax Planning on Excess Profits; How To Raise Money To Make Money; How Federal Tax Angles Multiply Real Estate Profits.

Casey was scarcely questioned by the members of the committee, who mostly fell over themselves to laud his sapience. But by December 1981 they had to report on him again. This time, the problem was his taste in Deputy Directors for Operations. Max Hugel, who had been handpicked by Casey for this sensitive post, was accused of dubious stock dealings by his former colleagues. When interviewed by the committee's special counsel, says the report dryly, "Mr. Hugel's responses were circumscribed." As for Casey, it found that he had forgotten to disclose at least nine investments valued at more than $250,000, personal debts and contingent liabilities of nearly $500,000, the fact that he had served on the boards of a number of corporations and foundations, four civil lawsuits in which he had been involved in the previous five years, and more than seventy clients he had represented in private practice in the same period. Among those "clients" were the governments of Indonesia and South Korea and an oil company named Pertamina, controlled by the Indonesian government. The committee, which went through the most abject contortions in order to give Casey the benefit of the doubt, ducked the question of whether his services to Indonesia should have required his registering under the Foreign Agents Registration Act—a formality with which he had not troubled himself. Actually, investigation shows that Casey "misled" the committee during his confirmation hearing: he was asked in writing whether he had been an attorney for a foreign government and gave a deceitful answer.

Casey remains because he is useful to his political seniors. He has always had the knack of being obliging, and it is surely this, rather than any aptitude for intelligence work, that has recommended him to President Reagan. In 1972, for instance, just before the election, he used his position as Chairman of the Securities and Exchange Commission to frustrate the inquiry into International Telephone and Telegraph. There were thirty-four boxes of ITT papers under his care, and Congress wanted to have a peek at them. There was loose talk at the time about ITT buying favors from the Nixon Administration. The thirty-four boxes were whisked from the SEC to the Justice Department, and thus withheld from the vulgar gaze. Casey lied about that as well, testifying to Congress that he had transferred the records at the request of Justice Department officials.

Casey's tenure at the SEC, in fact, showed us early on that he has two abiding qualities. One, a loyalty to the less fastidious element of the Republican Party. Two, a persistent inability to distinguish between the public and the private interest. He is, really, the only highly placed figure of the Watergate era to retain his prominence in politics. He remembers the heady days of testifying for John Mitchell and Maurice Stans about Robert Vesco. His confirmation hearings as SEC Chairman were full of the flavor of that epoch. Casey, it turned out, had been sued by an investor in his firm Advancement Devices Inc., which went broke a year after making a stock offering that the investor claimed was fraudulent and violated federal security laws. The offering circular was written by a man Casey introduced to the firm, who had once been disciplined by the SEC for price rigging; its fraudulent nature would have been discovered earlier had it been registered with the SEC, but Casey preferred not to inconvenience himself by doing that, claiming the offering was private. There are advantages in hiring a poacher as a gamekeeper, but it's easy to overstate them.

In an earlier lawsuit, Casey displayed all the qualities that serve him so well as head of the CIA. He was found guilty of purloining and plagiarizing a manuscript on taxation. The real author, Harry Fields, sued for and was awarded punitive damages. The jury found that Casey had acted with "malice and vindictiveness." His attorneys offered to pay a $20,500 out-of-court settlement if the verdict was expunged from the record. In the end, money changed hands and the court records of the case were sealed. Casey lied about this, too, during his confirmation hearings as SEC Chairman.

In April 1980, Casey told *The New York Times*, in his capacity as Ronald Reagan's campaign manager, "We expect Carter will try everything to get re-elected. So we'll be ready for everything." That may just have been tough talk. But it is perfectly clear that the Reagan-Bush campaign committee took very few chances and had very few scruples. It used stolen property as a crib. It has been cited by the Federal Election Commission, which "found a reason to believe that the law was violated" in point of contributions. Casey, again, says he knows nothing. He acts the part of the selfless Cincinnatus, abandoning his private life and his honest toil for the public weal. He has been attacked by liberals for confusing private and public transactions, though the truth is that he doesn't know the difference. And he has been criticized for constantly pleading ignorance even though he is in charge of the nation's intelligence network. One begins to suspect that, for Reagan, the problem of Casey is not that he remembers too little but that he knows too much.

(*The Nation*, August 6–13, 1983)

DOING GOOD:
The Neoliberals

❏

It's all too easy to sneer at neoliberals. But it is, I'm afraid, all too necessary. The movement that bears this smart little title has been in some danger of being taken too seriously. And, though its 1983 conference in Washington did something to deplete that seriousness, there is an evident need to say a few words before the memory fades.

First, what is neoliberalism? Its adherents beam with false modest when they are asked. They will not be so dogmatic as to attempt a definition. But I think I know what it is. In the November 1983 issue of *The Washington Monthly*, which sponsored the conference and which serves as the calendar and notice board of the movement, there appears a review by Charles Peters, who is founder and mentor of both. The review concerns the new book *Vietnam*, by Stanley Karnow, which is a companion to the series now running on PBS. It's a short notice, and it reads, in its entirety, thus:

> Everyone, right and left, will find fault with this book, but there is nothing better available now. It is unique in its understanding of the cultural differences between South and North Vietnam and China that might have served our legitimate ends much more effectively and humanely than bombing by B-52s and invasion by 500,000 troops.

Here is the essence of the neoliberal style. First comes the smarmy even-handedness ("right and left" are, of course, ideologies, and therefore untrustworthy). Then the vague but seductive idea that "cultural differences" can substitute for a definition of conflict. Then the invocation of "our legitimate ends," which are assumed. Finally, there is the criticism of military and bureaucratic ineptitude—with all the moral and political courage that such a stand requires.

Neoliberals are like that. They have a sort of pious earnestness. They hold opinions rather than convictions. They wear their lightness learnedly. They are easily disappointed by the efforts and the antics of common people. They have a slightly feigned nostalgia for the times of FDR and JFK. They practice risk-free iconoclasm. Their idea of bravery is to speak the unsayable, shocking thing. For example: "I know it's not fashionable to say this, but a lot of people really do cheat on welfare." Some of them actually want Ernest Hollings to be President. To spend a weekend with them was like living through, rather than sitting through, *The Big Chill*.

Cynics have compared the neoliberal tendency to the neoconservative one. I think that comparison must be counted as unfair. For one thing, neoconservatives are much more rigorous. For another, they are much more interesting. Neoconservatives believe in original sin, while neoliberals believe in the enervating effect of public spending programs. Neoconservatives are keenly interested in foreign policy, with its emphasis on tough choices, while neoliberals are oddly diffident about it. Neoconservatives have a sense of class struggle and know which side they are on. Neoliberals wish the word "class" had never been discovered and agree not to use it at all, ever, except when attacking radicals for being out of touch with what "ordinary people" want. Neoconservatism could occur in any country. Neoliberalism could, really, only occur in a country like America, which combines abundance with angst and has a vast population of overqualified graduate students, some of whom wish they had, after all, served in Vietnam.

In what I suppose I must call his keynote address, Peters laid out a testing agenda for this bright-eyed group, mugged as they are by unreality. We must be flexible on welfare and crime, he said, and not automatically oppose the Right. We must be ready to denounce trade unions. We must invigilate and audit the big spenders. We must beware "the special interests" (I was touched to hear a panelist describe women as one such). Nor is equality forgotten—the neoliberals, in their only egalitarian proposal, would collectivize young Americans by means of the draft.

There is, true, a striking coincidence between these points and the "ideas" of the President. There's also a coincidence in method (when Peters calls for educational reform, he does so because he believes it will make the United States able to "compete economically with other technologically advanced countries"). But neoliberals cannot help the time they live in, and I believe even they are a little embarrassed by these convergences. Still, it's partly their own fault. If you go around mouthing Chamber of Commerce clichés like (Peters again) "In Japan, auto workers think about how they can improve their products; in America; they think about filing grievances," you have earned your resemblance to the Great Purveyor of reactionary common sense.

The neoliberal style is a smartass one, and not without its effectiveness. The core of it is a species of gutless irony. You think public spending helps the poor? Check out Mike's coruscating piece in _____ . You still think aid to the Third World has a point? Get a load of Nick in _____ . Disarmament would be less risky than the arms race? Where have you been? Read Jim in _____ . Neoliberals like to puncture illusions, and one wishes them luck in that enterprise. But they never take aim at the huge, gaseous balloon that supports their own basket.

A perpetual theme at the conference was the reinstatement of family values, or at least the rescue of those values from the crass, coercive stress placed upon them by the Christian Right. There was much talk of responsibility and parenthood as the common thing, even the model thing. In fact, neoliberals seem to see the United States as a sort of family. They employ the word _we_ a lot, as in "our" industry, "our" military, and "our" political process. As I was moved to say at their conference, a family is collectivist as a society and socialist as an economy. It reveres the individual but it operates, approximately, on the principle "from each according to his or her ability and to each according to his or her need." If these socialist values are good enough for the rearing of American children, why are they not good enough for American society? The fact that no panelist answered my tiny question suggests to me that neoliberals have, at best, only the cowardice of their convictions.

(*The Nation*, November 5, 1983)

THE PRESIDENT

❑

One clue to the causes of the invasion of Grenada can be found in the captured internal minutes of the New Jewel Movement, which show where leftist sectarianism can lead. Another can be found in the pages of the most recent issue of *Conservative Digest*. Published just before the Marines splashed heroically ashore, it is given over to a scathing right-wing critique of Ronald Reagan. He is convicted of all kinds of feebleness, especially in answering the Soviet threat. Patrick Buchanan scornfully refers to *"The New York Times* foreign policy decked out in the rhetorical finery of the *National Review."* More significantly, Richard Viguerie writes about the fallacy of automatic conservative support for the President. It is not true, he warns, that conservatives have nowhere else to go. He calls for a new candidate or, failing that, a new party. A *Conservative Digest* poll of leading reactionaries shows similar sentiments predominating, and a decline in willingness to give time or money to Reagan's reelection. There is also an ominous map of the world, depicting all the countries that are lost to, or threatened by, communism. Grenada is listed as lost on the accompanying inventory, one of the nations "taken during the 'Era of Detente.' "

So the President has done some skillful repair work in that quarter. More depressing still, he has managed yet again to coerce and corrupt the wretched Democrats. The abject silence of Walter Mondale has been commented on enough. I wish Democratic Representative Michael Barnes had been as reticent. Returning from a fact-finding trip to Grenada in his capacity as Chairman of the House Subcommittee on Western Hemisphere Affairs, he announced he had concluded that the invasion was justified. He cited the position of the American students as the crucial element in his conversion. There are two things to be said here. First, even if the students were in danger, which seems at best arguable, their safety could warrant only a rescue mission. Neither the Israeli commando raid at Entebbe nor the American Desert One mission sought to overthrow the regimes of Uganda or Iran, nasty though they both were. Second, the students said they were relieved to be rescued from the fighting caused by the landing. That is a circular justification—somewhat like invading the island to capture the weapons that were stockpiled to resist an invasion.

Why do the Democrats persist in giving Ronald Reagan more benefit than doubt? It is perfectly clear that in foreign policy he has surrendered completely to the fanatics. This is partly because they cut with his own grain and partly because the fanatics are at least easy to understand. I have no time, personally, for jokes about the President's hearing aid or his other disabilities. But deafness can mask wider incomprehension, even an unwillingness to hear. As a tribute to Reagan's foreign-policy grasp, let me reproduce a transcript of an exchange he had at a lunchtime meeting with some carefully selected "minority" editors on October 18.

Q:	Are you going to put any kind of pressure on the Turkish government about giving a just solution to the Cyprus problem?
THE PRESIDENT:	To the which problem?
Q:	To the Cyprus problem.
THE PRESIDENT:	Oh. I wish the Secretary of State were here. We're aware of that but I don't know that we have involved ourselves directly and deeply in that. We have offered, as we always do, to be of help if we can, but right now I think more of our help is directed a little further east than that, on the shores of——
Q:	I am speaking of 200,000 refugees in Cyprus.
THE PRESIDENT:	Yes, I know, and I hope that we can find—and help in the settlement of that.
Q:	Mr. President, my name is Dr. Michael Szaz from the National Confederation of American Ethnic Groups. When are we going to break off diplomatic relations with the Soviet-imposed government in Afghanistan and extend more effective material assistance to the freedom fighters in Afghanistan?
THE PRESIDENT:	I have to say that I don't believe that breaking off diplomatic relations, even with the Soviet Union in our anger with them over this terrible deed with the Korean airliner——

Q:	It's Afghanistan.
THE PRESIDENT:	What?
Q:	It's Afghanistan, with the Soviet-imposed government in Kabul.
THE PRESIDENT:	Oh.
Q:	Do you still have the plan to visit South Korea? If so, what is the main purpose to visit South Korea?
THE PRESIDENT:	What?
Q:	South Korea?
THE PRESIDENT:	Yes.
Q:	Mr. President, does India fit into your schedule?
THE PRESIDENT:	What?
MS. SMALL [a Presidential aide]:	One more question, Mr. President.
Q:	Mr. President, my name is Keshishian from California. I would like to know if the American government has a stand on the Turkish genocide of the Armenians?
THE PRESIDENT:	The genocide of——
Q:	The Armenians in 1915.
MS. SMALL:	The Turkish and Armenian genocide.
THE PRESIDENT:	Oh. I—the only official stand that I can tell you we have is one opposed to terrorism on both sides. And I can't help but believe that there's virtually no one alive today who was living in the era of that trouble. And it seems to me we ought to be able to sit down now, an entirely new group of people who know only of that from reading it, to set down and work out our differences and bring peace at last to that segment of humanity.
MS. SMALL:	Thank you, Mr. President. Thank you very much.
MR. PRESIDENT:	Karna tells me I have to go. Thank you all very much. Thank you.

I never have met Karna, but I think she's absolutely right.

(The Nation, November 19, 1983)

KENNEDY LIES

❏

Like every one else of my generation, I can remember exactly where I was standing and what I was doing on the day that President John Fitzgerald Kennedy nearly killed me. In October 1962 I was in my first term at an English boarding school and was at least as ignorant of Cuba as Kennedy was. But I have a very vivid recollection of masters standing in unaccustomed huddles, of bluff reassurances from prefects and from (I think) the chaplain. I know that Richard Dimbleby signed off that night with a stiff-upper-lip injunction to parents to send their children to school the following day, but this didn't apply to my dormitory. Such was the relief at finding that the next day was not going to be the last that, like almost everybody else, I forgave Kennedy for gambling with my life. Such is the masochism of the human race.

But I have just finished reading an article in *The Washington Post*, entitled "How I Remember Jack." It is written by Senator Edward Kennedy, or at least signed by him. Every important contention in the article is a lie. And, already, one can feel all the Kennedy hangers-on, in the media and academe, gearing up for a great thirtieth-anniversary feast of sentimentality, maudlin grief, and false accounting.

The two major lies in Senator Kennedy's article are these, and I quote: "He [Jack] spent mornings working on *Profiles in Courage*, his Pulitzer Prize–winning book." Then: "He showed us that a President could stand up to the Soviet Union, as he did in the Cuban crisis, without sacrificing the ideals for which this nation must always stand."

In fact, *Profiles in Courage* was written by Theodore Sorensen, who also penned Kennedy's flatulent but memorable inauguration speech. And the Pulitzer Prize committee (never less than impressionable, as recent bogus awards have shown) was lobbied almost out of existence by Arthur Krock, the Establishment journalist who used the whole weight of the Kennedy family to get the prize for his friend and patron JFK.

In his outstanding book *The Kennedy Imprisonment*, the historian Garry Wills meticulously documents this episode, as well as the other myths and fabrications which have been popularized by courtiers and toadies like Arthur Schlesinger. Professor Wills is no fellow traveler—he started his career as an earnest toiler on William F. Buckley's *National Review*. But he is impatient with the flattery and stupidity which surround Kennedy's presidency, and he has written a chapter on the Cuba crisis which is imperishable. To summarize it is to diminish it, but here goes.

Kennedy got into trouble with the Russians over Cuba because he was waging a secret war against the Castro regime and lying about it to the American Congress, public, and press. He thus had no alternative but to present Russian aid to Cuba as an inexplicable and sinister move. He could not admit that Khrushchev was right when he charged that thousands of American agents were, in Wills's words,

> plotting his [Castro's] death, the destruction of his Government's economy, the sabotaging of his mines and mills, the crippling of his copper and sugar indus-tries. We had invaded Cuba once. Officials high in Congress and the executive department thought we should have followed up with overwhelming support for that invasion.

It is now commonplace in the United States to describe the Bay of Pigs invasion as a "fiasco." This description rather euphemizes the real event. The attempt to take over and run Cuba, to enlist the support of the Mafia in the assassination of Castro, to poison and devastate Cuban crops, and to land a mercenary army on Cuban shores would have been much more disastrous if it had succeeded than if it had failed. Kennedy, we now know, was told this by quite close advisers. Yet he persisted in the policy, deter-mined not to be outdone by a smaller country in his first term. And he repeatedly lied about the Soviet motives in supplying missiles to fortify the island, so that, as Professor Wills puts it, "the Kennedys looked like brave resisters of aggression, though they had actually been the causes of it."

In a deft passage of reasoning, Wills confronts the argument that the Soviet missiles were a threat to America in any case:

> Would he [Castro] launch his missiles in conjunction with a larger Russian attack—again, knowing that we could incinerate his island as a side-blow in our response to Russia? Even if Castro had wanted to immolate his nation that way, his missiles would not have helped the Russians—might, rather, have been a hindrance, because of the "ragged attack" problem. If missiles were launched simultaneously from Russia and Cuba, the Cuban ones, arriving first, would confirm the warning of Russian attack. Or, if Cuban missiles were to be launched later, radar warnings of the Russian ones firing would let us destroy the Cuban rockets in their silos.

Kennedy knew all this too. It was his swaggering desire publicly to outface the Russians, without publicly admitting his war on Cuba, that brought the world to the best view it has yet had of the gates of hell. And it was only the restraint of Khrushchev (another fact that Kennedy could not admit) that made the difference between a view and a death. It's well understood now that Khrushchev lost his job as a result—hardly the best news from the Kremlin in the postwar period.

Reviewing such behavior, a sycophant like Arthur Schlesinger wrote of the Cuba crisis, "It was this combination of toughness and restraint, of will, nerve and wisdom, so brilliantly controlled, so matchlessly calibrated, that dazzled the world."

It may be, and it probably is, a complete waste of time trying to undo the grandiose absurdity of the Kennedy myth. If Americans knew then what they know now about JFK—that he shared a mistress with a Mafia murderer, that he faked the authorship of "his" books, that he gave a fictitious account of the wartime PT-109 episode that made him a Hollywood hero, that he dissembled about Vietnam and lied in his sparkling teeth about Cuba—they might not have trusted him as they did. But, knowing all this now, they cannot quite relate it to the man they think they remember. Somehow, the drama of Dallas has sanctified and canceled everything. All the senior figures in the Democratic Party will be taking part in ostentatious mourning this week. They will also keep sneering at Ronald Reagan as a phony movie star more interested in media manipulation and cheap successes than in the serious business of politics and diplomacy. True enough, but the truth is that Reagan has not, in his entire presidency to date, acted with anything like the gun-slinging idiocy that the boy-hero did.

(*The Spectator*, November 19, 1983)

PERCEPTIONS AND SIGNALS

❏

There are two voguish current terms which make American political discourse extremely irritating. They occur routinely in every press conference, every current-affairs broadcast, every congressional debate, and almost every editorial comment. The terms are "perception" and "signal." The first is used as either a displacement or an evasion. The speaker need not say that he thinks the consequence of policy X will be harmful. That would be too definite and thus too risky. It is usual, then, for him to intone that policy X "will be perceived" as harmful. This has two political advantages: it takes longer to say and thus sounds more important; and it is ambiguous, having all the moral weight of the statement "It's not me, it's the neighbors."

"Signal" is the other standby of the cornered politico. In this case, the speaker refrains from saying that policy X will amount to appeasement of the Russians, the Cubans, the Nicaraguans, or whomever. Instead, he bleats that policy X would "send them the wrong signal." "They" in this sentence are usually the Russians, which makes one wonder what became of the hot line if we are reduced to international semaphore.

This has been a cheap and disgraceful week in foreign policy. The Reagan Administration, while attacking all the critics of its Lebanon policy as cowards and traitors, was all the while preparing its own withdrawal. The object, as we now learn from White House spokesmen, was to deal with the public "perception" that the Marines were being endangered for no purpose, without sending a "signal" to the Russians that American resolve had weakened. The use of massive offshore batteries was, literally as well as figuratively, to lay smoke over this policy in time for the evening news. There is, after all, no lobby in Washington to maintain that some of our best friends are Druze.

On February 3, 1984, in an interview with *The Wall Street Journal*, the President was asked about Speaker Tip O'Neill's call for withdrawal of the Marines. "He may be ready to surrender," sneered Reagan, "but I'm not." Four days later, he announced the pullout and flew off to the seclusion of his ranch in Santa Barbara. I have never seen such rage and contempt among normally mild-mannered Democratic congressmen; Speaker O'Neill may be a dim old tub of guts, but he is an extremely loyal and reasonably honest tub. He fought bravely and stupidly in his own party for a "national" approach to Lebanon, arguing for the tradition that "politics ends at the water's edge"—meaning you don't snipe at the commander in chief. For Reagan to accuse him of cowardice and desertion, on a day when he must have known that he himself was about to order a withdrawal, is unpardonable—or is at least widely "perceived" to be so.

The President's conduct has led many pundits to accuse him of inconsistency. This is tempting, but misleading. The withdrawal was all of a piece with the original commitment and with the whole unhappy experience of the eighteen-month presence. It was decided in a haphazard and jumpy fashion, as an improvised response to a situation that was eluding the control (and, it is fair to say, the comprehension) of the political leadership. A week after the Marines were landed, on September 28, 1982, Reagan said that they would remain in Lebanon until all foreign forces were withdrawn, "because I think that's going to come rapidly. I think we're going to see the withdrawal." Later he said that "the American forces will not engage in combat." Later still, "So it could be that they will be there for quite a period." By October 1983, the Marines were there to show that America could not be pushed around—a new objective, which was replaced a few days later with: "What exactly is the operational mission of the Marines? The answer is to secure a piece of Beirut, to keep order in their sector and to prevent the area becoming a battlefield."

But it all ended up with our old standby—a test of American will. This is normally, to borrow from the argot I have been criticizing, a "signal" that a scuttle is being prepared. In his weekly radio chat with the nation, the old maestro said bravely:

> Yes, the situation in Lebanon is difficult, frustrating and dangerous. But that is no reason to turn our back on friends and to cut and run. If we do, we'll be sending one signal to terrorists everywhere, they can gain by waging war against innocent people.

The friends, if they heard that, must have started packing for Switzerland on the instant. The "terrorists," who already know that violence pays, were presumably unimpressed. Speaker O'Neill, who had taken a real political risk in helping to get Reagan the September War Powers Resolution, authorizing another eighteen months in Beirut for the Marines, is just plain disgusted.

Within the White House, it seems that there is still division between those who favor withdrawal (or "redeployment") and those who feel that President Gemayel should be backed to the hilt. In the former camp are Caspar Weinberger and the Chief of Staff, James Baker. In the latter are George Shultz and Robert McFarlane, the National Security Adviser. Henry Kissinger, who is still maneuvering cannily for a place in the next Administration, has switched, in the space of one month, from saying that those who advocate withdrawal are preaching surrender to saying that the latest pullback is timely and statesmanlike.

The "signals" sent by all this to Moscow and Damascus are distinctly garbled. Neither government has ever doubted that the United States is capable of using force in the Middle East, but both may be marveling at the "seat-of-the-pants" way in which Reagan operates. Perhaps, by accident, the President has found his equivalent of Richard Nixon's "madman theory of war," where neither your enemies nor your friends have any idea what you may do next.

The "perceptions," in domestic terms, are extremely confused also. I wrote recently that Reagan's apparent honesty and amiability have enabled even his critics to give him the benefit of the doubt. Last week, I met more than a few people who thought they detected, for the first time, the rancid whiff of a Presidential doublecross. Are the Marines to be withdrawn, or are they not? Whose side are we on? If Lebanon is so vital, why isn't there a really serious troop commitment? If it isn't so vital, why are we shelling it in fits of pique? Above all, why say one thing and do another?

It is overlooked, in all this, that the Administration supported Begin and

Sharon when they invaded Lebanon and radicalized the Shiite Muslims while driving them north, along with the Palestinians, to Beirut. It is also over-looked that the Marines were committed to Beirut in the first place because of the Sabra and Shatila massacres, which were the last in a long line of General Sharon's broken promises. The blasting of the Marine barracks, and many subsequent miseries, can be viewed from one perspective as the re-venge for Reagan's endorsement of "Operation Peace for Galilee." Even the Israelis now regard that summer as one of their greatest mistakes. There has been no comparable accounting in Washington, but if ever there is, there may be some lasting changes in "perception."

Our final perception, if I may: President Reagan's first campaign speech was to the Association of Christian Broadcasters, a rather bovine and literal-minded group of evangelists who not only think that you can live twice, but believe that they themselves are already doing so. In his speech, the can-didate referred to the need to bring God back into life and society. He never misses the opportunity of accusing America's enemies of being atheists and materialists. Here is another "signal" that did not get through. His opponents in Lebanon may be many things, but "godless" they are not.

(The Spectator, February 18, 1984)

FINDING IT FUNNY

❑

In the memoirs of Ignazio Silone, which describe his mounting alienation from the communism of his youth, there is an anecdote of a visit he paid to Moscow. A British trade unionist who was in the city at the same time had objected to some proposed tactic of the Comintern. It would, he was alleged to have said, be "dishonest." At this, there was a roaring, boiling gale of laughter. It spread from the committee room, through the successive ech-elons of the party, all across the Kremlin. Stalin himself was said to have heard and savored the story by suppertime. Silone wrote that, "in judging a regime, said Togliatti who was with me, it is very important to know what it finds amusing."

In the last fortnight, the editorial and cartoon sections of the American press have been behaving as though they enjoyed Silone's moral authority. You might think, from reading the pompous and righteous comments, that Ronald Reagan's feeble microphone-testing gag about bombing Russia was a revelation of the real intentions of his regime. It was obviously, as any careful Reagan-watcher would admit, nothing of the kind. A man who can say to the surgeons, on the day that he cops a slug in the chest, "I hope you're all Republicans," and who can repeat the joke in his party's election-campaign film, is quite capable of an innocuous crack about genocide and extinction. The sanctimony of the editorialists is misplaced. But Reagan's sense of humor, and his free and easy way with facts and claims, may still be symptomatic and interesting.

He's got away with gallows humor before now, as when he told his radio audience, concerning Vietnam, that "we could pave the whole country and put parking stripes on it and still be home by Christmas." When the kidnappers of Patty Hearst demanded the distribution of free food surpluses to the poor of California, Reagan as Governor announced that he personally hoped for an outbreak of botulism. But he invests these utterances with such an "aw shucks, just kidding" flavor that it takes a heart of stone to condemn him. The same things, if said by, say, George Wallace, would sound ugly and nasty. Somehow, Reagan manages to escape this judgment.

Escape artistry is, in a sense, his political genius. Congresswoman Patricia Schroeder recently dubbed him "the Teflon President" because he seemed to be made of nonstick material. Here is a man who can fall asleep during an audience with His Holiness the pope and get away with it. Here is a man who could say, in 1982, that he didn't know there were still segregated schools in the United States. Here is a man who, in the same year, told a press conference that submarine-based missiles, such as Trident, were "conventional-type" weapons which, once launched, could be "recalled." Any one of these would have been enough to ruin Jimmy Carter or Gerald Ford. This President just rises above them.

In fact, like the legendary Antaeus, he is somehow strengthened by each defeat. He opposed the attempt by Congress to add a cost-of-living index to the social security system. He lost. Republican television ads in the 1982 midterm elections then showed a folksy, white-haired postman delivering the new improved social security checks to America's beloved senior citizens. "President Reagan kept his promise to the American people," the ad intoned. This is wizardry of a high order, which leaves the Democrats with their mouths opening and shutting like so many winded carp.

It is probably Reagan's gift for the anecdotal that gets him the benefit of the doubt. Like most people, he generalizes from personal experience, including the personal experience of rumor. Thus the story about Medicare paying for sex-change operations ("This one I'm sure will touch your heart"). Thus the tales about unemployed workers buying vodka with their food stamps. Thus his announced conviction, reminiscent of saloon-bar philosophers everywhere, that "if you are a slum dweller, you can get an apartment with 11-foot ceilings, with a 20-foot balcony, a swimming pool and gymnasium, laundry room and play room, and the rent begins at 113 and that includes utilities." I choose just three of the many Reagan assertions which have been checked out in detail and found to be quite baseless. From the habit of half-humorous exaggeration comes the more reprehensible practice of falsification and slander. A fair example is his sly assertion, two years ago, that the nuclear freeze was first proposed by Leonid Brezhnev. The President had every reason to know that the nuclear freeze had first been proposed by Mark Hatfield, a Republican senator. In 1980, Reagan pointlessly accused Jimmy Carter of "opening his campaign down in the city that gave birth to and is the parent body of the Ku Klux Klan," an accusation that would have been meaningless even if it were true.

The President's few lapses from bonhomie have occurred when he is challenged on points like this. Concerning the "bomb Russia" gaffe, he stupidly replied: "Isn't it funny? If the press had kept their mouth shut no one would have known I said it." This from the "great communicator," who owes so much to the indulgence of the mass media, even if he doesn't know a tautology when he sees one. In February 1982, asked by journalist Bruce Drake to account for some earlier statements, he became agitated.

> You don't really want to get into those mistakes you said that I made the last time, do you? I'd like you to know that the documentation proves that the score was five to one in my favor. I was right on five of them and I have the documentation with me.

Patient scribes later asked the White House for the "documentation" but were met with a refusal. Even his famous line "There you go again," which is supposed to have lost Jimmy Carter the 1980 election, was made in response to Carter's factually correct assertion that Reagan had opposed Medicare in 1965.

So it goes. "Governor, do you think homosexuals should be barred from public office in the United States?" "Certainly they should be barred from the department of beaches and parks." Just kidding. "We were told four years ago that seventeen million people went to bed hungry every night. Well, that was probably true. They were all on a diet." Whatsamatter, cantcha take a joke?

As one watched the orgiastic jingoism of the Republican Convention one got the queasy feeling that many of Ronald Reagan's audience don't even think he is joking. They agree, quite literally, with every word he says. Tip O'Neill is mistaken when he says that Reagan finds nuclear war funny. The problem is not that he finds it humorous (after all, Stanley

Kubrick milked it for laughs and became a liberal hero), but that he doesn't take it seriously.

(*The Spectator*, September 1, 1984)

REAGAN THE DEMOCRAT

❑

It is rare indeed for Walter Mondale to show anything resembling emotion. Even his closest associates have taken to nicknaming him "Norwegian wood." But there is one thing which infallibly gets him going, causes his waxen cheeks to redden and flat voice to rise. He can't stand it—in fact, he can't believe it—when Ronald Reagan invokes the name of John F. Kennedy.

It's an old trick, of course: a candidate who has switched his party allegiance can pretend to have lost his faith and found his reason. He can be pious about it ("I didn't leave my party. It left me"). He can be humorous about it ("What would the party of FDR, of Harry Truman, of Hubert Humphrey and JFK, say if they could see the Democrats now?"). Reagan uses this device on every possible occasion, partly to goad Mondale and partly because the polls show that it works. In particular, his ceaseless evocation of Kennedy goes over very well with first-generation voters, who have been brought up to view the Kennedy they never knew as a sort of Siegfried. The use of his name has talismanic quality, giving the President more the aura of a grand old man than of a has-been. The other day in Danbury, Connecticut, where JFK made one of his most famous outdoor appearances in the 1960 campaign, Ronald Reagan turned up on the exact anniversary. He spoke from the same balcony, quoted from the same speech, and delivered the same message of optimism. The effect, in a town where registered Democrats have predominated since the dawn of time, was electrifying. Something about Kennedy makes lumps form in the most leathery throat and brings that fateful pricking to the eyelids. Reagan milked it for all it was worth, and more. I have said that the voters love him for his faults, which is a good thing since he has so many of them. It is for various reasons just as well that the 1960 election has become a vague memory. Those who remember it well can recall that Ronald Reagan took an active part. In fact, he was one of the founders of a group called Democrats for Nixon. On July 15, 1960, he sent Nixon a handwritten letter, which concluded:

One last thought. Shouldn't someone tag Mr. Kennedy's bold new imaginative program with it's [sic] proper age? Under the tousled boyish haircut it is still old Karl Marx—first launched a century ago.There is nothing new in the idea of a government being Big Brother to us all. Hitler called his "state socialism" and way before him it was "benevolent monarchy."

I apologize for taking so much of your time, but I have such a yearning to hear someone come before us and talk specifics instead of generalities. You will be very much in my prayers in the days ahead.

Sincerely, Ronnie Reagan

I like this letter; I think it has everything. The idea that somebody, in 1960, should feel it necessary to urge Richard Nixon to call his opponents communists and fascists is a touching one. So is the "yearning" for specifics over generalities. The sign-off sentence is Ronnie at his eager and pleasing best. Who could dislike such a man?

The Democrats waited a long time before they released this treasure, because they know that personal attacks on the President do not play very well with the public. A spokesman for the White House press office was almost insolent in his insouciance about it. By any calculation, he said, more people would have heard Reagan's praise for Kennedy than would have read or noticed the letter. Therefore, it didn't count. This is the prevailing standard, and I suppose we had better get used to it.

This same White House press office deserves to have a medal struck in its name. This has been the week when American newspapers publish their Presidential endorsements. Reagan probably didn't expect the support of *The New York Times* or *The Washington Post*, both of which came out very strongly for Mondale. But he did pretty well. My favorite editorial was in the *Chicago Tribune*, which endorsed Reagan for a second term. It added that his "refusal to accept the linkage between the federal deficit and economic instability is threatening to bankrupt America and severely damage the free world economy." It went on to say that "his ignorance about the Soviet Union and his air-headed rhetoric on the issues of foreign policy and arms control have reached the limits of tolerance and have become an embarrassment and a danger." In other words, he is useless on the domestic front and a menace internationally. But he should be President for four more years because his philosophy "will result in less government growth and less government intrusion into the lives of citizens than would Walter Mondale's." So Mondale is Marx and Hitler all over again.

At the moment, there is only one historical figure who interests Walter Mondale in the least. That figure is Harry S Truman, who in 1948 made an idiot out of every pundit and pollster in the country by defeating Thomas Dewey. On his recent gallop through the Midwest, Mondale drew such large and happy crowds that there were those who thought a late surge was possible. And when Mondale mentioned Truman, at least he could honestly claim that he had supported him at the time. But it was during this very stage of the campaign, when things seemed to be picking up, that Mondale was told the bad news. His campaign chairman, Jim Johnson, took him aside in a Milwaukee hotel and informed him that no possible interpretation of the data could make him the next President of the United States. Truman, after all, did enjoy the advantage of being President already.

So that seems, to most people, to be that. When Mondale talks about the past of the Democratic Party, he is accused of living off memories and forgotten glories. When Ronald Reagan talks about Kennedy, he is credited with the capacity for vision. When Mondale insists that we should talk about "specifics" and not "generalities," he is accused of being a bore. When Reagan speaks, as he did in Oregon the other day, he is praised for raising America's sights. To the Oregonians, he said: "America will never stop. It will never give up its mission, its special mission. Never. There are new worlds on the horizon, and we're not going to stop until we get them all together." (This in a scripted and rehearsed appearance.) When Mondale talks about a very restricted nuclear freeze, he is accused of being credulous and gullible about the Russians. When Reagan says that he will share America's most advanced space technology with the Soviet Union, he is lauded for statesmanship and generosity.

I predict that, if Reagan does win, disillusionment will be swift. There are too many unredeemed pledges flying around and too many hangover-inducing binges behind us. Euphoria will stale. Future Republicans will be less inclined to quote the Reagan record. Nor will they want to mention their other past heroes, like Hoover, Nixon, and Ford. Instead, as they search for a peroration, they will tell lisping children and restless teenagers of the man who embodied all the American virtues. Generations yet unborn will be told, by leering phonies incandescent with insincerity, of how the Democratic Party has gone downhill since the plucky, thrifty, honest leadership of Walter F. Mondale.

(*The Spectator*, November 3, 1984)

DESTRUCTIVE ENGAGEMENT

❑

It's brass-monkey weather on Massachusetts Avenue, especially on that posh but exposed section which features the embassies of Britain and Brazil, and the fine vacant property that once housed the envoy of the Shah. Here stands the South African embassy and here, outside it, stands a permanent daily picket. District of Columbia law contains a simple protocol which states that anybody holding a placard within five hundred yards of a diplomatic legation will be arrested. A police tape is stretched to demarcate this limit for the convenience of demonstrators. Anyone taking the appropriate pace forward is guaranteed, after one warning, a ride in a car and a night in the cells.

With this guarantee comes the promise of an appearance on the nightly nationwide news. In the past fortnight, viewers have seen the black Mayor of Detroit, the black head of D.C. Council, and several Democratic congressmen escorted away by grave black policemen. On the night before I turned up, it was Douglas and Rory Elisabeth, the son and daughter of Bobby Kennedy, who volunteered themselves. Today, it's to be a trade-union official and a progressive nun. The picket line is swollen by three busloads of teachers' union members, most of them white and at least half of them female. And today, there's a new development. On the opposite corner stands a shivering man in a business suit, holding a homemade placard which reads: South Africa: Do Not Give In to Ignorant Mobs. You *Do* Have Support. This fellow is protected by his own personal posse of impassive black cops. In conversation, he says straightaway that he knows very little about South Africa but that he feels protest should be directed at the evils of black African governments. He accuses the demonstrators of being publicity seekers and looks genuinely blank when I ask him what he is seeking. "I'm completely unpolitical," he says, adding that he is a registered Republican and "a very strong Reagan supporter." These two statements are perhaps not as ill matched as they sound at first. "Anyway," he concludes, "those people should be concentrating on the problems we got right here at home."

It's difficult to think of any domestic issue that would unite this white Babbitt and the picketers yonder, but as a matter of record his words were an exact repeat of those offered me by the black cabbie who dropped me here. He too felt that his representatives might be better employed on the less glamorous business of the home-front political grind. And it's certainly true that the personalities arrested so far are a perfect cross-section of the forces—trade unions, urban blacks, and liberal Democrats—who were decisively repudiated by the electorate last month. It will take many renditions of "We Shall Overcome" and many evocations of the memory of Dr. King to obscure this simple truth. The nightly picket may be good for morale, and the Honk for Support placard draws hoots from about one car in three, which isn't bad. But this is a coalition of the defeated.

All the same, it has touched the Reagan Administration on an exposed spot. The ostensible reason for the picket is to draw attention to the seventeen black labor leaders recently detained in Johannesburg. But the real target is the increasingly warm relationship between Washington and Pretoria. Under the name of "constructive engagement," the Reagan Administration has relaxed the prohibition on the sale of arms, taken a "low profile" at the United Nations, and virtually dropped all criticism of the illegal occupation of Namibia. This has of course enraged black America, but it has embarrassed many other sectors too. The quid pro quo for "quiet diplomacy" was supposed to be a reform program in South Africa itself. Nothing worthy of that name has resulted, which makes the Administration here look foolish. In an astonishing development this week, thirty-five Republican congressmen, all of them declared Reaganites, delivered a letter to the South African ambassador. It said that "South Africa has been able to depend on conservatives in the United States to treat them [sic] with benign neglect. We serve notice that, with the emerging generation of conservative leadership, that is not going to be the case." This must have been something of a facer for the ambassador, more even than the message of sympathy which the picket line received from Governor George Wallace of Alabama, and certainly more than the news that Yale was selling its South African stocks.

Ronald Reagan has been unusually slow to sense this alteration in mood. After his meeting with Bishop Desmond Tutu, he was able to say no more than the usual platitudes. He told the waiting hacks that he had heard, from tribal chieftains in South Africa, how grateful they were for the boon of American investment. The tiny Tutu bears an uncanny resemblance to Bishop Abel Muzorewa, but if anybody had told the President that he sounded exactly like Ian Smith he would probably not have understood the reference. The concept of the loyal chieftain is too close to his generous heart.

For the clever right-wingers, though, the chieftain factor won't quite cover it. There's a concept here known variously as MoHo or MoHiG, which stands for "Moral High Ground." It is important to be seen to be in possession of this precious turf, and the Left has more or less monopolized it, in the case of South Africa, these many years. Ideologically speaking, apartheid makes nonsense of the celebrated distinction between authoritarian and totalitarian upon which conservatives base their human-rights policy. An authoritarian regime may repress dissent, but it is supposed to respect private life and private property, to allow its subjects to worship God in their own way, and to permit such free movement and intercourse as does not pose a threat to its rule. In practice, this is supposed to translate conveniently but not explicitly into "any dictatorship that is not Marxist-Leninist." But South Africa does make laws which rape the privacy of the individual, even as far as the bedroom. It confiscates the property of citizens, and it limits their right to travel and work even in the country of their birth. That all this is done on the basis of color and race doesn't make it any sweeter. By taking a sterner view of apartheid, then, the smarter Republicans are protecting a flank that has long been highly vulnerable.

In May 1981, Ronald Reagan defended South Africa by asking, absurdly:

"Can we abandon this country that has stood beside us in every war we've ever fought?" Leaving aside the numerous American wars in which South Africa took no part, and assuming that the President was chiefly referring to that greatest of all wars, we're forced to recall that the Afrikaaner Nationalist Party was on the wrong side in that one, and that imprisonment for pro-Nazi and anti-British activity was and is considered a badge of honor among its ruling circle. Reagan may not know this, but many people do. Here is a case which defies the normal Cold War and patriotic categories. The pickets on Embassy Row may be made up of today's political "out groups," and they may be whistling somewhat when they try to revive the spirit of Selma and Montgomery. But they have in common with their predecessors the firm tenancy of MoHo, and in America that will always count for something.

(*The Spectator*, December 15, 1984)

KENNEDY'S BEDROOM

❏

We can't pay you much, I'm afraid. But I can probably get you put up in the John F. Kennedy suite. You can fantasize there to your heart's content." I was to be the visiting speaker at the Institute of Politics at Harvard, which is attached to the Kennedy School of Government. On arrival, my friend and host handed me the keys with what I thought was a puckish look on his face. He repeated his injunction about fantasy and heart's content. I wondered how I could live up to this on my own. About whom was I supposed to fantasize? About Angie Dickinson, who once bashfully described an amour with JFK as "the most memorable fifteen seconds of my life"? Or about Kennedy himself, who told his friend Lem Billings that the advantage of Harvard was that "I can now get tail as often and as free as I want, which is a step in the right direction." With the help of an incredibly beautiful and utterly incurious girl, I managed to find the door to F14 of Winthrop House and, alone once more, to turn the key.

Erotic shades, if there were any, were taking the day off. I found myself in a comfy twin-bed setting, with an adjoining living room and small kitchen. A largish bookshelf held few books, all of them by or about a member of the Kennedy family. A plaque on the wall announced that JFK had shared this room with Torbert Macdonald, a fellow member of the Harvard intake of 1939–40. This was the year in which JFK, with the unacknowledged help of various court historians, produced his sonorous book *Why England Slept*, which is said by some to have had an oedipal bearing on his terrible father's pro-Nazi sympathies. A copy was laid beside my chaste cot. Not until I had lurched back from the seminar and the dinner did I notice the Visitors' Book.

It seemed to promise more bedside diversion than the lachrymose works of Arthur Schlesinger or the ghost-written juvenilia of the Great Man himself. I began at page one, and found that I could not put it down.

There is a space for remarks in this book, and at first my eye was taken by all those who had been unable to think of anything to say. The extant volume began in the winter of 1971. On November 22 of that year, the eighth anniversary of Dallas, Congressman John Brademas had signed without comment. A former Democratic whip, he is now president of New York University. Just before his entry, I found that of R. W. Apple, now London correspondent of *The New York Times* and one of the large cadre of American reporters who keep transmitting uplifting news about the SDP. He hadn't put anything either. Nor had Roy Hattersley or Gloria Emerson. There was the name of Allard Lowenstein, founder of the Dump Johnson movement in 1968 and the man credited with getting Bobby Kennedy to run against LBJ. Not long after I met him, Lowenstein was murdered in New York by an unhinged homosexual friend of his. A book published this month claims that he was working for the CIA all the time he was urging Bobby to take up the torch. No comment even from him.

Perhaps overcome by a sense of history, and perhaps not wishing to seem tongue-tied, Congressman Pete McCloskey of California makes the first stab. "The first day of peace," it says. I look at the date: April 30, 1975—the day Saigon fell. Is McCloskey one of those who think that Kennedy would never have continued the war he began? Something tells me that he is.

Emboldened by his example, the guests begin to commit themselves more. Frank Capra, a few months later, rather superfluously gives his address as "Hollywood." He writes, making a point of the capital letter, "I felt the Charisma." This is the first appearance made by the indispensable Kennedy-word. And on we go, with a certain John Vesey writing "Wow! The K-vibes are intense! 'Inspirational' sounds so put on, but it certainly is that. All right here." Exclamation marks are often a sign that the user is straining for effect. Can it be that Mr. Vesey wrote what he thought he should feel?

The years roll by, and Seymour Hersh, Congressman Charles Goodell, Ted Koppel, and others all come to stay without saying anything. In March 1977, I am stunned to notice, John B. Connally of Houston, Texas, passed a night here with his wife and left no inscription. I think, speaking purely for myself, that if I had featured in the most famous few frames of the century alongside the Dead Man, and if I had been his host at the time he was shot, I might have attempted a few words. But, then again, if anybody can be speechless, he can. More surprising is the modesty of Eugene McCarthy, one of America's most conceited men and the politician who eclipsed Robert Kennedy in 1968. Last I heard, McCarthy had become a Reaganite. But he prefers to stress the private poetry and aphorism which he produces in moments of solitude. The muse stood him up on this occasion.

But a burst of musing awaits. In quick succession we find Evangelos Averoff, leader of the Greek Right, who is moved to say, "Cozy and refined. Perfect." (I never did trust him.) Anne Armstrong, the Valkyrie-like ex-ambassadress to the Court of St. James's, gushes, "Thanks for kindness, stimulation and inspiration." Carl Oglesby, former SDS megaphone, gives his address as % the Assassination Information Bureau in Washington, D.C., and contributes, "One feels and imbibes the spirit of his life." Sean MacBride, Dan Rather, and Helen Suzman can't think how to follow that and pass on the whole thing. But with what pleasure does one find little Shirley Williams putting, "A la recherche des [sic] Temps Perdus."

Tough guys, on the whole, don't bother. William Webster, now head of the FBI, remains gruffly silent. So does James Buckley (brother of the famous Bill and now running Radio Liberty). Irving Kristol keeps his thoughts to himself, as, more surprisingly, does the loquacious Jack Valenti. Only with John V. Lindsay does the genius loci return. On November 20, 1980, just two days shy of the anniversary, this man, who was once said to be "Jack's inheritor," wrote the single word "Onward." Here, no exclamation mark is needed to emphasize the emptiness.

The Reagan years seem to have robbed some people of speech altogether. After 1980 there are mere hasty signatures from Judith Martin, who was presumably uncertain of the etiquette, from Hodding Carter, from Edwin Meese, from John Anderson, Barbara Tuchman, and C. L. R. Clifford. Garry Trudeau, creator of Doonesbury, was silent. Even I. F. Stone could do no better than "Very pleasant." The British and Irish take up the slack. On March 17, 1983, Harold McCusker boldly inscribes, "An Orangeman in Boston on St. Patrick's Day." He has the self-possession to omit the exclamation mark, which is more than can be said for the Irish Ambassador the day after, who writes, "The Irish Ambassador the day after." David Steel manages to say, in a schoolboy hand, "A marvellous experience!" Swell.

Lately, the Moral Majority have been staying here. Their press spokesman, Cal Thomas, has put "Jesus First." His deputy, an indecipherable Ed Someone from Lynchburg, has added (did they share the room?—the date is the same), "Ephesians 3:21." Look it up: I had to, because this is one of the few American guest rooms without a Bible. Inscriptions from the non-famous tend to be less self-conscious and more embarrassing. "Sic Transit Gloria," "A Whiff of History," "We will pay any price, bear any burden," and "Don't let it be forgotten that for one brief shining moment there was a spot known as Camelot." These are more like the humble slips lodged in some Wailing Wall.

So what became of Torbert Macdonald? He was adopted by his roommate and elected to Congress in 1954. The roommate's father had arranged for "Torby" to get a special job during the war. But the roommate's father later prevented Torby from inheriting Jack's Senate seat, which Jack had rashly promised him. The seat was pledged, after all, to Teddy. It was to Torby, who once asked him how he would prefer to die, that the young President said, after a pause, "Oh, a gun. You never know what's hit you. A gunshot is the perfect way."

After a couple of days, with the brilliant spring sunshine on the quad and the Charles River gleaming nearby, I began to develop a proprietary attitude toward the rooms where once Jack and Torby so grandly hung out. It's a wrench to pack the old bags. And there is the Visitors' Book, looking at me reproachfully. I want to be invited back. But one must be honest in the face of posterity. I pull the book toward me and begin, steadily, to write. . . .

(*The Spectator*, March 23, 1985)

USELESS IDIOTS

❑

In Isabel Allende's impressive novel *The House of the Spirits*, which is set in a barely fictional Chile, one of the best-drawn characters is a certain Esteban Trueba. Trueba is a grandee—a brawling, egotistical landowner and an almost likable prisoner of his own appetites. He devotes prodigious energy to rallying his class against the mob and to the struggle against Marxism. He is a senator when the workers' parties come legally to power, and he insists from the start that only violence will remove the danger to order and property. He smuggles guns into the country, solicits covert aid from the gringos, and addresses subversive meetings of young officers. On the glorious day of the military coup, he gets into his car and drives out to congratulate the soldiery.

> The officer received me with his boots up on the desk, chewing a greasy sandwich, badly shaven, with his jacket unbuttoned. He didn't give me a chance to ask about my son Jaime or to congratulate him for the valiant actions of the soldiers who had saved the nation; instead he asked for the keys to my car, on the ground that Congress had been shut down and that all Congressional perquisites had therefore been suspended. I was amazed. It was clear then that

they didn't have the slightest intention of reopening the doors of Congress, as we all expected. He asked me—no, he ordered me—to show up at the Cathedral at eleven the next morning to attend the Te Deum with which the nation would express its gratitude to God for the victory over Communism.

Trueba's veins contain real blood, not an insipid mixture of milk and holy water stiffened with liquid dollars. But as I read of his awakening to reality, I found I could clearly see the puffy, shifty, unctuous features of Arturo Cruz.

Cruz is, at one and the same time, the darling of the Reaganites and the icon of the liberals (one wishes he was the only such coincidence). It is he, and not the loutish Enrique Bermúdez or the sadistic Ricardo Lau, who is brought before the cameras like a performing seal. The face of the Contras as seen by the villagers of Nicaragua is that of the snarling, crop-burning fascist. The same face as seen by the U.S. news media and public is that of a sheep with a secret sorrow. Here comes Arturo again, with his nagging worries about the revolution betrayed. Naturally, we are drawn to sympathize with this troubled Everyman. But why are we not introduced to Bermúdez, the man at the cutting edge of our military aid? Next question.

Cruz doesn't have the pretext of innocence. He was on hand when Edgar Chamorro, spokesman of the so-called Nicaraguan Democratic Force, gave his testimony about widespread Contra atrocities and admitted that the aim of the mercenaries was the overthrow of the government. He knows that, for speaking those unwelcome truths, Chamorro was banished from the FDN ranks. Does he honestly think he would be treated differently? Does he dream of the day when "the boys" install him in the presidency of a liberal, democratic Nicaragua? Or would just plain "president" be enough?

Not long ago I attended a breakfast meeting in Washington that featured both Cruz and Edén Pastora. Cruz was reason itself, talking of the need to separate party from state and stressing the values of pluralism. He was skeptical about the Sandinista commitment to democracy and scornful of their election. Pastora was his usual "colorful" self, still battered from the bomb that had gone off at his jungle press conference. Both men could at least claim that they had once been Sandinistas, though the returns on this claim are diminishing with time and Bermúdez.

I admit to an animus against the heroic Pastora, for when that bomb exploded, he seized the only available rapid transport and fled, leaving a woman friend of mine (who had absorbed much of the blast meant for him) horribly wounded on a river bank. Still, I listened politely while he denounced Jesse Jackson for going to Cuba, describing him as one of Lenin's "useful idiots." The next question concerned Roberto d'Aubuisson, who had just paid a visit to Washington. What did Commander Zero think of him? Pastora preferred not to give an opinion because that would be "interfering in the internal affairs of El Salvador." At that point I interjected to ask why, in that case, did he feel so free to be personal about Jesse Jackson? He asked to have the question translated, and did not reply. Unimpressive. So, when you reflect on it, is the evolution of Arturo Cruz. He would not take part in an election that he felt to be insufficiently democratic, but he will take part in a war of sabotage and attrition that has no democratic pretenses at all.

This is the old "salami tactic," operating from the right. The Christian Democrats of Chile joined gleefully and mindlessly in the destruction of Salvador Allende because they believed that they would be the beneficiaries. And certain labor types helped in the overthrow of Jacobo Arbenz in Guatemala, hoping thereby to preserve "free trade unions." The alliance with fascists, murderers, and oligarchs was, of course, only temporary. Twelve years later in Chile and thirty years later in Guatemala, we can see who was using whom.

With Nicaragua, however, we don't have the excuse of hindsight. William Casey and his crew have picked Enrique Bermúdez and *his* crew, and have discarded the waverers. The installations and the infrastructure of a small underdeveloped country are being ruined and destroyed. The population is being subjected, after earthquake, war, and revolution, to a calculated campaign of demoralization, a modern attempt to create a Vendée. One can feel sympathy for the youths who leave the country to avoid the draft and the rationing, but it's asking a lot to expect us to regard the mercenaries, or their two-faced spokesmen, as brave democrats. The proper historical analogy for these people is not the Founding Fathers but Benedict Arnold.

It is, finally, Cruz and Pastora who are the dupes and the "useful idiots." Their time could come only under conditions that would consign them to the well-known dustbin of history. Counterrevolutions can also be betrayed. This one will devour its parents as well as its children.

(*The Nation*, April 27, 1985)

BITTER FRUIT

❑

The whole misery and disgrace of current U.S. involvement with the "wrong side" in Central America began with the invasion of Guatemala (sometimes described as the coup in Guatemala) in 1954. This invasion/coup was brought off by the usual suspects—Vice President Richard Nixon, the CIA, the

United Fruit Company, and other practitioners of destabilization. Even today, the more polished conservatives have to repress a shudder at the recollections of 1954 and its aftermath.

But in *Bitter Fruit*, their exemplary account of the Guatemalan intervention, Stephen Schlesinger and Stephen Kinzer also describe how solicitous the destabilizers were to the small but significant forces of liberalism and social democracy in the United States. They relate that Edward Bernays, chief lobbyist of the forces seeking to overthrow the elected government of Jacobo Arbenz,

> had an especially close relationship with *The New Leader*, a vigorously anti-Communist liberal weekly. . . . Bernays persuaded the United Fruit Company to sponsor public service advertisements on behalf of the Red Cross and U.S. Savings Bonds in the magazine at $1,000 a page, far above the going rate. *The New Leader* . . . carried numerous articles, both before and after the coup, justifying intervention against Arbenz's regime on the grounds that a Soviet takeover was imminent.

A managing editor of *The New Leader* in the 1950s, Daniel James, wrote a book entitled *Red Design for the Americas*, which provided a rationale for the destruction of Guatemalan democracy. United Fruit and the CIA cooperated to insure that this luminous work had a wide distribution.

I thought continually of this episode as I attended the national convention of Social Democrats, U.S.A., held in Washington from June 16. This organization, which might better be known as Social Democrats, U.S.A.! U.S.A.! and which has the crust to claim descent from the party of Debs and Thomas, is little understood or studied but highly influential. Combining the worst of Old Left sectarian venom with the cheapest line in neoconservative platitudes, SDUSA has provided the intellectual context for Jeane Kirkpatrick and some useful cover for other Humphrey-Jackson Democrats in transition. In transition to what? Well, their guru, Carl Gershman, held Kirkpatrick's fragrant coat at the United Nations for many years, served the Kissinger Commission on Central America, and now heads Reagan's National Endowment for Democracy. In other words, don't be fooled by the fact that the mode of address at SDUSA meetings is still "comrade."

There's a lot not to be fooled by at these affairs. Alfonso Robelo had been invited as the star guest, to do for the Contras what his 1954 predecessors did for Castillo Armas. He gave a bland speech, sounding for all the world as if the campaign against Nicaragua was being waged by members of the Young Social Democrats and the more highly evolved forces of the Socialist International. He lauded the Lew Lehrman coalition of anti-Soviet guerrillas (incidentally, I do not see how any of that bunch could have got into Angola without being taken through occupied Namibia by the South Africans).

When I asked him about the "social democratic" leadership of Colonel Enrique Bermúdez, he became ever so slightly less silky. To keep harping on about the Somoza National Guard, he said, was like saying that all the Wehrmacht were responsible for war crimes. This Bitburg reference, probably intended for a later speech at the convention of Young Americans for Fascism, may have just slipped out, but I didn't notice any of the Social Democrats objecting. They didn't even raise a murmur when Robelo claimed to have investigated all the former guardsmen in the FDN and found them blameless of atrocities under Somoza.

Your typical Social Democrat has a wised-up, pitying manner. You are looking at someone, he seems to say, who has left illusions behind him. No flies can settle on this smirking countenance. Don't you know, the face seems to ask, that the world is a dangerous place? Haven't you read *The Gulag Archipelago*? Ever heard of the boat people? Don't you want America to be strong? Aren't you aware that you can't demonstrate for nuclear disarmament in the Soviet Union? At about this point, and to distract myself from the overmastering desire to slap the face, I imagine myself demonstrating for nuclear disarmament in the Soviet Union and being locked up by someone with precisely those features and that tone of voice.

But, in fact, for all their worldly wisdom, the SDs are extremely naïve. They are the useful idiots of the Reagan revolution. They were the last political formation in America to realize that the Vietnam War was not being fought by democratic forces or for democratic ends. Many of them still feel that, with a bit more "political will" (favorite SD and neocon term), the trick might have been pulled off. They have a utopian and protective attitude toward Israel which in its myopia rivals that of any old party hack toward the Soviet Union. They think that Jean-François Revel is a new philosopher. They think that Aleksandr Solzhenitsyn is a social democrat, though some of them have suppressed worries about his attitude toward the Vlasovites. They think they "saw through" Carter and McGovern before anyone else did, but they modestly understate their role in Democrats for Nixon.

Intellectually contemptible though they may be, the Social Democrats shine like pearls among the Reaganite swine. Left to itself, the old conservative movement could not have come up with fluent twisters like Kirkpatrick, Elliott Abrams, and Max Kampelman, nor mastered a standard of apologetics anywhere near that of *Commentary* or the Committee for the Free World. A certain vital patina has thus been provided to this government of Christian bigots and thwarted militarists by an ostensibly secular, internationalist political tendency. As with Guatemala or Vietnam, the SDs will be somewhere else while the actual slaughtering is done—probably accusing the journalists who report it of "blaming America first." But, as with Guatemala and Vietnam, they show that every little bit helps.

(*The Nation*, July 6–13, 1985)

CHICKEN HAWKS

❏

When you've shouted "Rule Britannia,"
when you've sung "God save the Queen,"
When you've finished killing Kruger
with your mouth . . .

In Washington, it is the season of the white feather. A few months ago, Republican Congressman Bob Dornan attacked one of his Democratic opponents as a "draft-dodging wimp." On June 27, there was nearly a punch-up on the floor of the House when another young Reaganite, Dan Lungren, who bellows for everything from aid to the Contras to chemical warfare and Star Wars, shouted as he was restrained: "I do not have to fear for my physical being in this House. My avocations are weightlifting and *tae kwon do*, and I certainly do not have to worry about someone who is two decades older than I am." On television and in their syndicated columns, leading conservatives like George "Triumph of the" Will excoriate liberals for their reluctance to use force and for their generally bleeding-heart attitude. Meanwhile, the glistening pectorals of Sylvester Stallone have become inescapable as Rambo stalks the land, growling out of the side of his mouth about the stab in the back that "our boys" received from unnamed pointy-heads.

But, as Kipling showed long ago, patriotism and jingoism are not by any means the same thing. Jane Mayer in *The Wall Street Journal*, and the less surprising Jack Newfield in *The Village Voice*, decided to take a look at the leading white-feather distributors. What they found was what social scientists might call an inverse correlation. The louder a man shouts for bombing and strafing, the less likely he is to have felt the weight of a pack. There are pitiful examples of this, like the former Reaganite Congressman Bruce Caputo, who actually fabricated a Vietnam War record, deceived even his own staff, and was finally given the breeze by the electorate he had hoodwinked. And there are grandiose examples, like the President himself, who convinced Yitzhak Shamir that he had personally taken part in the liberation of the concentration camps, and who repeated the story to other auditors until his handlers and speechwriters admitted that he never left Hollywood between Pearl Harbor and Potsdam. Mostly, though, the proponents of militarism are simply inglorious.

Congressman Dornan, for example, turned out to have been rather a cautious reservist throughout the Vietnam War. Congressman Lungren, he of the Contras and the *tae kwon do,* was eligible for the draft between 1964 and 1970, but now says: "I had a knee injury from football." Newt Gingrich, who last year told Congress, "I am the very tough-minded son of a career soldier," was eligible from 1961 to 1969 but took the prudent course of a student deferment and told *The Wall Street Journal:* "What difference would I have made? There was a bigger battle in Congress than in Vietnam." Arguably true, but since he took part in neither . . . Best of all, from the esthetic point of view, is Sylvester Stallone himself. He dodged the draft in the most agreeable possible way, hiding in Switzerland as coach to a private school for girls. As he told an interviewer before *Rambo* was released:

> I got there because my mother was a great con-artist and she got me in as a physical instructor. This was a school for extremely wealthy and professionally spoiled children. The Shah of Iran's kid. The kid from the Hershey fortune, the kid whose father owned the Kimberley mines. . . . I didn't want to ski. I just wanted to get loaded and play pinball machines. Essentially I was the imported American sheepdog for these little lambs, these girls. I mean it.

I bet he does. And there's nothing wrong in wishing that you had had a good war, but something, well, *rum* about pretending that you did. Something rummer still about defaming those who opposed the last war or who are unenthusiastic about the next.

The green-eyed monster must be at work somewhere. As it happens, the leading "doves" (ludicrous term) have rather more to show on their chests and sleeves. The new senator from Massachusetts, for example, John Kerry, was a renowned officer in Vietnam but also helped found Vietnam Veterans Against the War. George McGovern was a decorated bomber pilot in World War II. Congressman Andrew Jacobs, who originated the idea of calling the rightist bluffers "war wimps," was a marine in Korea.

And the coincidences are extraordinary. Look into the past of any rabid patriot of the moment—and you will find that they wangled a job at the base. There never was such a collection of bad knees, weak lungs, urgent academic priorities, or, as in the case of Stallone, sheer bloody gall. Contrast this "hawkish" crew with Senator Albert Gore, the rather decent and skeptical Democratic senator from Tennessee. Of those who graduated from Harvard in 1969, Gore was practically the only one to enlist under his country's colors. As he put it in a recent interview—because this is the conversation topic of the moment—"I came from a small town of three thousand people. I concluded that if I didn't go, somebody else would have to go."

Which is the closest to a money-mouth relationship that anybody has got in this exchange. The open secret about the American Armed Forces is that, by rank and file, they are composed of poor blacks, Hispanics, and rural whites. The figure of Lieutenant Calley was shocking to enlightened Americans, not because they discovered him in Vietnam, but because he was the sort of person they never met at home. Both sides wage class war on the point: the Right by suggesting that the limousine liberals are out of touch with "grass-roots America" and the liberals by alleging that the Right only fancies the plebeians as cannon fodder.

The conservatives certainly asked for this riposte about their own war records, and they are definitely squirming as a result. But the Democrats should beware of their temporary field day. Congressman Lane Evans, for example, has proposed nicknaming the draft-dodging warmongers "chicken hawks," which is superficially amusing but is also, as I bet he knows perfectly well, a particularly nasty slang word for elderly pederasts. People like Jack Newfield, who don't think *anybody* should have gone to Vietnam, should beware of borrowing the philistine, vulgar speech with which antiwar spokesmen were slandered in those days. The white feather can be a more honorable thing to receive than to give.

The serious pacifist objects not to dying but to killing. The serious radical long ago got bored with endless jokes about socialists who went to private school, had a private income, were embarrassed by having servants, etcetera, etcetera, ad nauseam. Tom Wolfe built a whole reputation on this one tenuous gag, and Lord Stansgate nearly lost one. But everybody agrees, somewhere in his heart, that there ought to be *some* connection between what you believe and how you behave, what you advocate for others and how you live yourself. At the moment, the gap is more conspicuous in the case of the summer soldiers and sunshine patriots. So:

> *Pass the hat for your credit's sake and pay—*
> *pay—pay!*

(*The Spectator*, August 10, 1985)

STANDING TALL

❑

The standard image of President Ronald Reagan as a game but fuddled movie actor is an image so stale as to be rebarbative. It is the standby of the weary cartoonist, the flagging gag-writer, and the composer of hackneyed captions. It's been a boast of mine, during some years of writing from Washington, that I have never lampooned the old boy as a Wild West ham, an All-American kid, a granite-jawed GI, or any other of the stock repertoire. To fall for such instant "takes" is to be a hack oneself—like those who go to Republican conventions in Texas and dwell endlessly on the rhinestones and ten-gallon hats.

Now, as we lurch uncertainly into the second term, comes Professor Michael Rogin of the University of California with a serious thesis on Reagan and celluloid. And now I wish that I had paid more attention to the obvious. At the annual meeting of the American Political Science Association in New Orleans, Rogin gave a paper entitled "Ronald Reagan: The Movie." This paper makes the most blasé, acclimatized Washingtonian sit up and peer around. For example, I still remember the irritation I felt at my own emotion when Reagan last summer made his D-Day anniversary speech in Normandy. I knew that I was being got at, but I swallowed and blinked all the same when he asked the assembled leathery veterans: "Where do we find such men?" I might have been better armored had I recognized the line from *The Bridges at Toko-Ri*. Likewise, in the New Hampshire primary debates in 1980, when Reagan upstaged his rivals by chirruping, "I'm paying for this microphone," few of those present recognized the plagiarism of Spencer Tracy's *State of the Union*.

All the President's lines—but not all of them so subliminal. Launching his latest nuclear fantasy, he told the press corps, "The Force is with us." Then, rather oddly, he complained at having his "Strategic Defense Initiative" nicknamed Star Wars. Defending his inventive tax-reform bill, and challenging the Democrats to make something of it, he gurgled: "Make my day!" But comparisons between his style and that of Dirty Harry are daily discouraged by a pained, overworked White House press office.

The apotheosis of all this ("Where's the rest of me?" "Let's win this one for the Gipper!") came, Rogin believes, in 1981. "To confirm the President's faith in the power of film, John Hinckley, imitating the plot of the movie *Taxi Driver*, deliberately shot the President on the day of the Academy Awards." It so fell out that Reagan had already recorded a breezy, upbeat salute to the audience at the Oscar ceremony: "The television audience watching a screen saw a Hollywood audience watch another screen. One audience saw the other applaud a taped image of a healthy Reagan, while the real President lay in a hospital bed."

The point must come when one asks whether the President himself knows the difference. Perhaps it came recently when the Leader of the Free World took a gander at the impasse in Beirut and told the microphone (which he'd paid for): "I saw *Rambo* last night, and next time I'll know what to do." The whoop that echoed across the nation was one that had been building for some time. But, though I have been writing about *Rambo* for months, I am still uncertain about what has made it so much more successful than other chauvinist, paranoid spectaculars. The theme of captive "missing" Americans in Indochina might be thought to have been exhausted, in the last year alone, by at least three rival films. The idea that "we" could have won if it weren't for the press and the pointy-heads ("Weimar chic," as a friend put it to me sourly) is drearily familiar from a host of Monday-morning quarterbacks. The idea that "we" actually *did* win, in Vietnam and everywhere else, is even now being popularized by that great studio revisionist Menachem Golan, whose latest offering is a replay of the TWA Beirut hijack—where the U.S. Cavalry really does arrive at the last minute.

A possible explanation was offered to me unintentionally by a Vietnamese friend with whom I went to see *Rambo*. He took it with fair good humor, though he was generally rather appalled. He objected in particular to the portrayal of Vietnamese soldiers as Japanese—as, moreover, the cruel, kepi-wearing, buck-toothed Japanese of John Wayne vintage. Easy to see why any Vietnamese above the age of forty would resent such a vulgar confusion. But musing through a second screening, and seeing Mr. Minh's point afresh, I was struck by the final scene in which Sylvester Stallone howlingly machine-guns a whole roomful of his boss's high-tech computers, radios, and retrieval systems. To him, of course, they represent the power of the potbellied bureaucrat over the man in the field. But, to the blue-collar, semiemployed youths who yell for Rambo, may this moment not suggest the revenge on Sony, Nissan, Toyota, and Mitsubishi? Today's cold war with Asian capitalism excites scarcely less passion than did the hot one with Indochinese communism. Rambo as protectionist paradigm?

The screen, a smaller one this time, has also dominated the year's most emotional and enduring public debate. It is a very rare night that does not feature some strong footage from the Cape of Good Hope, usually succeeded by some strenuous punditry. American networks easily make up in technological sweetness what they have abandoned by way of political depth, and some real feats have been accomplished. By satellite, and by the deft use of separate studios (Apart-Aid?), Botha and Tutu have been presented as if they were actually arguing in the same room. An issue which was, until very recently, almost occluded in America has become *the* foreign-policy question. Its hard edge of moral choice and its pitiless focus on racialism have insured that there is scant hiding place for the undecided. This means that a lot of American clergymen are getting prime time without, for once, having to pay for it by the electronic collection plate.

In *The Eighteenth Brumaire* Marx said, rather aptly, that men learning a new language always begin by translating it back into the language they already know. Thus, the newly potent symbols of apartheid become instantly assimilated to the memory of Selma, Montgomery, and Memphis. Experienced South Africa hands like Jim Hoagland of *The Washington Post* (himself a white Southerner) have been arguing for years that the comparison is not even a comparison. But the temptation of analogy has proved too strong. For an entire hour the other night, the Reverend Jerry Falwell and the Reverend Jesse Jackson went at it as if the Freedom Riders were even now being bayed by Bull Connor. The two men still detest each other from that period, and neither of them seems to have read anything except the Bible (or "the babble," as they both call it) since. Falwell, though still able to please a racialist crowd while later saying, "Who, me?" now claims to have been delivered by the Lord from his earlier segregationist prison. Jackson, who set out as a rainbow warrior, has also kept company with bigots and claims to have been cleansed by the experience. Both know as much about South Africa as I do about molecular biology. It's a curious thing in American life that the most abject nonsense will be excused if the utterer can claim the sanction of religion. A country which forbids an established church by law is prey to any denomination. The best that can be said is that this is pluralism of a kind.

And I wonder, therefore, how James Atlas can have been so indulgent in his recent essay "The Changing World of New York Intellectuals." This rather shallow piece appeared in *The New York Times Magazine* and took us over the usual jumps. Gone are the days of *Partisan Review*, Delmore Schwartz, Dwight Macdonald, etcetera, etcetera. No longer the tempest of debate over Trotsky, *The Waste Land*, Orwell, blah, blah. Today the assimilation of the Jewish American, the rise of rents in midtown Manhattan, the erosion of Village life, yawn, yawn. The drift to the right, the rediscovery of patriotism, the gruesome maturity of the once-iconoclastic Norman Podhoretz, okay, *okay!* I have one question which Atlas in his much-ballyhooed article did not even discuss. The old gang may have had regrettable flirtations. Their political compromises, endlessly reviewed, may have exhibited naïveté or self-regard. But much of that record is still educative, and the argument did take place under real pressure from anti-Semitic and authoritarian enemies. Today, the alleged "neoconservative" movement around Jeane Kirkpatrick, *Commentary*, and *The New Criterion* can be found in unforced alliance with openly obscurantist, fundamentalist, and, above all, anti-intellectual forces. In the old days, there would at least have been a debate on the proprieties of such a united front, with many fine distinctions made and brave attitudes struck. As I write, nearness to power seems the only excuse, and the subject is changed as soon as it is raised. I wait for the agonized, self-justifying neoconservative essay about necessary and contingent alliances. Do I linger in vain?

The smart new metropolitan Right has more in common with the unpolished legions of Falwell and Rambo than it might care to acknowledge. Their shared psychology is one of superpower self-pity. Rambo sees the United

States as David to the Vietnamese Goliath. By slight contrast, the Committee for the Free World views America, in Nixon's famous, grizzling phrase, as "a pitiful, helpless giant." Never in history can any group of well-connected, well-heeled, well-advertised propagandists have complained so much, and through so many outlets, about being an oppressed minority. Seldom in history has such a wealthy, powerful, overbearing government represented itself so consistently as a victim—bullied now by the Lebanese and now by the Nicaraguans. Individual self-pity ("We want our country to love us— gulp—as much as we love our country") merges nicely with this lachrymose conception of country itself. I don't mind the fact that former liberals rush to repeat these old conservative commonplaces. It is, after all, one of the great themes of our time. But I do find it hard to be told, in the age of Reagan and Rambo, that it took *courage* for them to do so. "Where do we find such men?" Only too easily.

(*London Review of Books*, October 3, 1985)

SKIN OF THEIR TEETH

❏

During a particularly dismal phase of the Cyprus crisis, Aneurin Bevan was taunting the Tory front bench and happened to observe that they were, without knowing it, of two minds. Did they want, he inquired sarcastically, a base in Cyprus or Cyprus as a base? I have been told by those who witnessed the debate that you could actually see the ministerial visages change. As Bevan's point went home, they realized that the need for a strategic foothold did not commit them to an indefinite responsibility for an unpopular and repressive government. You could have one without the other. A brisk climbdown, some hasty constitutional arrangements, a bit of aid and goodwill and—generalized feelings of relief. Failure to see this opportunity would infallibly have resulted in the loss of both the island and the bases.

It is difficult to pinpoint with any certainty the moment at which the Reagan team was hit by the same blinding and obvious revelation about the Philippines. In the mind of Michael Armacost, Under Secretary of State for Political Affairs, the moment seems to have come when, as U.S. Ambassador in Manila, he had to read and write reports on the murder of Benigno Aquino. The experience convinced him that Ferdinand Marcos was terminally dis- honest and nasty and a great deal more trouble than he was worth. Returned to Foggy Bottom, he set about winning over his colleagues and superiors to this view. But, while the anti-Marcos faction in the State Department was growing steadily, the White House was still committed to its client in his capacity as the landlord for Clark Field and Subic Bay. It's only a short while since George Bush, toasting Marcos at a banquet, said: "We stand with the Philippines. We stand with you, sir. We love your adherence to democratic principles and to the democratic processes. We will not leave you in isolation. It would be turning our backs on history if we did."

Attacking Mondale's foreign-policy proposals during the second Presidential debate, Ronald Reagan chose the Philippines as a classic illustration of the rightness of his own world view. Better to "retain their friendship," he burbled, "rather than throwing them to the wolves and then facing a communist power in the Pacific." As late as February 10, 1986, the President said that he was unconvinced by reports of election fraud: "I'm sure even elections in our own country—there are some evidences of fraud in places and areas." It's so unusual for Reagan to say anything that even slightly denigrates America that one must judge his attachment to Marcos to have been pretty strong even at the eleventh hour.

Several things combined to make a lightning change possible. First, Marcos practically committed suicide on network television. Apparently he had no adviser brave enough to tell him how revolting, conceited, and deranged he looked. I say apparently, because he did keep coming on, arousing choruses of disgust across the nation. Second, there was, unlike in Nicaragua or Iran, an alternative "third force" available, led by presentable people. Third, and oddly unremarked, the Soviet Union decided for reasons of its own to defend Marcos, to attack American "interference" in the elections, and even to send its ambassador to congratulate the despot on his "victory." This made it harder to present Marcos as the only alternative to the expansionist Bear.

So the thing was done, and done with dispatch. The State Department won its first foreign-policy victory in a long time. All that now remains is for Ronald Reagan to succeed in giving the impression that the whole thing was his own idea.

This may prove more difficult than his other masterly credit takings have done. The least noticed but certainly the major casualty of the Marcos demission is that very theory which has, until now, been the Administration's guide. For six years, the ideas of Jeane Kirkpatrick have been the reigning wisdom. In the famous article that got her a place in Reagan's heart and, later, in his Cabinet, Kirkpatrick wrote that American liberalism had a suicidal tendency to respect "deep historical forces." It was not such forces, she argued, that brought down the Shah and Somoza. It was "lack of realism" in American decision-making coupled with "the pervasive and mistaken assumption that one can easily locate and impose democratic alternatives and the equally pervasive and equally flawed belief that change *per se* in autocracies is inevitable, desirable and in the American interest." The answer was to abandon the precepts of Jimmy Carter and Andrew Young, and to give ungrudging support to "positively friendly" authoritarians.

In the last few months, Kirkpatrick and her supporters have fought a long rearguard action in defense of Marcos. Norman Podhoretz, Robert Evans and Rowland Novak, Owen Harries, and the other syndicated neoconservatives echoed the same themes. They attacked "liberal meddling" in Filipino affairs. And they were taken up by Blas Ople, Marcos's official spokesman, who told American viewers that he "would like to paraphrase Jeane Kirkpatrick, who warned against a foreign policy of the United States dedicated literally to the subjugation of a friendly nation."

At the climax of the Filipino elections, Kirkpatrick's column urged that American interference cease lest the United States end up like Magellan, "hacked to death by the Philippine tribes." Just as her article was going to syndicated subscribers, Kirkpatrick tried to change it, hastily inserting some lines about "charges of fraud" that "destroyed the perception [that bloody word again] of a creditable election." Which column you might have read depended on which newspaper you bought. Put the two versions together, and you see the collapse of the neoconservative ascendancy in foreign policy.

By failing to take its own advice, the Reagan Administration has not only secured its enormous military bases in the Philippines, but it has won itself an immense grant of moral and political credit. That credit may be temporary, and there will be those who resent the last-minute nature of the metamorphosis. But it has all gone off incomparably better than anyone would have foreseen, and incomparably better than any of Jimmy Carter's brushes with authoritarianism. The Reagan people hate being mentioned in the same breath with Jimmy Carter, but in this case they'll just have to live with the fact that they did what he would have done. As Aneurin Bevan said on another occasion, conservatives are quite good at wearing the medals of their defeats.

(The Spectator, March 8, 1986)

LOONY TUNES

❑

If there is one thing that unites the Reaganites and their sickly circle of liberal admirers in Washington, it is the allegation that Nicaragua is a "revolution betrayed." The phrase has an honorable pedigree, deriving from Trotsky's mordant dissection of the Stalinist regime in the Soviet Union.

But, as employed by the White House propaganda team, it is an important element in the manufacture of a false consensus. If the term means anything in President Reagan's mouth, it means that everybody welcomed the anti-Somoza revolution but that some of the more sensitive comrades have become sickened and distressed since 1979—sickened and distressed enough to start burning the crops, murdering the peasants, and bombing the refineries of a wretchedly underdeveloped society (something the original Trotskyists were only *accused* of doing).

The record, like history, is pitiless. It shows what the Right would have you forget: that Reagan and his advisers were always pro-Somoza and anti-Sandinista, and that they started levying war on Nicaragua long before any of the incoming revolutionary tendencies had had a chance to establish or to differentiate themselves.

As a candidate in 1979, Ronald Reagan recorded numerous broadcasts for his political action committee, Citizens for the Republic. Tapes and cassettes of these gems were distributed to radio stations across the luckless nation. Here is what the man emitted between March and April 1979:

Senator Steve Symms of Idaho . . . made a nine-day trip, touching shore in Jamaica (our newest Marxist neighbor), the Dominican Republic and Cuba. His summation is blunt and to the point. He says the Caribbean is rapidly becoming a Communist lake in what should be an American pond. . . .

I'm sure he would agree that the troubles in Nicaragua bear a Cuban label also. While there are people in that troubled land who probably have justifiable grievances against the Somoza regime, there is no question but that most of the rebels are Cuban-trained, Cuban-armed and dedicated to creating another Communist country in this hemisphere.

A little later in the same period, as Somoza's government was approaching its death agony and inflicting death agony on thousands of its own people, Reagan took to the airwaves again. His target was the softhearted State Department:

Our State Department [has decided on] a cutback in economic aid to Nicaragua and the withdrawal of American personnel. This we are doing because, according to the State Department, President Somoza is in violation of our standards of human rights. He may be—I don't know.

So, right up until July 19, 1979, the date of the Sandinista revolution, there is no evidence that Reagan was anything but sympathetic to the deluded sadist Somoza, who bombed his own capital city before giving up. Nor was it long after the revolution that the American Right began to rattle the saber. The 1980 Republican platform, which was written less than a year after the fall of Somoza, read:

> We deplore the Marxist Sandinista takeover of Nicaragua and the Marxist attempts to destabilize El Salvador, Guatemala and Honduras. We do not support United States assistance to any Marxist government in this hemisphere, and we oppose the Carter Administration aid program for the government of Nicaragua. However, we will support the efforts of the Nicaraguan people to establish a free and independent government.

Credit for the insertion of this plank in the platform is taken by John Carbaugh, a former senior foreign-policy aide to Senator Jesse Helms and a man of such disordered reactionary temper that the Thatcher government had to ask him to leave the Zimbabwe independence talks in London, where, uninvited, he was urging Ian Smith to hang tough.

Even Carbaugh would have looked a little farouche at the May 1980 meeting of the Council for Inter-American Security in Santa Fe, New Mexico. The CIAS declaimed:

> Certainly, in war there is no substitute for victory; and the United States is engaged in World War III. The first two phases, containment and detente, have been overtaken by the Soviet scenario of double envelopment: surround the People's Republic of China and strangle the Western industrialized nations by interdicting their oil and ore. Southern Asia and Ibero-America are the actual areas of aggression.
>
> Latin America is vital to the United States: America's global power projection has always rested upon a cooperative Caribbean and a supportive South America. For the United States of America, isolationism is impossible. Containment of the Soviet Union is not enough. Detente is dead.
>
> Only the United States can, as a partner, protect the independent nations of Latin America from Communist conquest and help preserve Hispanic-American culture from sterilization by international Marxist materialism.

It was from among the authors of this swirling bullshit that candidate Reagan picked his advisers on the Panama Canal and Nicaragua. Roger Fontaine briefed him on the canal, became a special Central America adviser to the National Security Council, and now works for the Moonies at *The Washington Times*. Lewis Tambs is U.S. Ambassador to Costa Rica. L. Francis Bouchey, one of Roberto d'Aubuisson's hosts when he visited the United States in 1984, also has continual "input," as they say.

The rest is history. In March 1981, the Reaganites suspended Nicaraguan credits for the purchase of wheat. In April of the same year, they canceled the fifteen million dollars in aid that remained of President Carter's original seventy-five-million-dollar program. In September, the seven-million-dollar

AID loan was suspended, and, in November, the National Security Council met to approve an eight-point plan that included the initial nineteen million dollars for the Contras, and their training by officers of the Argentine junta.

And yet we are asked to believe that the Right has been driven by Sandinista excesses to support the Somacistas. If it had been up to the Reaganites, Somoza would never have been overthrown. Not since the days of the China lobby has an important foreign policy been so firmly in the hands of a fanatical clique—an ancien régime cabal of misfits and loony tunes.

(*The Nation*, April 19, 1986)

CASTING BREAD ON
THE SENATORS

❑

If there was ever a topic which the Reagan Administration spent a great deal of time not caring about, that topic was acid rain. It had everything that a hot Republican issue should not have: environmental and ecological overtones; the possibility of complex and restrictive legislation; the opening of an avenue of attack on the American Chamber of Commerce. There were no blue-collar votes in it either, or even middle-class residential ones. Wasn't the whole point of acid rain the fact that it drifted over into Canada? Everybody knows that there's lots of spare room in Canada, combined with a disagreeable tendency to whinge. Two or three years ago, I went to the Key Theater in Georgetown and sat through three unbearably dull Canadian films about the problem solely because the Administration had refused the films an import license. That was how much the White House, and most of the rest of Washington, cared about Canadian susceptibilities.

All of a sudden, however, there was action, Michael Deaver, the White House Deputy Chief of Staff, became all acid rain–conscious. The subject was moved to the top of the agenda when Reagan met Brian Mulroney in Quebec. Generous allocations were made to those old favorites, research and prevention. And, when Michael Deaver left the White House to put up his brass plate as a consultant, one of his first blue-chip clients was the government of Canada. "Indeed, my lord, it followed hard upon." Investigation shows that it was Deaver who had been pushing for a more "activist" policy while in office. He picked up his million-dollar retainer almost, as it were, on the way out. As a result, in spite of the fact that he was probably doing the right thing in a praiseworthy cause, Mr. Deaver is hauled before the cameras and the Congress for a "conflict of interest."

There isn't a single member of that great legislative body who does not know the meaning of the term. For as long as I live here, I shall never quite adjust to the loud, uncompromising way in which money talks. Deaver has argued publicly that he was not using the "revolving door" between public and private interest, and that he only did what many other insiders do. How right he is. American politics is choking and drowning in boodle.

The agreed villain is the political action committee, or PAC. These organizations evolved to circumvent the laws on campaign finance that followed the Watergate scandal. They allow individual interests and corporations to make enormous donations to candidates and incumbents, and to buy themselves audience in the Capitol. As I write, the Congress is debating tax reform and members are daily forced to run what's been called "the Gucci gauntlet," as sharply dressed lobbyists and loophole artists crowd the corridors. A congressman who doesn't want his eye to be caught will be in a weak position when he espies the face of a man who just wrote him a check for $75,000.

I am not exaggerating. There are twenty-seven senators seeking reelection this year, and in 1985 alone they accepted a total of $9.8 *million* in donations from political action committees. This is an elevenfold increase over 1979. Some senators are more candid about the situation than others. Senator Charles Grassley, a Republican from Iowa, told the *Los Angeles Times* that he's getting so much interest-group money these days that he has to keep a computer printout on his desk to remind him to whom he is indebted. Asked why he was suddenly in the money, Grassley deployed what Stanley Baldwin used to call "appalling frankness." He's on the Senate Finance Committee, he said, "and we didn't have a tax bill in 1983. Now, people are anticipating a major tax bill."

The situation is bad enough and blatant enough for (the retiring) Senator Barry Goldwater to introduce legislation limiting PAC payments. This would mean that a senator could accept "only" $750,000 from PACs. But it would make some other provisions as well. For example, the practice of "bundling" would be sharply restricted. Bundling? Bundling is a means for PACs to evade contribution limits by collecting serial amounts from their members in individual checks and handing the whole fistful or armful to the target candidate. A wonderful group named Align PAC—a group of insurance agents set up to lobby on the tax-reform bill—last year gave $215,000 in this fashion to Senator Robert Packwood of Oregon. He was Chairman of the Senate Finance Committee.

In the last election campaign, PACs kicked in $102 million to congressional candidates. (It took six million ordinary Americans and thousands of assorted celebrities several months to raise half that amount in the recent Hands

Across America ballyhoo.) And there were only four thousand PACs involved, which lends point to Goldwater's observation that "it is no longer 'we the people,' but PACs and the special interests they represent, who set the country's political agenda and control nearly every candidate's position on the important issues of the day."

If this money and these inducements were being made available to parties, it might be unfair but it would not be so suspicious. It is the singling out of individual candidates and incumbents, and the clear attempts made to suborn their votes and allegiances, that has become more than a "problem." There is no boring old balance rule in the American mass media. If you want air time at election time, you pay for it—and very steeply, too. If you don't want, then you don't want to get elected. Parties these days will simply not nominate men and women without funds of their own or access to the funds of others.

As if all this were not enough, we have the annual farce, just completed, of the "Honorarium Declaration." The law allows a senator to accept as much as one-third again of his or her salary in presents and fees, provided that the residue is given "to charity." The salary of a senator is $75,100 per annum, plus generous expenses for staff and research. Last week we learned that senators accepted $2.3 million in honoraria in 1985, passing on $723,000 of it to charities such as libraries in their own districts bearing their own names. Incredible groups like the American Pork Congress, which one never hears about most of the time, spend a good deal of money buying free holidays for senators and free facelifts for their overworked wives. If this is not bread on the waters, what is? Members of the House of Representatives copped $4.6 million in honoraria and lavished $847,000 of that on their favorite charities. The leading recipient (of honoraria, that is) was Dan Rostenkowski, Democratic Chairman of the Ways and Means Committee, who netted $137,500. The Ways and Means Committee is a tax-writing committee, and it was no surprise to find that its members attracted two and a half times the average in extramural receipts.

You don't have to be very precise about how you spend money given to you for campaign purposes, and, under one extra-generous clause in the law, you can keep any of it left over for your personal use if you were in office on January 8, 1980.

Goldwater is right. The voters are sickened by the way in which their Congress has been alienated from them by money. I think one could go further and say that the decadence of political language, the growing domination of discourse by ad men and media consultants, all the grooming and blow-drying and emasculation of candidates are largely attributable to the operations of pelf. It's no surprise that so few Americans think their vote counts, or even bother to register it.

Poor Michael Deaver. Like many former *chefs de cabinet*, he developed the illusion that his job was above politics. When next he comes for a solemn hearing on Capitol Hill, it will be interesting to see which senator casts the first bundle.

(*The Spectator*, May 31, 1986)

WATERGATE REVISITED:
The Greek Connection

❏

On June 17, 1986, it will be fourteen years since Richard Nixon's burglars were caught in the Watergate offices of the Democratic National Committee. These fourteen years have seen many changes, including an incomprehensible rehabilitation of Nixon himself. But we still lack an answer to one of the five cardinal questions of the investigator. We know who, we know what, we know where, and we know when—but we do not know why. What were the burglars after? What were President Nixon and Attorney General John Mitchell hoping they would find?

One footprint turns up at every stage of Richard Nixon's criminal career, from his election to the presidency in 1968, to the Watergate scandal, to the various attempts made to cover up that scandal. That footprint belongs to Thomas A. Pappas, an ultrareactionary Greek-American tycoon who lives in honorable retirement in Boston. The most succinct summary of Pappas's influence on the Nixon Administration occurs in J. Anthony Lukas's book *Nightmare*. Lukas quotes a February 9, 1973, conversation between Presidential counsel John Dean and Attorney General Mitchell, in which the thorny question of raising hush money for the burglars' defense was discussed. Dean asked, "Did you talk to the Greek?" Mitchell replied in the affirmative, and Dean then asked, "Is the Greek bearing gifts?" Mitchell said, "Well, I want to call you tomorrow on that." As Lukas takes up the tale:

The "Greek" was Thomas A. Pappas, a Greek immigrant to the United States who had returned to his native land in the 1960s to build an oil, shipping, and chemical empire. Pappas had been a major financial backer of his *landsman* Spiro Agnew while Agnew was still governor of Maryland, and has been credited with a prime role in the selection of Agnew as Nixon's running mate. Friendly with both the Greek junta then in power and the CIA—"I have worked for the

CIA anytime my help was requested," he once boasted—Pappas became virtually the official host for U.S. dignitaries visiting Athens in the early 1970s. He spent much of 1972 shuttling between Greece and the United States, helping to raise money for Nixon; and he himself contributed more than $100,000 before the April 7 deadline. Sometime during the winter of 1973, Dean says, [Mitchell's aide Frederick] LaRue told him to ask Pappas for $250,000–$300,000—as a *quid pro quo* for some import quotas Pappas needed to construct two crude-oil conversion plants in the United States or Canada. Both Mitchell and LaRue spoke with Pappas. On March 21 Dean told the President, "Pappas has agreed to come up with a single amount, I gather from Mitchell." (Later in the spring Nixon said, "Good old Tom is raising money. . . ." But Pappas insists he made no such contribution and there is no evidence that he did.)

Well, now there is evidence that he did. And that evidence, viewed in context, allows one to offer a general theory of the Watergate case. A Greek journalist named Elias P. Demetracopoulos, who is described in Central Intelligence Agency documents as "a scooper," and who was an active foe of the dictatorship in Athens, has been on this case for many years and recently unearthed some unpublished material from the Watergate special prosecutor's office. These papers show that on February 2 and February 5, 1974, Pappas was interviewed, in the presence of his lawyer, John Doukas, by four members of the special prosecutor's team. One of these, Roger M. Witten, wrote a memorandum about the interviews, dated February 7, 1974. It states:

Pappas met John and Martha Mitchell in their New York apartment after the election. Mitchell was watching the T.V., was upset, and was taking notes. Mrs. Mitchell was also very upset. Pappas stated that Mitchell did not ask him for funds or ask him to raise funds after the election.

The interview was continued on February 5, with Ben-Veniste, Volner, Koeltl, Witten, Pappas and Doukas present. *Pappas stated that Mitchell asked him for a $50,000 loan in late 1972, which he gave to Mitchell.* Pappas further stated that he was asked about contributing to the defendants in a discussion where LaRue and others were present. [Emphasis added.]

"The defendants" are unmistakably identified in the remaining text as the Watergate burglary conspirators. The same set of documents from the special prosecutor's office shows:

1. That Pappas, an admitted "asset" of the CIA and cochairman of the finance committee of the Committee to Re-Elect the President, solicited campaign contributions from corporations and individuals, including foreign nationals, in clear violation of U.S. law forbidding such donations.

2. That one of the foreign contributors was rewarded with a lucrative government contract. In return for a $15,000 donation to CREEP, and an

additional contribution of between $10,000 and $12,500, a Greek business-man named Nicholas Vardinoyiannis was awarded the fueling contract for the Sixth Fleet in the Mediterranean. The special prosecutor's memorandum speaks of six possible violations of American law in this instance alone.

3. That, although he had broken the law, Pappas was not prosecuted. Among the grounds given by Witten for this leniency was Pappas's age. Yet, in 1972 alone, Pappas flew to and from Greece no less than twenty-four times, making himself look pretty hale.

In order to appreciate the extent of the "Greek connection," it is necessary to go back in time a little. The story begins on October 31, 1968, in the closing stages of the Presidential campaign that first brought Richard Nixon and Spiro Agnew to power. On that day, Democratic national chairman Lawrence O'Brien called on Nixon and Agnew to explain their relationship with Pappas. He pointed to Pappas's role as "a key Republican fund-raiser, go-between for Nixon and Agnew, and an unofficial representative of the Greek junta." O'Brien's statement, which was issued from the Watergate headquarters of the Democratic National Committee, ended with the words, "I think that both Mr. Nixon and Mr. Agnew should explain their relation-ships with him [Pappas], and let the American people know what's going on."

It has since been established that O'Brien was more right than he knew. In secret testimony before the House Intelligence Committee in 1976, Henry Tasca, Nixon's ambassador to Greece in the years of the fascist dictatorship, confirmed that in 1968 money from that dictatorship was funneled to the Nixon-Agnew election campaign. The source of the money was Michael Roufogalis. Roufogalis, now serving a life sentence in Athens for high treason and for his part in the murder of dissidents under the junta, was then the strongman of the Greek CIA. Known and feared under the acronym KYP, this agency was founded and heavily subsidized by Langley, Virginia. The conduit for the money was—Thomas A. Pappas.

In other words, the Nixon camp had a dirty and dangerous secret, guarded by a few intimates, that dated back to 1968. A CIA asset was recycling CIA money from a particularly repulsive foreign dictatorship that wanted to in-fluence an American Presidential election. It seems fair to speculate that O'Brien's call for more information alarmed the President's men.

We do not know the exact sum the Greek dictators gave to the Nixon campaign. We do know that they got their money's worth. On September 27, 1968, forty-eight hours before the Athens junta was to hold a phony plebiscite legitimizing its rule, Spiro Agnew held a press conference at which he reversed his declared "neutrality" on the issue and praised the dictators for moving toward democracy. During the subsequent Nixon-Agnew years, the junta moved even further from democracy and was flooded with aid and goodwill from Washington.

O'Brien's call for clarification of the Pappas connection might have been a shot in the dark, or it might not. It became urgent for the President's men to find out what O'Brien knew, and simultaneously to block any further avenue of inquiry. This is where Demetracopoulos enters the story. It was he who first gave evidence to O'Brien, and it was he who kept up the campaign to ventilate the issue. In July 1971, he was invited to testify about Pappas before Representative Ben Rosenthal's Foreign Affairs Subcommittee on Europe.

Recent successful Freedom of Information Act lawsuits by Demetracopoulos against the Federal Bureau of Investigation and the CIA (which culminated on April 16, 1986, with the CIA's admission that it possessed "no derogatory information" about him) elicited documents showing that he was under extremely heavy surveillance during this period. A letter signed by FBI Director William Webster to Representative Don Edwards admits that "rather extensive" surveillance of Demetracopoulos was conducted between November 9, 1967, and October 2, 1969; between August 25, 1971, and March 14, 1973; and between February 19, 1974, and October 24, 1974.

Demetracopoulos did not know he was being invigilated, but he did know that he was drawing unwelcome atttention because of his efforts to highlight the Pappas connection. On September 7, 1971, Nixon's henchman and confidant Murray Chotiner told him bluntly over lunch at the fashionable Jockey Club: "Lay off Pappas. You can be in trouble. You can be deported. It's not smart politics. You know Tom Pappas is a friend of the President." On October 27, 1971, lunching with Robert Novak at the Sans Souci restaurant, Demetracopoulos was threatened by Pappas himself, who came over from an adjacent table to tell him and Novak that he knew their employers and had sufficient pull to make life hard for those who wanted him investigated.

These were pinpricks compared with the barrage unleashed by Attorney General Mitchell. My witness here is Louise Gore, who has a fair claim to be considered an unimpeachable source. She was a key member of the Republican Establishment in Maryland, a state senator, and one of those most responsible for getting Spiro Agnew the governorship. (It was also she who introduced him to Nixon.) She was a close friend of John and Martha Mitchell, and, at the time of which I am writing, had returned to Washington while still Richard Nixon's representative to UNESCO. On January 24, 1972, she sent a handwritten letter to Demetracopoulos, of which I possess a copy.

Dear Elias—
I went to Perle's [Perle Mesta's] luncheon for Martha Mitchell yesterday and sat next to John. He is *furious* at you—and your testimony against Pappas. He kept threatening to have you deported!!
    At first I tried to ask him if he had any reason to think you could be deported

and he didn't have any answer—But then tried to counter by asking me what I knew about you and why we were friends.

It really got out of hand. It was all he'd talk about during lunch and everyone at the table was listening. . . .

At the table were George Bush, then Ambassador to the UN, Hubert Humphrey's sister Frances Humphrey Howard, J. Willard Marriott, and numerous other diplomats and luminaries. In front of these people the Attorney General of the United States conceived it as his responsibility to make threats against a dissident for questioning the probity of the President's bagman. Demetracopoulos, ignoring Chotiner's warning, submitted the requested memorandum to Representative Rosenthal's subcommittee on September 17, 1971. He closed his testimony with these words: "Finally, I have submitted separately to the subcommittee items of documentary evidence which I believe will be useful." Those words, which were printed in the record of the hearing, caused what Rowland Evans and Robert Novak described as "extreme nervousness in the Nixon White House."

Why did they have that effect? The Nixonites had every reason to fear disclosure of their corrupt practice of taking money from the Greek junta for the 1968 campaign. What was their reaction? To try to debauch the 1972 campaign as well. On June 17, 1972, five months after his vulgar public outburst against Demetracopoulos at Perle Mesta's, John Mitchell ordered the burglars into the Watergate building.

Now, the uniqueness of the Pappas connection lies in the fact that it occurs in 1968, in 1972, and in the subsequent cover-up. Indeed, White House sensitivity to the mention of Pappas's name seems to have intensified at the same tempo as the Watergate investigation. A transcript of the Nixon tapes for April 26, 1973, which was not disclosed until 1977 by *Washington Post* reporters Bob Woodward and Scott Armstrong, indicates the President was seriously worried. He feared that in his upcoming testimony to Congress, John Dean might recall Nixon's earlier admission that Pappas had raised "hush money" for the burglars. In six hours of foul-mouthed shop talk with his Chief of Staff, H. R. Haldeman, Nixon brought up Pappas seven times. At one point the Leader of the Free World fretted, "I think it's a matter of fact though that somebody said be sure to talk to Pappas because he's being very helpful on the, uh, Watergate thing."

Dean's memory was as good as Nixon had feared, or nearly so. On June 27, 1973, he appeared before the Senate Watergate Committee and said, under questioning from Senator Edward Gurney:

There was at one point in time, after Mr. Moore [Richard A. Moore, a White House assistant] had been to visit with Mr. Mitchell in New York, following the La Costa meeting, an effort to have Mr. LaRue go and raise money. This had been discussed earlier and Mr. LaRue had done some activities of this nature. Mr. [John] Ehrlichman [domestic-affairs adviser to Nixon] mentioned to me the fact that someone ought to go to Mr. Pappas, who was a long-time supporter of the President, and see if he would be of any assistance. Apparently, Mr. LaRue and Mr. Pappas had had some business dealings and as a result of those business dealings, Mr. LaRue was encouraged that something might be able to be done. But he told me that Mr. Pappas might want to have some favorable considerations from the government on some oil matters that resulted from this mutual venture they were in.

The "La Costa meeting" refers to a gathering at Haldeman's California villa in February 1973. At that meeting, Ehrlichman asked what Dean, with his usual gift for phrase, called the "bottom-line" question: "Would the seven defendants remain silent through the Senate hearings?" The question was by no means an idle one. As Lukas puts it, "They all agreed that the strategy depended on continued silence, but Dean reported that the defendants were making new demands for hush money."

Lukas also reports:

One of those LaRue spoke with about the unidentified "White House project" was Carl H. Lindner, board chairman of the American Financial Corporation and chairman of the *Cincinnati Enquirer*. Lindner was willing to contribute $50,000–$100,000 but wanted to know what he was giving for. LaRue consulted Mitchell, who said they obviously couldn't tell him what it was for. So that source too was abandoned.

Precisely. One merit of the Pappas hypothesis is that nobody had to explain to him what the money was for. Pappas already knew about the 1968 fascist slush fund; already knew that the connection was in danger of exposure; already knew what the burglars had been after. Thus, Mitchell went to him for the money.

John Dean, like Lawrence O'Brien, was smarter than he himself realized. There were indeed "oil matters" and "favorable considerations" at stake, involving Nicholas Vardinoyiannis, the Sixth Fleet payoff contract, and the funds for CREEP from unauthorized foreigners. But they constituted, to borrow Nixon-Kissinger argot, a sideshow to the real Greek connection— the funneling of junta money through Pappas. And the concentration of sideshow aspects of the matter allowed Pappas to appear before a Watergate grand jury and deny that he had ever given money for the cover-up. That was perjury, as the special prosecutor's documents show. February 1974, when federal prosecutors questioned Pappas, after all, was several months before Nixon's abject resignation. How did the Pappas connection go undetected?

There were three attempts by congressional committees to probe Pappas's activities. They did, as Seymour Hersh puts it in *The Price of Power,* "raise the question of whether the CIA . . . was aware that some of its funds were being returned to the United States for use in the presidential election." All three congressional inquiries were terminated. Here is what happened to each.

The first was launched by Representative Wright Patman, a grizzled and combative veteran from Texas, who chaired the House Banking Committee. Within five days of the Watergate break-in, his staff had traced the numbered hundred-dollar bills found on the burglars through Mexico and all the way back to Maurice Stans and CREEP. Patman prepared a subpoena list, causing Richard Nixon to start talking out of the side of his mouth again. "The game has to be played awfully rough," said the President at a meeting in the Oval Office with Haldeman and Dean on September 15, 1972. "Tell Ehrlichman to get [Banking Committee member Garry] Brown in and [Gerald] Ford in, and then they can all work out something. But they ought to get off their asses and push it. No use to let Patman have a free ride here."

Political pressure was indeed brought to bear on Patman, through House minority leader (and future Watergate beneficiary) Gerald Ford. But ordinary political muscle was not thought sufficient. The FBI was instructed to "leak" poisonous information about Elias Demetracopoulos to members of the committee. That information, since admitted by the bureau to have been false and defamatory, accused him of being a dangerous communist. It also suggested that he had arranged a Wall Street speaking engagement for Patman at a fee of $1,500. Shown "in confidence" to committee members, this concatenation of falsehoods had the desired effect. Six Democrats joined the Republicans in voting to deny Patman subpoena powers. John Dean recalled later that "another sigh of relief was made at the White House that we had leaped one more hurdle in the continuing cover-up." (On May 6, 1986, the FBI released documents to Demetracopoulos which show that "upon closer examination" the fee paid to Patman "proved perfectly appropriate." Too late. The same papers show twelve "general indices at [FBI] New York office regarding Wright Patman." After each of these appears the single word "destroyed.")

In ordering the collection of slanderous information about Demetracopoulos, the State Department had urged that "the Department of Justice do everything possible to see if we can make a Foreign Agent's case, or any kind of a case for that matter." At whose request was this catch-all pseudo-investigation launched? None other than Henry Tasca's, Nixon's loyal ambassador to the Greek junta and a close personal friend of Tom Pappas, who knew the dirty secret about the dirty money of 1968. In July 1971, a few days after Demetracopoulos had testified before Representative Ben Rosenthal's committee, Tasca sent a four-page secret cable from Athens urging that "a way will be found to step up investigation of Demetracopoulos." The cable was addressed in the ordinary way to William Rogers at State but also, and most unusually, to Attorney General John Mitchell.

The second investigation was sidetracked in a manner that was scarcely less ignominious. Under the chairmanship of Frank Church, the Senate began an inquiry into the abuse of the democratic process by its alleged guardians in the CIA. There was every reason to ask whether the agency had violated its own charter forbidding domestic political operations, since all of the Watergate burglars were connected with the CIA. But, as Seymour Hersh also says in his study of the matter:

> This question [the Greek connection] was not looked into by the Senate Intelligence Committee during its CIA inquiries in 1975 and 1976. Sources close to the committee have said that its investigation was abruptly canceled at Kissinger's direct request.

Thus, the intervention in American internal affairs by foreign despots, themselves closely tied to the CIA, was thought too sensitive by a Senate committee appointed to consider such abuses.

The third investigation was prompted by George McGovern. He suspected the Greek connection from the start and, on October 29, 1976, asked Daniel Inouye, then Chairman of the Senate Select Committee on Intelligence, to investigate it. By McGovern's account, Elias Demetracopoulos

> incurred the animosity of both the Greek and American governments. In Washington, he was threatened with deportation by Attorney General John Mitchell, denounced in an anonymous State Department memorandum, his Wall Street employers were visited by FBI agents, the congressional committee before which he testified was visited by a Justice Department agent, and slanderous raw material and disinformation from CIA operatives about Demetracopoulos was given to reporters and free lance writers like Russell Howe and Sarah Trott.

McGovern added in a follow-up letter to Inouye dated June 7, 1977:

> It is also pertinent to note that in the material I supplied to you last October twenty-ninth there were intimations from a number of high officials, including Secretary of State Kissinger and former CIA Director William Colby, that the Agency's relationship with the Greek junta was such that if it were brought to light, that Administration's relations with the restored democratic government in Greece could be damaged.

Those in Washington who had hoped for a serious probe were to be disappointed. Inouye ceased to be chairman of the intelligence committee at the end of 1977, and subsequent hearings during the tenure of Birch Bayh were prevented from calling CIA witnesses by Vice-Chairman and later Chairman Barry Goldwater. In the words of one of his subordinates (the only name in this story I keep confidential), "Goldwater deep-sixed the Pappas investigation."

In October 1963, an interview with Goldwater had been published in the *Athens Daily Post*. The interviewer was Elias Demetracopoulos. In the midst of a call for more private capital in Greece, Goldwater said:

> The recently signed agreement between Tom Pappas of Boston and the Greek government for the investment of U.S. private capital of $160 million in Greece is an important beginning in this direction. I know Tom Pappas very well. He is one of my closest friends.

This distinguished friendship, which a new and more cynical world has learned to call conflict of interest, did not restrain Senator Goldwater from crushing the Pappas inquiry or impel him to reiterate his long and deep comradeship with its subject. Not to waste words, the Inouye probe into the Pappas question was unceremoniously flushed down the memory hole, where it joined its two promising predecessors.

Why not, just for once, take Gordon Liddy's word for it? He said that the purpose of the break-in was "to find out what O'Brien had of a derogatory nature about *us*, not for us to get something on *him* or the Democrats."

I know there are other hypotheses about the motive for the break-in. The most plausible, advanced by Michael Drosnin in *Citizen Hughes*, is that Nixon wanted to know what the Democrats knew about Howard Hughes and his payoffs. But Hughes was also paying off the Democrats, and there is no evidence that they ever planned to make a campaign issue out of him.

To summarize the reasons why Nixon, Mitchell, and Kissinger went into orbit at the very mention of Pappas's name:

Pappas, exploiting CIA connections, was the bagman for an illegal and shameful transfusion of campaign money in 1968.

The congressional investigation of this deed was edging closer to the truth in early 1972.

That investigation was opposed at every step, by means legal and illegal, by Nixon and Mitchell. The American Ambassador to Greece, a friend of Pappas and a man who knew the guilty 1968 secret, took a hand in this wrecking operation.

All of the burglars had CIA connections, which may explain how they knew what to look for and why they kept silent.

Pappas provided the only money we know about to John Mitchell for the burglars' hush money.

All three subsequent House and Senate probes into the Pappas connection were sidetracked by men with either CIA loyalties or connections to Tom Pappas, or both.

It's been fourteen years. It would be nice to say that there have been seven fat and seven lean ones. But here we are in 1986, and it is Nixon who has waxed fat, Kissinger who has waxed fat, Goldwater who has waxed fat. Those who modestly raised the banner of a discreet McGovern liberalism have seen history rewritten and their own cherished ideals defamed as anti-American by the heirs of a ghastly crook. As I write, *Newsweek* has a gloating cover story on Nixon, with the brainless headline HE'S BACK. That pushover Governor Cuomo says of Tricky Dicky that he is "a man of great intellect, unique experience and extraordinary political wisdom." Fill in the rest for yourself. But before you do so, be sure that you can answer the following questions:

Why was Thomas Pappas not prosecuted for his violations of U.S. law?

Why was John Mitchell never asked about his soliciting of $50,000 from a man who was known to work both for the CIA and for a foreign dictatorship, and who at the time was in breach of laws that Mitchell had taken his oath to uphold?

Why was the Senate Watergate Committee never informed of the Pappas-Mitchell transaction uncovered by the special prosecutor?

Did Henry Kissinger, who chaired the 40 Committee which oversaw covert action and whose members included John Mitchell (the first attorney general to serve as a 40 Committee member), know of this evidence when he killed the Church Committee's probe?

Did Barry Goldwater, a "close" friend of Pappas, know of this evidence when he dropped Senator Inouye's later inquiry?

If those questions could be answered candidly, then bygones could be bygones. But there isn't even a conspiracy of silence about such questions. Rather, we have a conspiracy of nervous and sickly applause. The fact remains that a popular Republican Administration succeeded in subverting the Constitution and the Bill of Rights, that it got away with it without ever taking the witness stand, and that the corrupt alliance with a foreign dictatorship was a crucial ingredient. Maybe that reminds you of something and maybe it doesn't, but there is still no legal obstacle to ex-convict John Mitchell stepping into the witness box and telling, at last, why he drummed up that fifty grand.

(*The Nation*, May 31, 1986)

WANTON ACTS OF USAGE

❑

Terrell E. Arnold is a consultant to the State Department on terrorism and Executive Director of the Institute on Terrorism and Subnational Conflict. In 1983 and 1984, he was Principal Deputy Director of the State Department's Office for Counter Terrorism and Emergency Planning. He is the co-editor, with Neil C. Livingstone, of *Fighting Back: Winning the War Against Terrorism*. He's also a very nice guy. On April 28, 1986, I spent an hour debating with him on C-SPAN, the cable TV network, before an audience of high-school students. I asked him plainly, perhaps half a dozen times, whether he could do the elementary service of defining his terms. Could he offer a definition of "terrorism" that was not:

Tautological or vacuous ("the use of violence for political ends," as Constantine Menges, late of the National Security Council, once put it) in a way that would cover any state, party, movement, or system not explicitly committed to pacifism;

A cliché ("an attack on innocent men, women, and children") of the kind that all warring states and parties have always used to attack all other warring states and parties; or

A synonym for "swarthy opponent of United States foreign policy."

My reason for asking so insistently was that the Reagan Administration has yet to define terrorism; the numerous institutes and think tanks which are paid to study it have yet to define terrorism; and the mass media which headline it have yet to define terrorism. I wasn't just looking for a debating point. I really—since this is an issue that might take us to war—wanted to know. Finally, Terrell E. Arnold, who is as I say a nice guy, decided to answer my question. He said: "Can I provide a universally acceptable definition of terrorism? I fear I have to say I cannot."

That was honest. So, in a clumsier way, was CIA Director William J. Casey, in the opening essay of *Hydra of Carnage: International Linkages of Terrorism—The Witnesses Speak*, edited by Uri Ra'anan, Robert L. Pfaltzgraff, Jr., Richard H. Shultz, Ernst Halperin, and Igor Lukes. Kicking off this volume, which seems to represent the distilled counterterrorist scholarship of the Fletcher School of Law and Diplomacy at Tufts University, Casey begins, promisingly: "In confronting the challenge of international terrorism, the first step is to call things by their proper names, to see clearly and say plainly who the terrorists are, what goals they seek, and which governments support them."

Yes, yes. Who, what, and which? Let's have it. Next sentence: "What the terrorist does is kill, maim, kidnap, and torture."

In other words, and if we are to believe the Director of the CIA, the terrorist is nothing new, and nothing different. Can that be right?

One turns to Robert C. McFarlane, former National Security Adviser to the President and, like so many who farm "terrorism" as a new academic discipline, a "counselor" at the Center for Strategic and International Studies at Georgetown University. In his foreword to the book edited by Livingstone and Arnold, McFarlane defines "acts of terrorism" as "calculated political crimes against people." Perhaps feeling that he should improve on a banality that would comprehend everything from Nazi storm troopers to the Teamsters union, and from the Khmer Rouge to the Contras, McFarlane went a touch further in *The Washington Post Book World* of May 18, 1986, and adopted the definition put forward in the book he was reviewing. The book was *Terrorism: How the West Can Win,* and was put together by Israel's UN Ambassador, Benjamin Netanyahu. Terrorism as here defined and seized upon by an impoverished McFarlane is "the deliberate and systematic murder, maiming, and menacing of the innocent to inspire fear for political ends." Did Casey, one wonders, raise a lofty eyebrow when he saw that kidnap and torture had been wholly left out of this account?

We don't do much better with *Terrorism as State-Sponsored Covert Warfare,* by Ray S. Cline and Yonah Alexander. Alexander turns out to be Director of the Institute for Studies in International Terrorism at the State University of New York at Oneonta and editor of *Terrorism: An International Journal.* Both he and Cline are attached to the Center for Strategic and International Studies at Georgetown. Early in the book, the two men state rather disarmingly: "There is no universal agreement about who is a terrorist because the political and strategic goals affect different states differently. There is no value-free definition."

The first sentence is no more than one could have said oneself. The second sentence imperils the whole rationale of the book and is thus discarded for the remaining hundred pages, wherein "terrorism" is quite easily used as if everybody agreed upon what it meant. For a sample of the depth of thinking and scholarship involved, I cite the Cline-Alexander analysis of the twentieth century:

> Domestic terrorism has risen to a high level of brutality at many times. Stalin's collectivization of agriculture and purges of party and armed forces of the 1920s and 1930s are prime examples. They are rivaled only, perhaps, by Mao Tse-tung's murderous Great Cultural Revolution of the 1960s and 1970s.

(A purist might say that this fails to mention another rather conspicuous example of domestic terror in this century.)

This book has jacket endorsements from, among others, Senator Richard Lugar of the Foreign Relations Committee, who says of Cline that "he has clearly defined the nature of terrorist acts, the role of states in utilizing terrorism, and the options which governments, such as ours, have to respond."

Finally, or at any rate lastly, to the Rand Corporation, which has made rather a good thing out of "terrorism" consultancy and which has produced a masterwork, *Trends in International Terrorism, 1982 and 1983*. The introduction to this pamphlet inquires, as well it might:

> What do we mean by terrorism? The term, unfortunately, has no precise or widely accepted definition. The problem of definition is compounded by the fact that *terrorism* has become a fad word that is applied to all sorts of violence.

Six scholars labored to produce this report for Rand, and they were obviously not about to let this piece of throat-clearing get in the way of their grants, trips, and fellowships. For the rest of the study, the word *terrorism* is used without qualification to mean whatever they want it to mean:

> In Rand's continuing research on this subject, *terrorism* is defined by the nature of the act, not by the identity of the perpetrators or the nature of the cause. Terrorism is violence, or the threat of violence, calculated to create an atmosphere of fear and alarm. All terrorist acts are crimes.

A connoisseur might savor the last grace note, given that the Rand study also states, "In Nicaragua, international terrorist violence during 1982–83 consisted only of four hijackings involving Nicaraguans seizing planes in which to flee the country." Aside from the obvious omissions, what is "international" about a Nicaraguan using force to leave Nicaragua?

My initial question is a simple one. How can a word with no meaning and no definition, borrowed inexpertly from the second-rate imitators of Burke and his polemic against the French Revolution of 1789—when *Terror* meant "big government"—have become the political and media buzzword of the eighties? How can it have become a course credit at colleges, an engine of pelf in the think tanks, and a subject in its own right in the press, on television, and at the movies?

Some people have noticed the obvious fact that the word carries a conservative freight. It is almost always used to describe revolutionary or subversive action, though there is no reason in any of the above "definitions" why this should be. And I think one could also add that it's taken on a faint but unmistakable racist undertone (or overtone), in much the same way as the word *mugger* once did. There's always the suspicion, to put it no higher, that the politician or journalist who goes on and on about "terrorism" has not got the South African police in mind, any more than the "law and order" bigmouth means business about the Mafia.

In a defensive reaction to this hypocritical and ideological emphasis, many liberals have taken simply to inverting the word, or to changing the subject. Typically, a sympathizer of the Palestinians will say that it is Ariel Sharon who is "the real terrorist"; a Republican Irishman, that it is the British occupier who fills the bill; and so on. Still others will point suavely to the "root cause" of unassuaged grievance. This is all right as far as it goes, which is not very far. You don't draw the sting from a brainless propaganda word merely by turning it around. The word *terrorist* is not—like *communist* and *fascist*—being abused; it is itself an abuse. It disguises reality and impoverishes language and makes a banality out of the discussion of war and revolution and politics. It's the perfect instrument for the cheapening of public opinion and for the intimidation of dissent.

In the *Oxford English Dictionary* there is only one useful citation of the term, once you get past the tautologies ("any one who attempts to further his views by a system of coercive intimidation"). This usage comes to us from that great and worldly nineteenth-century divine, the Reverend Sydney Smith. Smith, who once boasted that his sermons were "long and vigorous, like the penis of a jackass," defined a terrorist as "one who entertains, professes, or tries to awaken or spread a feeling of terror or alarm; an alarmist, a scaremonger."

This usage may seem perverse, but it's much more enlightening than any of the hysterical commonplaces that pass for definitions today. Consider the case of Syria. Here is a large country with a long history. It contains competing elites from at least three major strands of Islam, plus many Christians of varying stripes. Geopolitics has removed Lebanon and the Golan Heights from its territory in the last half-century. It has been through countless wars and coups and repressions. Not long ago, Ted Koppel devoted a rare half-hour to this country. What was the question asked and debated? How did the experts and Administration spokesmen approach the land of Aleppo and Damascus? Why, by asking "Is Syria *terrorist*?" This is the sort of question which insults the audience as much as the presumed victim or target. Yet it's the level of question to which this ridiculous word has reduced us.

What an astounding state of affairs. A great power and a purportedly educated and democratic intelligentsia have allowed themselves to be "terrorized," as the Reverend Smith would have put it, into viewing the world this way. Stalin was terrorist, Mao was terrorist, Arabs are terrorist; Europeans are soft on terrorism; Latins are riddled with it. Whisk, whisk . . . and there goes history, there goes inquiry, there goes proportion. All is terror.* The best that can be said for this method is that it economizes on thought. You simply unveil it like a Medusa's head and turn all discussion into stone.

This is a bit of a disgrace to language as well as to politics. English contains rather a number of words, each of them individually expressive, with which to describe violence and to suggest the speaker's attitude toward it. Any literate person could duplicate, expand, or contest the following set of examples:

1. One who fights a foreign occupation of his country without putting on a uniform: guerrilla or *guerrillero;* partisan; (occasionally) freedom fighter.
2. One who extorts favors and taxes on his own behalf while affecting to be a guerrilla: bandit; brigand; pirate.
3. One who wages war on a democratic government, hoping to make it less democratic: nihilist; (some versions of) fascist, anarchist, Stalinist.
4. One who gives his pregnant fiancée a suitcase containing a bomb as she boards a crowded airliner: psychopath; murderer.
5. One who cuts the throat of an unarmed civilian prisoner while he lies in a shallow grave and buries him still living after inviting an American photographer to record the scene: Contra.
6. One who makes a living by inspiring fear and temporary obedience in the weak and vulnerable: goon; thug; kidnapper; blackmailer; hijacker; hoodlum.
7. One who directs weapons of conventional warfare principally at civilian objectives: war criminal.
8. One who believes himself licensed to kill by virtue of membership in a religious or mystical fraternity: fanatic; (traditionally) assassin.

Only the fifth of these examples is mischievously propagandistic, and I include it both as a true incident and as a joke about the prevailing self-righteousness. Meanwhile, we have not even begun to parse the words *tyrant, despot, dictator, absolutist,* and *megalomaniac. Terrorist,* however, is a convenience word, a junk word, designed to obliterate distinctions. It must be this that recommends it so much to governments with something to hide, to the practitioners of instant journalism, and to shady "consultants."

I can give two examples of what I mean by "convenience word." When I was in Rhodesia years ago, the colonial government practiced a fairly light,

* A breathtaking example is provided here by Benjamin Netanyahu. In his essay "Defining Terrorism" in *Terrorism: How the West Can Win,* he compresses the Algerian revolution into the descriptive sentence: "Algeria [is] merely another of the many despotisms where terrorists have come to power."

inept, and porous form of censorship. It was not exactly illegal to advocate majority rule or to criticize repressive policy. News from the outside world was allowed in, despite numerous farcical exceptions and restrictions. But one thing was strictly forbidden. The names of Robert Mugabe and Joshua Nkomo, rival leaders of the black population who were then in an uneasy coalition, could not legally be published or broadcast. This meant that, when a bomb went off in an oil depot, say, it would be denounced in the press as the work of "an externally based terrorist leader." This simplified matters to some extent. The slang word *terr*, for example, did not have the ambiguity I just mentioned in connection with *mugger*. It *always* meant "troublesome black person." And there were no wearisome inquests about the propriety of journalists doing interviews with Mugabe or Nkomo and not turning them in to the police, because it was strictly illegal to publish such interviews. It also meant that everything that went wrong (plenty) could be blamed on "an externally based terrorist leader."

The policy turned out to be a sick joke on its defenders. The second most important fact about Rhodesia, after its status as a white-ruled colony, was the tribal and political division between Mugabe and Nkomo, Shona and Ndebele, ZANU and ZAPU, ZIPRA and ZANLA. So you heard settlers, white of skin and right of wing, asking one another anxiously which "externally based terrorist leader" the government meant that day. They needed and wanted to know, but were prevented by their own illusions from finding out. It wasn't unheard-of for quite well connected whites to get in touch with journalists—the same journalists they denounced in their clubs and their cups as morale-sapping liberals—and ask what Mugabe (or Nkomo) had really said the previous weekend. There were many sighs of relief when Rhodesia belatedly became Zimbabwe, and many must have rejoiced to be rid of the strain of calling all Africans "terrorists" or "terrorist sympathizers."

Another story: In March of 1976, I sat in Baghdad opposite Abu Nidal while he railed against imperialism, Zionism, and so forth. I sat up only when he issued a threat against somebody I knew. Said Hammami, who headed the PLO office in London at the time, had been writing articles for *The Times* calling for a territorial compromise over Palestine. Abu Nidal told me that if I saw Hammami I should warn him that he had attracted displeasure. I thus had the unusual experience, a short while later, of delivering (or at any rate passing on) a death threat. Hammami had heard this kind of talk before, of course. I don't think our conversation seemed as memorable to him at the time as it still is to me; but he was murdered in his Mayfair office not long afterward.

Most people recognized then that we had lost a very brave and thoughtful man, but by the standards that prevail today, nothing much had happened. One "terrorist" had perhaps killed or commissioned the killing of another "terrorist." The PLO is regarded as a terrorist organization by the United

States government, and that has the effect of making distinction and discrimination impossible. Is it possible that this is the intention of the term?

Stupidity here makes an easy bedfellow, as always, with racialism and with the offensive habit of referring to "the Arabs." All Arab states and all Arab parties and communities recognize the PLO as the representative of the Palestinians. Define the PLO as "terrorist" and what have you done? You've flattened the picture of the Middle East, for one thing. All Arabs are, *ex hypothesi*, terrorists or terrorist sympathizers. And what can't you do with terrorism? *Compromise* with it, that's what you can't do. *Anybody* knows that, for gosh sakes. So—no need to compromise with the Arabs, who have to keep apologizing for living in the Middle East too. This idiot syllogism is a joke only if you haven't seen the *Congressional Record* for May and June, 1986, and read the contributions of our legislators to the Saudi arms "debate." Like bootleggers smashed on their own hooch, the "antiterrorism" types were convoluted by their own propaganda.

You can see the same process at work if you turn the pages of the report issued by the Long Commission, set up by the Defense Department to find out "what went wrong" with the Marine expedition to Beirut. This document is a pitiful thing from whichever political or literary standpoint it is approached. It reeks of self-pity and self-deception. We learn that "it was anticipated that the [Marines] would be perceived by the various factions as evenhanded and neutral." Anticipated by whom? And which factions?

Later, according to the commission, the "environment could no longer be characterized as peaceful. The image of the [Marines], in the eyes of the factional militias, had become pro-Israel, pro-Phalange, and anti-Muslim." When would the "environment" of Beirut have been "characterized as peaceful"? Again, which factional militias? The same ones whose welcome was earlier "anticipated"? And were the militias right or wrong about the tendency of American allegiance, or was it, as the report says, an "image" problem? There would be no glue with which to hold this tenth-rate explanation together if the report did not use the words *terrorism* and *terrorist* 178 times. So that's all right then. We know our enemy.

The terrorist is always, and by definition, the Other. Call your enemy communist or fascist and, whatever your intentions, you will one day meet someone who proudly claims to be a communist or fascist. Define your foe as authoritarian or totalitarian and, however ill-crafted your analysis, you are bound to find a target that amplifies the definition. But "terrorist" is hardly more useful than a term of abuse, and probably less so.

One way of putting this simple point is to take the "antiterrorist" argument at its strongest. Random violence is one thing, say the well-funded experts, but it gets really serious when it's "state-sponsored" terrorism. The two words that are supposed to intensify the effect of the third actually have the effect, if we pause for thought, of diminishing it. It is terrifying to be held at gunpoint by a person who has *no demands*. A moment of *terror* is the moment when the irrational intrudes—when the man with the gun is hearing voices or wants his girlfriend back or has a theory about the Middle Pyramid. But if the gunman is a proxy for Syria or Iran or Bangladesh or Chile (the fourth being the only government mentioned here that has ever detonated a lethal bomb on American soil), then it isn't, strictly speaking, the irrational that we face. It may be an apparently unappeasable grievance, but it is, finally, political. And propaganda terms, whether vulgar or ingenious, have always aimed at making political problems seem one-sided.

Why should they not? That is the propagandist's job. What is frightening and depressing is that a pseudoscientific propaganda word like *terrorism* has come to have such a hypnotic effect on public debate in the United States. A word which originated with the most benighted opponents of the French Revolution; a word featured constantly in the antipartisan communiqués of the Third Reich; a word which is a commonplace in the handouts of the Red Army in Afghanistan and the South African army in Namibia; a word which was in everyday use during the decline of the British, French, Portuguese, and Belgian empires. Should we not be wary of a term with which rulers fool themselves and by which history is abolished and language debased? Don't we fool and console ourselves enough as it is?

(*Harper's*, September 1986)

HURRICANE ROBERTSON

❑

It was, on the face of it, rather difficult to find anything objectionable in Pat Robertson's rally at Constitution Hall. The entire evening, like most of Robertson's current flirtation with the electorate, was more an occasion for pitying mirth than for apprehension. One had only to look at the peerlessly fatuous face of an Oral Roberts, for example, to realize that the human race must be the product of evolution. None but the most heartlessly irresponsible deity would have "created" him like that, or filled his mouth with the strangulated nonsense to which he treated the crowd. It was also amusing, in a slightly awful way, to hear speaker after speaker—I particularly liked the unintentional sauciness of the star of *Annie*—as they depicted America as a drug-sodden, demoralized wilderness, filled with people "hurting and hungry like never before." All this after six years of the fabled Reagan revolution?

True, there was something vaguely sinister about the sexlessness of the

Victory Singers as they beamed through their patriotic medley and shamelessly appropriated "This Land Is Your Land." And I can't say I much care for the upflung hand salute with which enthusiasts make the Praise the Lord sign. The fixity of the grins can get you down, as can the Dale Carnegie rhetoric. But, in general, the suffocating corniness has the effect of deflating any drama.

However, there *is* something frightening about stupidity—more especially, about stupidity in its mass, organized form. I spent much of the time facing the audience, and it was disturbing to see the rows and rows of faces lit only by gullibility. One wonders how much they know of "Pat's" theology, as opposed to his trite invocations of family values.

The man who drew the job of introducing Robertson to the throng was Harald Bredesen. Probably very few of those who watched this character recognized him as Ronald Reagan's adviser on Armageddon. Bredesen is a more versatile chap than his appearance suggests. He is a self-defined "evangelical-charismatic," with alleged Pentecostal powers to speak in tongues. In 1970, accompanied by his co-thinker George Otis, he visited Reagan in Sacramento for a soul session. While Otis prophesied his accession to the presidency, the ghastly old thespian's arms "shook and pulsated" with the Holy Spirit. Wish I'd been there.

But there I go again, looking on the funny side. How amusing is it, really, that a well-funded and organized campaign is getting under way, led by a man who believes that we are approaching the End of Days? Robertson may try to squirm away from the question at press conferences, but he has gone repeatedly and unambiguously on the record about this. He maintains that the prophetic eschatology of the Book of Ezekiel is being fulfilled in today's Middle East and that we are squaring off for the final battle. Some people have said defensively that Robertson, unlike Jerry Falwell and Bailey Smith, is not given to attacking the Jews as infidels. True. All Robertson says is that all Jews who do not convert in time will be destroyed by the coming of the Lord. In the meantime, their sole purpose is to vindicate biblical injunctions by expanding from the Nile to the Euphrates and beckoning on a global holocaust. (If you think I exaggerate even slightly, look up Grace Halsell's book *Prophecy and Politics*.)

In a book with the limpidly brilliant title of *Answers to 200 of Life's Most Probing Questions*, Robertson writes: "Those who refuse to accept Christ will grow worse and worse in their wickedness. It will become increasingly difficult for the church and the world to coexist." Coupled with mounting sinfulness, he argues, is an expansion of "computers to monitor the behavior of populations and to control all of the world's money. These developments are fulfilling biblical prophecies. This tells me that we are getting very close to the time when God is going to say that the human race has gone far enough. He may be ready to step in to terminate this phase of human activity." There is more along those lines, culminating in the fantastic notion that microchips and electronic banking could make it easier to "fulfill what Revelation says: that people could not buy or sell without the mark of the Beast." "Pat" argues, with complete seriousness, that the numbers 666 will soon be stamped on the hand and forehead of every person on earth, but he urges people to cheer up because the reign of the Antichrist is the antechamber to the reign of people like himself.

Admittedly, the only concrete result of this flat-out, barking, foaming lunacy so far is a decline in the electoral prospects of Jack Kemp. So there may be a solid case for complacency. But it might also be wise to pay more attention to the workings of the irrational in our political life. As the year 2000 approaches, it is a safe bet that we will be treated to more superstition and barbarism of the Robertson sort, and that other unscrupulous demagogues will try to canalize the fears and doubts of those who have been let down by the education system. A few years ago, secular Israelis scoffed at the crackpots and cretins who called for a religious state and a holy war. Now they don't scoff. Robertson and his kind are the direct allies—political and financial—of those crackpots and cretins. They bear watching.

Another thing that bears watching is the gradual infiltration of Robertson's ideas into the Reagan Administration. The Secretary of Education, William Bennett, is an honored guest on *The 700 Club* and has appointed the most primitive fundamentalists to positions of influence in his department. William Rehnquist's view of the role of the Supreme Court might have been scripted by Robertson on an off day. Edwin Meese's view of public morality is borrowed from the salacious antipornographer Tim LaHaye, whose wife, Beverley, spoke at Constitution Hall for Roberston's candidacy. Of course, it would be appalling if a man like Robertson got his pudgy finger on the button. But what if the button is already being fingered by a man who thinks Robertson is full of the right stuff?

(The Nation, October 4, 1986)

WITH A LITTLE LUCK

❑

Ronald Reagan's meeting with his opposite number in Reykjavik this week had better be good. There are signs and portents, to put it no higher, of a diminution of his magical persuasive powers. Last Thursday, in particular, was a very bad day. Opinion polls showed that a vast majority of the American voters did not believe his denials of a "swap" in the affair of Nicholas Daniloff. It was hard to imagine, really, why the denial was made in the first place. If you don't want people to believe you are swapping, then don't release your spy on the day you get your journalist back. People who would happily have forgiven Daniloff, if they thought he was performing a bit of patriotic duty on the side, won't stand for being treated like kids when it comes to explanations.

Later in the day, a number of senior Republicans joined with the Democratic minority in the Senate to give Reagan his first serious, public, foreign-policy defeat. Again, people can be induced to believe that the President worries about Russian penetration of Africa. What they won't swallow is the pretense that his opposition to sanctions derives from his compassion for Mr. Botha's black subjects. It was only a few days since William F. Buckley had startled his readers by writing a column in which he said that if he were both black and South African he would be a member of the ANC.

Finally, there was the revelation in that day's *Washington Post* that most of the anti-Qaddafi material put out by American press and television since August was put in by a White House disinformation unit. Planted items included rumors of a new terror offensive and hints of another American military strike, as well as numerous fanciful items about coups, plots, and instability. This last effort seems to me the most egregious of the three. The Administration already had most of the press and public behind it, ready to believe anything about the dreaded Muammar. Why this heavy layer of gilt on the lily? I retired on Thursday evening wondering for the first time if the President's sureness of touch had begun to desert him. To have been caught out by the opinion polls, the Senate and the press corps all in one week seemed suspiciously like carelessness.

So, as I say, the "mini-summit" had better be good. But again, there are weird signs of hubris. The Republicans may well believe that a high-level meeting will win them votes in the November midterm elections. There is even an old political term for this kind of tactic, which goes by the name of "an October surprise." But is it wise to say, so openly, that this is the purpose of the exercise? Thomas Griscom, who presides over the largest political budget in history in his capacity as Director of the Republican Senatorial Campaign Committee, told the masses that "in off-year elections people look for reasons to vote against the President's party. The economy is in good shape and we've just defused the war and peace issue." That last sentence seems to me to contain a whole embassy full of hostages to fortune. The stock market is in a tailspin, the dollar is as soggy as fettuccine, the much-ballyhooed new tax bill has been found to make less than fifty dollars' difference to the average middle-income family, and the deficit continues to swell, while the "war and peace issue" is by its very nature more difficult to "defuse" than Mr. Griscom might like to think.

If Reagan wants to return from the frozen north with something that will keep his team in control of the Senate, he will need more than the snapshots and anecdotes that he brought back from Geneva. Conversely (or you might say similarly), if he brings back more than snapshots and anecdotes he will be in trouble with his own true believers. These people are already quite upset by the Daniloff deal and unmollified by those who point out that the terms of it were quite favorable. Their objection is not to the terms but to the deal itself, and their attitude to arms control and summitry is fairly analogous. If the Russians agree to something, there must, *ex hypothesi*, be something wrong with it. Daniloff's first television interview, in which he said that he thought the Soviet Union wanted to withdraw from Afghanistan, must have come as something of a facer to this faction. (As it did to the interviewer, who went on to ask if the Russians had put any drugs in Daniloff's bland but nourishing prison fare.)

"I am not," said Reagan, "in the giveaway business." He was speaking, inappositely enough, at the dedication of the Jimmy Carter Presidential Center in Atlanta, Georgia. Standing next to his old enemy for the first time since October 1981, when he sent him off to make a fool of himself as America's envoy to the funeral of Sadat, Reagan spoke of Carter's "passion and intellect and commitment." It is just this kind of soppy talk that mobilizes the hawks in the Pentagon and the think tank, and makes them rush to grab the Presidential elbow. Later in the same day, the elbow was back in Washington and a statement denying "cave-ins" to the Russians was made by its owner. As a matter of fact, it was Jimmy Carter who began the deployment of missiles in Europe, pushed ahead with the neutron bomb, and issued Presidential Directive 59 ordering a state of preparedness to fight and win a protracted nuclear war. He also cut off grain sales to the Soviet Union and boycotted their turn as host to the Olympic games. But no matter. Carter is tagged, seemingly forever, as a wimp and a pushover. His image haunts his successor. To act tough and yet look soft is quite a trick—the very worst of both worlds. To be tough enough to act soft without looking it is an achievement usually vouchsafed only to conservative statesmen with a hardened image to belie. Reagan has set himself the task of attending a minisummit which must lead to a macro-summit and avoid a test-ban treaty, and help his senatorial election candidates, and not remind people of Carter. According to Gordon Weihmiller, author of a study of the history of American-Soviet summits since 1955, this puts him at least initially in Gorbachev's hands. Reagan has grinned and wriggled out of tighter spots than that, of course. But that was when his luck seemed inexhaustible, and that, in turn, seems a little while ago.

(*The Spectator*, October 11, 1986)

"A BODYGUARD OF LIES"

❑

The straightest man in the Reagan Administration is undoubtedly George Shultz. He is no brighter than he looks, but, compared to some of the wide boys and wild men on hand in Washington, he is a model of sobriety and rectitude. It was he who single-handedly destroyed the President's plan for mandatory lie-detector tests by saying publicly and angrily that he would never agree to submit to one. If he wasn't trusted, he said, he had a perfectly good boardroom to go back to. The proposal to plug all bureaucrats into the polygraph was substantially amended.

Someday I want to write about the American faith in the polygraph and about the whole idea of a machine that tells or can tell the truth. For the moment, it's enough to note that, if there were such a machine, the President would have to avoid it like the plague. He lies with such ease and artistry that it has almost become part of his notorious charm. When Eugene Hasenfus was shot down over Nicaragua for all practical purposes wearing a U.S. Army uniform, Reagan denied categorically that he had any connection with the United States government. Shultz, invited to answer the same question, could not bring himself to lie so boldly. In a more scrupulously worded response, he simply said that he had asked the Defense and State departments, and they said they knew nothing.

The difference in style was also illustrated the previous week, when *The Washington Post* revealed that much of the "evidence" about Libyan terrorism which it had been printing was the result of a government-sponsored disinformation effort. A copy of the secret memo composed by the mysterious Admiral Poindexter, Reagan's National Security Adviser, showed an extensive planting job, designed to convince the American news media that Colonel Qaddafi was sponsoring a new wave of terrorism. *The Wall Street Journal*, *The Washington Post*, and ABC and CBS news have all apologized to their readers and viewers for passing on untreated government waste as if it were the result of an on-the-level, off-the-record briefing.

Confronted with this, Reagan denied that there had been any attempt to deceive or disinform. Shultz, less barefaced, implicitly confirmed the whole story by recalling Churchill's declaration that in wartime truth was so precious that it had to be secured by "a bodyguard of lies." To which one questioner asked why, in that case, there was no declaration of war on Qaddafi. "There damn near is," replied the hopelessly honest Shultz, as yet another yowling pussycat squirmed out of the bag. At least he'd got the bodyguard bit right.

State Department and CIA spokesmen are never happier than when pointing out the unfairness of it all. Here are the Russians, they say, with their closed society and their KGB "active measures," while *we* have to fight this implacable foe with Congress and the press breathing down our necks. There are, arguably, two dimensions missing from this reasoning. The first is psychological. Can it be healthy to regard an open society as in some sense a *disadvantage* in the ideological combat? The second is more practical. When, in fact, have Congress and the press failed to take the Administration's word for it? In the most obvious instance, which is that of Vietnam, it took almost fifteen years for skepticism to become general. And the Reagan Administration has, with the glaring exception of South Africa, had an almost uninterrupted run of indulgence from the other two Estates. In fact, seeing how eagerly the American press ingested every other and earlier horror story about Libya, there seems to have been no occasion to mount a special Poindextrous disinformation job on it.

There have, in recent history, been four successful CIA manipulations of the American press. At least, there have been four that we know about. Morton Halperin, who was a senior aide to Henry Kissinger until he found that his boss was tapping his home telephone, told Congress in 1978 of the four episodes known to him.

The first was an attempt to discredit domestic and foreign critics of the Warren Commission. That commission, set up to investigate the assassination of President Kennedy, relied heavily on the CIA for its generally reassuring and often contradictory conclusions. The agency gave a number of scurrilous background briefings, defaming those who had cast doubt on the findings. In testimony before the House of Representatives, Halperin said:

> One of the things they succeeded in getting which I do not mention in my statement was an article in *The Spectator,* a distinguished British publication, which apparently, according to the documents, was written in Langley, Virginia at the CIA headquarters, placed in the magazine by assets of the CIA in Britain. Now that is obviously a magazine widely read by Americans and one which could not have helped but to influence the debate within the United States on the Warren Commission report, as well as abroad.

Makes you proud. Halperin took pains to stress the circulation of *The Spectator* in America because the CIA's charter forbids it to carry out domestic operations.

The other occasions involved a briefing to *Time* magazine containing alarmist and derogatory material about the newly elected Salvador Allende of Chile, the exploitation of the murder of a CIA agent in Greece in order to derail a Senate investigation, and the circulation of black propaganda about a Greek dissident named Elias Demetracopoulos.

Since 1980, the climate has changed appreciably. The image of the CIA under Carter has become an analogue of the conservative image of America itself—a giant compelled to fight with one hand tied behind its back. Under William Casey's stewardship, the leash has been slipped and the old firm is doing business at the old stand. You can tell this from minor touches, such as the fact that Eugene Hasenfus was carrying a calling card from a little-known outfit named the Office of Humanitarian Assistance, while his airplane was loaded with lethal weaponry.

The point about this Administration's "bodyguard of lies" is that most of them are unnecessary. Nobody doubts or denies that the United States is directly involved in arming the Contras. For the President to pretend shock at the very idea is laughable and reduces his already slim chances of being believed when he chooses to tell the truth. The same goes for the effort to destabilize Qaddafi—an enterprise which, if openly admitted, could actually have recruited considerable popular support. For Shultz's Churchillian comparison to be dignified, one would have to have a people who were sure about their cause and its justice, and prepared to believe that their government was acting in principle for the best. No such assurance is available in the case of the dubious battles in Libya and Nicaragua, and so the lying there is nothing more than the inadvertent revelation of an uneasy conscience. If Shultz and Reagan are like any recent politicians in British history, they resemble Anthony Eden and Selwyn Lloyd in 1956 much more nearly than Winston Churchill and Clement Attlee in 1940.

(The Spectator, October 25, 1986)

REAGAN'S DECEMBER

❑

In *The Dean's December,* Saul Bellow's Albert Corde reviews the evidence of a colleague about lead poisoning in the United States:

> We had been "authoritatively assured" that lead levels were normal and tolerable. Far from it. Official standards are worse than incorrect, they are dangerously false. . . . Government agencies assigned the task of measurement and control were incompetent. The true magnitude of this deadly poisoning of water, vegetation and air was discovered by the pure sciences of geochronology, cosmology and nuclear geochemistry. A truly accurate method of detecting tiny amounts of lead led to the discovery that the cycle of lead in the earth had

been strongly perturbed. The conclusion: chronic lead insult now affects all mankind.

This is one of those things, thinks the dean at first, like the alleged depletion of the ozone layer by aerosols. But he is gradually won over by the weight of evidence. It now turns out, of course, that the doomsayers were right about the ozone layer. And last week Ronald Reagan's own Environmental Protection Agency announced that one in five Americans is ingesting more lead through the drinking water than any safety standard would permit. The report, which incidentally admitted that the safety standard was too lenient anyway, said that excess lead was responsible for the measurable decline in intelligence in 143,500 children every year, for pregnancy complications among 622,000 women, and for 118,400 cases of hypertension. I turned back to Bellow: ". . . millions of tons of intractable lead residues poisoning the children of the poor. They're the most exposed. The concentration is measurably heaviest in those old slum neighborhoods."

This may seem a rather oblique way to begin a consideration of a quite different phenomenon—the gradual political eclipse of Ronald Reagan. But there is something emblematic about the story. For one thing, it was not the Environmental Protection Agency that released the report. It was Ralph Nader who forced them to disgorge it. Nader probably symbolizes everything that has been "out" in Washington these past six years. Hard on the big boys, vigilant about corporate malfeasance, indifferent to personal income, identified with irksome controls and regulations, he and his kind have not even had a toe in the door. Meanwhile, the EPA staff was cut to the bone, and two of its senior directors faced charges of collusion with polluting companies. One of them is now in jail.

Poisoned drinking water is one of those cases where the public is not content with laissez-faire. Up until recently, Reagan had managed the trick of denouncing government while swelling its scope (and its deficit) and of getting people to distrust Washington while trusting him. Several things now point to a weariness with this prestidigitation.

Most obviously, the President failed in his attempt to cajole the electorate "one more time." He lost nine of the thirteen states in which he campaigned, and, while nobody actually called him a liar, nobody bought his success story about Reykjavik either. This despite a most intensive barrage of concerted, government-sponsored rewriting of the event.

Press skepticism about Reaganite claims has increased since Bernard Kalb resigned over the disinformation business, but there seems also to be somewhat less credulity among the public at large. Flippancy and arms control are—well—ill sorted. The light-hearted way in which the Administration this week announced that it would exceed the SALT II deployment limits is thought to be depressing George Shultz, on whose patient features are written the signs of increasing dissent. Embarrassed by the Libyan disinformation, exhausted and overruled at Reykjavik, he is now humiliated by his exclusion from the Teheran plot. Also ill sorted, for the matter of that, are flippancy and "terrorism."

It was the Reaganites who chose to make this term a talismanic one and to apply loyalty tests and sturdiness tests that were based upon their own definition of it. They cannot therefore escape the contempt that is their due for the double-dealing with Iran. A bit of private horse-trading for hostages might have been pardoned, but not the supply of high-tech weaponry to a nation which had been put in quarantine, for every allied nation except Israel, by Washington itself. All matters of principle aside, the deal puts in question the thrice-affirmed neutrality of the United States in the Gulf War. If this neutrality is to be abandoned, then the process of deliberation should be a bit more polished than the silly affair of disguises, cakes, and false noses that has just come to light.

On every hand, there is evidence of "wing and prayer" politics and sordid improvisation. It now appears, for example, that the man who acted as armorer and organizer of the doomed Eugene Hasenfus mission to Nicaragua was Luis Posada, a Cuban exile extremist who is still wanted for blowing up an airliner in midair in October 1976. Sure, you can't be choosy when you are waging a covert war. But did they have to choose Posada? Here is yet another revelation of incompetence mixed with irresponsibility (I euphemize only slightly), of the sort which Congress is no longer in a mood to ignore. Before the elections, the Administration might have got away with one or the other, and even perhaps both. But, just as nothing succeeded like success, nothing fails like failure.

It is entirely probable that within a few months it will be as fashionable to blame Reagan for everything as it has been to excuse him for everything. It is not really progress to teach a parrot a new word, and it won't be especially inspiring to see the rodents jumping ship. But there is some satisfaction to be had whenever the press and the electorate shake off their addiction to a formula or a slogan. The catch phrase these many years has been "Teflon," a nonstick substance of which the President is allegedly composed. Invented by his critics, this charge became a sort of perverse compliment, like Tory, suffragette, supply-sider, and impressionist in their day. Reagan's power of dissociation, of absence from the scene of trouble, served him well and saw him through two great election campaigns.

In the recent poll, as an unkind friend pointed out to me, it was revealed that his coattails were made of Teflon too. The hangers-on just didn't make it. From now on, there will be fewer volunteers to share the limelight with Reagan and more people prepared to point the identifying finger. Fewer issues will seem to dissolve under the famous emollience of the Presidential quip and grin. There is quite an agenda of tough questions to face, and these have a habit, like lead in the bones of children, of accumulating.

(*The Spectator*, November 15, 1986)

REALITY TIME

❏

If you wish to understand the fire that has broken out in the Washington zoo, and penetrate beyond the mere lowing and baying of the trapped and wounded beasts, you must master three key concepts in the capital's vernacular. These three—all of them coined by the White House itself—are "damage control," "the line of the day," and "reality time." Damage control is the art, perfected until recently by Donald Regan, of giving way without yielding an inch; of taking an inconvenient leak or revelation and placing it in quarantine. One may trump it, for example, with another leak less damaging but more newsworthy. One may change the subject by holding a press conference at which the President announces a bold new "initiative." And, of course, one leans heavily on the indubitable fact that the press and public opinion have distinctly short memories.

Essential to damage control is "the line of the day," a routine that was instituted at about the time that Regan became White House Chief of Staff. Blindingly simple, like all great ideas, it calmly stipulates that all members of the executive branch spend a few minutes each day coordinating their story. It is then fit for endless iteration, and the resulting front of unanimity will depress any bothersome scribbler or congressional invigilator. It need last, at a pinch, no longer than it takes to get to "reality time."

"Reality time" is the White House term for the seven-o'clock news. According to David Stockman, in his intestinal memoir of the Reagan style, this is when Meese, Reagan, Regan, Buchanan, *e tutti quanti* hold their breath. Once they are over the frail hurdle erected by Dan Rather, Peter Jennings, and the other stars, and the word *split* has not been employed, then the team can relax. They may not need a Presidential press conference after all.

The most brilliant illustration of the process was at Reykjavik, when even the dullest eye could see the woe on George Shultz's face and when there was keen speculation about failure and recrimination in high places. Damage control took over with a meeting that was actually held on Air Force One on the way home. A line of the day was established, which was that no "agreement" had ever been sought in Iceland. Iceland was a test of resolve on Star Wars, not the beginning of arms control at all. Division, what division? This line, repeated loudly and assertively and ad nauseam, just about got past the scrutiny of reality time. It held up through the midterm elections, though there was one nasty moment in Chicago when Reagan spoke of "building on the agreement we made in Iceland." Clarifications were issued, smokescreens were laid down, the subject was changed, and Reagan got through the entire campaign without giving one live press conference.

You can see why the Presidential press conference is considered a last resort. In the case of the Iranian arms fiasco, it came only after a flurry of denials, several artful changes in the line of the day (from humanitarian concern for hostages to the strategic importance of Iran and back again), and a full-blown autocue address by the President immediately after reality time on Thursday, November 13, 1986. It was only when opinion polls revealed a public sales resistance to the line of the day, and only after the line itself had been publicly broken by an outraged Shultz, that the gates of the White House were reluctantly opened to the questioners. And the harvest, on November 19, was the pitiful spectacle of a mad old tortoise at bay that has dominated the discussion ever since. Reagan, McFarlane, Shultz, Regan, and Speakes cannot all be telling the truth. In my opinion, they have all lied. But there is no line of the day, and reality time has turned all too real, and damage control is beyond repair.

Compare the Reykjavik lying with the Iran lying and you will see what makes the difference. Reagan said that the proposal in Iceland had been to ban all strategic missiles in five years, and that the arms sent to Iran were few and defensive, and could be carried on shoulders. Actually, the vanquished proposal in Reykjavik was for a ban on *ballistic* missiles within *ten* years; and the antitank weapons sent to Iran could equip three divisions, are hardly "defensive," given that Iran is pushing south, and are so heavy that they have to be mounted on jeeps. The first lie is complex and requires a sustained interest in the subject of arms control to reveal itself as an absurdity. The second is specific, checkable, and, in a sense, much more conscious. It is also much more readily detectable by an average newspaper reader. So is the claim that the weapons had nothing to do with the release of the three hostages—a release for which Reagan then claims his arms-sales policy is responsible! (I almost never employ exclamation marks, but that seemed to warrant one.)

Analogies with Watergate are too easily made, but they may turn out to be more profound than they first appear. Of course, Watergate involved the changing of the official story, the rendering "inoperative" of previous versions, and all the rest of it, to a point where nothing the President said was believed for a second. (It also involved, interestingly enough, a refusal by

George Shultz to supply Nixon with the tax returns and private invoices of his political critics.) But the often-forgotten genesis of Watergate was the need to conceal certain aspects of Nixonian foreign policy. The "plumbers" evolved as a squad for use against those who leaked the secret bombing of Cambodia and the other, even less decorative, initiatives of Henry Kissinger. That's where the bugging began.

It is also where congressional indulgence stopped. The fiascos and humiliations in Chile, Indochina, Cyprus, and Bangladesh led the House and Senate to retrieve much of the influence they had lost over war making and foreign intervention. You can read the entire "Reagan revolution" as a concerted attempt to roll back the gains made by the Fulbright and Church committees in the seventies. And, just as it was the later humbling of the United States in Teheran that shifted public opinion toward tougher, less circumscribed executive action, it is the Iranian imbroglio that has recalled a sleepwalking Congress to its responsibilities. From now on, it is very likely that the National Security Council—that bats' nest of Poindexters, McFarlanes, and Norths—will have to submit its mysterious membership to confirmation by the legislative branch. Reagan has not merely excluded Congress, he's excluded the State Department. We may not automatically do better, say the senators, but taking one consideration with another, we could scarcely do worse.

The question which, reiterated, brought down Richard Nixon was "What did this President know and when did he know it?" On Tuesday, Reagan claimed, astoundingly, that an operation involving Switzerland, Israel, the CIA, Iran, and Nicaragua had been conducted without his "full" knowledge. I don't care for that "full," and I think he will regret it. The secret war on Nicaragua has been "his" war in just the same way as the shady dealing with the mullahs was "his" deal. Henry Kissinger—the other unindicted Watergate survivor—has a maxim of real quality for these occasions. It is that anything which is going to have to be confessed *ultimately* should be confessed *now*, and anyone who is going to have to go eventually should go at once. Poindexter and North have gone—but they were military men who took orders rather than gave them.

All this will be the stuff of policy making and debate from now until the end of this presidency. But in looking ahead one mustn't be blasé about the story of the week. The story of the week is the final rumbling of Ronald Reagan. Readers of Dr. Oliver Sacks's wonderful casebook *The Man Who Mistook His Wife for a Hat* may recall the opening paragraph of the essay entitled "The President's Speech":

> *What* was going on? A roar of laughter from the aphasia ward, just as the President's speech was coming on, and they had all been so eager to hear the President speaking. . . .

There he was, the old Charmer, the Actor, with his practiced rhetoric, his histrionisms, his emotional appeal—and all the patients were convulsed with laughter. Were they failing to understand him? Or did they, perhaps, understand him all too well?

Sacks explains that the chief property of aphasia—the loss of word recognition—is accompanied by a compensation. With aphasics:

There has been a great change, almost an inversion, in their understanding of speech. Something has gone, has been devastated, it is true—but something has come in its stead, has been immensely enhanced, so that—at least with emotionally-laden utterance—the meaning may be fully grasped even when every word is missed.

In fact, as clinical neurologists will tell you, it is impossible to lie to an aphasic because aphasics have "an infallible ear for every vocal nuance, the tone, the rhythm, the cadences, the music, the subtlest modulations, inflections, intonations, which can give—or remove—verisimilitude to or from a man's voice." Sacks concludes, from the ridicule and contempt with which his patients greeted a Reagan broadcast, that

we normals—aided, doubtless, by our wish to be fooled, were indeed well and truly fooled ("Populus vult decipi, ergo decipiatur"). And so cunningly was deceptive word-use combined with deceptive tone that only the brain-damaged remained intact, undeceived.

For the past several years, I have been attempting to parse Reagan's speeches, to convey a sense of their falsity as well as their success. In this week of vindication, I am willing to admit to aphasia in order to join the suddenly swollen ranks of "the normals" who hasten to emphasize that they had, really, seen through him all along.

(The Spectator, November 29, 1986)

THE ERA OF GOOD FEELINGS

❏

The essence of the Reagan era has been a combination of unexampled slap-happy greed at home and squalid, surreptitious violence overseas. The essence of the current "scandal" (indeed, the only thing that makes it a scandal instead of business as usual) is that the unexampled greed and the surreptitious violence became temporarily fused. At about that point many people who had been feeling good about the cult of easy money and the celebration of cheap machismo began to feel a bit surfeited with both.

When the record of this sleazy, vicious Administration is written up for posterity, it will be asked, What did American liberal intellectuals have to say? How many of them were blown along by the gusts of the Era of Good Feelings? How, if at all, did they resist the impulses of chauvinism, pelf, and power worship? There are two instructive cases, both of them culminating as I write.

In the past few weeks, New Republic Books and its partner Holt, Rinehart and Winston have announced that they will no longer distribute their plum title, *Merger Mania*, by Ivan Boesky. And *Partisan Review* has admitted, rather grudgingly to be sure, that it has canceled a special symposium on foreign policy that would have appeared in its next issue. Centerpiece of the symposium was to have been a hysterical essay by Michael Ledeen, who as an "expert" in the State Department helped originate the blood-money deal that milked reaction in Iran in order to finance the counterrevolution in Nicaragua.

It would be hard to find two better symbols of the Reagan era than Boesky and Ledeen—the one up to his elbows in other people's money and the other up to his neck in other people's blood. At the intellectual and moral level, also, they are almost perfectly equivalent. But one cannot say that either *The New Republic* or *Partisan Review* ended its dalliance with these men because of any prompting of principle. On the contrary, it has been made perfectly clear by both sets of editors that they dropped their fair-weather friends because of a sudden sense of embarrassment. The Era of Good Feelings has also been an era of fashion-consciousness par excellence. It's no fault of Martin Peretz or William Phillips, respective stewards of these two formerly honorable titles, that their pals are so suddenly, catastrophically out of style.

The two instances are not precisely congruent. At *Partisan Review*, there was a protracted debate about the very idea of building an issue of the magazine around a figure like Ledeen (who is a frequent contributor to *The New Republic*). In the end, after a number of dissenting voices had been heard, Daniel Bell removed himself from the masthead and put an end to a long and intimate association with the editors. He was followed, some time after the Iran scandal broke, by Leon Wieseltier. But the decision to drop the January centerpiece was made only under the lash of events—events that would have made *Partisan Review* look ridiculous rather than unscrupulous.

Boesky was a little harder to detach from *The New Republic*. After all, had not Martin Peretz written an ode to the arbitrager in the March 25, 1985, issue and called it "Productive Predators"? Had not Boesky, along with Jeane Kirkpatrick and Henry Kissinger, been a guest of honor at the magazine's seventy-fifth–anniversary bash in the same year? True, the man's effusion was hastily dropped by New Republic Books. But, in the earlier week of Boesky's unmasking by the Securities and Exchange Commission, Peretz issued an edict that forbade any mention of the matter in the pages of the magazine. Celebrated for its yuppie coverage and its strong interest in the money culture, *The New Republic* saw its regular feature column on capitalism dropped for that week and displaced onto the op-ed pages of *The Washington Post*. The extra space was filled by stale pieces from Morton Kondracke and Charles Krauthammer, arguing desperately that democratic scrutiny should not be allowed to impair the cause of the Contras.

Given the din of events, is there any reason to care about this kind of thing? Yes. In conversation Bell mentioned rather wistfully the time that *Partisan Review* was associated with George Orwell. Before it fell into the philistine hands of Peretz, whose family had $8.3 million in Boesky's investment fund, *The New Republic* had been the paper of Walter Lippmann and Edmund Wilson. Now it's a vulgar echo chamber for the Contras and the corporate raiders.

So, though one might be tempted to say that Phillips and especially Peretz are mere bubbles of scum on the great boiling vat of Reaganism, it would be vulgar to dismiss them as such. By aligning their magazines with power and money, they shrink the arena in which argument about ideas can take place. Imperceptibly, this has the effect of cheapening the terms of debate. A journal of opposition like *The Nation* has no cause to rejoice at the decline of *Partisan Review* into neoconservatism or at the surrender of *The New Republic* to mercenary glitz. It's in our own interest to have honest and learned antagonists.

What has been observable over the last two administrations, however, is the uninteresting invertebrate style of so many of our rivals in the talking classes. Instead of warning about the threat to democracy at home that was created by adventures abroad, they joined in a chanting, taunting chorus about the "weakness" of those who held back. This barely counted as *trahison* because those who did it could barely count themselves *clercs*. But, as Conor Cruise O'Brien wrote in *Power and Consciousness*, before he himself became too familiar with the seats of the mighty, the retreat of the liberal

may become a rout, his disenchantment apostasy. Thus we may find that the man who has refused to make the decisive intellectual and moral sacrifices for the revolution will go on to make them for the status quo and in that cause proclaim: "This sham is true, these injustices are just, these oppressed have all the opportunities of the free world." These sacrifices, whether made for the revolution or the counterrevolution, constitute, of course, the abdication of the intellectual.

(*The Nation*, January 17, 1987)

BLABSCAM

❑

In the White House press office, there sits a woman named Denny E. Brisley. You may not know Ms. Brisley. But if you watch the Sunday-morning political chat shows, you know her work. To her falls the job of producing and editing the key segments of "This Week With David Brinkley," "Meet the Press," and "Face the Nation." If you ask why the taxpayer should be financing such a job, instead of the sturdy advertiser, then you probably believe that ABC, NBC, and CBS are engaged in relentless competition to beat each other to the truth.

In theory, the networks devote many hours to conversational television every week. That is to say, they self-consciously step aside from mere news gathering and open the screen to questioning, debate, and reflection. In point of fact, these pompous mini-seminars from the nation's capital are an insult in three ways. First, they are indistinguishable in style, supplying three identical brands of audio-visual chewing gum for the vacant mind. Second, they are so arranged as to act as an echo chamber for politicians and a tiny repertory of pundits. Third, they are fixed. Rigged.

It is a subtle process, but nevertheless one by which intellectual mediocrity and political conformism are guaranteed. Brisley, in her demanding job as TV impresario, must bear in mind a White House policy that was recently spelled out in *The Washington Post*, a policy which stipulates that President Reagan's Press Secretary, as well as Brisley, "must find out who is appearing with the administration official and get some idea of the format." "It is all done in a very sensitive, diplomatic-type language," says Brisley. "Things are said, but not said." Among the things "said" in this unspoken dialogue (which takes a TV producer about a week to learn for life) is something along these lines: "Don't even *think* about having X on the panel of questioners— or we'll go to another network with the Secretary and you'll look small." And thus it is assured that the questioning is anodyne and sycophantic, a form of helpful prompting. "Mr. Secretary, can you tell us anything more of your thinking about . . . ?"

Manipulation by the state, which dangles ratings and "heavyweight" prestige before the networks, is replicated lower down the scale with the other political talk shows. I have been a panelist or guest on almost all of them, and what follows is my report.

Take, first, "The McLaughlin Group," aired by the Public Broadcasting System and some NBC affiliates. Its eponymous chairman, the genial rogue John McLaughlin, is the Washington editor of *National Review* and a retooled priest, whose wife, Ann, was until recently Ronald Reagan's Under Secretary of the Interior. McLaughlin is also catholic with a small *c*; he likes to canvass all opinions from the extreme right to the moderate right. Pat Buchanan, now White House Director of Communications, was hired straight off the set of McLaughlin's show. Since his departure, the regular team has consisted of Robert Novak, Morton Kondracke, and Jack Germond. Novak is one of those ultrarightists who have made a good thing of Reaganism but still regard themselves as members of an oppressed and ignored minority. Kondracke is the kind of reformed liberal who worries that the Contras are being made to fight with one hand tied. Germond, the radical exhibit, breaks in every now and then to ask whatever happened to the great tradition of Harry Truman. For the show's rotating fourth seat, McLaughlin will often call on the born-again Christian Fred Barnes or some firebrand from *The Wall Street Journal*.

The dirty secret about the McLaugh-in, though, is not its intimacy with the reigning ideas and their spokesmen. It is that it declares itself to be "an unrehearsed program." The introductory voice-over makes this claim every week as the group surges into focus. Well, one wouldn't mind so much if they called it "unscripted." After all, knowing what Mort Kondracke is bound to say is not the same as coaching him to say it. But *unrehearsed* the McLaugh-in is not.

When I appeared as a guest, there were four stages to be gone through. First, an interview with the beaming McLaughlin himself, held in the *National Review*'s downtown suite. Second, a long talk with his "researcher" about the order in which questions and topics would be raised, and the order in which one would be invited to comment on them. Third, a telephone call from HQ on the morning of the taping day, alerting me to last-minute changes of subject and consequent changes of order ("John will come out on Bob Novak, and then turn to you, Chris, and ask . . ."). Finally, a rehearsal along the same lines just before we moved into the studio. And even that was not enough. At the end of the second segment of the show, as we were about to return to the air, another "researcher" rushed onto the set and hissed in my ear: "Prediction! Have you got a prediction ready? We forgot to tell you to have a prediction!" Having already watched the show in the privacy of my own home (which you might think to be rehearsal enough), I was able to suck a "prediction" out of my thumb in ten seconds.

But "McLaughlin" is Parnassus compared to "It's Your Business," which fills ABC's Sunday lunchtime slot and somehow attracts a surprising number of congressmen, scribes, and thinkers to its studio. Set up to look like a real network program, this is actually put together by the U.S. Chamber of Commerce and is produced in the C. of C.'s well-appointed building just north of Lafayette Square. Its tempestuous host, Meryl Comer, is in fact the straight woman to the permanent panelist, Dr. Richard Lesher, who basks in the Chamber's employ. My appearance on this show brought me together with Robert Novak, Robert Kuttner of *The New Republic*, and the good doctor. All of us but Lesher were told what questions we would be asked, in what order, and how long we would have to respond. Unfair to Lesher? Not exactly. Novak, if memory serves, was asked about Japan and protectionism. Kuttner was invited to speculate on the magnitude of the coming year's deficit. I drew some question about European currency fluctuations. Lesher, modestly taking his turn last, was challenged to say if he thought that recent developments did not illustrate the superiority of the free-enterprise system. He did his manly best to cope with this curveball.

And then there's the Cable News Network's "Crossfire," which awakes the adrenaline of millions of citizens each weekday evening—and is yet another phony homage to the notion of unfettered exchange. There is less time for rehearsal, but guests are subjected to lengthy telephone "pre-interviews" from faraway Atlanta. As the lights go up, a voice-over intones, "On the left—Tom Braden. On the right—Robert Novak." Then follow thirty minutes of frank and fearless debate. Debate? Actually, "Crossfire" is a tired show by the same old ragged repertory company. (Robert Novak inherited the right-wing chair from . . . Pat Buchanan.) And it has assimilated the prevailing values with the same ease as its more polished seniors. The conservative or the Administration case is put by people who believe in or are paid by it, respectively. "Balance" is satisfied by inviting an obscure radical onto the set when there has been a hijacking, say, or a Russian atrocity. "Now, Mr. Lefty, you're an apologist for the Soviets. What do you have to say about this?"

I've been down this path. One evening, as soon as I arrived at the "Crossfire" studios to do a show, I was invited to join the producer in his office. He told me to go easy on "Bob" Novak that evening or bid farewell to "Crossfire." This seemed odd, since prior to an earlier appearance I had been warned in the same office not to be upset if Novak was sometimes a bit crude. (And he was—I was accused of doing the KGB's dirty work before I had figured out which camera I was supposed to look into.) I refused to give any assurance of moderation. Novak thereupon vetoed my appearing on the show. I would not grizzle about this if "Crossfire" didn't advertise itself as a rough-and-tumble knock-down, drag-out spontaneous match, instead of a fixed fight where one of the permanent players doubles as referee.

It happens all the time. When George Will was being ridiculed in *Doonesbury*, he forbade Sam Donaldson to make even a joking reference to the fact in a run-through of "This Week With David Brinkley." The show aired in its normal pally mode. Is it any wonder that Reagan was six years into his presidency before he had a rough press conference? The entire media culture of Washington had been conditioned for soft lobs, first-name exchanges, and a jostle for the eye of Denny Brisley. And you still read articles about the "adversary relationship" between the press and the presidency. I'll start to believe that on the day that Ted Koppel forgets to call Henry Kissinger "Doctor."

(Harper's, March 1987)

FAULTY TOWER

❏

On May 16, 1986, Lieutenant Colonel Oliver North sent one of his computer messages to Vice Admiral John Poindexter. He did so by making use of the Professional Office System of the National Security Council (whose abbreviation, PROF, makes my earlier nomination "Profligate" seem uncanny in its prescience). The message read:

> I have no idea what Don Regan does or does not know re my private U.S. operation but the President obviously knows why he has been meeting with several select people to thank them for their "support for Democracy" in CentAm. [Illiteracies in original.]

The next day Poindexter responded by saying, "Don Regan knows very little of your operation and that is just as well."

The conclusion of the Tower Commission from this and a mass of similar and consistent evidence is that Don Regan is the villain and that North and Poindexter "do not seem to have sought the President's approval."

Note, here, the calculated insult to the human intelligence. First, what is the word *seem* doing in that evasive sentence? Is it not abundantly clear that they had no need to seek what they had already been granted? So why is Regan, who played a minimal part in the original blood-money deal and who merely made a hash of the cover-up, singled out for blame? The ridiculous Brent Scowcroft, while introducing the report, opined: "The problem at the heart was one of people, not of process. It was not that the structure

324	CHRISTOPHER HITCHENS

was faulty; it is that the structure was not used." When the President appointed a man like that to investigate the President, he certainly knew what
he was doing.

The report poses Juvenal's question *Quis custodiet ipsos custodes?* ("Who
shall guard the guardians themselves?"). This paradox of ruling-class damage
control has been stale since the time of the Caesars. A more intelligent
maxim is that of William of Occam, who early in the fourteenth century
observed keenly, *Pluralitas non est ponenda sine necessitate* ("Entities
should not be multiplied without necessity"). This is known to logicians as
Occam's razor.

The principle of Occam's razor is attractive and useful because it can
dispose of unnecessary assumptions. Consider the unnecessary assumptions
that must be made by someone who doubts the personal and direct culpa-
bility of Ronald Wilson Reagan in this matter. Such a person must claim to
be bewildered by the following facts:

1. Reagan appointed Poindexter and North, and he has not rescinded his
opinion that the latter is a "national hero," given after the disclosure of
North's illegal activities.

2. Reagan met frequently with donors to the Contra cause who had been
recruited by Carl Channell, a supporter of the John Birch Society. Channell
received a letter from Reagan on October 10, 1985, which said, "You and
your organization have made a remarkable contribution to the course of
democracy in Central America." That letter was used by North and Channell
to help raise several million dollars in illegal donations to the Contra death
squads. The office for this operation was in the White House.

3. Channell employed three of Reagan's former aides in the various front
organizations of his National Endowment for the Preservation of Liberty.
Richard Miller, director of broadcast services for the 1980 Reagan-Bush
campaign, was hired to spend $2 million on lobbying Congress for the Con-
tras. David Fischer, former special assistant to Reagan, was getting $10,000
a month. Lyn Nofziger, former chief political aide at the White House, was
paid $20,000 a month to provide information to the Channell operation.

4. International Business Communications, the firm retained by Channell
and run by Miller, received a $276,000 "classified contract" from the State
Department, ostensibly to help debrief defectors from Managua.

5. The Internal Revenue Service allowed Channell to make all his donations tax-deductible.

I could go on. But at what point would the Reaganite John Tower, the
Reaganite Brent Scowcroft, and the sheep-faced Carterite Edmund Muskie
cease to wag their slow heads in puzzlement at the President's lack of attention to detail? None of the above disclosures makes any sense, after all,

unless you assume that the President's attention to detail was in fact rather minute.

No sooner had the Tower Commission report fallen from the press than a queue of politicians and journalists formed up, all competing for the right to tell Reagan that he must "take charge." What can they imagine that he has been taking all this time? A more apt response might have been to point out that every speech and statement made by the President since the story broke has been a deliberate lie. But there is not one politician or editorialist who will make this simple observation. Instead, we hear servile bleats for the restoration of the master's "authority." Even the pathetic George Bush went unchallenged when he admitted in public on February 27 that there *had* been a swap of arms for hostages. ("We did not—repeat—did not trade weapons or anything else for hostages," said Reagan last November 13.) Said Bush of the policy of ransom and blood money, "It failed the American people, and it failed the President." Here we have, in its most rococo form, the growing consensus view that the author of the policy is really its victim.

Fearlessly, the Tower trio declares:

> The President did not seem to be aware of the way in which the operation was implemented and the full consequences of U.S. participation. . . . The President should have ensured that the N.S.C. system did not fail him. . . . At no time did he insist upon accountability and performance review.

And so on. Again, what is the word *seem* doing here? The trio could hardly omit it and say that the President was *not* aware, because the impressive circumstantial and documentary evidence of his involvement makes that impossible. So they have to create a mystery where none exists. Why did he fail to "insist upon accountability"? Well, jeepers creepers, we sure as hell don't know. And since it can't be that he was *frightened* by accountability . . .

(The Nation, March 14, 1987)

MIAMI VICE

❑

This time six months ago the political climate was more surreal than even the President can probably remember. After a goodish spring of bombing in North Africa ("firing into a continent," as Joseph Conrad put it in *Heart of Darkness*) and a pretty decent summer of tomfoolery and posturing around the Statue of Liberty, the Reaganites were still turning tricks and pulling rabbits. The two hypnotic subjects on which they had focused, dragging an enormous media entourage behind them, were terrorism and drugs.

No need to waste words on "terrorism," which has disappeared even from the shamefaced official vocabulary, and, no doubt by coincidence, from the news and op-ed pages as well. But what can explain the sudden silence on the subject of narcotics, the one topic on which there is no need for artifice? Agreement on the harm done by addiction and on the damage done to society by the filthy economy of crime it creates is probably the only sincere consensus in America.

Evidence is accumulating that the private economy of the Contra war is and was a function of the private economy of the drug lords. The Administration has not merely been turning a blind eye to the Contras' drug habit. It has made use of that habit to finance the counterrevolution. This is the disclosure that is waiting to be made in the Senate hearings and the special prosecutor's report.

On April 6, the CBS program "West 57th" led off with a densely documented segment about the CIA-Contra-narcotics connection. The flagships of the middlebrow press, with the honorable exception of *The Miami Herald*, have thus far avoided commenting on the contents of the program. Those contents were sensational, in the best sense of that word. Here is Mike Tolliver, a free-lance pilot and convicted drug smuggler, describing his life with the Reagan Administration's Nicaragua policy. In March 1986, he was contracted by the CIA to fly to Aguacate, a Contra supply base of the sort set up by Elliott Abrams and others in Honduras:

TOLLIVER: We had about twenty-eight thousand pounds of military supplies—guns, ammunition, things like that.
REPORTER: And when you landed in Honduras, no checking, no customs, no inspections?
TOLLIVER: Well, I didn't think the customs people were going to be out there in the jungle, to be honest with you.
REPORTER: What kind of cargo were you bringing back?
TOLLIVER: Twenty-five thousand and change, pot.
REPORTER: Twenty-five thousand pounds of pot?
TOLLIVER: Yeah, marijuana. Same plane.

Having established that the dope came from the same people who provided the original shipment of guns, Tolliver described his homeward run to South Florida:

REPORTER: Where in South Florida?
TOLLIVER: We landed at Homestead.
REPORTER: Homestead?
TOLLIVER: Air Force Base.

Tolliver is a jailbird, but he cannot hope to shorten his sentence by giving this testimony, or sweeten his relationship with the federal authorities. The plane he identified as the one he flew has been confirmed as the same plane hired by the Administration to fly "humanitarian" supplies to the Contras. The dates check out as well.

Another charmer, named George Morales, is a convicted cocaine smuggler. He affirms, again without hope of improving his legal position by doing so, that the CIA exploited his indictment as a drug lord to squeeze him for planes, pilots, and a three-million-dollar cash donation to the Contras. The Costa Rican airstrip that he identifies as the switchboard of guns for cocaine is owned by John Hull. As readers of even the lenient Tower Commission report will know, Hull has been recorded in several meetings with Oliver North.

The forensic standards of the CBS program were rigorous and certainly succeeded in showing that some individuals had run a lot of guns to the Contras, as well as a lot of drugs to American dealers and addicts (it would take an exact moralist to decide which set of CIA actions was the more offensive to humanity). You may say that this was a cowboy operation or, perhaps, a venomous exception to the general rule. You would not say that if you had read a forthcoming book by Peter Dale Scott, who has been researching the subject for the International Center for Development Policy in Washington. (The fact that the center recently had its documents rifled and burgled may or may not be strictly germane.)

Scott is also a scrupulous and scholarly researcher. He has a sophisticated analysis of the web of narcotics, weapons, and death squads in which the Administration has involved itself. Let me summarize his conclusions in order to emphasize the persuasiveness of his argument. We know, as he shows, that there was a CIA report in 1985 alleging that a "top commander" of the Contras in Costa Rica had used cocaine money to buy an arms shipment and a helicopter. We know that two Nicaraguan cocaine smugglers, convicted in the largest coke seizure in West Coast history, told of passing their cut to the Contras. We know that the Drug Enforcement Administration identified a leading Contra fund-raiser in 1984 as a major cocaine importer for the U.S. market.

Has the nerve of outrage gone as dead as the fatuous pundits say it has? When will cynicism turn to anger? When will one of our famous Democratic aspirants find the courage to make this—the corrupting of America to finance the ruin and torture of Nicaragua—the issue?

(The Nation, April 25, 1987)

ORIGINAL SIN

❑

Lieutenant Colonel Oliver North, we learn, has a benefactor named Albert Hakim, who set up a $200,000 trust fund for North's family and left him $2 million in his will. Testifying before Congress on June 4, 1987, the generous Hakim described North's hostage trading with Iran last fall and said that the colonel's "prime objective at that time was to support the President or the Republicans in the elections. . . . He wanted to gain the release of the hostages to enhance the position of the President."

This may not be the first time that such "enhancement" was planned. On January 20, 1981, Ronald Reagan was inaugurated as the fortieth President of the United States. On the same day, on the initiative of Hashemi Rafsanjani, Speaker of the Iranian Parliament, the U.S. diplomatic hostages were released from Teheran. Had they been released ten weeks earlier, it is highly unlikely that Reagan would have taken that oath of office.

On July 18, 1981, an Argentine CL-44 Turboprop plane crashed on the Soviet-Turkish border. It was loaded with weapons in transit from Israel to Iran. The United States, we have since been assured by high-level Israeli officials, knew and approved of the arms dealing that this crash exposed to view. The spare parts and ammunition were all American-made. But in July 1981 there were no U.S. hostages in Teheran or in Beirut.

Suppose that those shipments of weapons in the earliest days of the Reagan regime were in payment for hostages. Suppose that they were in payment for a hostage release that was delayed to influence the 1980 election. That would mean a deal between the Reagan team and the ayatollahs, made in the closing months of the Carter presidency. Keep the hostages until we have won, and we will supply you with weapons when we take power.

Cast your mind back to March 1984. In that month it was revealed that the 1980 Reagan campaign had got hold of President Carter's debate briefing book. How did the Reaganites come by it? According to Admiral Robert Garrick, who was head of plans and policy for the Reagan campaign, and to the subsequent congressional inquiry, there was a special team. The purpose of that team was to forestall any attempt at an "October surprise" on the part of Carter. And the only surprise they feared was a hostage release by the Iranians. That would have vindicated Carter's Rose Garden diplomacy and presumably secured him a second term.

The head of the special team was campaign director William Casey, who on July 15, 1980, described it as "an intelligence operation." Its members were "retired military officers." Who fits that description? Among others, Major General Richard Secord, who had spent much of the 1970s training the Iranian air force. Secord has since told Congress that he hoped to get back into government after his conflict-of-interest problems at the Pentagon procurement division. In 1981 he was made Deputy Assistant Secretary of Defense and, with Oliver North, was put in charge of lobbying for the AWACs deal for the Saudis. North, we have since learned, was a watcher on the Turkey–Iran border as the Carter-Brzezinski Desert One rescue came to grief.

Casey and Meese continually stressed, during the 1984 "Debategate" inquiry, that their "October surprise" team was made up of "retired" officers. But not all of their contacts were by any means retired. One of the papers revealed in the course of the inquiry was a memorandum from the Reagan-Bush election committee dated September 17, 1980. It reported that General Richard Ellis, then head of the Strategic Air Command, had requested "a sitdown" with Governor Reagan:

> Due to his rank and position he cannot formally institute the meeting, but if a meeting were requested by RR, he would be happy to sit down with him.
> . . . The General has said he "wants to blow Jimmy Carter out of the water."

The memorandum is headed "To Ed Meese—What Think?" It was passed to Meese through Max Hugel, who later became the CIA's Director of Covert Operations and who was removed, over Casey's protests, because of his malodorous business activities. (In 1981, General Ellis was appointed by Reagan to the U.S.–Soviet Standing Consultative Committee on compliance with nuclear-arms treaties.)

Meese, Casey, Secord, North . . . does this remind you of anything? All of them passionate Reagan loyalists. All of them part of a pattern of activity designed to trip up Jimmy Carter in the 1980 election. All of them agreeing that Iran was his weakest point. All of them appointed to key posts by Reagan immediately after the victory. All of them involved with the shipment of arms to Teheran at a time when there were no Americans being held.

At the time of Debategate, it was obvious that the White House and the Justice Department were extremely anxious to avoid an inquiry. The very suggestion of a special prosecutor caused convulsions. Upholding a motion for the appointment of a special prosecutor in the case, U.S. District Court Judge Harold Greene observed that the Attorney General had utterly misunderstood the Ethics in Government Act and strongly criticized the idea of "an information gathering apparatus employed by a Presidential campaign which uses former agents of the FBI and the CIA."

The head of the FBI's Washington field office, Theodore Gardner, rashly proposed giving lie-detector tests to Administration members in order to find out how they had "filched" (David Stockman's word) the briefing book. He was instantly transferred to Portland, Oregon. The man who ordered his transfer was Judge William Webster. In November 1986, Webster meekly accepted the assurance of Edwin Meese that there was no need for an FBI investigation into "possible lawbreaking" in the Iran-Contra scandal.

A theory that fits all the known facts usually has some merit. Many people wondered why Meese panicked on November 25, 1986. What secret did he fear would surface? Congress should start asking about the original sin in which this whole bloody Administration was conceived.

(*The Nation*, June 20, 1987)

A FEW QUESTIONS

❑

In the fall of 1968, the incumbent Democrats were making steady progress in the opinion polls. Despite their appalling record on Vietnam, they had a chance to win reelection by organizing a peace conference to end the war. The Nixon campaign had as its foreign-policy coordinator a man named Richard V. Allen. Allen made it his task to develop contact with moles in the government machine because, as Seymour Hersh wrote in *The Price of Power*, "Nixon knew the Johnson Administration was involved in a desperate attempt to get some kind of substantive peace talks under way in Paris, and thus improve Humphrey's chances in the election." With the help of these insiders, who included Henry Kissinger, and with the assistance of right-wing fanatics like Anna Chennault, a "backchannel" to the South Vietnamese was established. It was made plain to the South Vietnamese that they would get a better deal from a Nixon Administration.

On November 2, 1968, two days after the White House announced that he would be participating in the Paris peace talks and three days before the U.S. elections, President Nguyen Van Thieu of South Vietnam withdrew from the negotiations. His timing was disastrous for the talks—and for the Democratic ticket.

I recently suggested that the Reagan campaign in 1980 might have played a similar game with the mullahs in Teheran. Did it assure them that if they kept the American hostages until after the elections, a Reagan Administration would reward Iran with weapons? This would explain the timing of the hostage release and the almost-immediate shipment of arms via Israel to Iran when no hostages were being held and no "moderates" were on the horizon. Further evidence for this hypothesis follows.

In the first two weeks of October 1980, three prominent Reaganites met with an envoy of the Iranian regime. The meeting took place in the L'Enfant Plaza Hotel in Washington. It was arranged by Robert McFarlane (then working for Senator John Tower) and attended by Laurence Silberman, cochairman of the Reagan-Bush foreign-policy advisory group. Also present was the other cochairman, Richard V. Allen. Allen, who became Reagan's first National Security Adviser, now claims that his notes of the meeting have been "mislaid." But Abolhassan Bani-Sadr, who was president of Iran at the time, says that two ayatollahs did negotiate through intermediaries with the Reagan campaign, trading the humiliation of Carter for future arms deliveries. According to the excellent Alfonso Chardy of *The Miami Herald*, Bani-Sadr identifies the two as Hashemi Rafsanjani and Mohammed Beheshti. Rafsanjani has since emerged as the Iranian of choice in all the Reagan Administration's arms deals.

Barbara Honegger, who served as a researcher in the Reagan campaign and later as a policy analyst at the White House, says she was in the Reagan headquarters in Arlington, Virginia, on October 24 or 25, 1980, at about 11:00 P.M., when an excited staffer in the "operations center" said, "We don't have to worry about an 'October surprise.' Dick cut a deal." "Dick" was Richard Allen.

A memorandum in Allen's handwriting, printed in the House investigating committee's report on the theft of President Carter's campaign papers, is dated October 10, 1980. One entry reads, "FCI—Partial Release of hostages for parts." FCI are the initials of Fred C. Iklé, now an Under Secretary of Defense and then a member of one of Reagan's action groups on the "October surprise."

According to the House investigation, there were two teams that sought to deny President Carter an "October surprise" success in releasing the hostages. The first met in the Skyline House in Falls Church, Virginia, and consisted of Edwin Meese III, William Casey, Richard Wirthlin, Pete Dailey, and Admiral Robert Garrick. This was the group described by Casey as "an intelligence operation." The second team was convened by Allen and included Fred Iklé, John Lehman, and Admiral Thomas Moore.

Speaking before the House committee, which, alas, did not hold public hearings and did not compel testimony under oath, Meese, Casey, and James Baker III all confirmed that Admiral Garrick ran a network of serving and retired officers whose job was to watch U.S. bases for any signs of unusual activity that might suggest a rescue operation. Garrick confirmed this in his own testimony but claimed that he could not remember the names of his informants or the names of the bases. The committee found that "Garrick's lack of memory about his alleged 'network' is not credible."

Again according to the House investigation, secret documents from the U.S. embassy in Teheran were found in the files of Edwin Meese and Anthony Dolan, now Reagan's chief speechwriter. The committee determined that "these copies were obtained from Iran after being in the possession of Iranians." One of those documents, unearthed from Meese's file, has an attached handwritten note of acknowledgment from Reagan, signed "Ron." By way of the FBI, Reagan told the committee that he "was not certain who provided him with the documents."

A Reaganite staffer on the Senate Intelligence Committee, Angelo Codevilla, informed the House committee that he had been told of active-duty CIA agents who worked for the Bush campaign. Richard Allen's telephone log for October 13, 1980, reads: "1115 Angelo Codevilla—938-9702. DIA—Hostages—all back in compound, last week. Admin. embargoed intelligence. *Confirmed.*" As the committee's report dryly notes, "Neither Allen nor Codevilla could provide information concerning the meaning of this note."

Well, the hostages were released at just the right time, and the first shipments of weapons began the next month. You may wonder if the Reaganites were capable of making such a vile deal. But you don't really wonder that, do you? Let me give the last word to former President Bani-Sadr: "I don't know precisely why the timing of the release was so important to the Reagan apparatus. But it seems to me that his aides were trying to prepare the American public psychologically and symbolically for the era of Reaganism."

It is more than time that these questions got the special prosecutor they deserve.

(The Nation, July 4–11, 1987)

TRIUMPH OF THE WILL

❑

I have suggested that the paramilitary wing of the Reagan team was in business before the 1980 election. The operation on which this team cut its teeth was known as the "October surprise," a coordinated effort to deny President Carter the political kudos that would have accrued from a negotiated *or* a military deliverance of the hostages in Iran. For this purpose, and according to their own testimony, the paramilitary Reaganites divided into two wings. One was headed by William Casey and the other by Richard Allen. Both campaign managers were to step into command of "national security" when Reagan was elected.

In testimony before a lenient and torpid Congress, North revealed that it was Casey who had summoned Major General Richard Secord from the disgrace into which he had fallen after a procurement scandal at the Pentagon. And in a moist and loving profile of North in *The Washingtonian* for July 1987, two of the colonel's friends and fellow "terrorism experts" revealed that it was Allen who had talent-spotted him onto the National Security Council. It's of some interest, then, that both Secord and North were involved in the Desert One fiasco of April 1980. Secord, who had been in Iran from 1975 to 1978 as a dogged servant of the special relationship with the Shah, helped plan the air force's role in the absurdly named Eagle Claw operation that ended with smashed helicopters on the sand. North, for reasons nobody has been able to ascertain, was monitoring the disaster from the Turkish–Iranian border.

Moreover, and according to retired Lieutenant General Samuel Wilson, at least three leaders of the Desert One mission went on to wage Reagan's secret war in Nicaragua. Wilson was vice-chairman of the Pentagon review panel that conducted the literal and metaphorical postmortem on Eagle Claw. The panel found evidence of negligence that surprised even those who are hardened to military incompetence. By Wilson's account, the three Desert One operators who were later mobilized into illegal warfare in Nicaragua were Secord, Lieutenant Colonel Richard Gadd, and Colonel Robert Dutton. Dutton is a business associate of Secord. Gadd's American National Management Corporation employs former Special Forces Master Sergeant John Cupp, who recruited three other, unnamed, Desert One veterans for the operation that gave us Eugene Hasenfus.

All this, of course, may mean nothing. The American *Freikorps* is quite small, and the same names do keep turning up. But consider the coincidences against the background of two other bits of evidence. First, it has been established by numerous journalistic and diplomatic authorities present in Teheran in April 1980 that the Khomeini leadership knew a rescue operation was impending. The mullahs attributed the failure of Carter's expedition to God, but they don't say it was God who tipped them off. Second, we have the hysterical lying of Edwin Meese on November 25, 1986. At his now-famous press conference, he said that earlier Israeli shipments of weapons to Iran had been made without prior U.S. authorization. When he said that, he knew it to be part of a false cover story hastily crafted by William Casey. From the very beginning of this affair, there has been a desperate effort to avoid the question, Why did arms go to Iran so early, when there were no hostages in Teheran or Beirut and no prospective "moderates" either? It is on an answer to that question that the result of any inquiry must depend. And it seems that the shipments began the month after the inauguration of Ronald Reagan.

The unwillingness on the part of the press and Congress to ask that question has been general but not universal. A recently released NSC memorandum from North to Poindexter, dated June 3, 1985, speaks of the irritation caused to the secret government by Alfonso Chardy of *The Miami Herald*. North wrote:

> For several weeks now there have been rumors of stories being prepared which allege an NSC connection to private funding and other support to the Nicaraguan resistance. The rumors originally surfaced with a reporter Alfonso Chardi [*sic*]. . . . At my request [deleted] went to Chardi . . . and told Chardi that if he (Chardi) printed any derogatory comments about the FDN or its funding sources that Chardi would never again be allowed to visit FDN bases or travel with their units.

On July 5, 1987, in *The Miami Herald*, Chardy published three extraordinary disclosures about the career of Oliver North. The first was a "contingency plan," drawn up by North between 1982 and 1984, to suspend the Constitution and impose martial law. Among the "contingencies" that would license such a coup was mass opposition to a U.S. military operation overseas. The project drew alarmed protest even from a man as reactionary as Attorney General William French Smith, who minuted his opposition to such an "emergency czar" on August 2, 1984. Since the minute was addressed to Robert McFarlane, it fell on deaf ears.

The same article notes that, while at the NSC, North was assigned for a time to carry the "football," which contains the codes for fighting a nuclear war and which follows the President, as North did, everywhere. This experience cannot have been good for North's sense of proportion.

Finally, according to Chardy's sources, "the secret governing arrangement traces its roots to the last weeks of Reagan's 1980 campaign. Officials say the genesis may have been an October 1980 decision by Casey . . . to create an October Surprise Group." I think so too.

(*The Nation*, August 1–8, 1987)

THE KILLING BOTTLE

❑

State Penitentiary, Parchman, Mississippi

I had to come this far to see my first gas chamber. The apparatus is encased in a flagon-shaped container, rather like a man-sized version of the killing bottles used by lepidopterists. The killing bottle in turn is housed in a shed. And the shed is adjacent to a row of cells, in which the human specimens are kept for the bottle's convenience.

It ought to be the work of a moment to take a man out of a cell, whisk him into the bottle, and put him beyond the reach of earthly cares. But in some peculiar way the process is a protracted one. The man I had come to see, Edward Earl Johnson, had been kept waiting for eight years. During those eight years, which began shortly after his eighteenth birthday, he had seen and heard other men being fed into the bottle. When the bottle is being readied, the sound of the guards and technicians going about their tasks is clearly audible. They tend to whoop, with excitement or disappointment, when they "do the bunnies." "Doing the bunnies" involves inserting some experimental rabbits into the bottle and observing the effect of cyanide gas upon them. Sometimes the bunnies check out very rapidly. Other times, they linger. If you are in a cell waiting to be gassed yourself, you can gauge the probable speed of your own demise by the noises coming from the shed.

The last man to enter the bottle before Johnson was Jimmy Lee Gray. Even the prison authorities admit that his death was low on dignity and lacking in dispatch. Shortly after midnight on September 2, 1983, a switch was thrown, causing lethal fumes to rise from the cyanide crystals. Gray went into convulsions, which lasted for eight minutes. He was observed to gasp deeply eleven times and to smash his head repeatedly on the metal pole behind him. After those eight minutes, the guards lost their nerve and hustled the witnesses from the shed, where they had been gaping through the bottle's glass flanks. So nobody really knows how long it took Jimmy Lee to pay his ultimate debt to society. Johnson, who was gassed a few days after I said goodbye to him, survived in the bottle for a full fifteen minutes.

Jimmy Lee Gray was white and had pleaded guilty to the murder of a white child. Edward Earl Johnson was black and denied to the end that he had shot a white policeman. According to evidence recently accepted by the Supreme Court, a black man who kills a white is three times more likely to suffer the penalty of death than a white man who kills a white. A black man who kills a white is eleven times more likely to be slain by the state than a white man who kills a black. In my idealistic youth, this was known as racial discrimination or even racism. Now, says the majority on the Supreme Court, it is "a discrepancy that appears to correlate with race." However, as the justices went on to say, such "apparent disparities in sentencing are an inevitable part of our criminal justice system." If that last statement is true, it is rather a condemnation.

If you get hold of Amnesty International's report *The United States of America: The Death Penalty* (322 Eighth Avenue, New York, N.Y. 10001, $6), you can read a meticulous account of the operations of the capital-punishment system. The gas chamber, the firing squad, and the electric chair are employed on the mentally ill, on juveniles, on racial minorities, and, of course, on those who have committed no crime. State and regional variations in sentencing make a mockery of consistency and therefore of even the vaguest utility of that incoherent concept "the deterrent." The fashion for allegedly more humane execution by lethal injection has resulted in obscenely painful and grotesque episodes, and involves the corruption of the Hippocratic code of medical ethics. Yet, under the Reagan Administration, this death cult has been given every encouragement to spread.

Two additional objections struck me during my stay at Parchman. The first was so obvious that it took me some time to realize it. Edward Earl Johnson was not merely rotting under sentence of death; he was being tortured. I had never actually seen anyone being tortured before. Perhaps, as a member of the post-Nuremberg generation, I had naïvely supposed that the practice had been at least officially done away with. But if I was confined in a windowless cell shortly after my eighteenth birthday, and was kept waiting for eight years to know if I would live or go to the bottle, I would believe that I was in prison not *as* punishment but *for* punishment. That is torture. The state of Mississippi makes a big thing of the last-minute reprieve, or stay. (Justice Earl Warren once telephoned Parchman at midnight, only to be told that it was too late; now they wait a ritual extra ten minutes.) So you don't know, even when the men with masks and rubber gloves enter your cell, that it is really the end. And then it can take you quite a long time to die, with strangers watching. The tableau is made complete by the representatives of my two least favorite professions—the lawyer and the priest. These have been essential fixtures at the stake and the scaffold since medieval times. But we have no right to consider torture medieval while it is still legally practiced in the New World.

My second objection is that capital punishment strikes directly at democracy and due process. It can't be coincidence that it is used most frequently in countries that consider the citizen to be the property of the state. In a caste-bound or dictatorial system, the condemned can be taken from the dock to the execution yard, and that's that. At least the relatives of the victim (if the system has picked the right culprit) have the paltry satisfaction of swift justice. But democracy requires appeal procedures, mature consideration, review, and the possibility of clemency and revision. This, in the strict sense, is incompatible with the death penalty and, when combined with it, makes a charade of the legal system, turning ostensibly humane review into a protracted humiliation.

Racist, brutalizing, antidemocratic, sadistic, and thoughtless—is it any wonder that this special symbol of primitivism is undergoing a recrudescence in the era of Edwin Meese?

(*The Nation*, August 29, 1987)

THE TOLLING BELL

❑

To listen even very briefly to Ronald Reagan is to realize that here is a man upon whose synapses the termites have dined long and well. Lately, there has been evidence that his body is beginning to catch up with his mind. The most noticeable outward sign is the succession of plasters jauntily worn on the Presidential nose, which has been troubled with a recurring skin cancer. In July, when he warned his fellow Americans to stay out of the range of harmful rays, Reagan became the first Californian politician ever to speak against sunshine.

The President was not, on this occasion, being alarmist. Physicians are reporting a frightening increase in skin cancer, and linking it directly to the deterioration of the ozone layer. The ozone layer, like the rain forests and the ice caps and the whale population, is one of those issues that are often tagged as "green" and therefore slightly eccentric. But now it seems that we have to do some serious worrying about it. A large hole has opened in our protective atmospheric sheath, directly over the South Pole. The favored scientific explanation is the erosion of the ozone layer by chlorofluorocarbons of the kind employed in aerosols and certain industrial processes. Since human and animal life can't coexist for long with ultraviolet rays, we have the right to become agitated.

At a recent meeting of the United States Cabinet Council on Domestic Policy, Interior Secretary Donald Hodel adopted a "no sweat" strategy. Instead of the proposed thirty-one-nation treaty to ban chlorofluorocarbons from the atmosphere, he counseled a "personal protection" program involving the use of "hats, sunglasses and sunscreen lotion."

His chief executive, who is suffering from an environmental cancer, believes that "minimal government" is to be preferred to irksome regulation—rather as he believed that his own shooting by John Hinckley was an argument *against* handgun control. In a more complex mind, this would be known as cognitive dissonance. As it is, it represents a striking loyalty to dogma.

One is spoiled for choice in seeking ways to ridicule this attitude. Who will equip the children of Brazil or Bangladesh with designer sunglasses? Who will anoint the mammal population with tanning oil? Who will dish out *chapeaux* to the human race? If Mr. Hodel were not so very lacking in the distinctions, he might be accounted the Marie Antoinette of the environmental revolution. As it is, he is merely the Mad Hatter (or possibly a lobbyist for powerful headgear, sunglass, and lotion interests).

Folded inside Mr. Hodel's grotesque message is a real difference of principle. Are we, or are we not, all in the same boat? This homely British metaphor has its uses. The "same boat" can have first and steerage classes, as the *Titanic* has resurfaced to remind us.

But all the extra money in the world won't buy your son a place at a school with better ozone. And the total cost of hats, glasses, and cream for each theoretically individual consumer would far outweigh the expense of designing and enforcing a worldwide aerosol ban, *without* doing a thing to defend the ecosphere.

I bought an armful of socialist magazines in London recently, and was impressed by their dogged iteration of the new rage for free market, individualist formulae. There seems to be no limit to the revisionist enterprise. Once the intoxication of this "new thinking" has worn off, it will again become boringly clear that all macro questions are questions that confront society rather than the individual. This is true of the nuclear menace, which the dogmatists believe can be faced by back-yard, family-sized shelters. It is true of the imperiled web of nature and climate, which when messed around can lead to dustbowls in one province and floods in the neighboring one. It is true of the water that can bring lead into the blood and bone of children. There is no "minimal government" solution to any of these pressing matters.

One doesn't want or need to argue this with any relish. The idea of the individual should not be glibly counterposed to the idea of society. After all, what is society made up of, if not individuals? But there are two ways of facing collective responsibilities. One is to ignore them until it is too late, at which point things like rationing, conscription, and regimentation become the options, irrespective of whether the system is capitalist or socialist. The other is to recognize them in time and take the necessary measures freely and by consent. But there is no evading these responsibilities altogether, or of dismissing them as "One World sentimentality."

In a recent book, the American conservative historian Gertrude Himmelfarb has reasserted the ideal of the nineteenth-century English family and has thus appeared to underscore Mrs. Thatcher's famous invocation of "Victorian values." It might be a mistake to dismiss this particular bit of the revisionist canon. The family, so often piously invoked by Tories, is in fact an elementary form of socialism. It operates, without undue repression, on the principle of "from each according to his/her ability and to each according to his/her need."

In the Victorian and Thatcherite model, of course, the family is also necessary to protect its members from the encroachment of other families and thus to reinforce patriarchy and instill various kinds of competitive spirit, but this aspect of the model is not an essential one. The family core is the recognition that an injury to one is an injury to all—a precept that many people can recognize only when it is put to them in a self-interested way.

Yet there is an amazing persistence to the notion that everybody can, by his or her own efforts, become an autonomous proprietor. Surely this, rather than the socialist vision, is the real utopianism? At the moment, Wall Street is operating on the false promise, not of the usual well-worn casino metaphor, but of a casino *where nobody loses*. In Britain, it seems, everybody is to be the owner of a restaurant as well as the customer. Increasingly, it is the partisans of the unfettered enterprise culture who have to answer that old trick question—who's going to do the hard work?

This may seem a long digression from the ozone layer, but in fact there is more than one sense in which the sky is the limit. The lesions on Ronald Reagan's proboscis are a reminder that resources are finite, that individual actions have consequences for individuals beside oneself, and that even the most sophisticated consumers do not have sovereignty over the most basic things. They certainly do not have sovereignty over commodities, like air and sunlight, that they are forced to consume.

In the developed world there is at least a trade-off. We may get nuclear leaks, for example, but we also get the benefits of nuclear energy. This is more than can be said for the inhabitants of Bhopal, say, who died from inhaling a product that never even enriched them. But in the end we all move closer to the margin. So certain truisms are beginning to resound again. If we don't hang together, we *will* hang separately. The bell *does* toll for us all. It will not do to listen to the cheerleader business-politicians whose motto is "Only disconnect." The values of solidarity, collectivism, and internationalism are not so much desirable as they are actually mandated by nature and reality itself.

(*The Observer*, September 13, 1987)

DEAR OSCAR

❑

In England prisoners are detained "at Her Majesty's pleasure" and are often therefore ironically termed "guests of Her Majesty." After his years in Reading Gaol, during which he was witness to the flogging of a mentally deficient inmate and the dismissal of a warder who showed kindness to a child locked up for poaching rabbits, Oscar Wilde observed, "If this is how Her Majesty treats them, then she doesn't deserve to *have* any prisoners." I could not find this biting comment in Richard Ellmann's voluminous new biography of Wilde, nor could I detect this aspect of Wilde from any of the book's flattering reviews, most of which have represented him as a sort of sumptuous fop, possessed of a dangerous vanity, whose tale may be told as an example of hubris.

Yet the salient point about Wilde was the economy and address of his wit. He did not froth with bons mots like some second-rate charmer. He was a tough and determined Irishman who more than once flattened bullies with his fist, and most of the time—if we exempt pardonable and tempting sallies about blue china and decorative screens—his drawling remarks were not snobbish or mannered. I suppose that people need to see him as a species of languid dandy, which is why "The Soul of Man Under Socialism" is almost never discussed when dear Oscar's name comes up.

Try to find that essay in any of the current anthologies of Wilde. First published in 1891, it was geldingly retitled "The Soul of Man" while Wilde was in prison. It expressed the sensibility that had impelled him to take the side of the Irish rebels and, in particular, to oppose the British government's attempted frame-up of Charles Stewart Parnell, who, like Wilde, was destroyed on a charge of immorality when all else had failed. It gave Wilde the same distinction as that which he acquired by being the only writer in London to sign George Bernard Shaw's petition for the Haymarket martyrs. And it contains the following imperishable sentence:

> The chief advantage that would result from the establishment of Socialism is, undoubtedly, the fact that Socialism would relieve us from that sordid necessity of living for others which, in the present condition of things, presses so hardly upon almost everybody.

This is not the flippant remark that philistines might take it to be. It is in fact what is truly meant by "compassion," a word now made to sound sickening in the mouths of Democratic hypocrites.

What those hypocrites mean when they intone the hack word "compassion" is that we should not forget the needy and the desperate as we pursue our glorious path of self-advancement. This is the rough equivalent of the older injunction that we should remember the wretched in our prayers. Wilde was proposing something infinitely more daring and intelligent—that we regard poverty, ugliness, and the exploitation of others as something repulsive to ourselves. If we see a slum, a ghetto, a beggar, or an old person eating pet food, we should not waste pity on the victim. We should want the abolition of such conditions for our own sakes. The burden of enduring them is too much.

This is why early socialists were quite proud to be accused of spitting in the face of charity. The principle that an injury to one is an injury to all is not just talk; it is the expression of a solidarity that recognizes mutual interest. As Wilde also wrote, in his review of Edward Carpenter's *Chants of Labour*, "For to make men Socialists is nothing, but to make Socialism human is a great thing." His appreciation of paradox here makes an excellent match with his rejection of sentimentality.

There is another sense in which it would be nice to think that Wilde intended his insight about "living for others." In the great working-class novel *The Ragged Trousered Philanthropists*, the Irish laborer Robert Tressell describes the feelings of charity and gratitude that overwhelm the credulous, patriotic men who worked alongside him. They were content to spend their entire lives living for others—their betters—each of them confident of his own sturdy independence. This type did not disappear with the waning of the Industrial Revolution. You can meet him today, the despair of "progressive" intellectuals, as he bellies up to the bar with his "can't fool me" talk and proceeds to speak, sometimes using the very same phrases, in the tones of the President's last lying paean to native virtues. Praise for these philanthropists, especially at times when they are needed to be expended in war, is the only official rhetoric you hear that mentions the word "class." Almost the only place that class distinctions are stressed these days is at the Vietnam Veterans Memorial.

They deserve to be stressed more often. Society labors on, supporting both an enormously wealthy upper class, whose corporate holdings are frequently tax free or even tax subsidized, and a growing underclass, which is sporadically and pathetically cited as a spur to conscience. Never is it asked: What are these classes *for*?

A sort of moral blackmail is exerted from both poles. The underclass, one gathers, should be dulled with charity and welfare provision lest it turn nasty. The upper class must likewise be conciliated by vast handouts, lest it lose the "incentive" to go on generating wealth. A rising tide, as we have recently learned, does not lift all boats, nor does a falling tide sink them all. If people were to recognize that they are all in the same boat, they would take better care of its furnishings, its comfort, and its general décor. This is what Wilde meant by the importance of the aesthetic.

Radicals have been taught to distrust any too-great display of individualism, and where they forget this lesson there are always conservatives to remind them. Wilde himself was haunted by a Moral Majority-like chaplain in prison, who reported that the cell reeked of semen. (How could he tell?) We are in the debt of the brave man who taught us to ask, of their majesties, whether they deserve us, or our continued amiable subservience.

(*The Nation*, February 20, 1988)

PREPARED
FOR THE
WORST

❑

ON NOT KNOWING
THE HALF OF IT:
Homage to Telegraphist Jacobs

❏

In the early days of the December that my father was to die, my younger brother brought me the news that I was a Jew. I was then a transplanted Englishman in America, married, with one son, and, though unconsoled by any religion, a nonbelieving member of two Christian churches. On hearing the tidings, I was pleased to find that I was pleased.

One of the things about being English born and bred is the blessed lack of introspection that it can confer. An interest in genealogy is an admitted national quirk, but, where this is not merely snobbish or mercenary, it indulges our splendid and unique privilege of traceable, stable continuity. Englishmen do not have much time for angst about their "roots" or much of an inclination to the identity crisis. My paternal grandfather had a favorite joke, about a Wessex tenant in dispute with his squire. "I hope you realize," says the squire, "that my ancestors came over with William the Conqueror." "Yes," returns the yeoman. "We were waiting for you." It was from this millennial loam that, as far as I knew, I had sprung. I had long since let lapse my interest in family history, as being unlikely to prove any connection to title or fortune. For something to say, I would occasionally dilate on the pure Cornish origins of the name Hitchens, which had once been explained to me by A. L. Rowse in the course of a stuporous dinner at Oxford. The Celtic strain seemed worth mentioning, as representing a sort of romantic, insurgent leaven in the Anglo-Saxon lump. But having married a Greek (accepting confirmation in the Orthodox Church with about as much emotion as I had declined it in the Anglican one) and left England, I never expected any but routine news from the family quarter.

My brother's account was simple but very surprising. Our mother had died tragically and young in 1973, but her mother still lived, enjoying a very spry tenth decade. When my brother had married, he had taken his wife to be presented to her. The old lady later complimented him on his choice, adding rather alarmingly, "She's Jewish, isn't she?" Peter, who had not said as much, agreed rather guardedly that this was so. "Well," said the woman we had known all our lives as "Dodo," "I've got something to tell you. So are you."

My initial reaction, apart from pleasure and interest, was the faint but definite feeling that I had somehow known all along. Well used to being taken for English wherever I went, I had once or twice been addressed in Hebrew by older women in Jerusalem (where, presumably, people are looking for, or perhaps noticing, other characteristics). And, though some of my worst political enemies were Jewish, in America it seemed that almost all my best personal friends were. This kind of speculation could, I knew, be misleading to the point of treachery, but there it was. Then, most provoking and beguiling of all, there was the dream. Nothing bores me more than dream stories, so I had kept this one to myself. But it was the only one that counted as recurrent, and I had also experienced it as a waking fantasy. In this reverie, I am aboard a ship. A small group is on the other side of the deck, huddled in talk but in some way noticing me. After a while a member of the group crosses the deck. He explains that he and his fellows are one short of a quorum for prayer. Will I make up the number for a *minyan?* Smiling generously, and swallowing my secular convictions in a likable and tolerant manner, I agree to be the tenth man and stroll across the deck.

I hesitate to include this rather narcissistic recollection, but an account of my reactions would be incomplete without it, and I had had the dream recently enough to tell my brother about it. He went on to tell me that our grandmother had enjoined us to silence. We were not to tell our father, who was extremely unwell. He had not known that he had a Jewish wife, any more than we had known we had a Jewish mother. It would not be fair to tell him, at the close of his life, that he had been kept in the dark. I felt confident that he would not have minded learning the family secret, but it was not a secret I had long to keep. My father died a matter of weeks after I learned it myself.

The day after his funeral, which was held in wintry splendor at the D-Day Chapel overlooking our native Portsmouth, whence he had often set sail to do the king's enemies a bit of no good, I took a train to see my grandmother. I suppose that in childhood I had noticed her slightly exotic looks, but when she opened the door to me I was struck very immediately by my amazing want of perception. Did she look Jewish? She most certainly did. Had I ever noticed it? If so, it must have been a very subliminal recognition. And in England, at any rate in the milieu in which I had been brought up, Jew-consciousness had not been a major social or personal consideration.

We had family grief to discuss, and I was uncertain how to raise the other matter that was uppermost in my mind. She relieved me of the necessity. We were discussing my father's last illness, and she inquired his doctor's name. "Dr. Livingstone," I replied. "Oh, a Jewish doctor," she said. (I had thought Livingstone a quintessentially English or Scots name, but I've found since that it's a favorite of the assimilated.) At once, we were in the midst of a topic that was so familiar to her and so new and strange to me. Where, for a start, were we *from?*

Breslau. The home of B. Traven and the site of a notorious camp during the *Endlossung*. Now transferred to Poland and renamed Wroclaw. A certain Mr. Blumenthal had quit this place of ill omen in the late nineteenth century and settled in the English Midlands. In Leicester, he had fathered thirteen children and raised them in a scrupulously Orthodox fashion. In 1893, one of his daughters had married Lionel Levin, of Liverpool. My maternal grandmother, Dorothy Levin, had been born three years later.

It appeared that my great-grandparents had moved to Oxford, where they and their successors pursued the professions of dentistry and millinery. Having spent years of my life in that town as schoolboy and undergraduate and resident, I can readily imagine its smugness and frigidity in the early part of the century. Easy to visualize the retarding influence of the Rotary Club, and perhaps Freemasonry and the golf club, on the aspirations of the Jewish dentist or hatter. By the time of the Kaiser, the Levins had become Lynn and the Blumenthals, Dale. But I was glad to learn that, while they sought to assimilate, they did not renounce. Of a Friday evening, with drawn curtains, they would produce the menorah. The children were brought up to be unobtrusively observant. How then, could such a seemingly innocuous and familiar tale come to me as a secret? A secret which, if it were not for the chance of my grandmother outliving both my parents, I might never have learned?

Dodo told me the occluded history of my family. "Oxford," she said, materializing my suspicions, "was a very bad place to be Jewish in those days." She herself had kept all the Jewish feasts and fasts, but I was slightly relieved to find that, aged ninety-two, she was staunchly proof against the claims of religion. "Have any of your friends ever mentioned Passover to you?" she inquired. I was able to say yes to that, and to show some knowledge of Yom Kippur and Hanukkah too. This seemed to please her, though she did add that as a girl she had fasted on Yom Kippur chiefly to stay thin.

The moment had arrived to ask why this moment had arrived. Why had I had to bury my father to get this far? On the mantelpiece was a photograph of my mother, looking more beautiful than ever, though not as beautiful as in the photograph I possessed, which showed her in the Royal Navy uniform in which she had met my father. I had interrogated this photograph. It showed a young, blond woman who could have been English or (my fancy when a child) French. Neither in profile nor in curls did it disclose what Gentiles are commonly supposed to "notice."

"Your mother didn't much want to be a Jew," said Dodo, "and I didn't think your father's family would have liked the idea. So we just decided to keep it to ourselves." I had to contend with a sudden access of hitherto buried memories. Had my father shown the least sign of any prejudice? Emphatically not; he had been nostalgic for Empire and bleakly severe about the consequences of losing it, but he had never said anything ugly. He had been a stout patriot but not a flag waver, and would have found racism (I find I can't quite add "and chauvinism") an affront to the intelligence. His lifetime of naval service had taken him to Palestine in the 1930s (and had involved him in helping to put down a revolt in my wife's neighboring country of Cyprus in 1932), but he never droned on about lesser breeds, as some of his friends had done in my hearing when the gin bottle was getting low. If he had ever sneered at anyone, it had been Nasser (one of our few quarrels).

But I could recall a bizarre lecture from my paternal grandfather. It was delivered as a sort of grand remonstrance when I joined the Labour Party in the mid-1960s. *"Labour,"* my working-class ancestor had said with biting scorn, "just look at them. Silverman, Mendelson, Driberg, Mikardo . . ." And he had told off the names of the leading leftists of the party at that period. At the time, I had wondered if he was objecting to German names (that *had* been a continuous theme of my upbringing) and only later acquired enough grounding in the tones of the British Right to realize what it had meant. Imagining the first meeting between him and my maternal grandmother, as they discussed the betrothal, I could see that she might not have been paranoid in believing her hereditary apprehensions to be realized.

And then came another thought, unbidden. Oxford may have been a tough place to be a Jew, but on the European scale it did not rank with Mannheim or Salonika. Yet my parents had been married in April 1945, the month before the final liberation of Germany. It was the moment when the world first became generally aware of the Final Solution. How galling it must have been, in that month, to keep watch over one's emotions and to subsume the thought of Breslau in the purely patriotic rejoicing at the defeat of the archenemy.

"Well, you know," said Dodo, "we've never been liked. Look at how the press treats the Israelites. They don't like us. I know I shouldn't say it, but I think it's because they're jealous." The "they" here clearly meant more than the press. I sat through it feeling rather reticent. In January 1988— the month of which I am speaking—the long-delayed revolt in Gaza had electrified Fleet Street, more because some ambitious Thatcherite junior minister had got himself caught up in it than for any reason of principle. The following Sunday, I knew, *The Observer* was to publish a review of *Blaming the Victims,* a collection of essays edited by Edward Said and myself. This book argued that the bias was mostly the other way—even if, as Edward had once put it so finely in a public dialogue with Salman Rushdie, this was partly because the Palestinians were "the victims of the victims." I didn't know how to engage with my grandmother's quite differently stated conviction. But when I offered that the state she called "Israelite" had been soliciting trouble by its treatment of the Palestinians, she didn't demur. She just reiterated her view that this wasn't always the real reason for the dislike they—"we"—attracted.

Well, I knew *that* already. The Harold Abrahams character in *Chariots of Fire* says rather acutely of English anti-Semitism that "you catch it on the edge of a remark." Whether or not this is more maddening than a direct insult, I could not say from experience, but early in life I learned to distrust those who said, "Fine old Anglo-Saxon name," when, say, a Mr. Rubinstein had been mentioned. "Lots of time to spare on Sundays" was another thoughtless, irritating standby. This was not exactly *Der Stürmer,* but I began to ask myself: Had I ever let any of it go by? Had I ever helped it on its way with a smart remark? Had I ever told a joke that a Jew would not have told? (Plenty of latitude there, but everybody "knows" where it stops.) In this mood I bid farewell to my grandmother and, leaving her at her gate, rather awkwardly said, "Shalom!" She replied, "Shalom, shalom," as cheerfully and readily as if it had been our greeting and parting since my infancy. I turned and trudged off to the station in the light, continuous rain that was also my birthright.

Enough of this sickly self-examination, I suddenly thought. A hidden Jewish parentage was not exactly the moral equivalent of Anne Frank. Anti-Jewish propaganda was the common enemy of humanity, and one had always regarded it as such, as much by instinct as by education. To claim a personal interest in opposing it seemed, especially at this late stage, a distinct cheapening of the commitment. As the makers of Levy's rye bread had once so famously said, You don't have to be Jewish. You don't have to be Jewish to find a personal enemy in the Jew-baiter. You don't have to be a Palestinian to take a principled position on the West Bank. So what's new? By a celebrated and practiced flick of the lever, your enemies can transfer you from the "anti" column to the "self-hating." A big deal it isn't.

Well, then, why had my first reaction to the news been one of pleasure? Examining my responses and looking for a trigger, I turned back to *Daniel Deronda,* which I had thought when I first read it to be a novel superior even to *Middlemarch:*

"Then I *am* a Jew?" Deronda burst out with a deep-voiced energy that made his mother shrink a little backward against her cushions. . . . "I am glad of it," said Deronda, impetuously, in the veiled voice of passion.

This didn't at all meet my case. It was far too overwrought. For one thing, I had never had the opportunity to question my mother. For another, I had not (absent the teasing of the dream) had Deronda's premonitions. My moment in the Jerusalem bookshop, accosted by a matronly woman, did not compare with his in the Frankfurt synagogue. On the other hand, the response of Deronda's mother did seem to hit a chord:

"Why do you say you are glad? You are an English gentleman. I secured you that."

Another memory. I am sitting on the stairs in my pajamas, monitoring a parental dispute. The subject is myself, the place is on the edge of Dartmoor, and the year must be 1956 or so, because the topic is my future education. My father is arguing reasonably that private schooling is too expensive. My mother, in tones that I can still recall, is saying that money can be found. "If there is going to be an upper class in this country," she says forcefully, "then Christopher is going to be in it." My ideas about the ruling class are drawn from Arthurian legend at this point, but I like the sound of her reasoning. In any case, I yearn for boarding school and the adventure of quitting home. She must have had her way, as she customarily did, because a few months later I was outfitted for prep school and spent the next decade or so among playing fields, psalms, honors boards, and the rest of it. I thus became the first Hitchens ever to go to a "public" school, to have what is still called (because it applies to about one percent of the population) a "conventional" education, and to go to Oxford.

Until very recently, I had thought of this parental sacrifice—I was ever aware that the costs were debilitating to the family budget—as the special certificate of social mobility. My father had come from a poor area of Portsmouth, was raised as a Baptist, and had made his way by dint of scholarships and the chance provided by the navy. My mother—well, now I saw why questions about her background had been quieted by solemn references to Dodo's early bereavement. And now I wish I could ask my mother—Was all this effort expended, not just to make me a gentleman, but to make me an Englishman? An odd question to be asking myself, at my age, in a new country where all my friends thought of me as "a Brit." But an attractive reflection, too, when I thought of the Jewish majority among my circle and the special place of the Jews in the internationalist tradition I most admired. It counted as plus and minus that I had not had to sacrifice anything to join up. No struggle or formative drama, true, but no bullying at school, no taunting, not the least temptation to dissemble or to wish otherwise. In its review at the time, *The Tablet* (what a name!) had complained of *Daniel Deronda* that George Eliot committed "a literary error when she makes Deronda abandon, on learning the fact of his Jewish birth, all that a modern English education weaves of Christianity and the results of Christianity into an English gentleman's life." Nobody would now speak with such presumption and certainty about "the results of Christianity," but insofar as this abandonment would not be an act of supererogation on my part, it was by now impossible in any case. In other words, the discovery came to me like a free gift. Like Jonathan Miller in his famous writhe in *Beyond the Fringe*, I could choose to be "not a Jew, but Jew-ish."

Or could it be that easy? I had two further visitations of memory to cogitate. At the age of about five, when the family lived in Scotland, I had heard my mother use the term "anti-Semitism." As with one or two other words in very early life, as soon as I heard this one I immediately, in some indefinable way, *knew what it meant*. I also knew that it was one of those cold, sibilant, sinister-sounding words, innately repugnant in its implications. I had always found anti-Jewish sentiment to be disgusting, in the same way as all such prejudices but also in a different way, and somehow more so. To hear some ignorant person denouncing Pakistani or Jamaican immigrants in Britain was one thing—there would be foul-mouthed complaints about cooking smells, about body odors, and occasionally about sexual habits. This was the sort of plebeian bigotry that one had to learn to combat, in early days as an apprentice canvasser, as a sort of Tory secret weapon in the ranks of the Labour vote. But anti-Semitic propaganda was something else. More rarely encountered, it was a sort of theory: both pseudo- and anti-intellectual. It partook of a little learning about blood, soil, money, conspiracy. It had a fetidly religious and furtively superstitious feel to it. (Nobody accuses the blacks of trying to take over international finance, if only because racialists don't believe them capable of mounting the conspiracy.) When I came across Yevtushenko's poem *Babi Yar* at the age of sixteen, I realized that he had seized the essence of the horror that I felt: the backwardness and cunning that could be mobilized. I memorized the poem for a public reading that my school organized for the Venice in Peril Fund and can remember some lines even now without taking down the Peter Levi translation:

> *No Jewish blood runs among my blood,*
> *But I am as bitterly and as hardly hated*
> *By every anti-Semite*
> *As if I were a Jew.*

That seemed to me a fine ambition, even if easily affected at a civilized English boys' school. I know that it was at about this time that I noticed, in my early efforts at leftist propaganda, that among my few reliable allies in a fairly self-satisfied school were the boys with what I gradually understood were Jewish names. There was occasional nudging and smirking in chapel when we sang the line "Ye seeds of Israel's chosen race" in the anthem "Crown Him." What did it mean, *chosen?* Could it be serious? I hadn't then read *Daniel Deronda,* but I would have shared his stiff and correct attitude (antedating his discovery) that

> of learned and accomplished Jews he took it for granted that they had dropped their religion, and wished to be merged in the people of their native lands. Scorn flung at a Jew as such would have roused all his sympathy in grief and inheritance; but the indiscriminate scorn of a race will often strike a specimen who has well-earned it on his own account.

Oh, I was fair-minded all right. But strict fair-mindedness would suggest the conclusion that it didn't *matter* who was Jewish. And to say that it didn't matter seemed rather point-missing.

The second memory was more tormenting. Shortly before her death, and in what was to be our last telephone conversation, my mother had suddenly announced that she wanted to move to Israel. This came to me as a complete surprise. (My grandmother, when I told her fifteen years later, was likewise unprepared for the revelation.) Now I ransacked that last exchange for any significance it might retrospectively possess. Having separated from my father and approaching middle life, my mother was urgently seeking to make up for time lost and spoke of all manner of fresh starts. Her praise for Israel was of the sort—"It's a new country. It's young. They work hard. They made the desert bloom"—that one read in the gentile as well as the Jewish press. The year was 1973 and the time was just after the Yom Kippur War, and, in trying to moderate her enthusiasm, I spoke of the precariousness of the situation. This was slightly dishonest of me, because I didn't doubt Israel's ability to outfight its neighbors. But I suspected that any mention of the Palestinians would be a pointless expense of breath. Besides, I wasn't entirely sure myself how I then stood on that question.

In June 1967, I had sympathized instinctively with the Jewish state, though I remember noting with interest and foreboding a report from Paris which said that triumphalist demonstrators on the Champs Elysées had honked their car horns—*Is-ra-el vain-cra!*—to the same beat as the OAS *Al-gé-rie fran-çaise!* My evolution since then had been like that of thousands of other radicals: misery at the rise of the Israeli Right and enhanced appreciation of the plight of the Palestinians, whether in exile or under occupation. Several visits to the region meant that I had met Palestinians and seen conclusively through those who had argued that they did not "really" exist.

By the time I moved to the United States, the Left and even the liberals were thrown on the defensive. In America at least, a major part of the ideological cement for the Reagan-Thatcher epoch was being laid on by the neoconservative school, which was heavily influenced by the Middle East debate and which did not scruple to accuse its critics of anti-Semitism. My baptism of fire with this group came with the Timerman affair, which has been unjustly forgotten in the record of those years.

Even though Jacobo Timerman had been incarcerated and tortured *as a Jew*, his Argentine fascist tormentors were nonetheless felt, by the Reagan Administration and by the pre-Falklands Thatcherites, to be fundamentally on our side. (This in spite of the horridly warm relations between the Buenos Aires junta and the Soviet Union.) They did not count, in the new *kulturkampf*, as a tyranny within the meaning of the act. As a result, Jacobo Timerman had to be defamed.

He was accused of making up his story. He was reviled, in an attack that presaged a later hot-favorite term, of covert sympathy for "terrorism" in Argentina. He was arraigned for making life harder, by his denunciation, for Argentina's peaceable Jewish community. (This charge was given a special ironic tone by the accusation, made in parallel, that he had overstated the extent of anti-Semitism in that country.) Although some of this slander came from the Francoist Right, who were later to appear in their true colors under the banner of General Singlaub and Colonel North, the bulk of the calumny was provided by neoconservative Jewish columnists and publications. I shall never forget Irving Kristol telling a dinner table at the Lehrman Institute that he did not believe Timerman had been tortured in the first place.

I was much affected by Timerman's book *Prisoner Without a Name, Cell Without a Number*, partly because I had once spent a few rather terrifying days in Buenos Aires, trying to get news of him while he was incommunicado. Not even the most pessimistic person had appreciated quite what he was actually going through. As I read the account of his torture at the hands of the people who were later picked by Reagan and Casey to begin the training of the Contras, I was struck by one page in particular. An ideologue of the junta is speaking:

> Argentina has three main enemies: Karl Marx, because he tried to destroy the Christian concept of society; Sigmund Freud, because he tried to destroy the Christian concept of the family; and Albert Einstein, because he tried to destroy the Christian concept of time and space.

Here was the foe in plain view. As that pure Austrian Ernst Fischer puts it so pungently in his memoir *An Opposing Man:*

> The degree of a society's culture can be measured against its attitude towards the Jews. All forms of anti-Semitism are evidence of a reversion to barbarism.

Any system which persecutes the Jews, on whatever pretext, has forfeited all right to be regarded as progressive.

Here were all my adopted godfathers in plain view as well: the three great anchors of the modern, revolutionary intelligence. It was for this reason that, on the few occasions on which I had been asked if I was Jewish, I had been sad to say no, and even perhaps slightly jealous. On the other hand, when in early 1988 I told an editor my news, her response was sweet but rather shocking. "That should make your life easier," she said. "Jewish people are *allowed* to criticize Israel." I felt a surge of annoyance. Was that the use I was supposed to make of it? And did that response—typical, as I was to find—suggest the level to which the debate had fallen? It seemed to me that, since the Middle East was becoming nuclearized and since the United States was a principal armorer and paymaster, it was more the nature of a civic responsibility to take a critical interest. If Zionism was going to try to exploit gentile reticence in the post-Holocaust era, it might do so successfully for a time. But it would never be able to negate the tradition of reason and skepticism inaugurated by the real Jewish founding fathers. And one had not acquired that tradition by means of the genes.

As I was preparing for my father's funeral and readying a short address I planned to give to the mourners, I scanned through a wartime novel in which he had featured as a character. Warren Tute was an author of the *Cruel Sea* school and had acquired a certain following by his meticulous depiction of life in the Royal Navy. His best-known book, *The Cruiser,* had my father in the character of Lieutenant Hale. I didn't find anything in the narrative that would be appropriate for my eulogy. But I did find an internal monologue, conducted by the master-at-arms as he mentally reviewed the ship's complement of HMS *Antigone*:

> He knew that Stoker First Class Danny Evans would be likely to celebrate his draft by going on the beer for a week in Tonypandy and then spending the next three months in the Second Class for Leave. He knew that Blacksmith First Class Rogers would try and smuggle service provisions ashore for his mother and that telegraphist Jacobs was a sea lawyer who kept a copy of Karl Marx in his kitbag.

Good old telegraphist Jacobs! I could see him now, huddled defensively in his radio shack. Probably teased a bit for his bookishness ("a copy" of Marx, indeed), perhaps called "Four Eyes" for his glasses, and accused of "swallowing the dictionary" if he ever employed a long word. On shore leave at colonial ports, sticking up for the natives while his hearty shipmates rolled the taxi drivers and the whores. Perhaps enduring a certain amount of ragging at church parade or "divisions" (though perhaps not; the British lower deck is if anything overly respectful of "a man's religion"). Resorted to by his comrades in the mess when there was a dispute over the King's Regulations or the pay slips. Indefinitely relegated when promotion was discussed—a Captain Jacobs RN would have been more surprising than an Admiral Rickover. In those terrible days of war and blockade, where the air is full of bombast about fighting the Hun, or just fighting, Telegraphist Jacobs argues hoarsely that the enemy is fascism. Probably he has rattled a tin for Spain and collected bandages in the East End for the boys of the International Brigade (whose first British volunteers were two Jewish garment workers). When the wireless begins to use the weird and frightening new term *total war*, Telegraphist Jacobs already knows what it means. The rest of the time, he overhears the word *troublemaker* and privately considers it to be no insult.

My father never knew that he had a potential Telegraphist Jacobs for a son, but he hardly ever complained at what he did get, and I salute him for that. I also think with pleasure and pride of him and Jacobs, their vessel battered by the Atlantic and the Third Reich, as they sailed through six years of hell together to total victory. Commander Hitchens, I know, would never have turned a Nelson eye to any bullying. They were, much as the navy dislikes the expression, in the same boat.

As I'm told is common with elder sons, I feel more and more deprived, as the days pass, by the thought of conversations that never took place and now never will. In this case, having had the Joycean experience of finding myself an orphan and a Jew more or less simultaneously, I had at least the consolation of curiosity and interest. A week or so after returning from the funeral in England, I telephoned the only rabbi I knew personally and asked for a meeting. Rabbi Robert Goldburg is a most learned and dignified man, who had once invited me to address his Reform congregation in New Haven. He had married Arthur Miller to Marilyn Monroe (converting the latter to Judaism) but resisted the temptation to go on about it too much. After some initial banter about my disclosure ("Aren't you ashamed? Did you see Rabin saying to *break their bones?*"), he appointed a time and place. I wanted to ask him what I had been missing.

It may be a bit early to say what I learned from our discussion. The course of reading that was suggested is one I have not yet completed. No frontal challenge to my atheism was presented, though I was counseled to reexamine the "crude, Robert Ingersoll, nineteenth-century" profession of unbelief. Ever since Maimonides wrote of the Messiah that "he may tarry," Judaism seems to have rubbed along with a relaxed attitude to the personal-savior question and a frankly skeptical one about questions of wish-thinking such as the afterlife. A. J. Ayer once pointed out that Voltaire was anti-Semitic because he blamed the Jews for Christianity, "and I'm very much afraid to say that he was quite right. It *is* a Jewish heresy." When I had first heard him say that, I thought he might be being flippant. But as I discoursed more with Rabbi Goldburg, I thought that Judaism might turn out to be the most ethically sophisticated tributary of humanism. Einstein, who was urged on me as an alternative to Ingersoll, had allowed himself to speak of "the Old One" despite refusing allegiance to the god of Moses. He had also said that the Old One "does not play dice with the universe." Certainly it was from Jews like him that I had learned to hate the humans who thought themselves fit to roll the dice at any time.

Rabbi Goldburg's congregation was well-to-do, and when visiting them as a speaker I had been very impressed by the apparent contrast between their lifestyle, for want of a better term, and their attitudes. I say "apparent contrast" because it is of course merely philistine to assume that people "vote their pocketbook" all the time or that such voting behavior is hardheaded realism instead of the fatuity it so often is. The well-known Jewish pseudointellectual who had so sweetly observed that American Jews have the income profile of Episcopalians and the voting habits of Puerto Ricans was a perfect exemplar of Reaganism, of what Saul Bellow once called "the mental rabble of the wised-up world."

Anyway, what struck me when I addressed this highly educated and professional group was the same as what had struck me when I had once talked to a gathering of Armenians in a leafy suburb in California. They did not scoff or recoil, even when they might disagree, as I droned on about the iniquity and brutality, the greed and myopia that marked Reagan's low tide. They did not rise to suggest that the truth lay somewhere in between, or that moderation was the essential virtue, or that politics was the art of the possible. They seemed to lack that overlay of Panglossian emollience that had descended over the media and the Congress and, it sometimes seemed, over every damn thing. But nor did they bitch, as the English do, about how everything was getting worse, going to the dogs, and so on. That kind of plaintiveness is predicated on the myth of a golden past. Over drinks afterward, I suddenly thought: Of course. These people already know. They aren't to be fooled by bubbles of prosperity and surges of good feeling. *They know the worst can happen*. It may not be in the genes, but it's in the collective memory and in many individual ones, too.

Was this perhaps why I had sometimes "felt" Jewish? As I look back over possible premonitions, echoes from early life, promptings of memory, I have to suspect my own motives. I am uneasy because to think in this way is, in Kipling's frightening phrase, "to think with the blood." Jews may think with the blood if they choose: it must be difficult not to do so. But they—we—must hope that thinking with the blood does not become general. This irony, too, must help impart and keep alive a sense of preparedness for the worst.

Under the Nuremberg laws, I would have been counted a Blumenthal of

Breslau, and the denial of that will stop with me. Under the Law of Return, I can supposedly redeem myself by moving into the Jerusalem home from which my friend Edward Said has been evicted. We must be able to do better than that. We still live in the prehistory of the human race, where no tribalism can be much better than another and where humanism and internationalism, so much derided and betrayed, need an unsentimental and decisive restatement. [To be continued]

(Grand Street, Summer 1988)